Noah Webster

A Collection of Essays and Fugitiv Writings

On Moral, Historical, Political and Literary Subjects

Noah Webster

A Collection of Essays and Fugitiv Writings
On Moral, Historical, Political and Literary Subjects

ISBN/EAN: 9783337133542

Printed in Europe, USA, Canada, Australia, Japan

Cover: Foto ©ninafisch / pixelio.de

More available books at **www.hansebooks.com**

A

COLLECTION of ESSAYS

AND

FUGITIV WRITINGS.

ON

MORAL, HISTORICAL, POLITICAL and LITERARY

SUBJECTS.

BY NOAH WEBSTER, JUN.

ATTORNEY AT LAW.

Heureuses les villes qui, comme les individus, n'ont point encore pris
leur pli ! Elles seules peuvent aspirer à des loix unanimes, profondes
et sages.   TABLEAU DE PARIS.

PRINTED AT BOSTON, FOR THE AUTHOR,
BY I. THOMAS AND E. T. ANDREWS,
At FAUST'S STATUE, No. 45, Newbury Street.

MDCCXC.

SUBSCRIBERS

THE honorable John Adams, Efq. Vice Prezident of the United Sates, 2 copies.

The hon. Pierce Butler, Efq. }
The hon. Charles Carrol, Efq.
The hon. Oliver Ellfworth, Efq.
The hon. William Few, Efq.
The hon. Benjamin Hawkins, Efq.
The hon. John Henry, Efq. } Senators in Congrefs.
The hon. Ralph Izard, Efq.
The hon. William Samuel Johnfon, Efq.
The hon. Samuel Johnfton, Efq.
The hon. Rufus King, Efq.
The hon. Robert Morris, Efq.
The hon. George Read, Efq. }

Hon. Jonathan Trumbull, Efq. } Reprefentativs
Jeremiah Wadfworth, Efq. 2 copies. } in Congrefs.

A.
Nathaniel W. Appleton, Phyfician, *Bofton*.
John Allen, Efq. Attorney at Law, *Litchfield*.

B.
Ifaac Baldwin, Efq. Clerk of Court, *Litchfield*.
Ifaac Baldwin, jun. Efq. Attorney, do.
Mrs. Ruthy Barlow, *Greenfield*.
Mr. Jeffe Benedict, *Fairfield*.
Mr. Ifaac Bronfon, *Hartford*.
Mr. Caleb Bull, do.
Mr. James Burr, do.
Jonathan Brace, Efq. Attorney, *Glanftenbury*.
David Burr, Efq. Attorney, *Fairfield*.
Barna Bidwell, Efq. Attorney, *New Haven*.
John Bird, Efq. Attorney, *Salifbury*.

C.
Peter Colt, Efq. Treafurer of Connecticut, *Hartford*.
Mr. John M'Curdy, Merchant, do.
Richard M'Curdy, Efq. Attorney, *Lyme*.
John Caldwell, Efq. Alderman of the City of Hartford.
Mr. John Chenevard, jun. *Hartford*.

Hon.

Hon. John Chester, Esq. Judge of the County Court, *Wethersfield.*

Thomas Chester, Esq. Attorney, *Wethersfield.*

Edward Carrington, Physician, *Milford.*

Reverend Henry Channing, *New London.*

Joshua Coit, Esq. Attorney, do.

Mr. Lynde M'Curdy, Merchant, *Norwich.*

Messieurs Coit and Lathrop, Merchants, do.

Mason F. Cogswell, Physician and Surgeon, *Hartford.*

Reverend John Clarke, *Boston.*

D.

Samuel W. Dana, Esq. Attorney, *Middleton.*

David Daggett, Esq. Attorney, *New Haven.*

Mr. Benadam Dennison, *Norwich.*

E.

Pierpont Edwards, Esq. Attorney for Connecticut District, *New Haven.*

F.

Mr. Thomas Fanning, *Norwich.*

G.

William Greenleaf, Esq. *Boston.*

Chauncey Goodrich, Esq. Attorney, *Hartford.*

Elizur Goodrich, Esq. Attorney, *New Haven.*

Gideon Granger, jun. Esq. Attorney, *Suffield.*

Gaylord Griswold, Esq. Attorney, *Windsor.*

H.

His Excellency Samuel Huntington, Esq. Governor of Connecticut.

Lemuel Hopkins, Physician, *Hartford.*

Mr. Asa Hopkins, Druggist,   do.

Uriel Holmes, Esq. Attorney, *New Hartford.*

Colonel Ebenezer Huntington, Merchant, *Norwich.*

Mr. Joseph Howland,   do.

Mr. Andrew Huntington, Merchant,   do.

Mr. Levi Huntington,   do.

David Hull, Physician, *Fairfield.*

William Hillhouse, Esq. Attorney, *New Haven.*

Captain

Captain Pliny Hillyer, *Granby*.
Samuel Henshaw, Esq. *Northampton*.

I.
Jonathan Ingerfoll, Esq. Attorney, *New Haven*.

J.
William Judd, Esq. Attorney, *Farmington*, 2 copies.
John Coffin Jones, Esq. *Boston*.

K.
Mr. Isaac Kibby, Merchant, *Enfield*.
Ephraim Kirby, Esq. Attorney, *Litchfield*.
Mr. Joshua King, *Ridgefield*.

L.
Lynde Lord, Esq. Sheriff of Litchfield County, *Litchfield*.

M.
Reverend Jedidiah Morse, *Charlestown*.
William Moseley, Esq. Attorney, *Hartford*.
Samuel Marsh, Esq. Attorney, *Litchfield*.
Mr. John Morgan, Merchant, *Hartford*.
Mr. William Marsh,   do.
Eneas Munson, jun. Physician, *New Haven*.
Ashur Miller, Esq. Attorney, *Middleton*.
George R. Minot, Esq. Attorney, *Boston*.

N.
Hon. Roger Newberry, Esq. Judge of the County
Court, *Windsor*.

O.
Mr. Jacob Ogden, Merchant, *Hartford*.
Harrison Gray Otis, Esq. Attorney, *Boston*.

P.
Ralph Pomeroy, Esq. Controller of the Treasury,
Hartford.
Enoch Perkins, Esq. Attorney, *Hartford*.
Mr. Nathaniel Patten, Merchant, *Hartford*, 3 copies.
Colonel Joshua Porter, Judge of the County Court,
Salisbury.
Jonas Prentice, jun. Esq. *New Haven*.
Colonel Noah Phelps, *Symsbury*.
Giles Pettibone, Esq. *Norfolk*.   R.

R.

Hon. Jesse Root, Esq. Judge of the Superior Court, *Hartford.*

Nathaniel Rosseter, Esq. *Guilford.*

Ephraim Root, Esq. Attorney, *Hartford.*

Tapping Reeve, Esq. Attorney, *Litchfield.*

S.

Reverend Nathan Strong, *Hartford.*

Thomas Y. Seymour, Esq. Attorney,   do.

Mr. Isaac Sanford, Goldsmith,   do.

Reuben Smith, Esq. *Litchfield.*

Daniel Sherman, Esq. Chief Judge of County Court, *Woodbury.*

General Heman Swift, *Cornwall.*

Lewis B. Sturgis, Esq. Attorney, *Fairfield.*

Mr. James Smedley,   do.

Zephaniah Swift, Esq. *Windham.*

T.

John Trumbull, Esq. State Attorney for Hartford County.

Uriah Tracy, Esq. Attorney, *Litchfield.*

Nathaniel Terry, jun. Esq. Attorney, *Enfield.*

Mr. Thomas Tisdale, Merchant, *Hartford.*

W.

The Hon. Oliver Walcott, Esq. Lieutenant Governor of Connecticut, *Litchfield.*

John Williams, Esq. Attorney, *Wethersfield.*

William Williston, Esq. Attorney, *Symsbury.*

Mr. Joseph Williams, *Norwich.*

Mr. Ashbel Wells, Merchant, *Hartford.*

Alexander Wolcott, Esq. Attorney, *Windsor.*

Mr. Thomas Walley, Merchant, *Boston.*

Thomas Welsh, Physician, *Boston.*

T O

The PRESIDENT,
The VICE PRESIDENT,
The SENATORS, and
The REPRESENTATIVS
OF THE
UNITED STATES of AMERICA,
The following PUBLICATION,
Defigned to
Aid the PRINCIPLES of the REVOLUTION,
T O
Supprefs POLITICAL DISCORD,
AND TO
Diffufe a SPIRIT of ENQUIRY,
Favorable to MORALS, to SCIENCE, and TRUTH,
Is moſt humbly inſcribed,
As a TRIBUTE of RESPECT for their KARACTERS,
Of GRATITUDE for their PUBLIC SERVICES,
And a PLEDGE of ATTACHMENT
TO THE
Prefent CONSTITUTION
OF THE
AMERICAN REPUBLIC,
BY THEIR MOST OBEDIENT,
AND MOST HUMBLE SERVANT,

The Author.

HARTFORD, *June,* 1790.

As the author was absent from the press, and the copy, in some places, obscure or not correct, some errors have unavoidably escaped the notice of the printers. The following are the most material.

Page 47, line 7, after *corporate* add *body*.
  49, line 4 from bottom, for *cognized* reed *organized*.
  54, line 6 of note, for *would* reed *could*.
  53, line 7, for *contrary* reed *contracting*.
  146, last line, for *thousand* reed *hundred*.
  151, line 2 from bottom, for *jurisdiction* reed *usurpation*.
  263, line 13, for *do* reed *did*.
  275, line 5, for *Archorites* reed *Archontes*.
  283, line 14, for *leriquæ* reed *linguæ*, and for *dacedeni duodeni*.
  323, last line of text, for *godfather* reed *grandfather*.
  327, line 7 from bottom, for *change* reed *chance*.
  332, line 7 from bottom, for *masks* reed *marks*.
  334, line 22, place the full point after *equity*.
  349, line 1, for *district* reed *distinct*.
  350, line 2, for *mass* reed *map*.
  355, line 5, for *ilans* reed *elans*.
  365, line 9, for *the manners* reed *this manner*.
  375, line 3 and 4 from bottom, for *ilans* reed *ilands*.
  377, line 4, for *Koman* reed *Roman*.
  382, line 4 from bottom, for *necessarily* reed *necessary*.
  401, line 28, for *vormous* reed *enormous*.

PREFACE.

THE following Collection confifts of Effays and Fugitiv Peeces, ritten at various times, and on different occafions, az wil appeer by their dates and fubjects. Many of them were dictated at the moment, by the impulfe of impreffions made by important political events, and abound with a correfpondent warmth of expreffion. This freedom of language wil be excufed by the frends of the revolution and of good guvernment, who wil recollect the fenfations they hav experienced, amidft the anarky and diftraction which fucceeded the cloze of the war. On fuch occafions a riter wil naturally giv himfelf up to hiz feelings, and hiz manner of *riting* wil flow from hiz manner of *thinking*.

MOST of thoze peeces, which hav appeered before in periodical papers and Magazeens, were publifhed with fictitious fignatures ; for I very erly difcuvered, that altho the name of an old and refpectable karacter givs credit and confequence to hiz ritings, yet the name of a yung man iz often prejudicial to hiz performances. By conceeling my name, the opinions of men hav been prezerved from an undu bias arizing from perfonal prejudices, the faults of the ritings hav been detected, and their merit in public eftimation afcertained.

THE favorable reception given to a number of theze Effays by an indulgent public, induced

me

me to publiſh them in a volum, with ſuch alter‑
ations and emendations, az I had heerd ſuggeſt‑
ed by frends or indifferent reeders, together
with ſome manuſcripts, that my own wiſhes led
me to hope might be uſeful.

DURING the courſe of ten or twelv yeers, I
hav been laboring to correct popular errors, and
to aſſiſt my yung brethren in the road to truth
and virtue ; my publications for theze purpoſes
hav been numerous ; much time haz been ſpent,
which I do not regret, and much cenſure incur‑
red, which my hart tells me I do not dezerv.
The influence of a yung writer cannot be ſo
powerful or extenſiv az that of an eſtabliſhed
karacter ; but I hav ever thot a man's uſeful‑
neſs depends more on *exertion* than on *talents*.
I am attached to America by berth, education
and habit ; but abuv all, by a philoſophical
view of her ſituation, and the ſuperior advanta‑
ges ſhe enjoys, for augmenting the ſum of ſocial
happineſs.

I SHOULD hav added another volum, had not
recent experience convinced me, that few large
publications in this country wil pay a printer,
much leſs an author. Should the Eſſays here
preſented to the public, proov undezerving of
notice, I ſhal, with cheerfulneſs, reſign my oth‑
er papers to oblivion.

THE reeder wil obzerv that the orthography
of the volum iz not uniform. The reezon iz,
that many of the eſſays hav been publiſhed be‑
fore, in the common orthography, and it would
hav been a laborious taſk to copy the whole, for
the ſake of changing the ſpelling.

IN the effays, ritten within the laſt yeer, a conſiderable change of ſpelling iz introduced by way of experiment.   This liberty waz taken by the writers before the age of queen Elizabeth, and to this we are indeted for the preference of modern ſpelling over that of Gower and Chaucer.   The man who admits that the change of *houſbonde, mynde, ygone, moneth* into *huſband, mind, gone, month,* iz an improovment, muſt acknowlege alſo the riting of *helth, breth, rong, tung, munth,* to be an improovment. There iz no alternativ.   Every poſſible reezon that could ever be offered for altering the ſpelling of wurds, ſtil exiſts in full force ; and if a gradual reform ſhould not be made in our language, it wil proov that we are leſs under the influence of reezon than our anceſtors.

Hartford, June, 1790.

CONTENTS.

CONTENTS.

No. I.

On the Education of Youth in America.

No. IV.

On Guvernment.

No. V.

No. VI.

No. VII.

Remarks on the Manners, Guvernment and Debt of the United States.

No. VIII.

No. IX.

No. X.

No. XI.

No. XII.

No.

No.

On

A
COLLECTION of ESSAYS.

Nᵒ· I.

NEW YORK, 1788.

On the EDUCATION of YOUTH in AMERICA.

T HE Education of youth is, in all governments, an object of the firſt conſequence. The impreſſions received in early life, uſually form the characters of individuals ; a union of which forms the general character of a nation.

The mode of Education and the arts taught to youth, have, in every nation, been adapted to its particular ſtage of ſociety or local circumſtances.

In the martial ages, of Greece, the principal ſtudy of its Legiſlators was, to acquaint the young men with the uſe of arms, to inſpire them with an undaunted courage, and to form in the hearts of both ſexes, an invincible attachment to their country. Such was the effect of their regulations for theſe purpoſes, that the very women of Sparta and Athens, would reproach their own ſons, for ſurviving their companions who fell in the field of battle.

Among the warlike Scythians, every male was not only taught to uſe arms for attack and defence ; but was obliged to ſleep in the field, to carry heavy burthens, and to climb rocks and precipices, in order to habituate himſelf to hardſhips, fatigue and danger.

B   In

In Perfia, during the flourishing reign of the great Cyrus, the Education of youth, according to Xenophion, formed a principal branch of the regulations of the empire. The young men were divided into claffes, each of which had fome particular duties to perform, for which they were qualified by previous inftructions and exercife.

While nations are in a barbarous ftate, they have few wants, and confequently few arts. Their principal objects are, defence and fubfiftence ; the Education of a favage therefore extends little farther, than to enable him to ufe, with dexterity, a bow and a tomahawk.

But in the progrefs of manners and of arts, war ceafes to be the employment of whole nations ; it becomes the bufinefs of a few, who are paid for defending their country. Artificial wants multiply the number of occupations ; and thefe require a great diverfity in the mode of Education. Every youth muft be inftructed in the bufinefs by which he is to procure fubfiftence. Even the civilities of behavior, in polifhed fociety, become a fcience ; a bow and a curtefy are taught with as much care and precifion, as the elements of Mathematics. Education proceeds therefore, by gradual advances, from fimplicity to corruption. Its firft object, among rude nations, is fafety ; its next, utility ; it afterwards extends to convenience ; and among the opulent part of civilized nations, it is directed principally to fhow and amufement.

In defpotic ftates, Education, like religion, is made fubfervient to government. In fome of the vaft empires of Afia, children are always inftructed in the occupation of their parents ; thus the fame arts are always continued in the fame families. Such an inftitution cramps genius, and limits the progrefs of national improvement ; at the fame time it is an almoft immoveable barrier againft the introduction of vice, luxury, faction and changes in government. This is one of the principal caufes, which have operated in combining numerous millions of the human race under one form of government, and preferving national tranquillity

quillity for incredible periods of time. The empire of China, whofe government was founded on the patriarchical difcipline, has not fuffered a revolution in laws, manners or language, for many thoufand years.

In the complicated fyftems of government which are eftablifhed among the civilized nations of Europe, Education has lefs influence in forming a national character; but there is no ftate, in which it has not an infeparable connection with morals, and a confequential influence upon the peace and happinefs of fociety.

Education is a fubject which has been exhaufted by the ableft writers, both among the ancients and moderns. I am not vain enough to fuppofe I can fuggeft any new ideas upon fo trite a theme as Education in general; but perhaps the manner of conducting the youth in America may be capable of fome improvement. Our conftitutions of civil government are not yet firmly eftablifhed; our national character is not yet formed; and it is an object of vaft magnitude that fyftems of Education fhould be adopted and purfued, which may not only diffufe a knowlege of the fciences, but may implant, in the minds of the American youth, the principles of virtue and of liberty; and infpire them with juft and liberal ideas of government, and with an inviolable attachment to their own country. It now becomes every American to examin the modes of Education in Europe, to fee how far they are applicable in this country, and whether it is not poffible to make fome valuable alterations, adapted to our local and political circumftances. Let us examin the fubject in two views. Firft, as it refpects arts and fciences. Secondly, as it is connected with morals and government. In each of thefe articles, let us fee what errors may be found, and what improvements fuggefted, in our prefent practice.

The firft error that I would mention, is, a too general attention to the dead languages, with a neglect of our own.

This

This practice proceeds probably from the common use of the Greek and Roman tongues, before the English was brought to perfection. There was a long period of time, when these languages were almost the only repositories of science in Europe. Men, who had a taste for learning, were under a necessity of recurring to the sources, the Greek and Roman authors. These will ever be held in the highest estimation both for stile and sentiment; but the most valuable of them have English translations, which, if they do not contain all the elegance, communicate all the ideas of the originals. The English language, perhaps, at this moment, is the repository of as much learning, as one half the languages of Europe. In copiousness it exceeds all modern tongues; and though inferior to the Greek and French in softness and harmony, yet it exceeds the French in variety; it almost equals the Greek and Roman in energy, and falls very little short of any language in the regularity of its construction.*

In deliberating upon any plan of instruction, we should be attentive to its future influence and probable advantages. What advantage does a merchant, a mechanic, a farmer, derive from an acquaintance with the Greek and Roman tongues? It is true, the etymology of words cannot be well understood, without a knowlege of the original languages of which ours is composed. But a very accurate knowlege of the meaning of words and of the true construction of sentences, may be obtained by the help of Dictionaries and good English writers; and this is all that is necessary in the common occupations of life. But suppose there is some advantage to be derived from an acquaintance with the dead languages, will this compensate for the loss of five or perhaps seven years of valuable time? Life is short, and every hour should be employed to good purposes. If there are no studies of more consequence to boys, than those of Latin and Greek, let these languages employ their time; for idleness is the bane of youth.

But

---

* This remark is confined solely to *its construction*; in point of orthography, our language is intolerably irregular.

But when we have an elegant and copious language of our own, with innumerable writers upon ethics, geography, hiftory, commerce and government; fubjects immediately interefting to every man; how can a parent be juftified in keeping his fon feveral years over rules of Syntax, which he forgets when he fhuts his book; or which, if remembered, can be of little or no ufe in any branch of bufinefs? This abfurdity is the fubject of common complaint; men fee and feel the impropriety of the ufual practice; and yet no arguments that have hitherto been ufed, have been fufficient to change the fyftem; or to place an Englifh fchool on a footing with a Latin one, in point of reputation.

It is not my wifh to difcountenance totally the ftudy of the dead languages. On the other hand I fhould urge a more clofe attention to them, among young men who are defigned for the learned profeffions. The poets, the orators, the philofophers and the hiftorians of Greece and Rome, furnifh the moft excellent models of Stile, and the richeft treafures of Science. The flight attention given to a few of thefe authors, in our ufual courfe of Education, is rather calculated to make pedants than fcholars; and the time employed in gaining fuperficial knowlege is really wafted.

> " A little learning is a dangerous thing,
> " Drink deep, or tafte not the Pierian fpring."

But my meaning is, that the dead languages are not neceffary for men of bufinefs, merchants, mechanics, planters, &c. nor of utility fufficient to indemnify them for the expenfe of time and money which is requifite to acquire a tolerable acquaintance with the Greek and Roman authors. Merchants often have occafion for a knowlege of fome foreign living language, as, the French, the Italian, the Spanifh, or the German; but men, whofe bufinefs is wholly domeftic, have little or no ufe for any language but their own; much lefs, for languages known only in books.

There is one very neceffary ufe of the Latin language, which will always prevent it from falling into neglect;

neglect; which is, that it ferves as a common inter-
preter among the learned of all nations and ages.
Epitaphs, infcriptions on monuments and medals,
treaties, &c. defigned for perpetuity, are written in
Latin, which is every where underftood by the learned, and being a dead language is liable to no change.

But the high eftimation in which the learned languages have been held, has difcouraged a due attention
to our own.   People find themfelves able without
much ftudy to write and fpeak the Englifh intelligibly,
and thus have been led to think rules of no utility.
This opinion has produced various and arbitrary practices, in the ufe of the language, even among men of
the moft information and accuracy ; and this diverfity
has produced another opinion, both falfe and injurious
to the language, that there are no rules or principles
on which the pronunciation and conftruction can be
fettled.

This neglect is fo general, that there is fcarcely an
inftitution to be found in the country, where the Englifh tongue is taught regularly, from its elements to its
true and elegant conftruction, in profe and verfe.   Perhaps in moft fchools, boys are taught the definition of
the parts of fpeech, and a few hard names which they
do not underftand, and which the teacher feldom attempts to explain ; this is called *learning grammar.*
This practice of learning queftions and anfwers without acquiring any ideas, has given rife to a common
remark, *that grammar is a dry ftudy* ; and fo is every
other ftudy which is profecuted without improving the
head or the heart.   The ftudy of geography is equally
dry, when the fubject is not underftood.   But when
grammar is taught by the help of vifible objects ; when
children perceive that differences of words arife from
differences in things, which they may learn at a very
early period of life, the ftudy becomes entertaining, as
well as improving.   In general, when a ftudy of any
kind is tirefome to a perfon, it is a prefumptive evidence
that he does not make any proficiency in knowlege,
and this is almoft always the fault of the inftructor.

In

In a few inftances perhaps the ftudy of Englifh is thought an object of confequence; but here alfo there is a great error in the common practice; for the ftudy of Englifh is preceded by feveral years attention to Latin and Greek. Nay, there are men, who contend that the beft way to become acquainted with Englifh, is to learn Latin firft. Common fenfe may juftly fmile at fuch an opinion; but experience proves it to be falfe.

If language is to be taught mechanically, or by rote, it is a matter of little confequence whether the rules are in Englifh, Latin or Greek: But if children are to acquire *ideas*, it is certainly eafier to obtain them in a language which they underftand, than in a foreign tongue. The diftinctions between the principal parts of fpeech are founded in nature, and are within the capacity of a fchool boy. Thefe diftinctions fhould be explained in Englifh, and when well underftood, will facilitate the acquifition of other languages. Without fome preparation of this kind, boys will often find a foreign language extremely difficult, and fometimes be difcouraged. We often fee young perfons of both fexes, puzzling their heads with French, when they can hardly write two fentences of good Englifh. They plod on for fome months with much fatigue, little improvement, and lefs pleafure, and then relinquifh the attempt.

The principles of any fcience afford pleafure to the ftudent who comprehends them. In order to render the ftudy of language agreeable, the diftinctions between words fhould be illuftrated by the differences in vifible objects. Examples fhould be prefented to the fenfes, which are the inlets of all our knowlege. That *nouns are the names of things, and that adjectives exprefs their qualities*, are abftract definitions, which a boy may repeat five years without comprehending the meaning. But that *table* is the name of an article, and *hard* or *fquare* is its property, is a diftinction obvious to the fenfes, and confequently within a child's capacity.

There

There is one general practice in schools, which I censure with diffidence; not because I doubt the propriety of the censure, but because it is opposed to deep rooted prejudices: This practice is the use of the Bible as a school book.   There are two reasons why this practice has so generally prevailed: The first is, that families in the country are not generally supplied with any other book: The second, an opinion that the reading of the scriptures will impress, upon the minds of youth, the important truths of religion and morality. The first may be easily removed; and the purpose of the last is counteracted by the practice itself.

If people design the doctrines of the Bible as a system of religion, ought they to appropriate the book to purposes foreign to this design ? Will not a familiarity, contracted by a careless disrespectful reading of the sacred volume, weaken the influence of its precepts upon the heart ?

Let us attend to the effect of familiarity in other things.

The rigid Puritans, who first settled the New England States, often chose their burying ground in the center of their settlements.   Convenience might have been a motive for the choice ; but it is probable that a stronger reason was, the influence which they supposed the frequent burials and constant sight of the tombs would have upon the lives of men.   The choice, however, for the latter purpose, was extremely injudicious ; for it may be laid down as a general rule, that those who live in a constant view of death, will become hardened to its terrors.

No person has less sensibility than the Surgeon, who has been accustomed to the amputation of limbs. No person thinks less of death, than the Soldier, who has frequently walked over the carcasses of his slain comrades ; or the Sexton, who lives among the tombs.

Objects that affect the mind strongly, whether the sensations they excite are painful or pleasureable, always lose their effect by a frequent repetition of their impressions.

preffions.* Thofe parts of the fcripture, therefore, which are calculated to ftrike terror to the mind, lofe their influence by being too frequently brought into view. The fame objection will not apply to the hiftory and morality of the Bible; felect paffages of which may be read in fchools to great advantage. In fome countries, the common people are not permitted to read the Bible at all: In ours, it is as common as a newfpaper, and in fchools, is read with nearly the fame degree of refpect. Both thefe practices appear to be extremes. My wifh is not to fee the Bible excluded from fchools, but to fee it ufed as a fyftem of religion and morality.

These remarks fuggeft another error which is often committed in our inferior fchools: I mean that of putting boys into difficult fciences, while they are too young to exercife their reafon upon abftract fubjects. For example; boys are often put to the ftudy of math-ematics, at the age of eight or ten years; and before they can either read or write. In order to fhow the impropriety of fuch a practice, it is neceffary to repeat what was juft now obferved, that our fenfes are the avenues of knowlege. This fact proves that the moft natural courfe of Education is that which employs, firft the fenfes or powers of the body, or thofe faculties of the mind which firft acquire ftrength; and then proceeds to thofe ftudies which depend on the power of comparing and combining ideas. The art of writ-ing is mechanical and imitative; this may therefore employ boys, as foon as their fingers have ftrength fufficient

* The veneration we have for a great character, ceafes with an intimate acquaintance with the man. The fame principle is obfervable in the body. High feafoned food, without fre-quent intervals of abftinence, lofes its relifh. On the other hand, objects that make flight impreffions at firft, acquire ftrength by repetition. An elegant fimplicity in a building may not affect the mind with great pleafure at firft fight; but the pleafure will always increafe with repeated examinations of the ftructure. Thus by habit, we become exceffively fond of food which does not relifh at firft tafting; and ftrong attach-ments between the fexes often take place from indifference, and even from averfion.

ficient to command a pen. A knowledge of letters requires the exercise of a mental power, memory; but this is coeval almost with the first operations of the human mind; and with respect to objects of sense, is almost perfect even in childhood. Children may therefore be taught reading, as soon as their organs of speech have acquired strength sufficient to articulate the sounds of words.*

But those sciences, a knowlege of which is acquired principally by the reasoning faculties, should be postponed to a more advanced period of life. In the course of an English Education, mathematics should be perhaps the last study of youth in schools. Years of valuable time are sometimes thrown away, in a fruitless application to sciences, the principles of which are above the comprehension of the students.

There is no particular age, at which every boy is qualified to enter upon mathematics to advantage. The proper time can be best determined by the instructors, who are acquainted with the different capacities of their pupils.

Another error, which is frequent in America, is that a master undertakes to teach many different branches in the same school. In new settlements, where people are poor, and live in scattered situations, the practice is often unavoidable: But in populous towns, it must be considered as a defective plan of Education. For suppose the teacher to be equally master of all the branches which he attempts to teach, which seldom happens, yet his attention must be distracted with a multiplicity of objects, and consequently painful to himself and not useful to the pupils. Add to this the continual interruptions which the students of one branch suffer from those of another, which must retard the progress of the whole

---

* Great caution should be observed in teaching children to pronounce the letters of the alphabet. The labials are easily pronounced; thus the first words a child can speak are *papa* and *mama*. But there are some letters, particularly *l* and *r*, which are of difficult pronunciation, and children should not be pressed to speak words in which they occur. The difficulty may produce a habit of stammering.

whole fchool. It is a much more eligible plan to appropriate an apartment to each branch of Education,
with a teacher who makes that branch his fole employment.   The principal academies in Europe and America are on this plan, which both reafon and experience
prove to be the moft ufeful.

With refpect to literary inftitutions of the firft rank,
it appears to me that their local fituations are an object
of importance.   It is a fubject of controverfy, whether
a large city or a country village is the moft eligible fituation for a college or univerfity.   But the arguments
in favor of the latter, appear to me decifive.   Large
cities are always fcenes of diffipation and amufement,
which have a tendency to corrupt the hearts of youth
and divert their minds from their literary purfuits.
Reafon teaches this doctrine, and experience has uniformly confirmed the truth of it.

Strict difcipline is effential to the profperity of a public feminary of fcience ; and this is eftablifhed with
more facility, and fupported with more uniformity, in
a fmall village, where there are no great objects of curiofity to interrupt the ftudies of youth or to call their
attention from the orders of the fociety.

That the morals of young men, as well as their application to fcience, depend much on retirement, will
be generally acknowleged ; but it will be faid alfo, that
the company in large towns will improve their manners.
The queftion then is, which fhall be facrificed ; the advantage of an *uncorrupted heart* and an *improved head* ;
or of polifhed manners.   But this queftion fuppofes
that the virtues of the heart and the polifh of the gentleman are incompatible with each other ; which is by
no means true.   The gentleman and the fcholar are
often united in the fame perfon.   But both are not
formed by the fame means.   The improvement of the
head requires clofe application to books ; the refinement of manners rather attends fome degree of diffipation, or at leaft a relaxation of the mind.   To preferve
the purity of the heart, it is fometimes neceffary, and
always ufeful, to place a youth beyond the reach of bad
examples ;

examples ; whereas a general knowlege of the world, of all kinds of company, is requifite to teach a univerfal propriety of behavior.

But youth is the time to form both the head and the heart. The underftanding is indeed ever enlarging ; but the feeds of knowlege fhould be planted in the mind, while it is young and fufceptible ; and if the mind is not kept untainted in *youth*, there is little probability that the moral character of the *man* will be unblemifh-ed. A genteel addrefs, on the other hand, *may* be ac-quired at any time of life, and *muſt* be acquired, if ever, by mingling with good company. But were the culti-vation of the underftanding and of the heart, inconfift-ent with genteel manners, ftill no rational perfon could hefitate which to prefer. The goodnefs of a heart is of infinitely more confequence to fociety, than an elegance of manners ; nor will any fuperficial accom-plifhments repair the want of principle in the mind. It is always better to be *vulgarly right*, than *politely wrong*.

But if the amufements, diffipation and vicious ex-amples in populous cities render them improper places for feats of learning ; the monkifh mode of fequefter-ing boys from other fociety, and confining them to the apartments of a college, appears to me another fault. The human mind is like a rich field, which, without conftant care, will ever be covered with a luxuriant growth of weeds. It is extremely dangerous to fuffer young men to pafs the moft critical period of life, when the paffions are ftrong, the judgement weak, and the heart fufceptible and unfufpecting, in a fituation where there is not the leaft reftraint upon their inclinations. My own obfervations lead me to draw the veil of filence over the ill effects of this practice. But it is to be wifh-ed that youth might always be kept under the infpec-tion of age and fuperior wifdom ; that literary inftitu-tions might be fo fituated, that the ftudents might live in decent families, be fubject, in fome meafure, to their difcipline, and ever under the control of thofe whom they refpect.

Perhaps

Perhaps it may alfo be numbered among the errors in our fyftems of Education, that, in all our univerfities and colleges, the ftudents are all reftricted to the fame courfe of ftudy, and by being claffed, limited to the fame progrefs. Claffing is neceffary, but whether ftudents fhould not be removeable from the lower to the higher claffes, as a reward for their fuperior induftry and improvements, is fubmitted to thofe who know the effect of emulation upon the human mind.

But young gentlemen are not all defigned for the fame line of bufinefs, and why fhould they purfue the fame ftudies ? Why fhould a merchant trouble himfelf with the rules of Greek and Roman fyntax, or a planter puzzle his head with conic fections ? Life is too fhort to acquire, and the mind of man too feeble to contain, the whole circle of fciences. The greateft genius on earth, not even a Bacon, can be a perfect mafter of *every* branch ; but any moderate genius may, by fuitable application, be perfect in any *one* branch. By attempting therefore to teach young gentlemen every thing, we make the moft of them mere fmatterers in fcience. In order to qualify perfons to figure in any profeffion, it is neceffary that they fhould attend clofely to thofe branches of learning which lead to it.

There are fome arts and fciences which are neceffary for every man. Every man fhould be able to fpeak and write his native tongue with correctnefs ; and have fome knowlege of mathematics. The rules of arithmetic are indifpenfably requifite. But befides the learning which is of common utility, lads fhould be directed to purfue thofe branches which are connected more immediately with the bufinefs for which they are deftined.

It would be very ufeful for the farming part of the community, to furnifh country fchools with fome eafy fyftem of practical hufbandry. By repeatedly reading fome book of this kind, the mind would be ftored with ideas, which might not indeed be underftood in youth, but which would be called into practice in fome fubfequent period of life. This would lead the mind to the fubject of agriculture, and pave the way for improvements.   **Young**

Young gentlemen, defigned for the mercantile line, after having learned to write and fpeak Englifh correctly, might attend to French, Italian, or fuch other living language, as they will probably want in the courfe of bufinefs. Thefe languages fhould be learned early in youth, while the organs are yet pliable ; otherwife the pronunciation will probably be imperfect. Thefe ftudies might be fucceeded by fome attention to chronology, and a regular application to geography, mathematics, hiftory, the general regulations of commercial nations, principles of advance in trade, of infurance, and to the general principles of government.

It appears to me that fuch a courfe of Education, which might be completed by the age of fifteen or fixteen, would have a tendency to make better merchants than the ufual practice which confines boys to Lucian, Ovid and Tully, till they are fourteen, and then turns them into a ftore, without an idea of their bufinefs, or one article of Education neceffary for them, except perhaps a knowlege of writing and figures.

Such a fyftem of Englifh Education is alfo much preferable to a univerfity Education, even with the ufual honors ; for it might be finifhed fo early as to leave young perfons time to ferve a regular apprenticefhip, without which no perfon fhould enter upon bufinefs. But by the time a univerfity Education is completed, young men commonly commence *gentlemen* ; their age and their pride will not fuffer them to go thro the drudgery of a compting houfe, and they enter upon bufinefs without the requifite accomplifhments. Indeed it appears to me that what is now called a *liberal Education*, difqualifies a man for bufinefs. Habits are formed in youth and by practice ; and as bufinefs is, in fome meafure, mechanical, every perfon fhould be exercifed in his employment, in an early period of life, that his habits may be formed by the time his apprenticefhip expires. An Education in a univerfity interferes with the forming of thefe habits ; and perhaps forms oppofite habits ; the mind may contract a fondnefs for cafe, for pleafure or for books, which no efforts

can

can overcome. An academic Education, which fhould furnifh the youth with fome ideas of men and things, and leave time for an apprenticefhip, before the age of twenty one years, would in my opinion, be the moft eligible for young men who are defigned for activ employments.

The method purfued in our colleges is better calculated to fit youth for the learned profeffions than for bufinefs. But perhaps the period of ftudy, required as the condition of receiving the ufual degrees, is too fhort. Four years, with the moft affiduous application, are a fhort time to furnifh the mind with the neceffary knowlege of the languages and of the feveral fciences. It might perhaps have been a period fufficiently long for an infant fettlement, as America was, at the time when moft of our colleges were founded. But as the country becomes populous, wealthy and refpectable, it may be worthy of confideration, whether the period of academic life fhould not be extended to fix or feven years.

But the principal defect in our plan of Education in America, is, the want of good teachers in the academies and common fchools. By good teachers I mean, men of unblemifhed reputation, and poffeffed of abilities, competent to their ftations. That a man fhould be mafter of what he undertakes to teach, is a point that will not be difputed ; and yet it is certain that abilities are often difpenfed with, either thro inattention or fear of expenfe.

To thofe who employ ignorant men to inftruct their children, permit me to fuggeft one important idea : That it is better for youth to have *no* Education, than to have a bad one ; for it is more difficult to eradicate habits, than to imprefs new ideas. The tender fhrub is eafily bent to any figure ; but the tree, which has acquired its full growth, refifts all impreffions.

Yet abilities are not the fole requifites. The inftructors of youth ought, of all men, to be the moft prudent, accomplifhed, agreeable and refpectable. What avail a man's parts, if, while he is the " wifeft
and

and brighteſt," he is the "meaneſt of mankind ?" The
pernicious effects of bad example on the *minds* of youth
will probably be acknowleged ; but with a view to *improvement*, it is indifpenſably neceſſary that the teachers ſhould poſſeſs good breeding and agreeable manners.
In order to give full effect to inſtructions, it is requiſite
that they ſhould proceed from a man who is loved and
reſpected. But a low bred clown, or moroſe tyrant,
can command neither love nor reſpect ; and that pupil
who has no motive for application to books, but the
fear of a rod, will not make a ſcholar.

The rod is often neceſſary in ſchool ; eſpecially after
the children have been accuſtomed to diſobedience and
a licentious behavior at home. All government originates in families, and if neglected there, it will hardly
exiſt in ſociety ; but the want of it muſt be ſupplied
by the rod in ſchool, the penal laws of the ſtate, and the
terrors of divine wrath from the pulpit. The government both of families and ſchools ſhould be abſolute.
There ſhould, in families, be no appeal from one parent
to another, with the proſpect of pardon for offences:
The one ſhould always vindicate, at leaſt apparently,
the conduct of the other. In ſchools the maſter ſhould
be abſolute in command ; for it is utterly impoſſible
for any man to ſupport order and diſcipline among
children, who are indulged with an appeal to their parents. A proper ſubordination in families would generally ſuperſede the neceſſity of ſeverity in ſchools ; and
a ſtrict diſcipline in both is the beſt foundation of good
order in political ſociety.

If parents ſhould ſay, " we cannot give the inſtruct-
ors of our children unlimited authority over them, for
it may be abuſed and our children injured ;" I would
anſwer, they muſt not place them under the direction
of any man, in whoſe temper, judgement and abilities,
they do not repoſe perfect confidence. The teacher
ſhould be, if ſuch can be found, as judicious and rea-
ſonable a man as the parent.

There can be little improvement in ſchools, without
ſtrict ſubordination ; there can be no ſubordination,

without

without principles of efteem and refpect in the pupils ; and the pupils cannot efteem and refpect a man who is not in himfelf refpectable, and who is not treated with refpect by their parents. It may be laid down as an invariable maxim, that a perfon is not fit to fuperintend the Education of children, who has not the qualifications which will command the efteem and refpect of his pupils. This maxim is founded on a truth which every perfon may have obferved ; that children always *love* an *amiable* man, and always *efteem* a *refpectable* one. Men and women have their paffions, which often rule their judgement and their conduct. They have their caprices, their interefts and their prejudices, which at times incline them to treat the moft meritorious characters with difrefpect. But children, artlefs and unfufpecting, refign their hearts to any perfon whofe manners are agreeable, and whofe conduct is refpectable. Whenever, therefore, pupils ceafe to refpect their teacher, he fhould be inftantly difmiffed.

Refpect for an inftructor will often fupply the place of a rod of correction. The pupil's attachment will lead him to clofe attention to his ftudies ; he fears not the *rod* fo much as the *difpleafure* of his teacher ; he waits for a fmile, or dreads a frown ; he receives his inftructions and copies his manners. This generous principle, the fear of offending, will prompt youth to exertions ; and inftead of feverity on the one hand, and of flavifh fear, with reluctant obedience on the other, mutual efteem, refpect and confidence ftrew flowers in the road to knowlege.

With refpect to morals and civil fociety, the other view in which I propofed to treat this fubject, the effects of Education are fo certain and extenfiv, that it behooves every parent and guardian to be particularly attentiv to the characters of the men, whofe province it is to form the minds of youth.

From a ftrange inverfion of the order of nature, the caufe of which it is not neceffary to unfold, the moft important bufinefs in civil fociety, is, in many parts of America, committed to the moft worthlefs characters.

C- The

The Education of youth, an employment of more consequence than making laws and preaching the gospel,
because it lays the foundation on which both law and
gospel rest for success; this Education is sunk to a level
with the most menial services.   In most instances we
find the higher seminaries of learning intrusted to men
of good characters, and possessed of the moral virtues
and social affections.   But many of our inferior schools,
which, so far as the heart is concerned, are as important
as colleges, are kept by men of no breeding, and many
of them, by men infamous for the most detestable
vices.*   Will this be denied? will it be denied, that
before the war, it was a frequent practice for gentlemen
                                        to

    * How different this practice from the manner of educating
youth in Rome, during the flourishing ages of the republic !
There the attention to children commenced with their birth ;
an infant was not educated in the cottage of a hireling nurse,
but in the very bosom of its mother, whose principal praise
was, that she superintended her family.   Parents were careful
to choose some aged matron to take care of their children ; to
form their first habits of speaking and acting ; to watch their
growing passions, and direct them to their proper objects ; to
guard them from all immodest sports, preserve their minds innocent, and direct their attention to liberal pursuits.
    "—Filius—non in cella emptæ nutricis sed gremio ac sinu
matris educabatur, cujus præcipua laus, tueri domum, et in-
servire liberis. · Eligebatur autem aliqua major natu propin-
qua, cujus probatis spectatilque moribus, omnis cujuspiam
familiæ soboles committeretur, coram qua neque dicere fas erat
quod turpe dictu, neque facere quod inhonestum factu videre-
tur.   Ac non studia modo curasque, sed remissiones etiam lusus-
que puerorum, sanctitate quadam ac verecundia temperabat."
In this manner were educated the Gracchi, Cæsar, and other
celebrated Romans.   " Quæ disciplina ac severitas eo pertine-
bat, ut sincera et intergra et nullis pravitatibus detorta unius
cujusque natura, toto statem pectore, arriperet artes honestas."
——Tacitus de Orat. Dial. 28.
    The historian then proceeds to mention the corruption of
manners, and the vicious mode of Education, in the later ages
of Rome.   He says, children were committed to some maid,
with the vilest slaves ; with whom they were initiated in their
low conversation and manners.   " Horum fabulis et erroribus
teneri statim et rudes animi imbuuntur ; nec quis quam in toto
domo pensi habet, quid coram infante domino aut dicat aut
faciat."——Ibm. 29.

to purchafe convicts, who had been tranfported for their crimes, and employ them as private tutors in their families ?

Gracious Heavens ! Muft the wretches, who have forfeited their lives, and been pronounced unworthy to be inhabitants of a *foreign* country, be entrufted with the Education, the morals, the character of *American* youth ?

Will it be denied that many of the inftructors of youth, whofe examples and precepts fhould form their minds for good men and ufeful citizens, are often found to fleep away, in fchool, the fumes of a debauch, and to ftun the ears of their pupils with frequent blafphemy ? It is idle to fupprefs fuch truths ; nay more, it is wicked. The practice of employing low and vicious characters to direct the ftudies of youth, is, in a high degree, criminal ; it is deftructive of the order and peace of fociety; it is treafon againft morals, and of courfe, againft government ; it ought to be arraigned before the tribunal of reafon, and condemned by all intelligent beings. The practice is fo exceedingly abfurd, that it is furprifing it could ever have prevailed among rational people. Parents wifh their children to be *well bred*, yet place them under the care of *clowns*. They wifh to fecure their hearts from *vicious principles* and *habits*, yet commit them to the care of men of the moft *profligate lives*. They wifh to have their children taught *obedience* and *refpect* for fuperiors, yet give them a mafter that both parents and children *defpife*. A practice fo glaringly abfurd and irrational has no name in any language ! Parents themfelves will not affociate with the men, whofe company they *oblige* their children to keep, even in that moft important period, when habits are forming for life.*

Are

* The practice of employing low characters in fchools is not novel—Afcham, preceptor to Queen Elizabeth, gives us the following account of the practice in his time. " Pity it is that commonly more care is had ; yea and that among very wife men, to find out rather a cunning man for their horfe, than a cunning man for their children. They fay, nay, in word ; but

C 2   the

Are parents and guardians ignorant, that children always imitate thofe with whom they live or affociate? That a boy, bred in the woods, will be a favage? That another, bred in the army, will have the manners of a foldier? That a third, bred in a kitchen, will fpeak the language, and poffefs the ideas, of fervants? And that a fourth, bred in genteel company, will have the manners of a gentleman? We cannot believe that many people are ignorant of thefe truths. Their conduct therefore can be afcribed to nothing but inattention or fear of expenfe. It is perhaps literally true, that a wild life among favages is preferable to an Education in a kitchen, or under a drunken tutor; for favages would leave the mind uncorrupted with the vices, which reign among flaves and the depraved part of civilized nations. It is therefore a point of infinite importance to fociety, that youth fhould not affociate with perfons whofe manners they ought not to imitate; much lefs fhould they be doomed to pafs the moft fufceptable period of life, with clowns, profligates and flaves.

There are people fo ignorant of the conftitution of our natures, as to declare, that young people fhould fee vices and their confequences, that they may learn to

they do fo, in deed. For to one they will give a ftipend of two hundred crowns, and loth to offer the other two hundred fhillings. God, that fitteth in the Heaven, laugheth their choice to fcorn and rewardeth their liberality as it fhould: for he fuffereth them to have *tame* and *well ordered horfes*; but *wild* and *unfortunate children*: and therefore in the end they find more pleafure in their horfe, than comfort in their child.''

This is *old language*, but the facts ftated are *modern truths*. The barbarous Gothic practice has furvived all the attacks of common fenfe, and in many parts of America, a gentleman's groom is on a level with his fchoolmafter, in point of reputation. But hear another authority for the practice in England.

'' As the cafe now ftands, thofe of the firft quality pay their *tutors* but little above half fo much as they do their *footmen*.''—*Guardian*, No. 94.

'' 'Tis monftrous indeed that men of the beft eftates and families are more folicitous about the tutelage of a favorite *dog* or *horfe*, than of their *heirs male*.''—*Ibm*.

to deteſt and ſhun them.   Such reaſoning is like that
of the novel writers, who attempt to defend their de-
lineations of abandoned characters ; and that of ſtage
players, who would vindicate the obſcene exhibitions
of a theater ; but the reaſoning is totally falſe.*   Vice
always ſpreads by being publiſhed ; young people are
taught many vices by fiction, books or public exhibitions ; vices, which they never would have known, had
they never read ſuch books or attended ſuch public places. Crimes of all kinds, vices, judicial trials neceſſarily
obſcene, and infamous puniſhments, ſhould, if poſſible,
be concealed from the young.   An examination in a
court of juſtice may teach the tricks of a knave, the
arts of a thief, and the evaſions of hackneyed offenders,
to a dozen young culprits, and even tempt thoſe who
have never committed a crime, to make a trial of their
ſkill.   A newſpaper may ſpread crimes ; by commu-
nicating to a nation the knowlege of an ingenious trick
of villainy, which, had it been ſuppreſſed, might have
died with its firſt inventor.   It is not true that the effects of vice and crimes deter others from the practice ;
except when rarely ſeen.   On the other hand, frequent exhibitions either ceaſe to make any impreſſions
on the minds of ſpectators, or elſe reconcile them to a
courſe of life, which at firſt was diſagreeable.

> " Vice is a monſter of ſo frightful mein,
> As to be hated, needs but to be ſeen ;
> Yet ſeen too oft, familiar with her face,
> We firſt endure, then pity, then embrace."

For theſe reaſons, children ſhould keep the beſt of
company, that they might have before them the beſt
manners, the beſt breeding, and the beſt converſation.
Their minds ſhould be kept untainted, till their reaſoning faculties have acquired ſtrength, and the good principles which may be planted in their minds, have tak-
en deep root.   They will then be able to make a firm
                                                           and

* The fact related by Juſtin, of an ancient people, will apply univerſally.   " Tanto plus in illis proficit vitiorum ig-
noratio, quam in his cognitio virtutis."   An ignorance of vice
has a better effect, than a knowlege of virtue.

and probably a fuccefsful refiftance, againft the attacks
of fecret corruption and brazen libertinifm.

Our legiflators frame laws for the fuppreffion of vice
and immorality ; our divines thunder, from the pulpit, the terrors of infinite wrath, againft the vices that
ftain the characters of men. And do laws and preaching effect a reformation of manners ? Experience
would not give a very favorable anfwer to this inquiry.
The reafon is obvious ; the attempts are directed to
the wrong objects. Laws can only check the public
effects of vicious principles ; but can never reach the
principles themfelves ; and preaching is not very intelligible to people, till they arrive at an age when their
principles are rooted, or their habits firmly eftablifhed.
An attempt to eradicate old habits, is as abfurd, as to
lop off the branches of a huge oak, in order to root it
out of a rich foil. The moft that fuch clipping will
effect, is to prevent a further growth.

The only practicable method to reform mankind, is
to begin with children ; to banifh, if poffible, from their
company, every low bred, drunken, immoral character. Virtue and vice will not grow together in a great
degree, but they will grow where they are planted,
and when one has taken root, it is not eafily fupplant-
ed by the other. The great art of correcting mankind
therefore, confifts in prepoffeffing the mind with good
principles.

For this reafon fociety requires that the Education
of youth fhould be watched with the moft fcrupulous
attention. Education, in a great meafure, forms the
moral characters of men, and morals are the bafis of
government.* Education fhould therefore be the firft
care of a Legiflature ; not merely the inftitution of fchools,
but the furnifhing of them with the beft men for teachers. A good fyftem of Education fhould be the firft
article in the code of political regulations ; for it is
much eafier to introduce and eftablifh an effectual fyftem for preferving morals, than to correct, by penal
                                                    ftatutes,

* Plus ibi beni mores valent, quam alibi bonæ leges.
                                    Tac. de Mor. Germ. 19.

statutes, the ill effects of a bad syftem. I am fo fully
perfuaded of this, that I fhall almoft adore that great
man, who fhall change our practice and opinions, and
make it refpectable for the firft and beft men to fuperintend the Education of youth.

Another defect in our fchools, which, fince the revolution, is become inexcufeable, is the want of proper
books. The collections which are now ufed confift of
effays that refpect foreign and ancient nations. The
minds of youth are perpetually led to the hiftory of
Greece and Rome or to Great Britain ; boys are conftantly repeating the declamations of Demofthenes and
Cicero, or debates upon fome political queftion in the
Britifh Parliment. Thefe are excellent fpecimens of
good fenfe, polifhed ftile and perfect oratory ; but they
are not interefting to children. They cannot be very
ufeful, except to young gentlemen who want them as
models of reafoning and eloquence, in the pulpit or at
the bar.

But every child in America fhould be acquainted
with his own country. He fhould read books that
furnifh him with ideas that will be ufeful to him in
life and practice. As foon as he opens his lips, he
fhould rehearfe the hiftory of his own country ; he
fhould lifp the praife of liberty, and of thofe illuftrious
heroes and ftatefmen, who have wrought a revolution
in her favor.

A felection of effays, refpecting the fettlement and
geography of America ; the hiftory of the late revolution and of the moft remarkable characters and events
that diftinguifhed it, and a compendium of the principles of the federal and provincial governments, fhould
be the principal fchool book in the United States.
Thefe are interefting objects to every man ; they call
home the minds of youth and fix them upon the interefts of their own country, and they affift in forming
attachments to it, as well as in enlarging the underftanding.

" It is obferved by the great Montefquieu, that the
laws of education ought to be relative to the principles
of the government."* In

* Spirit of Laws. Book 4.

In defpotic governments, the people fhould have little or no education, except what tends to infpire them with a fervile fear. Information is fatal to defpotifm.

In monarchies, education fhould be partial, and adapted to the rank of each clafs of citizens. But " in a republican government," fays the fame writer, " the whole power of education is required." Here every clafs of people fhould *know* and *love* the laws. This knowlege fhould be diffufed by means of fchools and newfpapers; and an attachment to the laws may be formed by early impreffions upon the mind.

Two regulations are effential to the continuance of republican governments : 1. Such a diftribution of lands and fuch principles of defcent and alienation, as fhall give every citizen a power of acquiring what his induftry merits.* 2. Such a fyftem of education as gives every citizen an opportunity of acquiring knowlege and fitting himfelf for places of truft. Thefe are fundamental articles ; the *fine qua non* of the exiftence of the American republics.

Hence the abfurdity of our copying the manners and adopting the inftitutions of Monarchies.

In feveral States, we find laws paffed, eftablifhing provifion for colleges and academies, where people of property may educate their fons ; but no provifion is made for inftructing the poorer rank of people, even in reading and writing. Yet in thefe fame States, every citizen who is worth a few fhillings annually, is entitled to vote for legiflators.† This appears to me a moft glaring folecifm in government. The conftitutions are *republican*, and the laws of education are *monarchical*. The *former* extend civil rights to every honeft induftrious man ; the *latter* deprive a large proportion of the citizens of a moft valuable privilege.

In our American republics, where governments is

in

---

* The power of entailing real eftates is repugnant to the fpirit of our American governments.

† I have known inftructions from the inhabitants of a county, two thirds of whom could not write their names. How competent muft fuch men be to decide an important point in legiflation !

in the hands of the people, knowlege fhould be univerfally diffufed by means of public fchools. Of fuch
confequence is it to fociety, that the people who make
laws, fhould be well informed, that I conceive no Legiflature can be juftified in neglecting proper eftablifhments for this purpofe.

When I fpeak of a diffufion of knowlege, I do not
mean merely a knowlege of fpelling books, and the
New Teftament. An acquaintance with ethics, and
with the general principles of law, commerce, money
and government, is neceffary for the yeomanry of a
republican ftate. This acquaintance they might obtain by means of books calculated for fchools, and
read by the children, during the winter months, and
by the circulation of public papers.

"In Rome it was the common exercife of boys at
fchool, to learn the laws of the twelve tables by heart,
as they did their poets and claffic authors."*   What
an excellent practice this in a free government !

It is faid, indeed by many, that our common people
are already too well informed.   Strange paradox ! The
truth is, they have too much knowlege and fpirit to refign their fhare in government, and are not fufficiently
informed to govern themfelves in all cafes of difficulty.

There are fome acts of the American legiflatures
which aftonifh men of information ; and blunders in
legiflation are frequently afcribed to bad intentions.
But if we examin the men who compofe thefe legiflatures, we fhall find that wrong meafures generally proceed from ignorance either in the men themfelves, or
in their conftituents.   They often miftake their own
intereft, becaufe they do not forefee the remote confequences of a meafure.

It may be true that all men cannot be legiflators ;
but the more generally knowlege is diffufed among the
fubftantial yeomanry, the more perfect will be the laws
of a republican ftate.

Every fmall diftrict fhould be furnifhed with a fchool,
at leaft four months in a year ; when boys are not otherwife

* Middleton's life of Cicero, volume 1, page 14.

erwife employed. This fchool fhould be kept by the
moft reputable and well informed man in the diftrict.
Here children fhould be taught the ufual branches of
learning ; fubmiffion to fuperiors and to laws ; the
moral or focial duties ; the hiftory and tranfactions of
their own country ; the principles of liberty and government. Here the rough manners of the wildernefs
fhould be foftened, and the principles of virtue and good
behaviour inculcated. The *virtues* of men are of
more confequence to fociety than their *abilities* ; and
for this reafon, the *heart* fhould be cultivated with more
affiduity than the *head*.

Such a general fyftem of education is neither impracticable nor difficult ; and excepting the formation
of a federal government that fhall be efficient and permanent, it demands the firft attention of American
patriots. Until fuch a fyftem fhall be adopted and
purfued ; until the Statefman and Divine fhall unite
their efforts in *forming* the human mind, rather than in
loping its excreffences, after it has been neglected ; until Legiflators difcover that the only way to make good
citizens and fubjects, is to nourifh them from infancy ;
and until parents fhall be convinced that the *worft*
of men are not the proper teachers to make the *beft* ;
mankind cannot know to what a degree of perfection
fociety and government may be carried. America affords the faireft opportunities for making the experiment, and opens the moft encouraging profpect of fuccefs.*   In

* It is worthy of remark, that in proportion as laws are favorable to the equal rights of men, the number of crimes in a
ftate is diminifhed ; except where the human mind is debafed by
extreme fervitude, or by fuperftition. In France, there are but
few crimes ; religion and the rigor of a military force prevent
them ; perhaps alfo, ignorance in the peafantry may be affigned as another reafon. But in England and Ireland the human
mind is not fo depreffed, yet the diftribution of property and
honors is not equal ; the lower claffes of people, bold and independent, as well as poor, feel the injuries which flow from
the feudal fyftem, even in its relaxed ftate ; they become defperate, and turn highwaymen. Hence thofe kingdoms produce more culprits than half Europe befides.

                                                      The

In a fyftem of education, that fhould embrace every part of the community, the female fex claim no inconfiderable fhare of our attention.

The women in America (to their honor it is mentioned) are not generally above the care of educating their own children. Their own education fhould therefore enable them to implant in the tender mind, fuch fentiments of virtue, propriety and dignity, as are fuited to the freedom of our governments. Children fhould be treated as children, but as children that are, in a future time, to be men and women. By treating them as if they were always to remain children, we very often fee their childifhnefs adhere to them, even in middle life. The filly language called *baby talk*, in which moft perfons are initiated in infancy, often breaks out in difcourfe, at the age of forty, and makes a man appear very ridiculous.* In the fame manner, vulgar, obfcene and illiberal ideas, imbibed in a nurfery or a kitchen, often give a tincture to the conduct through life. In order to prevent every evil bias, the ladies, whofe province it is to direct the inclinations of children on their firft appearance, and to choofe their nurfes, fhould be poffeffed, not only of amiable manners, but of juft fentiments and enlarged underftandings.

But the influence of women in forming the difpofitions

The character of the Jews, as fharpers, is derived from the cruel and villanous profcriptions, which they have fuffered from the bigotry of Chriftians in every part of Europe.

Moft of the criminals condemned in America are foreigners. The execution of a native, before the revolution, was a novelty. The diftribution of property in America and the principles of government favor the rights of men ; and but few men will commence enemies to fociety and government, if they can receive the benefits of them. Unjuft governments and tyrannical diftinctions have made moft of the villains that ever exifted.

* It has been already obferved that a child always imitates what he fees and hears : For this reafon, he fhould hear no language which is not correct and decent. Every word fpoken to a child, fhould be pronounced with clearnefs and propriety. Banifh from children all diminutive words, all whining and all bad grammar. A boy of fix years old may be taught to fpeak as correctly, as Cicero did before the Roman Senate.

tions of youth, is not the fole reafon why their education fhould be particularly guarded ; their influence in
controling the manners of a nation, is another powerful reafon.   Women, once abandoned, may be inftrumental in corrupting fociety ; but fuch is the delicacy
of the fex, and fuch the reftraints which cuftom impofes
upon them, that they are generally the laft to be corrupted.   There are innumerable inftances of men, who
have been reftrained from a vicious life, and even of
very abandonded men, who have been reclaimed, by
their attachment to ladies of virtue.   A fondnefs for
the company and converfation of ladies of character,
may be confidered as a young man's beft fecurity a-
gainft the attractives of a diffipated life.   A man who
is attached to *good* company, feldom frequents that
which is *bad*.   For this reafon, fociety requires that
females fhould be well educated, and extend their influence as far as poffible over the other fex.

But a diftinction is to be made between a *good* education, and a *fhowy* one ; for an education, merely fuperficial, is a proof of corruption of tafte, and has a mif-
chievous influence on manners.   The education of females, like that of males, fhould be adapted to the principles of the government, and correfpond with the ftage
of fociety.   Education in Paris differs from that in
Peterfburg, and the education of females in London
or Paris fhould not be a model for the Americans to
copy.

In all nations a *good* education, is that which renders
the ladies correct in their manners, refpectable in their
families, and agreeable in fociety.   That education is
always *wrong*, which raifes a woman above the duties
of her ftation.

In America, female education fhould have for its
object what is *ufeful*.   Young ladies fhould be taught
to fpeak and write their own language with purity and
elegance ; an article in which they are often deficient.
The French language is not neceffary for ladies.   In
fome cafes it is convenient, but, in general, it may be
confidered as an article of luxury.   As an accomplifhment,

ment, it may be studied by those whose attention is not employed about more important concerns.

Some knowlege of arithmetic is necessary for every lady. Geography should never be neglected. Belles Letters learning seems to correspond with the dispositions of most females. A taste for Poetry and fine writing should be cultivated; for we expect the most delicate sentiments from the pens of that sex, which is possessed of the finest feelings.

A course of reading can hardly be prescribed for all ladies. But it should be remarked, that this sex cannot be too well acquainted with the writers upon human life and manners. The Spectator should fill the first place in every lady's library. Other volumes of periodical papers, tho inferior to the Spectator, should be read; and some of the best histories.

With respect to novels, so much admired by the young, and so generally condemned by the old, what shall I say? Perhaps it may be said with truth, that some of them are useful, many of them pernicious, and most of them trifling. A hundred volumes of modern novels may be read, without acquiring a new idea. Some of them contain entertaining stories, and where the descriptions are drawn from nature, and from characters and events in themselves innocent, the perusal of them may be harmless.

Were novels written with a view to exhibit only one side of human nature, to paint the social virtues, the world would condemn them as defective: But I should think them more perfect. Young people, especially females, should not see the vicious part of mankind. At best novels may be considered as the toys of youth; the rattle boxes of sixteen. The mechanic gets his pence for his toys, and the novel writer, for his books; and it would be happy for society, if the latter were in all cases as innocent play things as the former.

In the large towns in America, music, drawing and dancing, constitute a part of female education. They, however, hold a subordinate rank; for my fair friends will pardon me, when I declare, that no man ever marries a woman for her performance on a harpsichord, or

her

her figure in a minuet. However ambitious a woman
may be to command admiration *abroad*, her real merit
is known only at *home*. Admiration is ufelefs, when it
is not fupported by domeftic worth. But real honor
and permanent efteem, are always fecured by thofe who
prefide over their own families with dignity.*

Before I quit this fubject, I beg leave to make fome
remarks on a practice which appears to be attended
with important confequences; I mean that of fending
boys to Europe for an education, or fending to Europe
for teachers This was right before the revolution; at
least

---

* Nothing can be more fatal to domeftic happinefs in America, than a tafte for copying the luxurious manners and a-
mufements of England and France. Dancing, drawing and
mufic, are principal articles of education in thofe kingdoms;
therefore every girl in America muft pafs two or three years
at a boarding fchool, tho her father cannot give her a farthing when fhe marries. This ambition to educate females a-
bove their fortunes pervades every part of America. Hence
the difproportion between the well bred females and the males
in our large towns. A mechanic or fhopkeeper in town, or a
farmer in the country, whofe fons get their living by their
father's employments, will fend their daughters to a boarding
fchool, where their ideas are elevated, and their views carried
above a connexion with men in thofe occupations. Such an education, without fortune or beauty, may poffibly pleafe a girl
of fifteen, but muft prove her greateft misfortune. This fatal miftake is illuftrated in every large town in America. In
the country, the number of males and females, is nearly e-
qual; but in towns, the number of genteelly bred women is
greater than of men; and in fome towns, the proportion is, as
three to one.

The heads of young people of both fexes are often turned
by reading defcriptions of fplendid living, of coaches, of plays,
and other amufements. Such defcriptions excite a defire to
enjoy the fame pleafures. A fortune becomes the principal
object of purfuit; fortunes are fcarce in America, and not eafily acquired; difappointment fucceeds, and the youth who
begins life with expecting to enjoy a coach, clofes the profpect with a fmall living, procured by labor and economy.

Thus a wrong education, and a tafte for pleafures which our
fortune will not enable us to enjoy, often plunge the Americans into diftrefs, or at leaft prevent early marriages. Too
fond of fhow, of drefs and expenfe, the fexes wifh to pleafe
each other; they miftake the means, and both are difap-
pointed.

leaft fo far as national attachments where concerned ; but the propriety.of it ceafed with our political relation to Great Britain.

In the firft place, our honor as an independent nation is concerned in the eftablifhment of literary inftitutions, adequate to all our own purpofes ; without fending our youth abroad, or depending on other nations for books and inftructors.   It is very little to the reputation of America to have it faid abroad, that after the heroic atchievements of the late war, thefe independent people are obliged to fend to Europe for men and books to teach their children A B C.

But in another point of view, a foreign education is directly oppofite to our political interefts, and ought to be difcountenanced, if not prohibited.

Every perfon of common obfervation will grant, that moft men prefer the manners and the government of that country where they are educated. Let ten American youths be fent, each to a different European kingdom, and live there from the age of twelve to twenty, and each will give the preference to the country where he has refided.

The period from twelve to twenty is the moft important in life. The impreffions made before that period are commonly effaced ; thofe that are made during that period *always* remain for many years, and *generally* thro life.

Ninety nine perfons of a hundred who pafs that period in England or France, will prefer the people, their manners, their laws, and their government, to thofe of their nativ country. Such attachments are injurious, both to the happinefs of the men, and to the political interefts of their own country. As to private happinefs, it is univerfally known how much pain a man fuffers by a change of habits in living. The cuftoms of Europe are and ought to be different from ours ; but when a man has been bred in one country, his attachments to its manners make them, in a great meafure, neceffary to his happinefs. On changing his refidence, he muft therefore break his former habits, which is always a painful

sacrifice ;

facrifice ; or the difcordance between the manners of his own country, and his habits, muft give him inceffant uneafinefs ; or he muft introduce, into a circle of his friends, the manners in which he was educated. Thefe confequences may follow, and the laft, which is inevitable, is a public injury. The refinement of manners in every country fhould keep pace exactly with the increafe of its wealth ; and perhaps the greateft evil America now feels is, an improvement of tafte and manners which its wealth cannot fupport.

A foreign education is the very fource of this evil ; it gives young gentlemen of fortune a relifh for manners and amufements which are not fuited to this country ; which however, when introduced by this clafs of people, will always become fafhionable.

But a corruption of manners is not the fole objection to a foreign education : An attachment to a *foreign* government, or rather a want of attachment to our *own*, is the natural effect of a refidence abroad, during the period of youth. It is recorded of one of the Greek cities, that in a treaty with their conquerors, it was required that they fhould give a certain number of *male children* as hoftages for the fulfilment of their engagements. The Greeks abfolutely refufed, on the principle that thefe children would imbibe the ideas and embrace the manners of foreigners, or lofe their love for their own country : But they offered the fame number of *old* men, without hefitation. This anecdote is full of good fenfe. A man fhould always form his habits and attachments in the country where he is to refide for life. When thefe habits are formed, young men may travel without danger of lofing their patriotifm.   A boy who lives in England from twelve to twenty, will be an *Englifhman* in his manners and his feelings ; but let him remain at home till he is twenty, and form his attachments, he may then be feveral years abroad, and ftill be an *American.** There may be exceptions to this obfervation ; but
living

* Cicero was twenty eight years old when he left Italy to travel·into Greece and Afia.   " He did not ftir abroad," fays
Dr.

living examples may be mentioned to prove the truth of the general principle here advanced, refpecting the influence of habit.

It may be faid that foreign univerfities furnifh much better opportunities of improvement in the fciences than the American. This may be true, and yet will not juftify the practice of fending young lads from their own country. There are fome branches of fcience which may be ftudied to much greater advantage in Europe than in America, particularly chymiftry. When thefe are to be acquired, young gentlemen ought to fpare no pains to attend the beft profeffors. It may, therefore, be ufeful, in fome cafes, for ftudents to crofs the atlantic to *complete* a courfe of ftudies ; but it is not neceffary for them to go early in life, nor to continue a long time. Such inftances need not be frequent even now ; and the neceffity for them will diminifh in proportion to the future advancement of literature in America.

It is, however, much queftioned, whether, in the ordinary courfe of ftudy, a young man can enjoy greater advantages

Dr. Middleton, " till he had completed his education at home ; for nothing can be more pernicious to a nation, than the neceffity of a foreign one."—*Life of Cicero, vol.* 1. *p.* 48.

Dr. Moore makes a remark precifely in point. Speaking of a foreign education, propofed by a certain Lord, who objected to the public fchools in England, he fays, " I have attended to his Lordfhip's objections, and after due confideration, and weighing every circumftance, I remain of opinion, that no country but Great Britain is proper for the education of a Britifh fubject, who propofes to pafs his life in his own country. The moft important point, in my mind, to be fecured in the education of a young man of rank of our country, is to make him an Englifhman ; and this can be done no where fo effectually as in England." See his *View of Society and Manners, &c.* vol. 1, page 197, where the reader will find many judicious remarks upon this fubject. The following are too pertinent to be omitted.—" It is thought, that by an early foreign education, all ridiculous Englifh prejudices, will be avoided. This may be true ; but other prejudices, perhaps as ridiculous, and much more detrimental, will be formed. The firft cannot be attended with many inconveniencies ; the fecond may render the young people unhappy in their own country when they return, and difagreeable to their countrymen all the reft of theirlives." Thefe remarks, by a change of names are applicable to America.

D

advantages in Europe than in America. Experience inclines me to raife a doubt, whether the danger to which a youth muft be expofed among the fons of dif-fipation abroad, will not turn the fcale in favor of our American colleges. Certain it is, that four fifths of the great literary charaĉers in America never croffed the atlantic.

But if our univerfities and fchools are not fo good as the Englifh or Scotch, it is the bufinefs of our rulers to improve them, not to endow them merely ; for en-dowments alone will never make a flourifhing femin-ary ; but to furnifh them with profeffors of the firft abilities and moft affiduous application, and with a com-plete apparatus for eftablifhing theories by experiments. Nature has been profufe to the Americans, in genius, and in the advantages of climate and foil. If this country, therefore, fhould long be indebted to Europe for opportunities of acquiring any branch of fcience in perfeĉion, it muft be by means of a criminal negleĉ of its inhabitants.

The difference in the nature of the American and European governments, is another objeĉion to a foreign education. Men form modes of reafoning, or habits of thinking on political fubjeĉs, in the country where they are bred ; thefe modes of reafoning may be found-ed on faĉ in all countries ; but the fame principles will not apply in all governments, becaufe of the infinite variety of national opinions and habits. Before a man can be a good Legiflator, he muft be intimately ac-quainted with the temper of the people to be governed. No man can be thus acquainted with a people, without refiding amongft them and mingling with all companies. For want of this acquaintance, a Turgot and a Price may reafon moft abfurdly upon the Conftitutions of the American ftates ; and when any perfon has been long accuftomed to believe in the propriety or impropriety of certain maxims or regulations of government, it is very difficult to change his opinions, or to perfuade him to adapt his reafoning to new and different circum-ftances.

One

One half the European Proteftants will now contend that the Roman Catholic religion is fubverfive of civil government. Tradition, books, education, have concurred to fix this belief in their minds ; and they will not refign their opinions, even in America, where fome of the higheft civil offices are in the hands of Roman Catholics.

It is therefore of infinite importance that thofe who direct the councils of a nation, fhould be educated in that nation.   Not that they fhould reftrict their perfonal acquaintance to their own country, but their firft ideas, attachments and habits fhould be acquired in the country which they are to govern and defend.   When a knowlege of their own country is obtained, and an attachment to its laws and interefts deeply fixed in their hearts, then young gentlemen may travel with infinite advantage and perfect fafety.   I wifh not therefore to difcourage travelling, but, if poffible, to render it more ufeful to individuals and to the community.   My meaning is, that *men* fhould travel, and not *boys*.

It is time for the Americans to change their ufual route, and travel thro a country which they never think of, or think beneeth their notice : I mean the United States.

While thefe States were a part of the Britifh Empire, our intereft, our feelings, were thofe of Englifhmen ; our dependence led us to refpect and imitate their manners, and to look up to them for our opinions. We little thought of any national intereft in America ; and while our commerce and governments were in the hands of our parent country, and we had no common intereft, we little thought of improving our acquaintance with each other, or of removing prejudices, and reconciling the difcordant feelings of the inhabitants of different Provinces. But independence and union render it neceffary that the citizens of different States fhould know each others characters and circumftances ; that all jealoufies fhould be removed ; that mutual refpect and confidence fhould fucceed, and a harmony of views and interefts be cultivated by a friendly intercourfe.

A tour thro the United States ought now to be confidered as a neceffary part of a liberal education. Inftead of fending young gentlemen to Europe to view curiofities and learn vices and follies, let them fpend twelve or eighteen months in examining the local fituation of the different States; the rivers, the foil, the population, the improvements and commercial advantages of the whole; with an attention to the fpirit and manners of the inhabitants, their laws, local cuftoms and inftitutions. Such a tour fhould at leaft precede a tour to Europe; for nothing can be more ridiculous than a man travelling in a foreign country for information, when he can give no account of his own. When, therefore, young gentlemen have finifhed an academic education, let them travel thro America, and afterwards to Europe, if their time and fortunes will permit. But if they cannot make a tour thro both, that in America is certainly to be preferred; for the people of America, with all their information, are yet extremely ignorant of the geography, policy and manners of their neighbouring States. Except a few gentlemen whofe public employments in the army and in Congrefs, have extended their knowlege of America, the people in this country, even of the higher claffes, have not fo correct information refpecting the United States, as they have refpecting England or France. Such ignorance is not only difgraceful, but is materially prejudicial to our political friendfhip and federal operations.

Americans, unfhackle your minds, and act like independent beings. You have been children long enough, fubject to the control, and fubfervient to the intereft of a haughty parent. You have now an intereft of your own to augment and defend: You have an empire to raife and fupport by your exertions, and a national character to eftablifh and extend by your wifdom and virtues. To effect thefe great objects, it is neceffary to frame a liberal plan of policy, and build it on a broad fyftem of education. Before this fyftem can be formed and embraced, the Americans muft *believe*, and *act* from the belief, that it is difhonorable to wafte life in mimicking the follies of other nations and bafking in the funfhine of foreign glory.   [The

[The following fhould have been added, in a note, on page 5, after the fecond paragraph.

In our colleges and univerfities, ftudents read fome of the ancient Poets and Orators ; but the Hiftorians, which are perhaps more valuable, are generally neglect-ed. The ftudent juft begins to read Latin and Greek to advantage, then quits the ftudy. Where is the fem-inary, in which the ftudents read Herodotus, Thucy-dides, Xenophon, Polybius, Dionyfius Halicarnaffeus, Livy, Velleius, Paterculus and Tacitus ? How fuper-ficial muft be that learning, which is acquired in four years ! Severe experience has taught me the errors and defects of what is called a liberal education. I could not read the beft Greek and Roman authors while in college, without neglecting the eftablifhed claffical ftud-ies ; and after I left college, I found time only to dip into books, that every. fcholar fhould be mafter of; a circumftance that often fills me with the deepeft regret. " Quis enim ignorat et eloquentiam et cæteras artes defciviffe ab ifta vetere gloria, non inopia hominum, fed defidia juventutis, et negligentia parentum, et infcientia præcipientium, et oblivione moris antiqui ?—Nec in auctoribus cognofcendis, nec in evolvenda antiquitate, nec in notitia vel rerum, vel hominum, vel temporum fa-tis operæ infumitur."—*Tacitus, de Orat. Dial.* 28. 29.]

No. II.

No. II.

NEW YORK, 1788.

PRINCIPLES of GOVERNMENT and COMMERCE.

ALL mankind are, by nature, free, and have a right to enjoy life, liberty and property.

One perfon has no right to take from another his life, health, peace, or good name; to take away or leffen his freedom of thinking and acting, or to injure his eftate in the fmalleft degree.

A collection of individuals forms a *fociety* ; and every fociety muft have *government*, to prevent one man from hurting another, and to punifh fuch as commit crimes. Every perfon's fafety requires that he fhould fubmit to be governed ; for if one man may do harm without fuffering punifhment, every man has the fame right, and no perfon can be fafe.

It is neceffary therefore that there fhould be laws to control every man. Laws fhould be made by confent or concurrence of the greateft part of the fociety.

The whole body of people in fociety is the fovereign power or ftate ; which is called, the body politic. Every man forms a part of this ftate, and fo has a fhare in the fovereignty ; at the fame time, as an individual, he is a fubject of the ftate.

When a fociety is large, the whole ftate cannot meet together for the purpofe of making laws ; the people therefore agree to appoint deputies, or reprefentativs, to act for them. When thefe agents are chofen and met together, they reprefent the whole ftate, and act as the fovereign power. The people refign their own authority to their reprefentativs ; the acts of thefe deputies are in effect the acts of the people ; and the people have no right to refufe obedience.

It is as wrong to refufe obedience to the laws made by our *reprefentativs*, as it would be to break laws made

by

by *ourfelves*. If a law is bad and produces general harm, the people may appoint new deputies to repeal it ; but while it is a law, it is the act and will of the fovereign power, and ought to be obeyed.

The people in free governments, make their own laws by agents or reprefentativs, and appoint the executiv officers. An executiv officer is armed with the authority of the whole ftate and cannot be refifted. He cannot do wrong, unlefs he goes beyond the bounds of the laws.

An executiv officer can hardly be too arbitrary ; for if the laws are good, they fhould be ftrictly executed and religioufly obeyed : If they are bad, the people can alter or repeal them ; or if the officer goes beyond his powers, he is accountable to thofe who appoint him. A neglect of good and wholefome laws is the bane of fociety.

Judges and all executiv officers fhould be made as much as poffible, independent of the will of the people at large. They fhould be chofen by the reprefentativs of the people and anfwerable to them only : For if they are elected by the people, they are apt to be fwayed by fear and affection ; they may difpenfe with the laws, to favor their friends, or fecure their office. Befides, their election is apt to occafion party fpirit, cabals, bribery and public diforder. Thefe are great evils in a ftate, and defeat the purpofes of government.

The people have a right to advife their reprefentativs in certain cafes, in which they may be well informed. But this right cannot often be exercifed with propriety or fafety : Nor fhould their inftructions be binding on their reprefentativs : For the people, moft of whom live remote from each other, cannot always be acquainted with the general intereft of the ftate ; they cannot know all the reafons and arguments which may be offered for, or againft a meafure, by people in diftant parts of the ftate ; they cannot tell at home, how they *themfelves* would think and act, in a general affembly of *all* the citizens.

In this fituation, if the people of a certain diftrict, bind their reprefentativ to vote in a particular manner, they

they may bind him to do *wrong*. They make up their minds, upon a partial view of facts, and form a refolution, which they themfelves, on a fair ftate of all the facts, in the general affembly, might fee reafons to change. There have been inftances, in which thefe binding, pofitiv inftructions, have obliged a reprefentativ to give his vote, contrary to the conviction of his own mind and what he thought the good of the ftate ; confequently his vote was a violation of his oath.

But the opinions of the people fhould, if poffible, be collected ; for the general fenfe of a nation is commonly right. When people are well informed, their general opinion is perhaps always right. But they may be uninformed or mifinformed and confequently their meafures may be repugnant to their own intereft. This is often the cafe, with particular diftricts of people ; and hence the bad policy of giving binding inftructions to reprefentativ. The fenfe of a nation is collected by the opinions of people in particular diftricts ; but as fome of thefe opinions may be wrong, a reprefentativ fhould be left with difcretionary powers to act for the good of the ftate.

Reprefentativs are chofen by the inhabitants of certain diftricts, becaufe this is moft convenient : But when they act as lawgivers, they act for the whole ftate. When a man is confidering the propriety of a general meafure, he is not to be influenced by the intereft of a fingle diftrict or part of a ftate ; but by the collectiv intereft of the whole ftate. A good lawgiver will not afk folely what is *my* intereft, or the intereft of *my* town or conftituents ? but, what will promote the intereft of the community ; ' *what will produce the greateft poffible good, to the greateft number of people ?*'

When a legiflativ body makes *laws*, it acts for *itfelf* only, and can alter or repeal the laws when they become inconvenient. But when it makes *grants* or *contracts*, it act as a party, and cannot take back its grant, or change the nature of its contracts, without the confent of the other party. A ftate has no more right to neglect or refufe to fulfil its engagements, than an individual.

There

There may be an exception in the case of a grant, for if a state has made a grant, which, contrary to its expectations, clearly endangers the safety of the community, it may resume that grant. The public safety is a consideration superior to all others. But the danger must be great and obvious ; it must be generally seen and felt, before the state can be justified in recalling its grant. To take back a gift, or break a contract, for small causes or slight inconveniencies, is a most wanton abuse of power. Bargains, conveyances, and voluntary grants, where two parties are concerned, are *sacred things*; they are the supports of social confidence and security ; they ought not to be sported with, because one party is stronger than the other ; they should be religiously observed.

As the state has no right to break its own promises, so it has no right to alter the promises of individuals. When one man has engaged to pay his debt in wheat, and his creditor expects the promise to be fulfiled, the legiflature has no right to say, the debt shall be paid in flax or horses. Such an act saps all the supports of good faith between man and man ; it is the worst kind of tyranny.

For this reason, all *tender laws*, which oblige a creditor to take, for his debt, some article which he never intended nor engaged to take, are highly *unjust* and *tyrannical*. The intention of the contracting parties should be strictly regarded ; the state may enforce that intention, but can never have a right to interfere and defeat it. A legiflature has no right to put a bargain on any footing, but that on which the parties *have* placed it or *are willing* to place it.

If a state is poor, and people owe more money than can be procured, a legiflature may perhaps go so far as to suspend the collection of debts ; or to ordain that a certain part only of the debts shall be recoverable immediately, and the payment of the remainder suspended. This may ease the debtors ; but can be justified in extreme cases only, when the people are generally and greatly involved.

A

A people fhould not generally be in debt : The con-
fumers of goods fhould not get credit.   Heavy and numerous debts are great evils to a ftate.   If the people
will giv and take extenfiv credit, the ftate fhould check
their imprudence, by putting debts out of the protection
of law.   When it becomes a practice to collect debts
by law, it is a proof of corruption and degeneracy among
the people.   Laws and courts are neceffary to fettle
controverted points between man and man ; but a man
fhould pay an acknowledged debt, not becaufe there is a
law to oblige him, but becaufe it is *juft* and *honeft*, and
becaufe he has PROMISED to pay it.

Money, or a medium in trade, is neceffary in all great
ftates ; but *too much* is a greater evil than *too little*.
When people can get money without labor, they neglect bufinefs and become idle, prodigal and vicious ;
and when they have nothing but money, they are poor
indeed.   Spain was ruined by its mines of gold and filver in South America.   That kingdom poffeffed all the
money in Europe, and yet was the *pooreft* ; it will never
be rich and flourifhing, till its mines are exhaufted.
The difcovery of rich mines in this country, would be
the greateft misfortune, that can befall the United States.

Money is a mere reprefentativ of property ; it is the
change which facilitates trade.   But the *wealth* of a country is its *produce* ; and its ftrength confifts in the number of its induftrious inhabitants.   A man cannot become rich, unlefs he earns more than he fpends.   It is
the fame with a country.   The labouring men are the
fupport of a nation.

The value of money depends on the quantity in circulation.   A medium of trade refpects all commercial
nations ; and like water, it will find its level.   Money
will go where it is wanted, if the people have any thing
to purchafe it.   If one ftate or country has more money
than another, it is a proof that the people are more induftrious or faving. It would be happy for the world, if
no more money could be made : There is already too
much.   Silver is become very burdenfome, merely becaufe there is too much in the world.   If there were but
                                                    one

one quarter of the money which now circulates, one quarter of a dollar would buy as much as a dollar will now.

Hence the mistaken policy of those people who attempt to increase the medium of trade by coinage or by a paper currency. They can add to the quantity, as much as they please ; but not to the value. If America were shut out from all intercourse with other nations, and ten millions of dollars were circulating in the country, every article of life would have a certain price. If in this case, wheat should be one dollar a bushel, let the money be instantly doubled, the price of wheat would then be two dollars, and the price of every article would rise in the same proportion. So that twenty millions of dollars would be worth no more than ten, because they would buy no more of the useful commodities : America would be no richer in the one case than in the other.

But as there is a communication with other nations, a million of dollars, added to the circulating specie, does not increase the permanent medium in quantity ; for just so much money as is added, will leave the country. If there is too much money in a country, the price of labor will rise, and the produce cannot find market abroad without a loss. This was the case with American produce, at the close of the war. If money is scarce in a country, the price of labor will be low, and consequently the produce of that country will be cheap at home, and a great profit will be made on the exportation. This profit will be returned, partly in goods and partly in money, and the country is enriched.

But the great principle, which should constitute the corner stone of government, is *public justice*. The fountain head should be pure, or the streams will be foul indeed. That Legislatures, or bodies politic, should make laws, annex penalties for disobedience, institute courts for deciding controversies and trying offenders, and execute punishments on those that are convicted ; yet at the same time neglect to do justice themselves by paying their own debts ; this is of all absurdities the

most

moſt glaring.   To compel individuals to perform contracts and yet break their own ſolemn promiſes ; to
puniſh individuals for neglect, and yet ſet a general example of delinquency, is to undermine the foundation
of ſocial confidence, and ſhake every principle of commutativ juſtice.

Theſe are general principles in government and trade,
and ought to be deeply impreſſed upon the minds of
every American.

No. III.

No. III.

NEW YORK, 1788.

BILLS *of* RIGHTS.

ONE of the principal objections to the new Federal Conflitution, is, that it contains no *Bill of Rights*. This objection, I prefume to affert, is founded on ideas of government that are totally falfe. Men feem determined to adhere to old prejudices, and reafon *wrong*, becaufe our anceftors reafoned *right*. A Bill of Rights againft the encroachments of Kings and Barons, or againft any power independent of the people, is perfectly intelligible ; but a Bill of Rights againft the encroachments of an electiv Legiflature, that is, againft our *own* encroachments on *ourfelves*, is a curiofity in government.

The Englifh nation, from which we defcended, have been gaining their liberties, inch by inch, by forcing conceffions from the crown and the Barons, during the courfe of fix centuries.* *Magna Charta*, which is called the palladium of Englifh liberty, was dated in 1215, and the people of England were not reprefented in Parliament till the year 1265. Magna Charta eftablifhed the rights of the Barons and clergy againft the encroachments of royal perogativ ; but the commons or people were hardly noticed in that deed. There was but one claufe in their favor, which ftipulated, that " no villain or ruftic fhould, by any fine, be bereaved of his carts, plows and inftruments of hufbandry." As for the reft, they were confidered as a part of the property belonging to an eftate, and were transferred, as other moveables, at the will of their owners. In the fucceeding reign, they were permitted to fend Reprefentativs

* Not that the Englifh nation was originally in flavery ; for the primitiv Saxons and Germans were free. But the military tenures, eftablifhed by the Gothic conquefts, depreffed the people ; fo that under the rigor of the feudal fyftem, about the date of Magna Charta, the King and Nobles held their tenants in extreme fervitude. From this depreffion, the Englifh have gradually emerged into ancient freedom..

tativs to Parliament ; and from that time have been gradually affuming their proper degree of confequence in the Britifh Legiflature. In fuch a nation, every law or ftatute that defines the powers of the crown, and circumfcribes them within determinate limits, muft be confidered as a barrier to guard popular liberty. Every acquifition of freedom muft be eftablifhed as a *right*, and folemnly recognized by the fupreme power of the nation ; left it fhould be again refumed by the crown under pretence of ancient prerogativ : For this reafon, the habeas corpus act paffed in the reign of Charles 2d, the ftatute of the 2d of William and Mary, and many others which are declaratory of certain privileges, are juftly confidered as the pillars of Englifh freedom.

Thefe ftatutes are however not efteemed becaufe they are unalterable ; for the fame power that enacted them, can at any moment repeal them ; but they are efteemed, becaufe they are barriers erected by the Reprefentativs of the nation, againft a power that exifts independent of their own choice.

But the fame reafons for fuch declaratory conftitutions do not exift in America, where the fupreme power is *the people in their Reprefentativs.* The *Bills of Rights*, prefixed to feveral of the conftitutions of the United States, if confidered as affigning the reafons of our feparation from a foreign government, or as folemn declarations of right againft the encroachments of a foreign jurifdiction, are perfectly rational, and were doubtlefs neceffary. But if they are confidered as barriers againft the encroachments of our own Legiflatures, or as conftitutions unalterable by pofterity, I venture to pronounce them nugatory, and to the laft degree, abfurd.

In our governments, there is no power of legiflation, independent of the people ; no power that has an intereft detached from that of the public ; confequently there is no power exifting againft which it is neceffary to guard. While our Legiflatures therefore remain electiv, and the rulers have the fame intereft in the laws, as the fubjects have, the rights of the people will be perfectly fecure without any declaration in their favor.

But

But this is not the principal point. I undertake to prove that a ftanding *Bill of Rights* is *abfurd*, becaufe no conftitutions, in a free government, can be unalterable. The prefent generation have indeed a right to declare what *they* deem a *privilege*; but they have no right to fay what the *next* generation fhall deem a privilege. A State is a fupreme corporate that never dies. Its powers, when it acts for itfelf, are at all times equally extenfiv; and it has the fame right to *repeal* a law this year, as it had to *make* it the laft. If therefore our pofterity are bound by our conftitutions, and can neither amend nor annul them, they are to all intents and purpofes our flaves.

But it will be enquired, have we then no right to fay, that trial by jury, the liberty of the prefs, the habeas corpus writ, and other invaluable privileges, fhall never be infringed nor deftroyed? By no means. We have the fame right to fay that lands fhall defcend in a particular mode to the heirs of the deceafed proprietor, and that fuch a mode fhall never be altered by future generations, as we have to pafs a law that the trial by jury fhall never be abridged. The right of Jury trial, which we deem invaluable, may in future ceafe to be a privilege; or other modes of trial more fatisfactory to the people, may be devifed. Such an event is neither impoffible nor improbable. Have we then a right to fay that our pofterity fhall not be judges of their own circumftances? The very attempt to make *perpetual* conftitutions, is the affumption of a right to control the opinions of future generations; and to legiflate for thofe over whom we have as little authority as we have over a nation in Afia. Nay we have as little right to fay that trial by jury fhall be perpetual, as the Englifh, in the reign of Edward the Confeffor, had, to bind their pofterity forever to decide caufes by fiery Ordeal, or fingle combat. There are perhaps many laws and regulations, which from their confonance to the eternal rules of juftice, will always be good and conformable to the fenfe of a nation. But moft inftitutions in fociety, by reafon of an unceafing change of circumftances, either become

altogether

altogether improper, or require amendment ; and every nation has at all times, the right of judging of its cir‑cumſtances and determining on the propriety of chang‑ing its laws.

The Engliſh writers talk much of the omnipotence of Parliament ; and yet they ſeem to entertain ſome ſcru‑ples about their right to change particular parts of their conſtitution. I queſtion much whether Parliament would not heſitate to change, on any occaſion, an article of Magna Charta. Mr. Pitt, a few years ago, attempt‑ed to reform the mode of repreſentation in Parliament. Immediately an uproar was raiſed againſt the meaſure, as *unconſtitutional*. The repreſentation of the kingdom, when firſt eſtabliſhed, was doubtleſs equal and wiſe ; but by the increaſe of ſome cities and boroughs, and the depopulation of others, it has become extremely *unequal*. In ſome boroughs there is ſcarcely an elector left to en‑joy its privileges. If the nation feels no great incon‑venience from this change of circumſtances, under the old mode of repreſentation, a reform is unneceſſary. But if ſuch a change has produced any national evils of mag‑nitude enough to be felt, the preſent form of electing the Repreſentativs of the nation, however *conſtitutional*, and venerable for its antiquity, may at any time be amended, if it ſhould be the ſenſe of Parliament. The *expediency* of the alteration muſt always be a matter of opinion ; but all ſcruples as to the right of making it are totally groundleſs.

Magna Charta may be conſidered as a contract be‑tween two parties, the King and the Barons, and no contract can be altered but by the conſent of both par‑ties. But whenever any article of that deed or contract ſhall become inconvenient or oppreſſiv, the King, Lords and Commons may either amend or annul it at pleaſ‑ure.

The ſame reaſoning applies to each of the United States, and to the Federal Republic in general. But an important queſtion will ariſe from the foregoing re‑marks, which muſt be the ſubject of another paper.

No. IV.

No. IV.

NEW YORK, 1788.

On GOVERNMENT.

THE important queſtion I propoſed to diſcuſs in this number, is this : " Whether, in a free State, there ought to be any diſtinction between the powers of the people, or electors, and the powers of the Repreſentativs in the Legiſlature." Or in other words, " whether the legiſlativ body is not, or ought not to be, a ſtanding convention, inveſted with the whole power of their conſtituents."

In ſupporting the affirmativ of this queſtion, I muſt face the opinions and prejudices of my countrymen ; yet if we attend cloſely to the merits of the queſtion, ſtripped of all its ſpecious covering, we ſhall perhaps find more arguments in favor of the opinion, than we at firſt ſuſpect.

In the firſt place, a Legiſlature muſt be the ſupreme power, whoſe deciſions are laws binding upon the whole State. Unleſs the Legiſlature is the ſupreme power, and inveſted with *all* the authority of the State, its acts are not laws, obligatory upon the whole State.* I am ſenſible that it is a favorite idea in this country, bandied about from one demagogue to another, that *rulers are the ſervants of the people.* So far as their buſineſs is *laborious* and *embarraſſing*, it implies a degree of ſervitude ; but in any other view, the opinion is totally falſe. The people ought at leaſt to place their rulers, who are generally men of the firſt abilities and integrity, on a level with themſelves ; for that is an odd kind of government indeed, in which, *ſervants* govern their *maſters.*

The

---

* The firſt convention of deputies in a ſtate, is uſually deſigned to direct the mode in which future legiſlatures ſhall be cognized. This convention cannot abridge the powers of future legiſlatures, any further than they are abridged by the moral law, which forbids all wrong in general.

E

The truth is, a Reprefentativ, as an individual, is on a footing with other people ; as a Reprefentativ of a State, he is invefted with a fhare of the fovereign authority, and is fo far a *governor* of the people. In fhort, the collectiv body of the Reprefentativs, is the collectiv fenfe and authority of the people ; and fo far are the members from being the *fervants* of the people, that they are juft as much *mafters, rulers, governors*, whatever appellation we give them, as the people would be themfelves in a convention of the whole State.

But in the fecond place, the public good or fafety requires that the powers of a Legiflature fhould be coextenfiv with thofe of the people. That a Legiflature fhould be competent to pafs any law that the public fafety and intereft may require, is a pofition that no man will controvert. If therefore it can be proved that the refervation of any power in the hands of the people, may at times interfere with the power of the Legiflature to confult the public intereft, and prevent its exercife, it muft be acknowleged, that fuch a refervation is not only impolitic, but unjuft. That a Legiflature fhould have unlimited power to do *right*, is unqueftionable ; but fuch a power they cannot have, unlefs they have all the power of the State ; which implies an unlimited power to do *wrong*. For inftance, fuppofe the conftitution of any ftate to declare, that no ftanding army fhall be kept up in time of peace ; then the Legiflature cannot raife and maintain a fingle foldier to guard our frontiers, without violating the conftitution. To fay that new enliftments every year will fave the conftitution, is idle ; for if a body of troops raifed for thirty years is a ftanding army, then a body raifed for twenty years, or for fix months, is a ftanding army ; and the power to raife troops for a year, is a power to raife them at any time and maintain them forever ; but with the addition of much trouble and a load of expenfe. Since therefore there never was, and probably never will be a time, till the millenium fhall arrive, when troops will not be neceffary to guard the frontiers of States, a claufe in a conftitution, reftricting a Legiflature

lature from maintaining troops in time of peace, will unavoidably difable them from guarding the public interest. That a power to raife and equip troops at pleafure, may be abufed, is certain ; but that the public fafety cannot be eftablifhed without that power, is equally certain. The liberty of a people does not reft on any refervation of power in their hands paramount to their Legiflature ; it refts fingly on this principle, *a union of interefts between the governors and governed.* While a Legiflator himfelf, his family and his property, are all liable to the confequences of the laws which he makes for the State, the rights of the people are as fafe from the invafion of power, as they can be on this fide heaven. This union of intereft depends partly on the laws of property ; but moftly on the *freedom of election.* The right of electing rulers is the people's prerogativ ; and while this remains unabridged, it is a fufficient barrier to guard all their other rights. This prerogativ fhould be kept facred ; and if the people ever fuffer any abridgment of this privilege, it muft be their own folly and an irrecoverable lofs.

Still further, I maintain that a people have no right to fay, that any civil or political regulation fhall be perpetual; becaufe they have no right to make laws for thofe who are not in exiftence. This will be admitted ; but ftill the people contend that they have a right to prefcribe rules for their Legiflature, rules which fhall not be changed but by the people in a convention. But what is a convention ? Why a body of men chofen by the people in the manner they choofe the members of the Legiflature, and commonly compofed of the fame men ; but at any rate they are neither wifer nor better. The fenfe of the people is no better known in a convention, than in the Legiflature.* But

* The *nominal* diftinction of *Convention* and *Legiflature* was probably copied from the Englifh ; but the American diftinction goes farther, it implies, in common acceptation, a difference of *power.* This difference does not exift in G. Britain. The affembly of Lords and Commons which reftored Charles II, and that which raifed the Prince of Orange to the throne, were

But admit the right of establishing certain rules or principles which an ordinary Legislature cannot change, and what is the consequence? It is this, a change of circumstances m⬤ supersede the propriety of such rules, or render alterations necessary to the safety or freedom of the State ; yet there is no power existing, but in the people at large, to make the necessary alterations. A convention then must be called to transact a business, which an ordinary Legislature can transact just as well ; a convention differing from the Legislature merely in name, and in a few formalities of their proceedings. But when people have enjoyed a tolerable share of happiness under a government, they will not readily step out of the common road of proceeding ; and evils insensibly increase to an enormous degree, before the people can be persuaded to a change. The reservation therefore of certain powers may, by an imperceptible change of circumstances, prove highly pernicious to a State. For example : When the Commons of England were first admitted to a share in the legislation of that kingdom, which was probably in the reign of Henry III, in 1265,* the representation was tolerably equal. But the changes

were called *Conventions*, or *parliamentary Conventions.* But the difference between these Conventions and an ordinary Parliament, is merely a difference in the manner of assembling ; a *Convention* being an assembly or meeting of Lords and Commons, on an emergency, without the King's writ, which is the regular constitutional mode of summoning them, and by custom necessary to render the meeting a *Parliament.* But the powers of this assembly, whether denominated a *Convention* or a *Parliament*, have ever been considered as coextensive and supreme. I would just remark further, that the impossibility of establishing perpetual, or even permanent forms of government, is proved already by the experience of two States in America. Pensylvania and Georgia, have suffered under bad Constitutions, till they are glad to go thro the process of calling a new Convention. After the new forms of government have been tried some time, the people will discover new defects, and must either call a third Convention, or let the governments go on without amendment, because their Legislatures, which ought to have supreme power, cannot make altertations.——[1789.]

* This is the date of the first writs now extant, for summoning the Knights and Burgesses.

changes in the population of different parts of the king-dom have deftroyed all equality. The mode of election therefore fhould be reformed. But how fhall it be done? If there is a conftitution in that kingdom, which fettles the mode of election, and that conftitution is an act of the people, paramount to the power of the Par-liament, and unchangeable by them, a convention of the people muft be called to make an alteration which would be as well made in Parliament. This would occafion infinite trouble and expenfe.

But the danger is, that as an evil of this kind increaf-es, fo will the lethargy of the people, and their habits of vice and negligence. Thus the difeafe acquires force, for want of an early remedy, and a diffolution enfues. But a Legiflature, which is always watching the public fafety, will more early difcover the approaches of dif-orders, and more fpeedily apply a remedy. This is not precifely the cafe with the Britifh conftitution; for it was not committed at once to parchment and ratified by the people. It confifts rather of practice, or com-mon law, with fome ftatutes of Parliament. But the Englifh have been too jealous of changing their practice, even for the better. All the writers on the Englifh conftitution agree, that any Parliament can change or amend every part of it; yet in practice, the idea of an *unalterable conftitution* has had too much influence in preventing a reform in their reprefentation.

But we have an example nearer home directly in point. The charter of Connecticut declares that each town fhall have liberty to fend *one* or *two* deputies to the General Court; and the conftant practice has been to fend *two*. While the towns were few, the number of Reprefentativs was not inconvenient; but fince the com-plete fettlement of the State, and the multiplication of the towns, the number has fwelled the Legiflature to an unwieldly and expenfive fize. The houfe of Repre-fentativs confifts of about 170 members: An attempt has been made, at feveral feffions, to leffen the repre-fentation, by limiting each town to one Deputy. A queftion arifes, have the Affembly a right to leffen the
reprefentation?

reprefentation ? In moft States, it would be decided in the negativ. Yet in that State it is no queftion at all ; for there is a ftanding law exprefsly delegating the *whole* power of all the freemen to the Legiflature. But I bring this inftance to prove the poffibility of changes in any fyftem of government, which will require material alterations in its fundamental principles ; and the Legiflature fhould always be competent to make the neceffary amendments, or they have not an unlimited power to do right.*

The diftinction between the *Legiflature* and a *Convention* is, for the firft time, introduced into Connecticut, by the recommendation of the late convention of States, in order to adopt the new conftitution. The Legiflature of the State, without adverting to laws or practice, immediately recommended a convention for that purpofe. Yet a diftinction between a *Convention* and a *Legiflature* is, in that State, a palpable abfurdity, even by their own laws ; for there is no conftitution in the State, except its laws, which are always repealable by an ordinary Legiflature ; and the laws and uniform practice, from the firft organization of the government, declare that *the Legiflature has all the power of all the people.* A convention therefore can have no more power, and differs no more from an ordinary Legiflature, than one Legiflature does from another. Or rather it is no more than a Legiflature chofen for *one particular purpofe* of fupremacy ; whereas an ordinary Legiflature is competent to *all* purpofes of fupremacy.

But

---

* In Penfylvania, after the late choice of Delegates to Congrefs by the people, one of the Gentlemen fent his refignation to the Prefident and Council, who refered it to the Legiflature then fitting. This body, compozed of the fervants of the people, I fuppoze, folemnly refolved, that there was no power in the State which would accept the refignation. The refolv was grounded on the idea that the power of the people is paramount to that of the Legiflature ; whereas the people hav no power at all, except in choofing reprefentativs. All Legiflativ and Executiv powers are vefted in their Reprefentativs, in Council or Affembly, and the Council fhould have accepted the refignation and iffued a precept for another choice. Their compelling the man to ferve was an act of tyranny.

But had the Legiflature of that State ratified or rejected the new conftitution, without confulting their conftituents, their act would have been valid and binding. This is the excellence of the conftitution of Connecticut, that the *Legiflature* is confidered as the *body of the people*; and the people have not been taught to make a diftinction which fhould never exift, and confider themfelves as *mafters* of their *rulers*, and their power as paramount to the laws. To this excellence in her frame of government, that State is indebted for uniformity and ftability in public meafures, during a period of one hundred and fifty years; a period of unparalleled tranquillity, never once difturbed by a violent obftruction of juftice, or any popular commotion or rebellion. Wretched indeed would be the people of that State, fhould they adopt the vulgar maxim, that their rulers are their *fervants*. We then may expect that the *laws* of thofe *fervants* will be treated with the fame contempt, as they are in fome other States.*

But from the manner in which government is conftituted, it is evident that there is no power refiding in the State at large, which does not refide in the legiflature. I know it is faid that government originates in *compact*; but I am very confident, that if this is true, the *compact* is different from any other kind of compact that is known among men. In all other *compacts*, *agreements* or *covenants*, the affent of every perfon concerned, or who is to be bound by the compact, is requifite to render it valid and obligatory upon fuch perfon.

---

* This pernicious error fubverts the whole foundation of government. It refembles the practice of fome Gentlemen in the country, who hire a poor ftrolling vagabond to keep a fchool, and then let the children know that he is a mere *fervant*. The confequence is, the children defpife him and his rules, and a conftant war is maintained between the mafter and his pupils. The boys think themfelves more refpectable than the mafter, and the mafter has the rod in his hand, which he never fails to exercife. A proper degree of refpect for the man and his laws, would prevent a thoufand hard knocks. This is *government in miniature*. Men are taught to believe that their rulers are their *fervants*, and then are rewarded with a prifon and a gallows for defpifing their laws.

fon.   But I very much queftion whether this ever takes place in any conftitution of government.

Perhaps fo far there is an *implied compact* in government, that every man confents to be bound by the opinion of a majority ; but this is all a *fuppofition* ; for the confent of a hundredth part of a fociety is never obtained.

The truth is, government originates in *neceffity* and *utility* ; and whether there is an implied compact cr not, the opinions of the *few* muft be overruled, and fubmit to the opinions of the *many*.   But the opinions of a majority cannot be known, but in an Affembly of the whole fociety ; and no *part* of the fociety has a right to decide upon a meafure which equally affects the *whole*, without a confultation with the whole, to hear their arguments and objections.   It is faid that *all* power refides in the *people* ; but it muft be remembered, that let the fupreme power be where it will, it can be exercifed only in an *Affembly of the whole State*, or in an *Affembly of the Reprefentativs of the whole State*.

Suppofe the power to refide in the people, yet they cannot, and they have no right to exercife it in their fcattered diftricts, and the reafon is very obvious ; it is impoffible that the propriety of a meafure can be afcertained, without the beft general information, and a full knowlege of the opinions of the men on whom it is to operate.

By opinions here I would not be underftood to mean, the various opinions formed on a view of a particular intereft, for thefe opinions may be obtained by fending to each diftrict, and collecting inftructions ; but I mean the *opinions* of the *whole fociety*, formed on the *information* and *debates* of the *whole fociety*.   Thefe opinions can be formed no where but in a Convention of the *whole State*, or of their *Reprefentativs*.   So far therefore are the people from having a power paramount to that of their Reprefentativs in Convention, that they can exercife no act of fupremacy or legiflation at all, but in a Convention of the whole State by Reprefentativs.*   Unlefs
                                                    therefore,

* "In a democracy there can be no exercife of fovereignty but by fuffrage : In England, where the people do not debate in a
                                                    collective

therefore, it can be proved that a *Convention*, so called, which is composed mostly of the same men as a Legislature, possesses some wisdom, power or qualifications, which a Legislature *does not* and *cannot*, then the distinction is useless and trifling. A Legislature is supposed to consist of men whom the people judge best qualified to superintend their interests ; a convention cannot be composed of better men ; and in fact we find it generally composed of the *same men*. If therefore no act of sovereignty can be exercised but in an Assembly of Representativs, of what consequence is it, whether we call it a *Convention* or a *Legislature ?* or why is not the Assembly of Representativs of a people, at all times a *Convention*, as well as a *Legislature ?*

To me it appears that a distinction is made without a difference ; but a distinction that will often prevent good measures, perpetuate evils in government, and by creating a pretended power paramount to the Legislature, tend to bring laws into contempt.

POSTSCRIPT.——This reasoning applies solely to the individual States, and not to the United States, before they were formed into a federal body.   An important distinction must be observed between the *Constitution of a sovereign State*, and of *thirteen distinct sovereignties*.   In a sovereign State, whatever they may suggest to the contrary, the voices of a majority are binding upon the minority, even in framing the first plan of government.   In general, a majority of the votes of the *Representativs* in Legislature or Convention have been admitted as obligatory upon every member of the State, in forming and establishing a Constitution : But when the Constitution has been submitted to the people, as it is called, in town meetings or other small assemblies, the assent of every individual could not be expressly obtained ; and the dissent of any number, less than half the freemen present, who might not be one half the whole number in the State, could not prevent
the

collective body, but by representation, the exercise of this sovereignty consists in the *choice of Representatives*." *Blackstone's Com.* *b.* 1. *ch.* 2.   This is the sole power of the people in America.

the eftablifhment of the government, nor invalidate the obligation of *every man* to fubmit peaceably to its operation. The members of a ftate or community, cannot *from neceffity*, be confidered as parties to a contract, where the affent of every man is neceffary to bind him to a performance of the engagement. But the feveral States, enter into a negociation 'like *contrary parties*; they agree that the affent of every individual State, fhall be requifite to bind that State; and the frame of government, fo agreed upon, is confidered as a compact between independent fovereignties, which derives its binding force from the mutual and unanimous confent of the parties, and not merely from a neceffity that the major part of the people fhould compel the reft to fubmiffion.

But in this very compact, the States have refigned their independent fovereignty, and become a fingle body or ftate, as to certain purpofes; for they have folemnly contracted with each other, that *three fourths of* their number may alter and amend the firft compact. They are therefore no longer feparate individuals and contracting parties; but they form a fingle State or body politic; and a majority of three fourths can exert every act of fovereignty, except in two or three particulars, exprefsly referved in the compact.

No. V.

No. V.

NEW YORK, 1788.

On GOVERNMENT.

THE conftitution of Virginia, like that of Connecticut, ftands on the true principles of a Republican Reprefentativ Government. It is not fhackled
with a Bill of Rights, and every part of it, is at any time,
alterable by an ordinary Legiflature. When I fay *every
part* of the conftitution is alterable, I would except the
right of elections, for the Reprefentativs have not power
to prolong the period of their own delegation. This
is not numbered among the rights of legiflation, and
deferves a feparate confideration. This right is not
vefted in the Legiflature; it is in the people at large;
it cannot be alienated without changing the form of
government. Nay the right of election is not only the
bafis, but the *whole frame* or effence of a republican conftitution; it is not merely *one*, but it is the *only* legiflativ or conftitutional act, which the people at large can
with propriety exercife.

The fimple principle for which I contend is this,
" That in a reprefentativ democracy, the delegates
chofen for Legiflators ought, at all times, to be competent to every poffible act of legiflation *under that form of
government*; but not to *change that form*." Befides it
is contrary to all our ideas of *deputation* or *agency for
others*, that the perfon acting fhould have the power of
extending the period of agency beyond the time fpeci-
fied in his commiffion. The Reprefentativ of a people is, as to his powers, in the fituation of an Attorney,
whofe letters commiffion him to do every thing which
his conftituent would do, where he on the fpot; but
for a limited time only. At the expiration of that time
his powers ceafe; and a Reprefentativ has no more
right to extend that period, than a plenipotentiary has
to renew his commiffion. The Britifh Parliament, by
prolonging

prolonging the period of their exiftence from one to three, and from three to feven years, committed an un-juft act ; an act however which has been confirmed by the acquiefcence of the nation, and thus received the higheft conftitutional fanction.   I am fenfible that the Americans are much concerned for the liberties of the Britifh nation ; and the act for making Parliaments feptennial is often mentioned as an arbitrary, oppreffiv act, deftructiv of Englifh liberty.*   The Englifh are doubtlefs obliged to us for our tender concern for their happinefs ; yet for myfelf I entertain no fuch ideas : The Englifh have generally underftood and advocated their rights as well as any nation, and I am confident that the nation enjoys as much happinefs and freedom, and much more tranquillity, under feptennial Parliaments, than they would with annual elections.   Corruption to obtain offices will ever attend wealth ; it is generat-ed with it, grows up with it, and will always fill a country with violent factions and illegal practices.   Such are the habits of the people, that money will have a principal influence in carrying elections ; and fuch vaft fums are neceffary for the purpofe, that if elections were annual, none but a few of the wealthieft men could de-fray the expenfe ; the landholders of moderate eftates would not offer themfelves as candidates ; and thus in fact annual elections, with the prefent habits of the people, would actually diminifh the influence of the Commons, by throwing the advantage into the hands of a corrupt miniftry, and a few overgrown nabobs. Before annual elections would be a bleffing to the Eng-lifh, their habits muft be changed ; but this cannot be effected by human force.   I wifh my countrymen would believe that other nations underftand and can guard their privileges, without any lamentable outcries from this fide of the Atlantic.   Government will always take its complexion from the habits of the people ; habits are continually changing from age to age ; a body of Legiflators taken from the people, will generally repre-

fent

---

* The feptennial act was judged the only guard againft a Popifh reign, and therefore highly popular.

fent thefe habits at the time when they are chofen :
Hence thefe two important conclufions, 1ft, That a legiflativ body fhould be frequently renewed and always
taken from the people : 2d, That a government which
is perpetual, or incapable of being accommodated to
every change of national habits, muft in time become a
bad government.

With this view of the fubject, I cannot fupprefs my
furprife at the reafoning of Mr. Jefferfon on this very
point.*   He confiders it as a defect in the conftitution
of Virginia, that *it can be altered by an ordinary Legiflature.*   He obferves that the Convention which framed
the prefent conftitution of that State, " received no
powers in their creation which were not given to every
Legiflature before and fince.   So far and no farther au-
thorifed, they organized the government by the ordinance entitled a Conftitution or form of government.
It pretends to no higher authority than the other ordinances of the fame feffion ; it does not fay, that it fhall
be perpetual ; that it fhall be unalterable by other Legiflatures ; that it fhall be tranfcendant above the powers
of thofe, who they knew would have equal powers with
themfelves."

But fuppofe the framers of this ordinance had faid,
that it fhould be *perpetual* and *unalterable* ; fuch a declaration would have been void.   Nay, altho the people
themfelves had individually and unanimoufly declared
the ordinance perpetual, the declaration would have
been invalid.   One Affembly cannot pafs an act, binding upon a fubfequent Affembly of equal authority ;†
and the people in 1776, had no authority, and confequently could delegate none, to pafs a fingle act which
the people in 1777, could not repeal and annul.   And
Mr. Jefferfon himfelf, in the very next fentence, affigns
a reafon, which is an unanfwerable argument in favor
of my pofition, and a complete refutation of his own.
Thefe are his words.   " Not only the filence of the inftrument is a proof they thought it would be alterable,

but

* Notes on Virginia, page 197. Lond. Edit.   Query 13.

†Contracts, where a Legiflature is a party, are excepted.

but their own practice also : For this very Convention,
meeting as a House of Delegates in General Assembly
with the new Senate in the autumn of that year, passed
acts of Assembly in contradiction to their ordinance of
government ; and *every Assembly from that time to this,
has done the same.*"

Did Mr. Jefferson reflect upon the inference that
would be justly drawn from these facts ? Did he not
consider that he was furnishing his opponents with the
most effectual weapons against himself ? The acts passed
by *every subsequent Assembly in contradiction to the first ordinance*, prove that all the Assemblies were *fallible* men ;
and consequently not competent to make *perpetual Constitutions* for future generations.   To give Mr. Jefferson, and the other advocates for *unchangeable Constitutions*, the fullest latitude in their argument, I will suppose every freeman of Virginia, could have been assembled to deliberate upon a form of government, and that
the present form, or even one more perfect, had been
the result of their Councils ; and that they had declared it unalterable.   What would have been the consequence ? Experience would probably have discovered,
what is the fact ; and what forever will be the case ;
that *Conventions* are not possessed of *infinite wisdom* ; that
the wisest men cannot devise a perfect system of government.   After all this solemn national transaction, and
a formal declaration that their proceedings should be
unalterable, suppose a single article of the Constitution should be found to interfere with some national benefit, some material advantage ; where would be the
power to change or reform that article ? In the same
general Assembly of all the people, and in no other body.
But must a State be put to this inconvenience, to find
a remedy for every defect of constitution ?

Suppose, however, the *Convention* had been empowered
to declare the form of government *unalterable* : What
would have been the consequence ? Mr. Jefferson himself has related the consequence.   Every succeeding Assembly has found errors or defects in that frame of government, and has happily applied a remedy.   But had
                                                      not

not every Legiflature had power to make thefe alterations, Virginia muft have gone thro the farce, and the
trouble of calling an *extraordinary* Legiflature, to do that
which an *ordinary* Legiflature could do juft as well, in
their annual feffion ; or thofe errors muft have remained in the conftitution, to the injury of the State.

The whole argument for Bills of Rights and unalterable Conftitutions refts on two fuppofitions, viz. that
the Convention which frames the government, is *infallible* ; and that future Legiflatures will be *lefs honeft,
lefs wife,* and *lefs attentiv to the intereft of the State,* than
a prefent Convention : The firft fuppofition is *always
falfe,* and the laft is *generally* fo.   A declaration of perpetuity, annexed to a form of government, implies a
fuppofition of *perfect wifdom and probity* in the framers ;
which is both arrogant and impudent ; and it implies a
fuppofed power in them, to abridge the power of a fucceeding Convention, and of the future ftate or body
of people.   The laft fuppofition is, in every poffible
inftance of legiflation, *falfe* ; and an attempt to exercife
fuch a power, a high handed act of tyranny.   But fetting afide the argument, grounded on a want of power
in one Affembly to abridge the power of another, what
occafion have we to be fo jealous of future Legiflatures ?
Why fhould we be fo anxious to guard the future
rights of a nation ? Why fhould we not diftruft the people and the Reprefentativs of the prefent age, as well as
thofe of future ages, in whofe acts we have not the fmalleft intereft ? For my part, I believe that the people and
their Reprefentativs, two or three centuries hence, will
be as honeft, as wife, as faithful to themfelves, and will
underftand their rights as well, and be as able to defend
them, as the people are at this period.   The contrary
fuppofition is abfurd.

I know it is faid, that other nations have loft their
liberties by the ambitious defigns of their rulers, and we
may do the fame.   The experience of other nations,
furnifhes the ground of all the arguments ufed in favor
of an unalterable conftitution.   The advocates feem
determined that pofterity fhall not lofe their liberty,

even

even if they fhould be willing and defirous to furrender
it. If a few declarations on parchment, will fecure a
fingle bleffing to pofterity, which they would otherwife
lofe, I refign the argument, and will receive a thoufand
declarations. Yet fo thoroughly convinced am I of
the oppofite tendency and effect of fuch unalterable declarations, that, were it poffible to render them valid, I
fhould deem every article an infringement of civil and
political liberty. I fhould confider every article as a
reftriction which might impofe fome duty which in time
might ceafe to be ufeful and neceffary, while the obligation of performing it might remain ; or which in its
operation might prove pernicious, by producing effects
which were not expected, and could not be forefeen.
There is no one fingle right, no privilege, which is commonly deemed fundamental, which may not, by an unalterable eftablifhment, preclude fome amendment,
fome improvement in future adminiftration of government. And unlefs the advocates for unalterable conftitutions of government, can prevent all changes in the
wants, the inclinations, the habits, and the circumftances of people, they will find it difficult, even with all
their declarations of unalterable rights, to prevent
changes in government. A paper declaration is a very
feeble barrier againft the force of national habits, and
inclinations.

The lofs of liberty, as it is called, in the kingdoms of
Europe, has, in feveral inftances, been a mere change of
government, effected by a change of habits, and in fome
inftances this change has been favorable to liberty.
The government of Denmark, was changed from a
mixed form, like that of England, to an abfolute monarchy, by a folemn deliberate act of the people or States.
Was this a lofs of liberty? So far from it, that the
change removed the oppreffions of faction, reftored liberty to the fubject and tranquillity to the kingdom. The
change was a bleffing to the people. It indeed lodged
a power in the Prince to difpofe of life and property ;
but at the fame time it lodged in him a *power to defend
both* ; a power which before was lodged *no where* ; and
                                                      it

it is infinitely better that fuch a power fhould be vefted
in a *fingle hand*, than that it fhould *not exift at all*.   The
monarchy of France has grown out of a number of petty ftates and lordfhips; yet it is a fact, proved by hiftory
and experience, that the fubjects of that kingdom have
acquired liberty, peace and happinefs, in proportion to
the diminution of the powers of the petty fovereignties,
and the extenfion of the prerogativs of the Monarch.
It is faid that Spain loft her liberties under the reign of
Charles Vth; but I queftion the truth of the affertion;
it is probable that the fubject has gained as much by an
abridgement of the powers of the nobility, as he loft by
an annihilation of the Cortez.   The United Netherlands fought with more bravery and perfeverance to
preferve their rights, than any other people fince the
days of Leonidas; and yet no fooner eftablifhed a government, fo jealoufly guarded as to defeat its own
defigns, and prevent the good effects of government,
than they neglected its principles; the freemen refigned
the privilege of election, and committed their liberties
to a rich ariftocracy.   There was no compulfion, no
external force in producing this revolution; but the
form of government, which had been eftablifhed on
paper, and folemnly ratified, was not fuited to the genius of the fubjects.   The burghers had the right of
electing their rulers; but they neglected it voluntarily;
and a *bill of rights*, a *perpetual conftitution* on parchment,
guaranteeing that right, was a ufelefs form of words, becaufe oppofed to the temper of the people.   The government affumed a complexion, more correfpondent to
their habits, and tho in theory no conftitution is more
cautioufly guarded againft an infringement of popular
privileges, yet in practice it is a real ariftocracy.
   The progrefs of government in England has been the
reverfe: The people have been gaining freedom by in-
trenching upon the powers of the nobles and the royal
prerogativs. Thefe changes in government do not proceed from *bills of rights*, *unalterable forms* and *perpetual
eftablifhments*; liberty is never fecured by fuch paper
declarations, nor loft for want of them.   The truth is,

F   Government

Government originates in neceffity, and takes its form
and ftructure from the genius and habits of the people ;
and if on paper a form is not accommodated to thofe
habits, it will affume a new form, in fpite of all the
formal fanctions of the fupreme authority of a State.
Were the monarchy of France to be diffolved, and the
wifeft fyftem of republican government ever invented,
folemnly declared, by the King and his council, to be
the conftitution of the kingdom ; the people with their
prefent habits, would refufe to receive it ; and refign
their privileges to their beloved fovereign.   But fo oppofite are the habits of the Americans, that an attempt
to erect a monarchy or an ariftocracy over the United
States, would expofe the authors to the lofs of their
heads.*   The truth is, the people of Europe, fince they
have become civilized, have, in no kingdom, poffeffed
all the true principles of liberty.   They could not therefore lofe what they never poffeffed.   There have been,
from time immemorial, fome rights of government,
fome prerogativs vefted in fome man or body of men,
independent of the fuffrages of the body of the fubjects.
This circumftance diftinguifhes the governments of
Europe and of all the world, from thofe of America.
There has been in the free nations of Europe an inceffant ftruggle between freedom or national rights, and
hereditary prerogativs.   The conteft has ended varioul-
ly in different kingdoms ; but generally in depreffing
the power of the nobility ; afcertaining and limiting
the prerogativs of the crown, and extending the privileges of the people.   The Americans have feen the records of their ftruggles ; and without confidering that
the objects of the conteft *do not exift in this country* ; they
are laboring to guard rights which there is no party to
attack.   They are as jealous of their rights, as if there
exifted here a King's prerogativs, or the powers of nobles,
independent of their own will and choice, and ever eager

to

---

* Some jealous people ignorantly call the propofed Conftitution of Federal Government, an *ariftocracy*.   If fuch men are
honeft, their honefty deferves pity : There is not a feature of
true ariftocracy in the Conftitution ; the whole frame of Government is a pure Reprefentativ Republic.

to fwallow up their liberties.   But there is *no man* in America, who claims any rights but what are common to *every man*; there is no man who has an intereft in invading popular privileges, becaufe his attempt to curtail another's rights, would expofe his own to the fame abridgement.   The jealoufy of people in this country has no proper object againft which it can rationally arm them ; it is therefore directed *againft themfelves*, or againft an invafion which they *imagine* may happen in future ages.   The conteft for *perpetual bills of rights* againft a future tyranny, refembles Don Quixote's fighting windmills ; and I never can reflect on the declamation about an *unalterable conftitution* to guard certain rights, without wifhing to add another article, as neceffary as thofe that are generally mentioned; viz. " that no future Convention or Legiflature fhall cut their own throats, or thofe of their conftituents."   While the habits of the Americans remain as they are, the people will choofe their Legiflature from their own body ; that Legiflature will have an intereft infeparable from that of the people, and therefore an act to reftrain their power in any article of legiflation, is as unneceffary as an act to prevent them from committing fuicide.

Mr. Jefferfon, in anfwer to thofe who maintain that the form of government in Virginia is unalterable, becaufe it is called a *conftitution*, which, ex vi termini, means an act above the power of the ordinary Legiflature, afferts that *conftitution*, *ftatute*, *law* and *ordinance*, are fynonymous terms, and convertible as they are ufed by writers on government.   Conftitutio dicitur jus quod a principe conditur.   Conftitutum, quod ab imperatoribus refcriptum ftatutumve eft.   Statutum, idem quod lex.*   Here the words *conftitution*, *ftatute* and *law*, are defined by each other ; they were ufed as convertible terms by all former writers, whether Roman or Britifh ; and before the terms of the civil law were introduced, our Saxon anceftors ufed the correfpondent Englifh words, *bid* and *fet*.†   From hence he concludes
that

* Calvini Lexicon Juridicum.
† See Laws of the Saxon Kings.
F 2

that no inference can be drawn from the meaning of the word, that a *conſtitution* has a higher authority than a law or ſtatute.   This concluſion of Mr. Jefferſon is juſt.

He quotes Lord Coke alſo to prove that any parliament can abridge, ſuſpend or qualify the acts of a preceeding Parliament.   It is a maxim in their laws, that " Leges poſteriores priores contrarias abrogant." After having fully proved that *conſtitution, ſtatute, law* and *ordinance*, are words of ſimilar import, and that the conſtitution of Virginia is at any time alterable by the ordinary Legiſlature, he proceeds to prove the danger to which the rights of the people are expoſed, for want of an *unalterable form of government.* The firſt proof of this danger he mentions, is, the power which the Aſſembly exerciſes of determining its own quorum. The British Parliament fixes its own quorum : The former Aſſemblies of Virginia did the ſame.   During the war the Legiſlature determined that *forty* members ſhould be a quorum to proceed to buſineſs, altho not a fourth part of the whole houſe.   The danger of delay, it was judged, would warrant the meaſure.   This precedent, our writer ſuppoſes, is ſubverſive of the principles of the government, and dangerous to liberty.

It is a dictate of natural law that a *majority ſhould govern* ; and the principle is univerſally received and eſtabliſhed in all ſocieties, where no other mode has been arbitrarily fixed.   This natural right cannot be alienated *in perpetuum* ; for altho a Legiſlature, or even the body of the people, may reſign the powers of government to forty, or to four men, when they pleaſe, yet they may likewiſe reſume them at pleaſure.

The people may, if they pleaſe, create a dictator on an emergency in war, but his creation would not *deſtroy*, but merely *ſuſpend* the natural right of the *Lex majoris partis.*   Thus forty members, a minority of the Legiſlature of Virginia, were empowered during a dangerous invaſion, to legiſlate for the State ; but any ſubſequent Aſſembly might have diveſted them of that power. During the operation of the law, veſting them with this

power,

power, their acts were binding upon the State ; becaufe
their power was derived from the general fenfe of the
State ; it was actually derived from a legal majority.
But that majority could, at any moment, refume the
power and practice on their natural right.

It is a ftanding law of Connecticut, that forty men fhall
be a quorum of the Houfe of Reprefentativs, which confifts of about 170 members. This law, I am confident,
never excited a murmur, or a fufpicion that the liberties of
the people were in danger ; yet this law creates an oligarchy ; it is an infringement of natural right ; it fubjects
the State to the poffibility, and even the probability of being governed at times by a minority. The acquiefcence
of the State, in the exiftence of the law, gives validity,
and even the fanction of a majority, to the acts of that
minority ; but the majority may at any time refume
their natural right, and make the affent of more than
half of the members, neceffary to give validity to their
determinations.

The danger therefore arifing from a power in the Affembly to determine their own quorum, is merely ideal,
for no law can be perpetual ; the authority of a majority of the people, or of their Reprefentativs, is always
competent to repeal any act that is found unjuft or inconvenient. The acquiefcence however of the people
of the States mentioned, and that in one of them for a
long courfe of years, under an oligarchy ; or their fubmiffion to the power of a minority, is an inconteftible
proof of what I have before obferved, that *theories* and
forms of government are *empty things* ; that the fpirit of a
government fprings immediately from the temper of the
people, and the exercife of it will generally take its tone
from their feelings. It proves likewife that a *union of
interefts* between the rulers and the people, which union
will always coexift with free elections, is not only the
beft, but the *only* fecurity for their liberties which they
can wifh for and demand. The Government of Connecticut is a folid proof of thefe truths. The Affembly
of that State, have always had power to abolifh trial by
jury, to reftrain the liberty of the prefs, to fufpend the
habeas

habeas corpus act, to maintain a standing army, in short to command every engine of despotism ; yet by some means or other, it happens that the rights of the people are not invaded, and the subjects have generally been better satisfied with the laws, than the people of any other State. The reason is, the Legislature is a part of the people, and has the *same interest*. If a law should prove bad, the Legislature can repeal it ; but in the *unalterable* bills of rights in some of the States, if an article should prove wrong and oppressiv, an ordinary Legislature cannot repeal or amend it ; and the State will hardly think of calling a special Convention for so trifling a purpose. There are some articles, in several of the State Constitutions, which are glaring infractions of the first rights of freemen ; yet they affect not a majority of the community ; and centuries may elapse before the evil can be redressed, and a respectable class of men restored to the enjoyment of their rights.*

To prove the want of an *unalterabbe Conflitution* in Virginia, Mr. Jefferson informs us that in 1776, during the distressed circumstances of the State, a proposition was made in the House of Delegates to create a Dictator, invested with every power, legislativ, executiv and judicial, civil and military. In June, 1781, under a great calamity, the proposition was repeated, and was near being passed. By the warmth he discovers in reprobating this proposal, one must suppose that the creation of a Dictator even for a few months, would have buried every remain of freedom. Yet he seems to allow that the step would have been justified, had there existed an *irresistible neceffity*.

Altho

---

* Such is the article, which excludes the clergy from a right to hold civil offices. The people, might, with the same propriety, have declared, that no merchants nor lawyers should be eligible to civil offices. It is a common opinion that the business of the clergy is wholly *spiritual*. Never was a grosser error. A part of their business is to inform the minds of people on all subjects, and correct their morals ; so that they have a direct influence on government. At any rate they are subjects of law, and ought as freemen to be eligible to a seat in the Legislature ; provided the people incline to choose them.

Altho it is poffible that a cafe may happen, in which
the creation of a Dictator might be the only refort to
fave life, liberty, property and the State, as it happened
in Rome more than once ; yet I fhould dread his power
as much as any man, were I not convinced that the
fame men that appointed him, could, in a moment,
ftrip him of his tremendous authority.   A Dictator,
with an army fuperior to the ftrength of the State, would
be a defpot ; but Mr. Jefferfon's fears feem grounded
on the authority derived from the Legiflature.   A con-
ceffion of power from the Legiflature, or the people,
is a voluntary fufpenfion of a natural *unalienable* right ;
and is refumeable at the expiration of the period fpeci-
fied, or the moment it is abufed.   A State can never
alienate a *natural right* ; for it cannot legiflate for thofe
who are not in exiftence.   It may confent to fufpend
that right for great and temporary purpofes ; but were
every freeman in Virginia to affent to the creation of a
perpetual Dictator, the act in itfelf would be void.   The
expedient of creating a Dictator is dangerous, and no
free people would willingly refort to it ; but there may
be times when this expedient is neceffary to fave a State
from ruin, and when every man in a State would cheer-
fully give his fuffrage for adopting it.   At the fame
time, a temporary inveftiture of unlimited powers in
one man, may be abufed ; it may be an influential precedent ; and the continuance of it, may furnifh the
Dictator with the means of perpetuating his office.   The
diftrefs of a people muft be extreme, before a ferious
thought of a Dictator can be juftifiable.   But the people who create, can annihilate a Dictator ; their right to
govern themfelves cannot be refigned by any act whatever, altho extreme cafes may vindicate them in fuf-
pending the exercife of it.   Even prefcription cannot
exift againft this right ; and *every* nation in Europe has
a *natural* right to depofe its King, and take the government into its own hands ; altho it may forever be in-
expedient for any of them to exercife the right.

VI.

No. VI.

NEW YORK, 1788.

On GOVERNMENT.

I HAVE faid,* " that the people ought not to give binding inftructions to Reprefentativs." " That they cannot exercife any act of fupremacy or legiflation at all but in a Convention of the whole State, or of the Reprefentativs of the whole State." And " That the right of election is the *only* conftitutional right which they can with propriety exercife." That thefe pofitions, however repugnant to the. received opinions of the prefent age, are capable of political demonftration, is to me unqueftionable. They all convey nearly the fame idea, and if true, they contravene, in fome meafure, a fundamental maxim of American politics, which is, that " the fovereign power refides in the people."

I am not defirous of fubverting this favorite maxim ; but I am very defirous it fhould be properly qualified and underftood ; for the abufe of it is capable of fhaking any government ; and I have no doubt that the miftakes which this maxim has introduced, have been the principal fources of rebellion, tumult and diforder in feveral of the American States.

It is doubtlefs true, that the individuals who compofe a political fociety or ftate, have a fovereign right to eftablifh what form of government they pleafe in their own territories. But in order to deliberate upon the fubject, they muft all convene together, as in Rome and Athens ; or muft fend deputies, vefted with powers to act for them, as is the practice in England and America. If they adopt the firft method, then the Supreme Legiflativ power refides, to all intents and purpofes, in the whole body of the people. If, from the local circumftances of the people, the whole body cannot meet for deliberation,

* No. II. IV. V.

eration, then the Legiſlativ powers do not reſide in the people at large, but in an aſſembly of men delegated by the whole body.

To prove this laſt poſition, it is neceſſary to enquire, what is the object of law, and on what principles ought it to be founded ? A law, if I underſtand the term, is an act of the *whole State*, operating upon the *whole State*, either by command or prohibition : It is thus diſtinguiſhed from a *reſolve* which more properly reſpects an individual or a part of the State.* The object of a law is to prevent poſitiv evil or produce poſitiv good to the *whole State* ; not merely to a particular part. The principle therefore on which all laws ſhould be founded, is, *a regard to the greateſt good which can be produced to the greateſt number of individuals in the State.* The principle is ſo obvious, that I preſume it will not be controverted. Permit me then to enquire, whether the people of any diſtrict, county or town, in their local meetings, are competent to judge of this *general good ?* A law, which is, in its operation *general*, muſt be founded on the beſt *general information :* The people themſelves have no right to conſent to a law, without this general information : They have no right to conſent to a law, on a view of a local intereſt ; nor without hearing the objections and arguments, and examining the amendments, ſuggeſted by every part of the community, which is to be affected by that law. To maintain the contrary

---

* It is a capital defect in ſome of the States, that the government is ſo organized as not to admit ſubordinate acts of legiſlation in ſmall diſtricts. In theſe States, every little collection of people in a village muſt petition the Legiſlature for liberty to lay out a highway or build a bridge ; an affair in which the State at large has very little intereſt, and of the neceſſity and utility of which the Legiſlature are not ſuitable judges. This occaſions much trouble for the State ; it is a needleſs expenſe. A State ſhould be divided into inferior corporations, veſted with powers competent to all acts of local police. What right have the inhabitants of Suffolk to interfere in the building of a bridge in Montgomery† ? Who are the moſt competent judges of a local convenience ; the whole State, or the inhabitants of the particular diſtrict ?

† This was written in New York.

trary is to defend the moſt glaring contradictions. But
can the inhabitants, in detached aſſociations, be acquainted with theſe objections and arguments ? Can they
know the minds of their brethren at the diſtance of three
or five hundred miles ? If they cannot, they do not poſſeſs the right of legiſlation. Little will it avail to ſay, that
the people acquire the neceſſary information by newſpapers, or other periodical publications : There are not
more than two States in the thirteen, where one half the
freemen read the public papers. But if every freeman read the papers, this would not give him the information neceſſary to qualify him for a Legiſlator ; for
but a ſmall part of the intelligence they contain is official,
which alone can be the ground of law ; nor can the
collectiv ſenſe of a nation or ſtate be gathered from newſpapers.   The whole body of people, or Repreſentativs of the whole body, are the only vehicles of information which can be truſted, in forming a judgement of
the true intereſt of the whole State.

If the *collectiv ſenſe* of a State is the baſis of law, and
that ſenſe can be known officially no where but in an
Aſſembly of all the people or of their Repreſentativs ;
or in other words, if there can be no ſuch thing as a *collection of ſentiments* made in any other manner, than by
a Convention of the whole people or their Delegates,
where is the right of *inſtructing Repreſentativs ?* The
ſenſe of the people, taken in ſmall meetings, without a
general knowlege of the objections, and reaſonings of
the whole State, ought not to be conſidered as the true
ſenſe of the State ; for not being poſſeſſed of the beſt
general information, the people often form wrong opinions of their own intereſt. Had I the journals of the ſeveral Legiſlatures in America, I would prove to every
man's ſatisfaction, that moſt of the ſchemes for paper
money, tender laws, ſuſpenſion of laws for the recovery
of debts, and moſt of the deſtructiv meaſures which have
been purſued by the States, have originated in towns and
counties, and been carried by poſitiv inſtructions from
conſtituents to Repreſentativs.   The freemen, in theſe
caſes, have wrong ideas of their own intereſt ; their error,

ror, in the firſt inſtance, is aſcribeable merely to ignorance, or a want of that juſt information, which they
themſelves would obtain in a General Aſſembly.* The
right therefore of preſcribing rules to govern the votes
of Repreſentativs, which is ſo often aſſumed, frequently
amounts to a right of doing infinite miſchief, with the
beſt intentions. There is perhaps no caſe in which the
people at large are ſo capable of knowing and purſuing
their own intereſt, as their Delegates are when aſſembled
for conſultation and debate. But the practice of giving binding inſtructions to Repreſentativs, if it has any
foundation, is built on this maxim, that the conſtituents, on a view of their local intereſts, and either with
none, or very imperfect information, are better judges
of the propriety of a law, and of the general good, than
the moſt judicious men are (for ſuch generally are the
Repreſentativs) after attending to the beſt official information from every quarter, and after a full diſcuſſion
of the ſubject in an Aſſembly, where claſhing intereſts
conſpire to detect error, and ſuggeſt improvements.
This maxim is obviouſly falſe ; and a practice built on
it, cannot fail to produce laws, inaccurate, contradictory, capricious and ſubverſive of the firſt rights of men.
Perhaps no country, except America, ever experienced
the fatal effects of this practice, and I bluſh to remark,
what candor itſelf muſt avow, that few arbitrary governments, have in ſo ſhort a period, exhibited ſo many
legal infractions of ſacred right ; ſo many public invaſions
of private property ; ſo many wanton abuſes of legiſlativ powers ! Yet the people are generally honeſt ; and
as well informed as the people of any country. Their
errors proceed from ignorance ; from falſe maxims of
governments. The people attempt to legiſlate without
the neceſſary qualifications for lawgivers ; yes, *they legiſlate at home !* and while this practice ſubſiſts, our public meaſures will be often weak, imperfect, and changeable ; and ſometimes *extremely iniquitous.* From theſe
                                                   conſiderations,

* An error, originating in miſtake, is often purſued thro ob-
ſtinacy and pride ; and ſometimes a familiarity with *falſehood,*
makes it appear like *truth.*

considerations, it appears that the powers of a Representativ fhould be wholly difcretionary when he acts as a
Legiflator ; but as an agent for a town or fmall fociety,
he may have pofitiv inftructions.   His conftituents, in
the laft cafe, are competent to inftruct him, becaufe they
are the whole body concerned ; but in the firft inftance,
they are but a part of the State, and not competent to
judge fully of the intereft of the whole.

'To place the matter in the ftrongeft point of light, let
us.fuppofe a fmall State, in which the whole body of
people meet for the purpofe of making laws. Suppofe
in this democracy, the people of a town or other diftrict fhould defire a particular act, for inftance, a tender
law. Would the inhabitants of this town, have a right
to meet a few weeks before the General Affembly, where
they all would expect to be prefent, to debate and vote ;
and in this town meeting take an oath, or otherwife
bind themfelves to vote for the act ? Would they have
a right to fhut their ears againft argument ; to lay a reftraint upon their own minds ; to exclude the poffibility
of conviction, and folemnly fwear to vote in a certain
manner, whether right or wrong ! If in this cafe, the
people of a diftrict have no right to lay a reftraint upon
themfelves before they enter the General Affembly,
neither have they a right, in reprefentativ democracies,
to lay fuch a reftraint upon their Delegates.   The very
reafon why they are incompetent to direct their *Deputies*, is that they cannot determine how to act *themfelves*, till they come into the Affembly. The very
doctrine of reprefentation in government excludes the
right of giving binding inftructions to Deputies. 'The
defign of choofing Reprefentativs is to *collect the wifdom of the State* ; the Deputies are *to unite* their Councils ; *to meet* and *confult for* the public fafety : But pofitiv inftructions prevent this effect ; they are dictated
by local interefts, or opinions formed on an imperfect
view of facts and arguments ; in fhort they totally
counteract the good effects of public deliberations, and
prevent thofe falutary meafures which may refult from
united Councils.   They make the opinions of a fmall
                                                  part

part of the State a rule for the whole ; they imply a decifion of a queftion, before it is heard ; they reduce a
Reprefentativ to a mere machine, by reftraining the exercife of his reafon ; they fubvert the very principles of
republican government.

But let us attend to the inconfiftency of the practice.
The oath required of a Reprefentativ, before he takes
his feat, binds him to vote or act from a regard to the
public good, *according to his judgement* and *the beft of his
abilities*. Some of the Conftitutions contain an oath
that binds a Reprefentativ, *not to affent to, or vote for, any.
act that he fhall deem injurious to the people*. But what
opinion, what judgement can a man exercife, who is
under the reftraint of pofitiv inftructions ? Suppofe a
man fo inftructed fhould in confcience believe that a bill,
if enacted, would be prejudicial to his conftituents, yet
his orders bind him to vote for it ; how would he act
between his oath and his inftructions ? In his oath he
has fworn to act according to his judgment, and for the
good of the people ; his inftructions forbid him to ufe
his judgment, and bind him to vote for a law which he
is convinced will injure his conftituents.   He muft then
either abandon his orders or his oath ; perjury or difobedience is his only alternativ.

This is no imaginary fituation ; I prefume that many
men have experienced it.   One very worthy member
of the Legiflature in this State* a few years fince, was
in that very predicament ; and I heard him exprefs
great anxiety upon the occafion.

How noble was the conduct of that gentleman in
Sandwich (Maff.) who, being chofen to reprefent the
town in the late Convention, and inftructed to vote
againft the Conftitution, *at all events ; notwithftanding any
thing that might be faid in favor of it* ; rather than fubmit to be fettered in this manner, refigned his appointment. The name of this gentleman, THOMAS BOURN,
Efq. ought to be held in veneration by every true friend
to his country, and his addrefs to the electors on that
occafion, ought to be written in letters of gold.   It is

recorded

* New York.

recorded in thefe words : " Fellow Townfmen—The line of conduct which has appeared to me right, I have ever wifhed to purfue. In the decline of life, when a few revolving funs at moft will bring me to the bar of impartial juftice, I am unwilling to adopt a different, and lefs honeft mode of acting. It is true, my fentiments at prefent are not in favor of the Conftitution ; open however to conviction, they may be very different, when the fubject is fairly difcuffed by able and upright men. To place myfelf in a fituation, where conviction could be followed only by a bigotted perfiftence in error, would be extremely difagreeable to me. Under the reftrictions with which your Delegates are fettered, *the greateft ideot may anfwer your purpofe as well as the greateft man.* The fuffrages of our fellow men, when they neither repofe confidence in our integrity, nor pay a tribute of refpect to our abilities, can never be agreeable. I am therefore induced pofitivly to decline accepting a feat in Convention, whilft I fincerely wifh you, gentlemen, and my countrymen, every bleffing which a wife and virtuous adminiftration of a free government can fecure."

Such a bold and honeft independence of mind are the marks of a good Legiflator. With fuch men as Mr. Bourn, in the legiflativ department, our lives, liberties and properties are fafe. Such a genius, rifing amidft the obfcurity of errors and falfe maxims, like a ftar emerging from chaos, fpreads the rays of truth and illuminates the furrounding hemifphere. Confidering the circumftances in which this gentleman was then placed, I had rather be the author of that fhort addrefs, than of all the labored differtations which have been written upon the propofed conftitution.

Another error, which is connected with the practice of inftructing Reprefentativs, and may perhaps be one caufe of it, is the opinion that a Deputy chofen by a certain number of freemen, is *their Reprefentativ only* or *particularly* : It feems to be believed that a Reprefentativ is bound to attend to the *particular intereft of the men who elect him*, rather than to the *general intereft*. If this

were

were true, it would obviate, in some measure, the objections against instructions. But with respect to every
general act, the opinion is *clearly false*. The reason why
men are chosen by small societies of freemen, and not
by the whole body, is, that the whole body cannot be
well acquainted with the most able men in the different
parts of the State. It is the best expedient to correct
the defects of government, or rather, it is the best *practi-*
cable mode of election. To render the mode perfect,
the *whole body of freemen* should be at liberty to choose
their Delegates from the *whole body*. This would des-
troy, in a great measure, the local views and attachments which now embarrass government ; every Representativ would be chosen by the whole body ; and the
interest of the whole number of constituents would be
his object.

This mode is either impracticable or hazardous ;
notwithstanding this, when a Delegate is elected by a
part of the State, he is really the Representativ of the
whole, as much as if he were *elected* by the whole. The
constituents of every Representativ are not solely those
who *voted* for him, but the *whole State*, and the man that
acts from a *local* interest, and attends merely to the
wishes of those men who elected him, violates his oath,
and abuses his trust. Hence the absurdity of instructions, which are generally dictated by a partial interest,
and can perhaps in no case be the sole rule of a Legisla-
tor's conduct. When therefore a Representativ says,
such is the wish of my constituents ; such are their directions ;
his declaration is but partially true ; for his instructions
are the wishes of a *part* only of his constituents. His
constituents, whom he actually represents, and whose
greatest interest is the sole rule of his conduct, are *the*
whole body of freemen. This is an important truth, and
I must repeat it ; the man who is deputed to make laws
for a State, and suffers a local interest to influence his
conduct, abuses a sacred trust ; and the Representativ
who obeys his instructions, in opposition to the conviction of his own mind, arising from a general view of
public good, *is guilty of a species of perjury*.

Such

Such are the opinions, which after long deliberation, I have formed refpecting the principles of a republican government. I feel a diffidence in publifhing fentiments fo repugnant to the principles received by my countrymen, and recognized by fome of the State Conftitutions. But a ftrong perfuafion of the truth of thefe opinions, acquired by reafoning, and confirmed by feveral years obfervations, forbids me to fupprefs them.

A fummary of the truths, deduced from the foregoing reafoning, is this : That the power of a State is at all times equal ; that neither the people themfelves, nor a Convention of their Delegates, have either the power or the right to make an unalterable Conftitution ; that the power of creating a legiflativ body, or the fovereign right of election, is folely in the people ; but the fovereign power of making laws is folely in an Affembly of their Reprefentativs ; that the people have no right to give binding inftructions to their Reprefentativs ; confequently a diftinction between a *Convention* and a *Legiflature,* can be merely a difference of *forms*; that Reprefentativs have no right to prolong the period of their delegation ; that being taken from the mafs of the people, and having a common intereft with them, they will be influenced, even by private intereft, to promote the public good ; and that fuch a government, which is a novelty on earth, is perhaps the beft that can be framed, and the only form which will always have for its object, the general good.

No. VII.

No. VII.

PHILADELPHIA, 1787.

REMARKS on the MANNERS, GOV-ERNMENT, and DEBT of the UNITED STATES.

SINCE the declaration and eftablifhment of a general peace, and fince this country has had an opportunity to experience the effects of her independence, events have taken place, which were little expected by the friends of the revolution. It was expected, that on the ratification of peace, by the belligerent powers, America would enjoy perfect political tranquillity. The ftatefman in his clofet, and the divine in his addreffes to heaven, predicted and anticipated the happy period, when every man would reft, unmolefted, under his own vine and his own fig tree. The merchant forefaw, in vifion, the ports of all nations open to his fhips, and the returns of a favorable commerce pouring wealth into his coffers. The honeft laborer, in the fhop and the field, was told that independence and peace would forever remove the fears of oppreffion, would lighten his burthen, and give him legal fecurity for the uninterrupted poffeffion of his rights. This flattering profpect infpired an irrefiftible enthufiafm in war. The contention for freedom was long and arduous ; the prize was obtained ; the delufion vanifhed, and America is furprized at the difappointment.

Inftead of general tranquillity, *one* State has been involved in a civil war, and moft of them are torn with factions, which weaken or deftroy the energy of government. Inftead of a free commerce with all the world, our trade is every where fettered with reftraints and impofitions, dictated by foreign intereft : and inftead of pouring wealth into our country, its prefent

G   tendency

tendency is, to impoverish both the merchant and the public. Instead of legal security of rights under governments of our own choice, and under our own control, we find property at least unsafe, even in our best toned government. Our charters may be wrested from us without a fault, our contracts may be changed or set aside without our consent, by the breath of a popular Legislature. Instead of a dimunition of taxes, our public charges are multiplied ; and to the weight of accumulating debts, we are perpetually making accessions by expensiv follies. Instead of a union of States and measures, essential to the welfare of a great nation, each State is jealous of its neighbor, and struggling for the superiority in wealth and importance, at the hazard even of our federal existence.

This is the dark side of our public affairs ; but such are the facts. The public and private embarrassments, which are both seen and felt, are the topics of incessant declamation. The rhapsodies of orators, and the publications in gazettes, from the northern to the southern extremity of the United States, concur in deprecating the present state of this country, and communicate the intelligence of our distresses to the whole civilized world. Nor are newspapers the only heralds of our calamities. The contempt of government among one class of men, the silent murmurs of poverty in the peaceful cottage, and numerous bankrupts in every quarter, are irresistible evidence to a thinking mind, that something is wrong.

But declamation is idle, and murmurs fruitless. Time has been when the minds of people were alarmed at the approaches of despotism : Then harangues roused attention ; then mobs raised the temple of freedom, and declared themselves ready to be sacrificed upon her altar. But violent passions in the public as well as in the human body, are always transitory. That enthusiasm which was called *public spirit, heroic virtue, and love of country*, has long ago subsided, and is absorbed in the general steady principle, private interest. That enthusiasm is not to be rekindled. The expos-

tulations

tulations of our rulers and patriotic writers, have no more effect in reviving public spirit, than the attraction of a meteor in raising a tide.

Men, who embraced revolution principles, because independence might save a few shillings in taxes, or extend the imaginary sphere of freedom ; who expected that peace would place them in a paradise of blessings, where they might riot without the fatigue of exertion ; such men had narrow views of the consequence of detaching America from a transatlantic jurisdiction. They viewed but a small part of the great event : They are, they *ought to be* disappointed. , Such men expect effects without causes, and are ready to despond, or commence enemies to a glorious event, because miracles are not wrought to verify their ill founded predictions.

In this view, this insect view of things, the revolution ought to be considered as extremely unfortunate ; for to the present generation, it must certainly prove so.

But on the general scale of human happiness, every man of reflection must rejoice at the illustrious event. Even the propriety of the independence of these States, is so obviously dictated by their local situation, that a generous European ought to have consented to the measure on this single principle. But taking into consideration the vast field which is here opened for improvements in science, in government, in religion, and in morals ; the philosopher will felicitate himself with the prospect of discoveries favorable to arts and happiness ; the statesman will rejoice that there is a retreat from the vassalage of Europe ; the divine will bless God that a place has been reserved for an uncorrupted church ; and the philanthropist, who compares the yeomanry of America with the peasantry of Europe, will congratulate himself on an event which has removed millions of people from the ambition of princes, and from a participation of the vices, which mark the decline of nations.

The revolution of America, whatever may be the present effects, must, on the universal scale of policy,

prove

prove fortunate, not only for the parties, but for mankind in general. The period, however, when this
country will realize the happy confequences of her feparation, muft be remote ; probably beyond the lives of
the prefent generation.

It is worth our curiofity to inquire into the caufes of
our prefent political evils ; not the more obvious caufes, which every man fees and laments, but thofe radical
caufes which lie hid from common obfervation ; whofe
operations are imperceptible, but whofe effects are vifible, even to a vulgar eye.

A fundamental miftake of the Americans has been,
that they confidered the revolution as completed, when
it was but juft begun.   Having raifed the pillars of the
building, they ceafed to exert themfelves, and feemed
to forget that the whole fuperftructure was then to be
erected.   This country is independent in government ;
but totally dependent in manners, which are the bafis
of government.   Men feem not to attend to the difference between Europe and America, in point of age
and improvement ; and are difpofed to rufh, with heed-
lefs emulation, into an imitation of manners, for which
we are not prepared.

Every perfon tolerably well verfed in hiftory, knows
that nations are often compared to individuals and to
vegetables, in their progrefs from their origin to maturity and decay.   The refemblance is ftriking and
juft.   This progrefs is as certain in nations as in vegetables ; it is as obvious, and its caufes more eafily underftood ; in proportion as the fecret fprings of action
in government are more eafily explained, than the mechanical principles of vegetation.

This progrefs therefore being affumed as a conceded
fact, fuggefts a forcible argument againft the introduction of European manners into America.   The bufinefs of men in fociety is, firft, to fecure their perfons
and eftates by arms and wholefome laws ; then to procure the conveniencies of life by arts and labor ; but it
is in the laft ftages only of national improvement, when
luxury and amufements become public benefits, by
                                             diffipating

diffipating accumulations of wealth, and furnifhing employment and food for the poor.   And luxury then is not beneficial, except when the wealth of a nation is wafted within itfelf.   It is perhaps always true, that an old civilized nation cannot, with propriety, be the model for an infant nation, either in morals, in manners or fafhions, in literature or in government.

The prefent ambition of Americans is, to introduce as faft as poffible, the fafhionable amufements of the European courts.   Confidering the former dependence of America on England, her defcent, her connexion and prefent intercourfe, this ambition cannot furprife us.   But it muft check this ambition to reflect on the confequences.   It will not be denied, that there are vices predominant in the moft polite cities in Europe, which are not only unknown, but are feldom mentioned in America; and vices that are infamous beyond conception.   I prefume it will not be denied that there muft be an amazing depravation of mind in a nation, where a farce is a publication of more confequence than Milton's Poem; and where an opera dancer, or an Italian finger, receives a falary equal to that of an Ambaffador.   The facts being known and acknowleged, I prefume the confequence will not be denied. Not that this charge is good againft every individual; even in the worft times, there will be found many exceptions to the general character of a nation.

If thefe vices and the depravation of mind do actually exift, it is a proof of a gradual corruption; for there was a time when they did not exift.   There was a time when decency was a virtue, even at Venice.   The progrefs is alfo flow, unlefs haftened by fome external circumftances.   It was more than two thoufand years from the building of Rome to the pontificate of Alexander the VIth whofe naked revelings filled the meafure of public vice, and ftrike the human mind with horror.

A conftant increafe of wealth is ever followed by a multiplication of vices: This feems to be the deftiny of human affairs; wifdom, therefore, directs us to retard,

if

if poffible, and not to accelerate the progrefs of corruption.   But an introduction of the fafhionable diverfions of Europe into America, is an acceleration of the
growth of vices which are yet in their infancy, and an
introduction of new ones too infamous to be mentioned.   A dancing fchool among the Tufcaroras, is not a
greater abfurdity than a mafquerade in America.   A
theater, under the beft regulations, is not effential to
our public and private happinefs.   It may afford entertainment to individuals ; but it is at the expenfe of
private tafte and public morals.   The great misfortune
of all exhibitions of this kind is this ; that they reduce
all tafte to a level.   Not only the vices of all claffes of
people are brought into view, but of all ages and nations.   The intrigues of a nobleman, and the fcurrility
of fhoe blacks, are prefented to the view of both fexes,
of all ages ; the vices of the age of Elizabeth and of
Charles IId are recorded by the mafterly pens of a
Shakefpeare and a Congreve, and by repeated reprefentation, they are " hung on high," as the poet ex-
preffes it, " to poifon half mankind."   The fact is,
that all characters muft be prefented upon a theater,
becaufe all characters are fpectators ; and a nobleman
and a failor, a dutchefs and a wafher woman, that attend conftantly on the exhibitions of vice, become
equally depraved ; their taftes will be nearly alike as to
vice ; the one is as prepared for a crime as the other.
It is for this reafon, that many of the amufements of
nations more depraved than ourfelves, are highly pernicious in this country.   They carry us forward by
hafty ftrides, to the laft ftages of corruption ; a period
that every benevolent man will deprecate and endeavor
to retard.   This circumftance, the difference in the
ftages of our political exiftence, fhould make us fhun
the vices which may be politic and even neceffary in
older ftates ; and endeavor to preferve our manners by
being our own ftandards.   By attaching ourfelves to
foreign manners, we counteract the good effects of the
revolution, or rather render them incomplete.   A revolution in the form of government, is but a revolution

in

in name; unlefs attended with a change of piinciples and manners, which are the fprings of government.

This leads me to treat more particularly of the influence of fafhions on the interefts of thefe States; an article in which the ladies are deeply interefted.

Fafhion in itfelf is a matter of indifference, as affecting neither morals nor politenefs. It is of no confequence whether a lady is clad with a gown or a frock; or whether a gentleman appears in public with a cap or a wig. But there may be times and fituations in which the moft trifling things become important. The practice of imitating foreign modes of drefs, cannot coft America lefs than 100,000l. a year. I fpeak not of the neceffary articles of drefs; but merely of changes of fafhions.

To underftand this fact, it is neceffary to advert to the different circumftances of this country, and of the European kingdoms, which we take as our models.

Two circumftances diftinguifh moft of the commercial countries of Europe from America; a feudal divifion of real property, and manufactures. Where vaft eftates are hereditary and unalienable, a great part of the people are dependent on the rich, and if the rich do not employ them, they muft ftarve. Thus in England and France, a great landholder poffeffes a hundred times the property that is neceffary for the fubfiftence of a family; and each landlord has perhaps a hundred families dependent on him for fubfiftence. On this ftatement, if the landlord fhould live penurioufly, and fupply his own family only with neceffaries, all his dependents muft ftarve. In order to fubfift the ninety nine families, he muft create wants, which their employment muft fupply; for the natural wants of a few rich people will not furnifh employment for great multitudes of poor. Hence the good policy, the neceffity of luxury in moft European kingdoms. Hence originate all the changes and varieties of fafhion. A gentleman or lady in London muft not appear in public twice in the fame fuit. This is a regulation of cuftom, but it is highly political; for were the nobility and rich

rich gentry to wear out all their clothes, one half the people muſt be beggars. The faſhions of England and France are not merely matter of fancy : Fancy may dictate new and odd figures in dreſs ; but the general deſign of frequent and continual changes of faſhion, is wiſe ſyſtematic policy, at the courts of London and Paris.

But let us ſee with how little diſcretion and policy *we* adopt foreign luxuries. America is a young country, with ſmall inequalities of property, and without manufactures. Few people are here dependent on the rich, for every man has an opportunity of becoming rich himſelf. Conſequently few people are ſupported by the luxuries of the wealthy ; and even theſe few are moſtly foreigners.

But we have no body of manufacturers to ſupport by diſſipation. All our ſuperfluities are imported, and the conſumption of them in this country enriches the merchants and ſupports the poor of Europe. We are generous indeed ! generous to a fault. This is the pernicious, the fatal effect of our dependence on foreign nations for our manners. We labor day and night, we ſacrifice our peace and reputation, we defraud our public creditors, involve ourſelves in debts, impoveriſh our country : Nay, many are willing to become bankrupts and take lodgings in a priſon, for the ſake of being as fooliſh as thoſe nations which ſubſiſt their poor and grow rich and reſpectable by their follies.

No objection can be made to rich and elegant dreſſes among people of affluent circumſtances. But perhaps we may ſafely calculate that one third of the expenſes incurred by dreſs in this country, add nothing either to convenience or elegance.

A new dreſs is invented in London or Paris, not for the ſake of ſuperior elegance, becauſe it frequently happens that a new dreſs is leſs rich and elegant than an old one ; but for the ſake of giving food to manufacturers. That new faſhion is ſent acroſs the Atlantic ; let it be ever ſo troubleſome and uncouth, we admire its novelty ; we adopt it becauſe it is faſhionable ; and

                                        merely

merely for a change, that may be made in half an hour by a tailor or a milliner, 20, 30, or 50,000 pounds are drawn from the capital stocks of property in America, to enrich nations which command our commerce and smile at our folly.

But it is not only the wealth of this country that is sacrificed by our servile imitation of other nations ; our complaisance often requires us to dispense with good taste.

It will probably be admitted that amidst the infinite variety of dresses which are fashionable, during a course of ten or fifteen years, some of them must be more convenient and elegant than others. True taste in dress consists in setting off the person to the best advantage. That dress which unites the articles of convenience, simplicity and neatness, in the greatest perfection, must be considered as the most elegant. But true taste goes farther ; it has reference to age, to shape, to complexion, and to the season of the year. The same dress which adorns a miss of fifteen, will be frightful on a venerable lady of seventy. The same dress will embellish one lady and disfigure another. But the passive disposition of Americans in receiving every mode that is offered them, sometimes reduces all ages, shapes and complexions to a level.

I will not undertake to say that people ought not, in the article of dress, to sacrifice taste to national interest. A sacrifice of that kind, in a manufacturing country, may be laudable ; it will at least be pardonable. But in a reverse of situation, in America, where a waste of property and a group of political evils accompany a bad taste, the sacrifice admits of no apology.

It is not unfrequent to hear ladies complain severely of the inconvenience of fashion. Their good sense disapproves and their taste revolts at incumbrances. And yet where is the lady who would not sooner submit to any fatigue, rather than be ridiculous. I speak of ladies particularly ; in point of expense, the gentlemens' dresses are exceptionable as well as the ladies ; in point of convenience, the ladies are the greatest sufferers by
fashion,

fashion, as their dress admits of the greatest variety of incumbrances.

Perhaps the trouble of conforming entirely to the fashions of Europe is as great a tax upon the ladies, as the expense is to their husbands and parents.

One society of people, the Friends, are happily re-leased from the tyranny and inconveniencies of fashion. However disagreeable the restraints of their religion may appear in other respects, it must be acknowledged that, in point of dress, the rules of their society con-form to purity of taste.

Perhaps we may safely estimate, that the ladies of that society dress with two thirds of the expense which other ladies incur, even when the articles of their dress are equally rich and expensiv; the difference is saved by neglecting superfluous finery. And are not their taste in dress, their simplicity and neatness, universally ad-mired? Does it not set off their persons to the best ad-vantage? Do not gentlemen almost universally give the preference to the taste of Quaker ladies? Nay, I would ask, whether other ladies themselves, under a strong bias in favor of a tawdry dress, are not fre-quently lavishing encomiums on the superior elegance and convenience of the Friends' dresses? And how of-ten do they sigh beneath the trouble of their own dress, and wish that particular articles would go out of fash-ion.

If there is any thing on earth, which can make a ra-tional mind disgusted with society, it is that cruel ne-cessity, which obliges a person to sacrifice both his in-terest and his taste, or run the hazard of being laughed at for his singularity.

In some Asiatic countries, people never change their modes of dress. This uniformity, which continues for ages, proceeds from the same principles as the monthly changes in England and France; both pro-ceed from necessity and policy. Both arise from good causes which operate in the several governments; that is, the manners of each government are subservient to its particular interest. The reverse is true of this
country.

country. Our manners are wholly fubfervient to the
intereft of foreign nations. Where do we find, in
drefs or equipage, the leaft reference to the circumftances of this country ! Is it not the fole ambition of the
Americans to be juft like other nations, without the
means of fupporting the refemblance ? We ought not
to harbor any fpleen or prejudice againft foreign kingdoms. This would be illiberal. They are wife, they
are refpectable. We fhould defpife the man that
piques himfelf on his own country, and treats all others with indifcriminate contempt. I wifh to fee much
lefs jealoufy and ill nature fubfifting between the Americans and Englifh. But in avoiding party fpirit and
refentment on the one hand, we fhould be very careful
of fervility on the other. There is a manly pride in
true independence, which is equally remote from info-
lence and meannefs ; a pride that is characteriftic or
great minds. Have Americans difcovered this pride
fince the declaration of peace ? We boaft of independence, and with propriety. But will not the fame men,
who glory in this great event, even in the midft of a
gafconade, turn to a foreigner and afk him, " what is
the lateft fafhion in Europe !" He has worn an elegant fuit of clothes for fix weeks ; he might wear it a
few weeks longer, but it has not fo many buttons as the
laft fuit of my lord ——— : He throws it afide, and gets
one that has. The fuit cofts him a fum of money ;
but it keeps him in the fafhion, and feeds the poor of
Great Britain or France. It is a fingular phenomenon, and to pofterity it will appear incredible, that a
nation of heroes, who have conquered armies, and raifed an empire, fhould not have the fpirit to fay—*we will
wear our clothes as we pleafe.*

Let it not be thought that this is a trifling fubject ;
a matter of no confequence. Mankind are governed
by opinion ; and while we flatter ourfelves that we enjoy independence, becaufe no foreign power can impofe
laws upon us, we are groaning beneath the tyranny of
opinion ; a tyranny more fevere than the laws of mon-
archs ; a dominion voluntary indeed, but for that rea-
                                                fon,

fon, more effectual; an authority of manners which commands our fervices, and fweeps away the fruits of our labor.

I repeat the fentiment with which I began; the revolution of America is yet incomplete. We are now in a fituation to anfwer all the purpofes of the European nations; independent in government, and dependent in manners. They give us their fafhions, they direct *our* tafte to make a market for *their* commodities; they engrofs the profits of our induftry, without the hazard of defending us, or the expenfe of fupporting our civil government. A fituation more favorable to *their* intereft, or more repugnant to our *own*, *they* could not have chofen for us, nor *we* embraced.

If fuch is the ftate of facts, and if the influence of foreign manners does actually defeat the purpofes of the revolution; if our implicit fubmiffion to the prevailing tafte of European courts, involves individuals and the public in unneceffary expenfes, it is in the power of a few influential characters in each of our commercial cities to remedy the whole evil. And in a reformation of this kind, the ladies would have no inconfiderable fhare.

It is really a matter of aftonifhment, that the pride of the Americans has fo long fubmitted tamely to a foreign yoke. Afide of all regard to intereft, we fhould expect that the idea of being a nation of apes would mortify minds accuftomed to freedom of thought, and would prompt them to fpurn their chains.

Have the ladies in America no ingenuity, no tafte? Do they not underftand what dreffes are moft convenient and elegant? What modes are beft adapted to the climate, or other circumftances of this country? They moft certainly do. Foreigners acknowlege that the nativ beauty and underftanding of the American ladies are not excelled in any country, and equalled in very few. And one would imagin that the modes of embellifhing fo many perfonal charms ought not, in all cafes, to be prefcribed by the milliners and manteau makers on the other fide of the Atlantic. A noble

pride

pride fhould forbid that ladies of birth and breeding fhould be wholly indebted to the tafte of others, for the decorations of their beauty.

When the gentlemen in America fhall exercife fpirit enough to be their own judges of tafte in drefs : When they have wifdom to confult the circumftances of this country, and fortitude enough to retain a fafhion as long as their *own intereft* requires, inftead of changing it when *other nations* direct :   When the ladies fhall exercife the rights of their fex, and fay, we will *give* the laws of fafhion to our *own nation*, inftead of *receiving* them from *another*, we will perform our part of the revolution : When both fexes fhall take more pride and pleafure in being their own ftandards, than in being the humble imitators of thofe who riot on the profits of our commerce ; we fhall realize a new fpecies of independence ; an independence flattering to generous minds, and more productive of wealth than all the laws of power, or the little arts of national policy.   And in this revolution of manners, there needs not any facrifice of real drefs.   I will venture to eftimate, that the retrenching of fuperfluous articles ; articles which conftitute no part of drefs, and ferve but to disfigure an elegant perfon ; articles that are made and fent to us to fupport the fixpenny day laborers of Europe ; I fay, a retrenching of thefe trifling articles only, would be an annual faving to America fufficient to pay one half of the intereft of our federal debt.   We can throw no blame on foreign nations ; they are wife, · and profit by our want of fpirit and tafte.

On the footing that all mankind are brethren, perhaps it is generous in us to affift foreigners, who are a part of the Great Family.

It is to be wifhed, however, that we might firft difcharge our honeft debts : That the foldier, whofe labor and blood have purchafed our empire, and whofe fervices have been repaid with a fhadow of reward, might be indemnified by the juftice of his country : That the widow and orphan might at leaft receive the ftipulated fatisfaction for loffes which money cannot repair. Yes,

let

let us firſt be *juſt*, and then *generous*.   When we have
no better uſe for our ſuperfluous property, then let us
beſtow it upon our wretched brethren of the human
race.   They will repay our charity with gratitude, and
bleſs God that he has peopled one half the world with
a race of freemen, to enrich the tyrants, and ſupport
the vaſſals of the other.

In another particular, our dependence on nations farther advanced in ſociety than ourſelves, has a very unhappy effect.

I aſſume it as a fact, conceded by all philoſophers
and hiſtorians, that there has been, in every civilized
nation, a particular period of time, peculiarly favorable
to literary reſearches ; and that in this period, language
and taſte arrive to purity ; the beſt authors flouriſh,
and genius is exerted to benefit mankind.

This period in Greece was the age of Themiſtocles,
immediately after the invaſion of Xerxes.   In Rome,
it was the reign of Auguſtus Cæſar, when a revolution
had left the empire in a ſtate of tranquillity.   In France,
the reign of Louis the XIVth was diſtinguiſhed for the
number and eminence of its authors, and the correct-
neſs of taſte.   The correſponding period of taſte in
England, commenced about the middle of the ſixteenth
century, and ended with the reign of George the IId.
Scotland was later in improvement ; but perhaps has
now ſeen its meridian ſplendor.

There ſeems to be a certain point of improvement
beyond which every ſtep in refinement is corruption ;
moral ſentiment is poſtponed to wit, and ſenſe is ſacrific-
ed to ſound.   This has been the caſe in all nations, and
is now true of England.   The candid among the nation
acknowlege and lament the decline of true taſte and ſcience.   Very few valuable writings appear in the preſent age ; plays, novels, farces, and compilations fill the
catalogue of new publications ; and the library of a
man of faſhion conſiſts of Cheſterfield's Letters, Triſ-
tram Shandy, and a few comedies.

A gentleman in high office in London, in a letter to
an eminent literary character in America, which I had
the

the honor to read, informs, " that fo low is the tafte of
the nation, that were Milton's Poem to be now firft
publifhed, it would not find purchafers : Mufic and.
painting are the only arts that have royal encouragement." He fays further, " that there is a national
combination to oppofe the fame of every American
art, production and character." I would hope that
this account is an exaggeration of the truth ; but we
have the beft teftimony to convince us that every thing
is facrificed to amufement and pleafure.

We ought not therefore to form our tafte after fuch
models : In order to write, think and act with propriety, we fhould go back half a century, to the ftyle and
morality of Addifon.and his cotemporaries ; there we
may find the moft perfect models.

By making the prefent tafte of Europe our ftandards,
we not only debafe our own, but we check the attempts
of genius in.this country.

Eminence is fometimes apt to impofe errors upon
people, whofe refpect for the character may filence all
fcruple, and prevent them from examining into the
grounds of his opinion. Such is the implicit confidence repofed in the opinions of certain celebrated
writers, that when an American ventures to call in
queftion a received principle or opinion of theirs, his
countrymen charge him with arrogance, and exclaim,
how fhould this man be as good a judge of the fubject
as a foreigner ! Such falfe notions of the perfection of
particular characters, fetter the mind, and in concert
with credulity and idlenefs, prepare it for the reception
of any errors, however enormous.

This fame veneration for eminent foreigners, and
the bewitching charms of fafhion, have led the Americans to adopt the modern corruptions of our language.
Very feldom have men examined the ftructure of the
language, to find reafons for their practice. The pronunciation and ufe of words have been fubject to the
fame arbitrary or accidental changes, as the fhape of
their garments. My lord wears a hat of a certain fize
and fhape ; he pronounces a word in a certain man-
                                                ner ;

ner ; and both muft be right, for he is a fafhionable
man.   In Europe this is right in drefs ; and men who
have not an opportunity of learning the juft rules of
our language, are in fome degree excufeable for imitating thofe whom they confider as fuperiors.   But in
men of fcience, this imitation can hardly be excufed.

Our language was fpoken in purity about eighty years
ago ; fince which time, great numbers of faults have
crept into practice about the theater and court of London.   An affected erroneous pronunciation has in
many inftances taken place of the true ; and new words
or modes of fpeech have fucceeded the ancient correct
Englifh phrafes.

Thus we have, in the modern Englifh pronunciation,
their natfhures, conjunctfhures, conftitfhutions, and
tfhumultfhuous legiflatfhures ; and a long catalogue of
fafhionable improprieties.   Thefe are a direct violation of the rules of analogy and harmony ; they offend
the ear, and embarrafs the language.   Time was,
when thefe errors were unknown ; they were little
known in America before the revolution.   I prefume
we may fafely fay, that our language has fuffered more
injurious changes in America, fince the Britifh army
landed on our fhores, than it had fuffered before, in the
period of three centuries.   The bucks and bloods tell
us that there is no proper ftandard in language ; that
it is all arbitrary.   The affertion, however, ferves but
to fhow their ignorance.   There are, in the language
itfelf, decifive reafons for preferring one pronunciation
to another ; and men of fcience fhould be acquainted
with thefe reafons.   But if there were none, and every
thing refted on practice, we fhould never change a general practice without fubftantial reafons : No change
fhould be introduced, which is not an obvious improvement.

But our leading characters feem to pay no regard to
rules, or their former practice.   To know and embrace every change made in Great Britain, whether
right or wrong, is the extent of their inquiries, and the
height of their ambition.   It is to this deference we
                                                    may

may afcribe the long catalogue of errors in pronunciation and of. falfe idioms which disfigure the language
of our mighty fine fpeakers. And fhould this imitation continue, we fhall be hurried down the ftream of
corruption, with older nations, and our language, with
theirs, be loft in an ocean of perpetual changes. The
only hope we can entertain is, that America, driven by
the fhock of a revolution, from the rapidity of the current, may glide along near the margin with a gentler
ftream, and fometimes be wafted back by an eddy.

The foregoing-remarks fuggeft fome of the caufes
which operate to defeat the true end of the revolution.
Every man fees and feels our political embarraffments ;
the foes of the revolution afcribe them all to that event,
and the friends charge them upon the enmity and refentment of our parent country. Both are wrong.
The revolution is, and will ultimately prove, a happy
event for us and for the world. The Englifh, as a
nation, are wife and refpectable : As citizens of the
world, we fhould efteem them : As a commercial people, we fhould cultivate a friendly intercourfe with
them ; but as a foreign nation, whofe political circumftances are very different from ours, we fhould not
make them, in all cafes, our ftandard. I repeat the
declaration I before made : The independence of this
country is incomplete : There has been a total change
in government, with little or no change in the principles which give energy to the operations of government.

In the preceding remarks, I have endeavored to fhew
in what refpect the revolution of America is yet incomplete, and that an independence of manners and
opinion is neceffary to give full effect to an independence of government. I propofe now to make fome
remarks on government, to ftate the effects of the revolution on the morals of people, and the influence of
money on mens' fenfe of juftice and moral obligation.

It is perhaps a fundamental principle of government,
that men are influenced more by habit, than by any
abftract ideas of right and wrong. Few people exam-

H   in

in into the propriety of particular ufages or laws ; or if they examin, few indeed are capable of comprehending their propriety.' But every man knows what is a law or general practice, and he conforms to it, not becaufe it is right or beft, but becaufe it has been the practice. It is for this reafon that habits of obedience fhould not be difturbed. There are perhaps in every government, fome laws and cuftoms, which, when examined on theoretical principles, will be found unjuft and even impolitic. But if the people acquiefce in thofe laws and cuftoms, if they are attached to them by habit, it is wrong in the Legiflature to attempt an innovation which fhall alarm their apprehenfions. There are multitudes of abfurdities practifed in fociety, in which people are evidently happy. Arraign thofe abfurdities before the tribunal of examination ; people may be convinced of their impropriety ; they may even be convinced that better fchemes may be projected ; and yet it might be impoffible to unite their opinions fo as to eftablifh different maxims. On the other hand, there are many good inftitutions, in which, however, there may be theoretical faults, which, if called into public view, and artfully reprefented, might fhake the beft government on earth.

Speculativ philofophers and hiftorians have often defcribed, and fometimes ridiculed the warmth with which nations have defended errors in religion and government. With the moft profound deference for wife and refpectable men, I muft think they are guilty of a miftake ; and that the errors which nations fight to defend, exift only in the heads of thefe theorifts. Whatever fpeculation may tell us, experience and the peace of fociety, require us to confider every thing as right, which a nation believes to be fo. Every inftitution, every cuftom, may be deemed juft and proper, which does not produce inconveniencies that the bulk of mankind may fee and feel. The tranquillity of fociety therefore fhould never be difturbed for a philofophical diftinction.

It

It will perhaps be objected, that thefe doctrines, if practifed, would prevent all improvements, in fcience, religion and government. By no means ; but they point out the method in which all improvements fhould be made, when opinion and fixed habits are to be overthrown, or changed. They fhow that all reformation fhould be left to the natural progrefs of fociety, or to the conviction of the mind. They fhow the hazard and impracticability of making changes, before the minds of the body of the people are prepared for the innovation. I fpeak not of defpotic governments, where the will of the prince is enforced by an army ; and yet even abfolute tyrants have been affaffinated for not attending to the fpirit and habits of their fubjects.

In vain do rulers oppofe the general opinion of the people. By fuch oppofition, Philip IId, of Spain, kept one part of his fubjects, for half a century, butchering the other, and in the end, loft one third of his dominions. By not regarding the change of habits in the nation, Charles Ift, of England, loft his head. By carrying his changes too far, Cromwell began to oppofe the fpirit of the nation, and had he lived to profecute his fyftem, that fpirit would, in a few years, have brought his neck to the block. The general fpirit of the nation reftored to the throne, the fon of the prince, whom that fpirit had but a few years before arraigned and condemned. By oppofing that fpirit, James was obliged to leave his kingdom, and the fenfe of the nation ftill excludes the family which, by their own law of fucceffion, has the beft title to the throne. But there is no prefcription againft general opinion ; no right that can enter the lift againft the fenfe of a nation ; that fenfe, which after all our reafoning, will forever determin what is beft.

The truth of thefe remarks is proved by examples in this country. An immenfe revenue might have been drawn from America without refiftance, in almoft any method but that which the Britifh parliament adopted. But their firft attempts were made upon articles of

common

common neceffity ; the attempts were too vifible ; the people felt and refifted. Their apprehenfions were a-larmed ; their fears, whether well founded or imaginary, were multiplied and confirmed by newfpaper rhapfo-dies, and finally produced a combined oppofition to all Britifh taxation. Then Great Britain fhould have compounded ; fhe did not ; fhe oppofed the general fenfe of three millions of her fubjects, and loft the whole.

A difpute exifted between Connecticut and Penfyl-vania, refpecting a tract of land ; a federal court decid-ed the jurifdiction, or State claim, in favor of Penfylva-nia ; five thoufand inhabitants, feated on the lands, ac-knowlege the jurifdiction, but contend that their original purchafe, and fubfequent labor, entitle them to the lands. Notwithftanding the invalidity of their State claim, the fettlers determin to maintain their lands. The queftion of right is at once fufpended, and the only inquiry is, which is the beft policy, to indemnify a few individuals by a pecuniary compofi-tion, or facrifice five thoufand fubjects. This queftion, left to the commonwealth, would be decided by a great majority, in favor of the fettlers, and againft the very principles of right on which the State holds the jurif-diction.

I am not competent to judge of the merits of the difpute between New York and Vermont ; but if the ufurpation of Vermont were a conceded fact, and that ufurpation to be defended by arms, and the queftion of granting them independence were left to the State of New York, I am confident that nine tenths of the peo-ple would decide for the independence of Vermont againft their own rights.

Thus it often happens, that a general opinion, grounded on rational expediency, will, and ought to decide political queftions, contrary to the ftrict princi-ples of juftice and equity.

I would, by no means, be underftood to defend, by fuch doctrines, the infurrections of a neighboring State. I reprobate every thing that wears the leaft appearance
of

of oppofition to lawful authority. It is evident however, that the Legiflature of Maffachufetts were too
inattentive to the general fpirit of the State. The
murmurs of the people were heard long before they
broke out into rebellion, and were treated with too
much negleft. They were a proof at leaft that fomething was wrong. This the Legiflature acknowleged
in their late acts, and the complaints of the populace
might once have been filenced by fuch conciliatory
meafures.

But an oppofition fo violent muft fuddenly ceafe, or
acquire fyftem. In the latter cafe, the demands of the
infurgents will rife in proportion to their ftrength ; they
will afk unreafonable conceffions, and the fword muft
decide their claims. The infurgents took wrong
fteps to obtain redrefs ; they fhould have refted their
agrievances on petitions, and the event of an election ;
but one rafh ftep leads to a fecond, and to a third. Thefe
fatal effects of popular difcontent afford one ufeful lef-
fon, that rulers fhould not attempt to carry a meafure
againft the general voice of a people.* But a queftion
will arife, how far may the people be oppofed, when
their fchemes are evidently pernicious ? I anfwer, this
can never happen thro defign ; and errors, even of
the populace, may gradually be removed. If the people cannot be convinced, by reafon and argument, of
the impolicy or injuftice of a favorite fcheme, we have
only to wait for the confequences to produce conviction. All people are not capable of juft reafoning on
the great fcale of politics ; but all can feel the inconveniencies .

* Some have fufpected from thefe fentiments, that I favor
the infurrection in Maffachufetts. If it is neceffary to be
more explicit than I have been in the declaration, "*I reprobate,*
&c." I muft add, that in governments like ours, derived from
the people, I believe there is no *poffible fituation* in which violent oppofition to laws can be juftified ; becaufe it can never
be neceffary. *General evils* will always be legally redreffed,
and *partial evils* muft be borne, if the majority require it. A
tender law, which interferes with *paft* contracts, is perhaps
the wickedeft act that a Legiflature can be guilty of ; and yet I
think the people in Rhode Ifland have done right, in not oppofing their's, in a violent manner.

niencies of wrong meafures, and evils of this kind generally furnifh their own remedy.   All popular Legiflatures are liable to great miftakes.   Many of the acts
of the American Legiflatures, refpecting money and
commerce, will, to future generations, appear incredible.   After repeated experiments, people will be better
informed, and aftonifhed that their fathers could make
fuch blunders in legiflation.

If the people of this State* are not already convinced, they certainly will be, that the addition of 150,000l.
of paper, to the current fpecie of the State, did not increafe the permanent value of circulating medium a
fingle farthing.   They were perhaps told that fuch a
fum of paper would fhut up the fpecie, or enable the
merchant to export it ; but their jealoufy made them
believe thefe the fuggeftions of intereft ; and nothing
but the experiment could fatisfy their wifhes.   Every
man of reflection muft regret that he is fubject to the
evils confequent on popular miftakes in judgement ; but
this is the price of our independence and our forms of
government.

Let us attend to the immediate and neceffary confequences of the American revolution.

So great an event as that of detaching millions of
people from their parent nation, could not have been
effected without the operation of powerful caufes.
Nothing but a feries of real or imaginary evils could
have fhaken the habits by which we were governed,
and produced a combined oppofition againft the power
of Great Britain.   I fhall not enumerate any of thefe
evils ; but obferve that fuch evils, by twenty years operation upon the fears or feelings of the Americans,
had alienated their affections or weakened thofe habits
of refpect, by which they were predifpofed to voluntary
obedience.   When a government has loft refpect, it
has loft the main pillar of its authority.   Not even a
military force can fupply the want of refpect among
fubjects.   A change of fentiment prepares the way for
a change of government, and when that change of fentiment

* Penfylvania.

timent had become general in America, nothing could have prevented a revolution.

But it is more eafy to excite fears than to remove them. The jealoufy raifed in the minds of Americans againft the Britifh government, wrought a revolution; but the fpirit did not then fubfide; it changed its object, and by the arts of defigning men, and the real diftreffes confequent on fuch a political ftorm, was directed againft our own governments. The reftraints impofed by refpect and habits of obedience were broken thro, and the licentious paffions of men fet afloat.

Nothing can be fo fatal to morals and the peace of fociety, as a violent fhock given to public opinion or fixed habits. Polemic difputes have often deftroyed the friendfhip of a church, and filled it, not only with rancor, but with immorality. Public opinion therefore in religion and government, the great fupports of fociety, fhould never be fuddenly unhinged. The feparation of America, however, from all dependence on European government, could not have been effected without previoufly attacking and changing opinion. It was an effential ftep, but the effects of it will not eafily be repaired. That independence of fpirit which preceded the commencement of hoftilities, and which victory has ftrengthened; that love of dominion, inherent in the mind of man, which our forms of government are continually flattering; that licentioufnefs of inquiry which a jealoufy of rights firft produced and ftill preferves, cannot be controled and fubdued, but by a long feries of prudent and vigorous meafures.

Perhaps the prefent age will hardly fee the reftoration of perfect tranquillity. But the fpirit and principles, which wrought our feparation from Great Britain, will moftly die with the prefent generation; the next generation will probably have new habits of obedience to our new governments; and habits will govern them, with very little fupport from law.

The force of habit in government is moft ftrikingly illuftrated by the example of Connecticut. Moft of the laws, cuftoms and inftitutions, which the people
brought

brought with them from England, or which they introduced, on their firſt ſettlement, remain to this day, with ſuch ſmall alterations only as would naturally be made in the progreſs of ſociety and population.

The government of Connecticut had formerly little more than a nominal dependence on England; independence therefore required but a little change of the old conſtitution. The habits of the people have not been materially changed; their reſpect for the government has not been ſuſpended nor diminiſhed. It would therefore be extremely difficult to raiſe an inſurrection in that State againſt their own government;* for they have not been accuſtomed to diſpute the propriety of their eſtabliſhed maxims and laws. Whatever alterations in their conſtitution, a diſcerning Legiſlator might ſuggeſt, it would be highly impolitic to attempt any changes, which ſhould diſturb public opinion or alarm apprehenſion. When a law or cuſtom becomes inconvenient, the people will feel the evil and apply a remedy.

Moſt of the other States had new conſtitutions of government to form; they had a kind of interregnum; an interval, when reſpect for all government was ſuſpended; an interval fatal in the laſt degree, to morals and ſocial confidence. This interval between the abolition of the old conſtitution and the formation of a new one, laſted longer in Maſſachuſetts than in the other States, and there the effects are moſt viſible. But perhaps it is impoſſible to frame a conſtitution of government, in the cloſet, which will ſuit the people; for it is frequent to find one, the moſt perfect in theory, the moſt objectionable in practice. Hence we often hear popular complaints againſt the preſent governments in America: And yet theſe may proceed rather from the novelty of the obedience required, than from any real

errors

* This aſſertion may ſeem to be contradicted by the oppoſition of Connecticut to the half pay act; but that oppoſition did not even threaten violence or arms: It was conducted in a peaceable manner; and I do not know that the State has furniſhed an inſtance of a tumultuous interruption of law.

errors or defects in the systems : It may be nothing but the want of habit which makes people uneasy ; the same articles which now produce clamors and discontent, may, after twenty years practice, give perfect satisfaction. Nay, the same civil regulation, which the present generation may raise a mob to resist, the next generation may raise a mob to defend.

But perhaps a more immediate and powerful cause of a corruption of social principles, is a fluctuation of money. Few people seem to attend to the connexion between money and morals ; but it may doubtless be proved to the satisfaction of every reflecting mind, that a sudden increase of specie in a country, and frequent and obvious changes of value, are more fruitful sources of corruption of morals than any events that take place in a community.

America began the late war without funds of money, and its circulating specie was very inconsiderable. Commerce was regular, and *speculation*, a term unknown to the body of the people.

The emission of paper was an obvious and necessary expedient ; yet it was bad policy to throw vast sums into circulation without taking some measures to recall it. It was the fate of America to receive in bills of credit, and in the course of three or four years, about twenty times the nominal value of its current specie ; the bills depreciated in the same proportion, and the real value of the medium continued the same.

The first visible effect of an augmentation of the medium and the consequent fluctuation of value, was, a host of jockies, who followed a species of itinerant commerce ; and subsisted upon the ignorance and honesty of the country people ; or in other words, upon the difference in the value of the currency, in different places. Perhaps we may safely estimate, that not less than 20,000 men in America, left honest callings, and applied themselves to this knavish traffic. A sudden augmentation of currency flattered people with the prospect of accumulating property without labor.

The

The firſt effect of too much money is to check manual labor, the only permanent ſource of wealth. Induſtry, which ſecures ſubſiſtence and advances our intereſt by ſlow and regular gains, is the beſt preſervative of morals ; for it keeps men employed, and affords them few opportunities of taking unfair advantages.   A regular commerce has nearly the ſame effect as agriculture or the mechanic arts ; for the principles are generally fixed and underſtood.

Speculation has the contrary effect.   As its calculations for profit depend on no fixed principles, but ſolely on the different value of articles in different parts of the country, or accidental and ſudden variations of value, it opens a field for the exerciſe of ingenuity in taking advantage of theſe circumſtances.   The ſpeculator may begin with honeſt intentions ; and may juſtify his buſineſs, by ſaying, that he injures no man, when he givs the current value of an article in one place, and ſells it for its current value in another ; altho in this caſe he is a uſeleſs member of ſociety, as he livs upon the labor of others, without earning a farthing.   But he does not ſtop here ; he takes an advantage of ignorance and neceſſity ; he will, if poſſible, monopolize an article to create a neceſſity.   Repeated opportunities of this kind gradually weaken the force of moral obligation ; and nine perſons of ten, who enter into the buſineſs of ſpeculation with a good character, will, in a few years, loſe their principles, and probably, their reputation.

Speculation is pernicious to morals, in proportion as its effects are extenſiv.   Speculation in the Engliſh funds is practiſed on principles deſtructiv of juſtice and morals ; but it conſiſts in the transfer of large ſums ; the contingencies on which it depends are not frequent, and the buſineſs is confined to a few ſharpers in the metropolis.   Such a ſpeculation affects not the body of the people.   The medium circulating in the kingdom, has a fixed permanent value, and affords no opportunities for irregular gains.

Very

Very different is fpeculation in America. Here its
objects are in every perfon's hands ; changes of value
are frequent ; opportunities of gain, numberlefs ; and
the evil pervades the community. The country
fwarms with fpeculators, who are fearching all places,
from the ftores of the wealthy, to the receffes of indi-
gence, for opportunities of making lucrativ bargains.
Not a tavern can we enter, but we meet crowds of
thefe people, who wear their character in their counte-
nances.

But the fpeculators are not the only men whofe
character and principles are expofed by fuch a ftate of
the currency ; the honeft laborer and the regular merchant are often tempted to forfake the eftablifhed principles of advance. Every temptation of this kind attacks the moral principles, and expofes men to fmall
deviations from the rectitude of commutativ juftice.

Such are the fources of corruption in commercial intercourfe. A relaxation of principle, in one inftance,
leads to every fpecies of vice, and operates till its caufes
ceafe to exift, or till all the fupports of focial confidence
are fubverted. It is remarked by people very illiterate
and circumfcribed in their obfervation, that there is not
now the fame confidence between man and man, which
exifted before the war. It is doubtlefs true ; this diftruft of individuals, a general corruption of manners,
idlenefs, and all its train of fatal confequences, may be
refolved into two caufes : The fudden flood of money
during the late war, and a conftant fluctuation of the
value of the currencies.

The effects of a fudden augmentation of the quantity of money in circulation were fo obvious, during the
war, and the example is fo recent, that the fubject requires no illuftration, but a recollection of facts. Yet
there is an example recorded in the Hiftory of France,
fo exactly in point, that I cannot omit it.

During the regency of the Duke of Orleans, one
Law, who had fled from punifhment in Scotland, and
taken refuge in France, obtained, by his addrefs, a great
fhare of confidence in the councils of the regent. He
formed

formed a plan of drawing all the specie from circulation, and issuing bills upon the royal treasury. It is
not necessary to name the expedients he used to effect
his purpose. It is sufficient to observe, that by various
methods, he drew most of the specie of the kingdom
into the public treasury, and issued bills to about one
hundred times the value of the specie, which had before circulated. The notes or securities depreciated as
they were thrown into circulation, like our continental
currency. The nature of a medium of trade, it seems,
was not well understood : Such a sudden depreciation
was a surprising phenomenon at that period ; men of
property, who were the holders of the paper, were a-
larmed ; the kingdom was in confusion. When the
bills had sunk to a fifth of their value, a royal edict was
issued, ordaining that the remaining specie in circulation should be sunk to a level with paper. This resembles, in some respects, the regulation of prices in
America. An edict, so rash and absurd, increased the
evils it was meant to remedy, and filled the kingdom
with clamor.

In a short time, the paper was sunk as low as our
continental currency, before its death.

The confusion was general ; the regent and Law
were obliged to fly the kingdom ; and both died in ob-
scurity, the one in Italy, and the other, if I mistake not,
in the Netherlands. In France there was a total change
of property ; poor men made fortunes by speculation,
and the rich were beggared. The result of the whole
was, that the paper was called in at a discount, by means
similar to the *forty for one* act of the United States.

But the principal view I have in stating this example
is, to show the effect of a sudden inundation of money
upon industry and morals. No sooner did the nation
feel an increase of the quantity of money, but the kingdom was overrun with speculators ; men who left useful occupations, for the prospect of rapid accumulations
of wealth. Knavery, over reaching, idleness, prodi-
gality, and every kind of vice prevailed, and filled the
kingdom with distress, confusion, and poverty.

The

'The South Sea bubble, in England, was a farce of a similar kind, but its effects were lefs extenfiv.

The continental currency was not the fole caufe of the idlenefs and fpeculation, which prevailed in this country, about the years 1780, 1781, and 1782. Vaft quantities of fpecie were introduced by the French army, by the Spanifh trade, and by a clandeftine intercourfe with the Britifh garrifons. At the clofe of the war, there was more than double the quantity of gold and filver in the country, which was neceffary for the purpofes of a regular commerce.

This extraordinary circulation of fpecie had its ufual, its certain effect; it prompted multitudes to quit manual labor for trade. This circumftance, in conjunction with the difbanding of the army, which left great numbers of men without employment, and with a rage for foreign goods, which was always ftrong, and was then increafed by a long war, filled our commercial towns with hofts of adventurers in bufinefs. The confequent influx of goods and enormous credit neceffary to obtain them, are evils that deeply affect this country. I will not attempt a detail of the ftate of commerce in the United States; but obferve that the neceffary exportation of fpecie was the happieft event that could befal the United States; the only event that could turn induftry into its proper channel, and reduce the commerce of the country to a proportion with the agriculture.

Diffipation was another confequence of a flood of money. No country perhaps on earth can exhibit fuch a fpirit of diffipation among men, who derive their fupport from bufinefs, as America. It is fuppofed by good judges, that the expenfes of fubfiftence, drefs and equipage, were nearly doubled in the commercial towns, the two firft years of the peace. I have no doubt the fupport of the common people was enhanced twenty five per cent. This augmentation of expenfes, with a dimunition of productiv induftry, are the confequences of too much money, and a fcarcity is our only remedy.

Short

Short fighted people complain of the prefent fcarcity; but it is the only hope of our political falvation;
and that Legiflature which ventures to remove popular
complaints, by a coinage of great quantities of fpecie,
or by its fubftitute, paper, checks induftry, keeps alive
a fpirit of diffipation, and retards the increafe of folid
wealth.   If this has been neceffary, it is a neceffity fincerely to be lamented.

But there is one fource of idlenefs and corruption,
which is general in America, and bids fair to be of
long duration.   I refer to the different fpecies of federal and State fecurities, which are every where diffufed,
and of fluctuating value.   Thefe evidences of our
debts open fuch profpects for rapid accumulations of
property to every clafs of people, that men cannot with-
ftand the temptation : Thoufands are drawn from
ufeful occupations into a courfe of life, which cannot
poffibly benefit fociety; which muft render them ufelefs, and probably will render them bad men, and dangerous members of a community.

What remedy can be applied to fo great an evil, it is
not for me to determin.   But if I may offer my fentiments freely, I muft acknowlege that I think no meafure can produce fo much mifchief, as the circulation of
a depreciated changeable currency.   Let all our debts
be placed on the footing of bank ftock, and made transferable only at the treafury; or let the prefent evidences of it be called in, and new notes iffued, payable only
to the creditor or original holder ; or let the fecurities
be purchafed at their current difcount, let fome method
be adopted to draw them from circulation; for they
deftroy public and private confidence; they cut the
finews of induftry; they operate like a flow poifon,
diffolving the *ftamina* of government, moral principles.

No paper fhould circulate in a commercial country,
which is not a reprefentativ of ready cafh ; it muft at
leaft command punctual intereft, and fecurity of the
principal when demanded.   Without thefe requifits,
all notes will certainly depreciate.   Moft of our public
fecurities want all the requifits of a paper currency.

But

But if they did not ; if they were equal ·in value to bank notes or fpecie, ftill the fums are much too large for a circulating medium in America.   The amount of the continental and State certificates, with the emif-fions of paper by particular States, cannot be lefs than feventy millions of dollars, which is feven times the fum neceffary for a circulation.

Were they equal in value to gold and filver, the whole medium would depreciate, fpecie as well as pa-per.   But as they want every requifit of a paper currency, the whole depreciation falls upon the fe-curities.

An alarming confequence of the State of our public debt remains to be confidered.   Want of confidence in the public, added to the vaft quantity of paper, has funk it to a third, fixth, or eighth part of its nominal value.   Moft of the creditors of the public have parted with their fecurities at a great difcount, and are thus robbed of the monies which they earned by the fweat of the brow.   Men of property have purchafed them for a trifle, and in fome States receive the intereft in fpecie.   In Maffachufetts, this is the cafe with refpect to fome part of the State debt.   When a man buys a note of twenty fhillings value for five, and receives the intereft, fix per cent. in fpecie, he in fact receives twen-ty four per cent. on his money.

This is one fource of the infurrection in Maffachu-fetts.   The people feel the injuftice of paying fuch an intereft to men who earned but a fmall part of it, and whofe fole merit is, that they have more money than their fellow citizens who fuffer the lofs by depreciation. Thofe men in particular, who fought for our inde-pendence, or loaned their property to fave the country, ·view with indignant refentment, that law which obliges them to pay twenty four per cent. intereft on the fecu-rities, which they have fold for a fourth, or an eighth part of their honeft demands.

This cannot juftify the violent fteps taken by the people ; becaufe petitions, and united firmnefs in a conftitutional way, would have procured redrefs.   But

I ftate

I ftate the facts to fhew the effects of fpeculation, or rather, of the want of faith in public engagements.

Such are the confequences of a variable medium ; neglect to induftry ; application to irregular commerce ; relaxation of principles in focial intercourfe ; diftruft of individuals ; lofs of confidence in the public, and of refpect for laws ; innumerable acts of injuftice between man and man, and between the State and the fubject ; popular uneafinefs, murmurs and infurrections.   And fuch effects will exift till their caufe fhall be removed. Not the creation of a Supreme Power over the United States, is an object of more importance, than the annihilation of every fpecies of fluctuating currency.

That inftability of law, to 'which republics are prone, is another fource of corruption.   Multiplication and changes of law have a great effect in weakening the force of government, by preventing or deftroying habits.   Law acquires force by a fteady operation, and government acquires dignity and refpect, in proportion to the uniformity of its proceedings.   Neceffity perhaps has made our federal and provincial governments frequently fhift their meafures, and the unforefeen or unavoidable variations of public fecurities, with the impoffibility of commanding the refources of the continent, to fulfil engagements, all predict a continuation of the evil.   But the whole wifdom of Legiflatures fhould be exerted to devife a fyftem of meafures which may preclude the neceffity of changes that tend to bring government into contempt.

A mild or lax execution of law may alfo have a bad effect in leffening the refpect for its officers.   In a monarchy, there is no reafoning with the executive ; the will of the prince infpires terror.   In our governments, the officers are often familiar, and will even delay juftice as long as poffible to affift the prifoner.

· In fome of the eaftern States, the frequency and mildnefs of laws, have introduced very fingular habits. The people of Connecticut refpect the laws as much as any people ; they would not be guilty of difobedience ; they mean generally to pay their debts, but are

not

not very anxious to be punctual. They fuppofe a creditor can wait for his money longer than the period when it is due, and think it hard if he will not.*

This mild execution of law, and a confequential habit of dilatorinefs, which arife from the fpirit of e-quality, are ftill prevalent amongft the body of the people. Thefe gave rife to the late incorporation of fever-al commercial towns, with large powers; an expedient which has anfwered the purpofe of giving to commerce the advantage of energy and difpatch in the collection of debts. As moft of the bufinefs is done in the cities, this effect will gradually extend itfelf, and form differ-ent habits.

The great misfortune of the multiplicity of laws and frequency of litigation, is, that they weaken a refpect for the executiv authority, deftroy the principle of honor, and transfer the difgrace, which ought to fol-low delinquency in payment, from a man's reputation, to the adminiftration of juftice. The lawyers and courts are impeached, when the whole blame ought to fall upon the debtor for his impunctuality. Honor, a fubftitute for honefty, has more influence upon men than law; for in the one cafe, a man's character is at ftake, and in the other, his property. When a man's character fuffers not, by a failure of engagements, and by a public profecution, the collection of debts muft be flow. But when a man's reputation is fufpended on the punctual difcharge of his contracts, he will fpare no pains to do it; and this is or ought to be the cafe in all commercial countries.

Extenfiv credit, in a popular government, is always pernicious, and may be fatal. When the people are deeply or generally involved, they have power and ftrong temptations to introduce an abolition of debts; an agrarian law, or that modern refinement on the Ro-man plan, which is a fubftitute for both, a paper cur-rency, iffued on depreciating principles. Rhode Ifland
is

* Thefe remarks are not applicable to the mercantile part of the people, who, fince the revolution, have been diftinguifhed by their punctuality.

I

is a melancholy proof of this truth, and New Hampſhire
narrowly eſcaped the deplorable evils. In governments
like ours, it is policy to make it the intereſt of people
to be honeſt.   In ſhort, the whole art of governing
conſiſts in binding each individual by his particular intereſt, to promote the aggregate intereſt of the community.

Maſſachuſetts affords a ſtriking example of the danger incurred by too many private debts.   During the
war the operation of juſtice was neceſſarily ſuſpended,
and debts were conſtantly multiplying and accumulating. When law came to be rigorouſly enforced, the
people were diſtreſſed beyond meaſure, particularly in
the weſtern counties, where people are poorer than in
the parts of the State better ſettled, and nearer to market.   Theſe private debts crowded hard, and operated
with the demands of the federal creditors, to puſh the
people into violent meaſures.

The planters in Virginia owe immenſe ſums of
money to the Britiſh merchants.   What is the conſequence ? a law, ſuſpending the collection of Britiſh
debts.   The loſs of their ſlaves is the oſtenſible excuſe
for this law ; but a more ſolid reaſon muſt be, the utter
impoſſibility of immediately diſcharging the debts.   In
our governments the men who owe the money, make
the laws ; and a general embarraſſment of circumſtances
is too ſtrong a temptation to evade or ſuſpend the performance of juſtice.   For this reaſon, the wiſdom of
the Legiſlature might cooperate with the intereſt of the
merchant, to check a general credit.   In ſome caſes it
might be ſafe and wiſe to withdraw the protection of
law from debts of certain deſcriptions.   It is an excellent law in one State, which ordains, that no tavern
debt, of more than two days ſtanding, ſhall be recoverable by law.   It prevents tavern haunting and its conſequences, idleneſs, drunkenneſs and quarrels.   Perhaps laws of this kind have the beſt effect in introducing punctual payments.   Their firſt effect is to prevent credit ; but they gradually change a man's regard
for his property, to a more activ and efficient principle, an attention to his character.   In

In the prefent anarchy in Maffachufetts, monied men get credit with the merchant, and are punctual to fulfil engagements, as they are fenfible that the merchant relies folely on their honor. The certain ultimate tendency of withdrawing the protection of law from particular kinds of debts, is to difcourage tricks and evafions, and introduce habits of punctuality in commerce.

The prefent ftate of our public credit hath the fame effect. Repeated violations of public faith, the circulation of a variable medium of trade, the contempt of law, the perpetual fear of new legiflativ fchemes for difcharging our debts, and of tender laws, have made men very cautious in giving credit, and when they do give it, they depend more on the honor of a man than on any fecurity derived from law. This one happy effect of want of confidence in the public, is fome fmall confolation for an infinite variety of political evils and diftreffes.

Laws to prevent credit would be beneficial to poor people. With refpect to the contraction of debts, people at large, in fome meafure, refemble children ; they are not judges even of their own intereft. They anticipate their incomes, and very often, by mifcalculation, much more than their incomes. But this is not the worft effect ; an eafy credit throws them off their guard in their expenfes. In general we obferve that a flow, laborious acquifition of property, creates a caution in expenditures, and gradually forms the mifer. On the other hand, a fudden acquifition of money, either by gambling, lotteries, privateering, or marriage, has a tendency to open the heart, or throw the man off his guard, and thus makes him prodigal in his expenfes. Perhaps this is ever the cafe, except when a penurious habit has been previoufly formed.

An eafy and extenfiv credit has a fimilar effect. When people can poffefs themfelves of property without previous labor, they confume it with improvident liberality. A prudent man will not ; but a large proportion of mankind have not prudence and fortitude

I 2   enough

enough to refift the demands of pride and appetite.
Thus they often riot on other men's property, which
they would not labor to procure. They form habits
of indolence and extravagance, which ruin their families, and impoverifh their creditors.

Another effect of extenfiv credit, is a multitude of
lawyers. Every thing which tends to create difputes,
to multiply debts, weaken a regard to commercial engagements, and place the collection of debts on law,
rather than on honour, increafes the encouragement of
lawyers. The profeffion of law is honorable, and the
profeffors, I fcruple not to aver, as liberal, honeft and
refpectable, as any clafs of men in the State. But their
bufinefs muft be confidered as a public evil, except in
the drafting of legal inftruments, and in fome real important difputes. Such is the habit of trufting to law,
for the recovery of debts, that, in fome of the eaftern
States, one half or two thirds of the lawyers are mere
collectors. They bring forward fuits for fmall debts,
that are not difputed; they recover judgement upon
default, they take out executions, and live upon their
fees.

The evil is not fo great in the middle States; but it
is great in all the States. Never was there fuch a rage
for the ftudy of law. From one end of the continent
to the other, the ftudents of this fcience are multiplying
without number. An infallible proof that the bufinefs
is lucrativ.

The infurgents in Maffachufetts enumerate lawyers
among their grievances. They wifh the Legiflature to
limit their number and their demands. Short fighted
mortals! They feem not to confider that lawyers grow
out of their own follies, and that the only radical remedy for the evil is, to contract no more debts than they
can pay, with ftrict punctuality.

The number of profeffional men in a State fhould
be as few as poffible; for they do not increafe the property of the State, but liv on the property acquired by
others.

There

There is little danger that the number of clergymen will be too great. In a few inftances, religious parties may have multiplied their teachers to too great a number, and perhaps in fome parts of the country, a few more minifters of the gofpel would be very ufeful.

Phyficians will multiply in proportion to the luxuries and idlenefs of men. They cannot be limited by law, for people will be as intemperate and as lazy as they pleafe.

But an artful Legiflature will take away fome of the caufes of litigation, and thus curtail the number of lawyers. We may always determin the degree of corruption, in commercial habits, by the number of civil fuits in the courts of law. The multiplication of lawyers is a proof of private embarraffments in any State ; it is a convincing proof that in America thefe embarraffments are numberlefs. The evil is of fuch magnitude in *fome* States, as to fufpend the operation of law, and in *all* it produces diftruft among men, renders property unfafe, and perplexes our mutual intercourfe. In this fituation, with popular governments, and an unbounded rage for magnificent living, perhaps the only effectual remedy for a multitude of public evils, is the reftraining of credit. It might even be ufeful to deftroy all credit on the fecurity of law, except debts of certain defcriptions, where mortgages might be given. This would not check bufinefs, but it would oblige people to exercife a principle of honor, and to have recourfe to induftry, and ready payment for articles which their neceffities or their fancies require. We fhould then be better able to determin, whether bucks and bloods, in high life, " who roll the thundering chariot o'er the ground," are fporting with their own property, or that of honeft creditors.

I cannot clofe thefe remarks without obferving how much this country owes to particular claffes of people for the practice of the commercial virtues. To the Friends, the Germans and the Dutch, this country is indebted for that induftry and provident economy, which

which enables them to fubfift without anxiety, and to be honeft and punctual, without embarraffment.

Happy would it be for this country, if thefe virtues were more generally practifed. Paper money and foreign credit are mere temporary expedients to keep up the *appearance of wealth* and fplendor ; but they are miferable fubftitutes for folid property. The only way to become rich at home and refpectable abroad, is to become induftrious, and to throw off our flavifh dependence on foreign manners, which obliges us to facrifice our opinions, our tafte, and our intereft, to the policy and aggrandizement of other nations.

No. VIII.

On PAPER MONEY.

[Publiſhed at *Baltimore*, Auguſt 9, 1785.]

Meſſrs. PRINTERS,

I OBSERVED a paragraph of intelligence in your Journal, of the 26th of July, reſpecting the circulation of paper currency in North Carolina. I am not diſpoſed to diſpute the truth of the fact, that paper currency paſſes in that State at par with ſpecie; but I ſhould be very ſorry to ſee it drawn into a precedent for other States.

The ſcarcity of caſh is a general complaint, and ſuperficial obſervers impute the evil to a wrong cauſe, while ſhallow reaſoners would remedy it by an emiſſion of paper credit.

The real ſtate of our commerce is this; ſince the ratification of peace, the quantity of goods imported into the United States has been much greater than what was neceſſary for the conſumption of the inhabitants. Perhaps I ſhall not be wide of the truth, when I ſuppoſe that one third of the importations would ſupply the demands of people. The conſequence is, the other two thirds continue on hand as a ſuperfluity. The merchant finds no market for his goods, and erroneouſly imputes the evil to a ſcarcity of caſh. But the real truth is, people do not want his goods; they purchaſe what they want, and find caſh or produce to make payment; but the ſurplus remains in ſtore.

In every trading nation, there ought to be a due proportion between the commercial intereſt, the agricultural and the manufacturing. Whenever the farmers and manufacturers are too numerous for the merchants, produce and manufactures will be plentiful and cheap; trade will of courſe be lucrativ. Whenever the merchants are too numerous for the laborers, the importations of
the

the former will exceed the wants of the latter ; of course goods will not find vent ; and the merchant who owes nothing may lie and sleep in indolence, while the merchant who deals on credit *must fail.* The experience of almost every day proves the *truth of this reasoning.* I will suppose that the number of merchants, and the quantity of goods in Baltimore, are double to what they were two years ago ; and the market for goods is nearly the same. The effect will be, that the same profit of business will be divided among double the number of men, while, at the same time, rents and the price of provision in market will be double. The clear profit of the merchant will therefore be reduced to one fourth part of what it was two years ago. I submit to the inhabitants of this *flourishing* town, whether this is a mere supposition, or a moderate state of facts ; and whether this reasoning will not, in a greater or less degree, apply to every commercial town in the United States.

But is not money scarce ? With respect to the quantity of goods in store, *money is very scarce :* With respect to the produce of the country, there is *money enough.* Almost every article of home produce will command cash ; but the merchant cannot get cash for his goods. Money is the representativ of goods bought and sold. I will suppose, for the sake of argument, that two years ago there was cash enough in the country to purchase all the goods in market at the usual advance. I will suppose that the quantity of goods has been trebled since that time. In this case, had the quantity of money continued the same, there would have been cash enough to purchase just one third of the goods. But suppose what is true, that at the time the quantity of goods increases in this proportion, the quantity of money in circulation diminishes in the same proportion. In this case there will be but one third of the cash to purchase three times the goods. Thus but one sixth part of the goods can be purchased by the circulating cash. The merchant must then lower the price of his goods to one sixth of their value, or keep

them

them on hand. This reafoning, however mathematical, is juft, and applies to all commercial countries. It is a fair ftate of facts in America. But though the quantity of money is greatly diminifhed, yet there is fufficient to reprefent the produce of the country, which in quantity continues the fame. The price is however lowered by the diminution of the quantity of circulating cafh.

Whether the quantity of cafh is diminifhed, and the quantity of goods increafed in the exact proportion above ftated, is not material, the foregoing reafoning being fufficient to illuftrate the principle. The probability is, that the difproportion between the goods in market and the cafh in circulation, is greater than I have fuppofed.

The following propofitions, I venture to affert, are generally, if not univerfally, true :

1. That the imports of a country fhould never exceed its exports. In other words, the value of the goods imported fhould never exceed the value of the fuperfluous produce, or that part of the produce which the inhabitants do not want for their own confumption.

2. That too great a quantity of cafh in circulation, is a much greater evil than too fmall a quantity.

3. That too much money in a commercial country will inevitably produce a fcarcity.

4. That the wealth of a country does not confift in cafh, but in the produce of induftry, viz. in agriculture and manufactures.

5. That in a commercial country, where people are induftrious, there can never be, for any long time, a want of cafh fufficient for a medium.

The firft propofition is univerfally acknowleged to be true.

The fecond is lefs obvious, but equally true. Too much money raifes the price of labor and of its effects ; deprives us confequently of a foreign market ; produces indolence and diffipation ; than which greater evils cannot happen to a State. The fudden increafe

creafe of money, by large emiffions of paper credit, at
the beginning of the late war, produced more luxury,
indolence, corruption of morals, and other fatal effects,
than all other caufes that ever took place in America.
We feel thefe evils to this moment. On the other
hand, a fcarcity of cafh, tho it cramps commerce for a
moment, always checks the evils before mentioned, low-
ers the price of labor, and produce will of courfe find a
profitable market ; it produces economy and induftry,
and confequently preferves the morals of the people ;
for induftry goes further in preferving purity of morals,
than all the fermons that were ever preached.

This leads to an illuftration of the third propofition.
If too much money in a country raifes the price of labor and of produce, the confequence is, that people
will go abroad for articles, becaufe they are cheaper in
foreign markets, and they will purchafe as long as they
can get cafh. Importations will be multiplied till the
country is drained of cafh, and then bufinefs will return to a new channel. The hiftory of trade in A-
merica, the laft two years, is an illuftration of this propofition.

The fourth propofition, alfo, is illuftrated by facts.
I will fuppofe that ten millions of dollars are fufficient
for a medium in America : Let that fum be inftanta-
neoufly augmented to twenty millions, and the country
is not a farthing richer, for the price of goods will be
immediately doubled. *Two* dollars, in the latter cafe,
purchafe no more than *one* in the former. People ignorantly fuppofe that goods rife in value ; when the
fact is, money falls in value. Continental currency
was a proof of this. There was cafh enough for a
medium in the country before the war ; and the addition of two hundred millions of dollars did not increafe the wealth of the country one farthing ; nor
would the whole purchafe more than the ten millions
of fpecie which circulated before the war. Had the
paper all been Spanifh milled dollars, the effect would
have been the fame, had they continued in the country, and not been hoarded.

                                                    The

The fifth propofition depends on this fimple fact, that money is a fluid in the commercial world, rolling from hand to hand wherever it is wanted, and there is any thing to purchafe it. Let the produce of a country excel, in the leaft degree, the confumption, and it will never want money.

Admitting the foregoing obfervations to be true, both the neceffity and policy of emitting paper, vanifh at once. Suppofing paper currency to preferve its credit, ftill fo far from increafing the medium of trade, that in a few months it will drive all the fpecie from the country. Bank notes and bills of exchange are ufeful in facilitating a change or conveyance of property; but to iffue paper credit, merely with a view to increafe the circulating medium, in a country where the people may have juft as much gold and filver as they are pleafed to work for, is the height of folly. If people are indolent, or extravagant, all the paper currency under heaven will not make them rich, or fupply their wants of cafh. If people are induftrious and frugal, and purchafe no more foreign goods than they can pay for in fuperfluous produce, they will ever have cafh enough. Their whole fyftem of commerce ftands on thefe fingle facts.

If the merchants bring more goods than people want, bufinefs *muft be dull*; money with them *muft be fcarce*. At the clofe of the war, cafh was plentiful and goods fcarce. This made bufinefs lively, till people had procured a fupply. Remittances were made in cafh, fo long as it could be obtained. That period is paft, and the merchant muft now look for remittances where alone they ought ever to be found, in the produce of the country. Bufinefs is juft now returning into its proper channel, from which it had been diverted by the violence of war, and the fluctuations of paper credit. The rapid population of a country is an agreeable circumftance; but every profeffion ought to increafe in a due proportion. Suppofing ten thoufand carpenters were to land in Baltimore at once, would they have bufinefs? Or would they not exclaim, *bufinefs is dull,*
money

money is fcarce ?   Every one might have a trifle of bufinefs, but they could not *all make fortunes.*

An event fimilar to this has taken place in Baltimore.   The reputation for bufinefs which Baltimore
had acquired juft at the clofe of the war, brought merchants here from every part of the world, and almoft
one half of the town has been built within two years.
How, in the name of common fenfe, do the merchants
expect to find bufinefs ?   The people who come to
this market, multiply gradually, and double in about
thirty years.   But the merchants who fupply the goods
have doubled, if not trebled, in numbers and ftock,
within three years.   There is, however, an expedient
which will yet enable them all to liv by trade.   Let
every merchant fend abroad to Ireland or Germany,
and bring over his hundred able induftrious farmers,
and fix them on the fertile lands of Maryland, which
now lie ufelefs and uncultivated in the hands of the
Nabobs :   Or let three fourths of the traders quit the
bufinefs.   Either of thefe expedients will make cafh
plentiful ; and one of them muft take place.

I will juft make one further remark ; the want of a
proper *union* among the States, will always render our
commerce fluctuating and unprofitable.   We may do
as much bufinefs as we pleafe ; but if the duties and
reftrictions on our trade remain, and the flag of the
United States is infulted as it has been, and each State
is laying duties on the trade of its neighbor, our commerce cannot be reduced to a fyftem, and our profits
muft be uncertain.   The want of a *Continental Power*
to guard the honor of the whole body, and reduce our
meafures to one uniform fyftem, is the great fource of
endlefs calamities.   We fhall feel national abufe, till
Congrefs are vefted with powers fufficient to *govern*
and *protect* us ; and till that period, foreigners, like fo
many harpies, will prey upon our commerce, and dif-
appoint the exertions of our induftry.

No.

No. IX.

On REDRESS *of* GRIEVANCES.

NEWBURY PORT, 1786.

BY some resolves of the discontented people of this State, (Massachusetts) it appears that the true cause of public grievances is mistaken, and consequently the mode of redress will be mistaken. It is laughable enough to hear the people gravely resolving, that the sitting of the general court at Boston is a grievance, when every body may recollect that about twelve years ago, the removal of the Legislature to Cambridge, was a grievance; an unconstitutional stretch of power, that threw the province into a bustle. A great change, since Hutchinson's time! Boston then was the only proper seat of the Legislature.

Lawyers, too, are squeezed into the catalogue of grievances. Why, sir, lawyers are a consequence; not a cause of public evils. They grow out of the laziness, dilatoriness in payment of debts, breaches of contract, and other vices of the people; just as mushrooms grow out of dunghills after a shower, or as distilleries spring out of the *taste* for New England rum. The sober, industrious, frugal Dutch, in New York, and the Quakers and Germans in Pensylvania, have no occasion for lawyers; a collector never calls upon them twice, and they feel no grievances. Before the war, there was, in Orange county, New York, but one action of debt tried in eighteen years. O happy people! happy times! no grievances.

Mr. Printer, I saw a man the other day, crying a bushel or two of flaxseed. Flaxseed is a cash article, and cash pays taxes. The man wanted cash to pay his taxes; he *must* have cash; but, Mr. Printer, half an hour afterwards, I saw him half drunk, and his saddle bags filled with coffee. But, sir, coffee pays no taxes.

Another,

Another, a few days ago, brought a lamb to market. Lambs command cafh, and cafh pays taxes ; but the good countryman went to a ftore, and bought a feather ; five fhillings for a feather, Mr. Printer, and feathers pay no taxes. Is it not a *grievance*, fir, that feathers and ribbands, and coffee and new rum, will not pay taxes ?

Now, Mr. Printer, in my humble opinion, there are but two effectual methods of redreffing grievances ; one depends on the people as individuals, and the other on the Supreme Executiv authority.

As to the firft, let every perfon, whether farmer, mechanic, lawyer, or doctor, provide a fmall box, *(a fmall box* will be big enough) with a hole in the lid. When he receives a fhilling, let him put fix pence into the box, and ufe the other fix pence in providing for his family ; not rum or feathers, but good bread and meat. Let this box remain untouched, until the collector fhall call. Then let it be opened, the tax paid, and the overplus of cafh may be expended on gauze, ribbands, tea, and New England rum. Let the box then be put into its place again, to receive pence for the next collector. This method, Mr. Printer, will redrefs all grievances, without the trouble, noife and expenfe of town meetings, conventions and mobs.

As to the other method, fir, I can only fay, were I at the head of the Executiv authority, I fhould foon put the queftion to a decifiv iffue. It fhould be determined, on the firft infurrection, whether our lives and our properties fhall be fecure under the law and the conftitution of the State, or whether they muft depend on the mad refolves of illegal meetings. Honeft men then would know whether they may reft in fafety at home, or whether they muft feek for tranquillity in fome diftant country.

No.

No. X.

The DEVIL *is in you.*[*]

PROVIDENCE, 1786.

THAT the political body, like the animal, is liable to violent difeafes, which, for a time, baffle the healing art, is a truth which we all acknowlege, and which moft of us lament. But as moft of the diforders, incident to the human frame, are the confequence of an intemperate indulgence of its appetites, or of neglecting the moft obvious means of fafety ; fo moft of the popular tumults, which difturb government, arife from an abufe of its bleffings, or an inattention to its principles. A man of a robuft conftitution, relying on its ftrength, riots in gratifications which weaken the *ftamina vitæ* ; the furfeiting pleafures of a few years deftroy the power of enjoyment ; and the full fed voloptuary feels a rapid tranfition to the meagre valetudinarian. Thus people who enjoy an uncommon fhare of political privileges, often carry their freedom to licentioufnefs, and put it out of their power to enjoy fociety by deftroying its fupport.

Too much health is a *difeafe*, which often requires a very ftrict regimen ; *too much liberty* is the worft of *tyranny* ; and *wealth* may be accumulated to fuch a degree as to *impoverifh* a State. If *all* men attempt to become *mafters*, the *moft* of them would neceffarily become *flaves* in the attempt ; and could *every man* on earth poffefs millions of joes, *every man* would be *poorer* than *any man* is now, and infinitely more wretched, becaufe they could not procure the neceffaries of life.

My countrymen, it is a common faying now, that *the devil is in you.* I queftion the influence of the devil, however, in thefe affairs. Divines and politicians agree in this, to father all evil upon the devil ;
but

[*] Publifhed in Rhode Ifland, fhortly after the preceding letter.

but the effects afcribed to this prince of evil fpirits, both
in the moral and political world, I afcribe to the wick-
ednefs and ignorance of the human heart. Taking
the word *Devil* in this fenfe, he is *in* you, and *among*
you, in a variety of fhapes.

In the firft place, the *weaknefs of our federal government
is the devil.* It prevents the adoption of any meafures
that are requifit for us, as a nation ; it keeps us from
paying our honeft debts ; it alfo throws out of our power all the profits of commerce, and this drains us of
cafh. Is not this the devil ? Yes, my countrymen,
an empty purfe is the *devil.*

You fay you are jealous of your rights, and dare not
truft Congrefs. Well, that jealoufy is an evil fpirit,
and all evil fpirits are *devils.* So far the devil is in you.
You act, in this particular, juft like the crew of a fhip,
who would not truft the helm with *one* of their number, becaufe he might *poffibly* run her afhore, when by
leaving her without a pilot, they were *certain* of fhip-
wreck. You act juft like men, who in raifing a building, would not have a mafter workman, becaufe he
might give out wrong orders. You will be mafters
yourfelves ; and as you are not all ready to lift at the
fame time, one labors at a ftick of timber, then another, then a third ; you are then vexed that it is not
raifed ; why let a mafter order thirteen of you to take
hold together, and you will lift it at once. Every family has a *mafter* (or a *miftrefs*—I beg the ladies' pardon.)
When a fhip or a houfe is to be built, there is a mafter ; when highways are repairing, there is a mafter ;
every little fchool has a mafter ; the continent is a great
fchool ; the boys are numerous, and full of roguifh
tricks, and there is no *mafter.* The boys in this great
fchool play truant, and there is no perfon to chaftife
them. Do you think, my countrymen, that America
is more eafily governed than a fchool ? You do very
well in fmall matters ; extend your reafon to great
ones. Would you not laugh at a farmer who would
faften a cable to a plough, and yet attempt to draw a
houfe with a cobweb ? " And Nathan faid unto David,
                                                    thou

thou art the 'man." You think a mafter neceffary to govern *a few* harmlefs children in a fchool or family ; yet leave thoufands of great rogues to be governed by *good advice.* Believe me, my friends, for I am *ferious* ; you *lofe rights*, becaufe you will not giv your magif-trates authority to *protect them*. Your liberty is defpo-tifm, becaufe it has no control ; your power is noth-ing, becaufe it is not united.

But further, luxury rages among you, and luxury is *the devil.* The war has fent this evil demon to impov-erifh people, and embarrafs the public. The articles of rum and tea alone, which are drank in this country, would pay all its taxes. But when we add, fugar, cof-fee, feathers, and the whole lift of baubles and trink-ets, what an enormous expenfe ? No wonder you want paper currency. My countrymen are all grown very tafty ! Feathers and jordans muft all be imported ! Certainly gentlemen, the devil is among you. A Hampfhire man, who drinks forty fhillings worth of rum in a year, and never thinks of the expenfe, will raife a mob to reduce the governor's falary, which does not amount to three pence a man per annum. Is not this the devil ?

My countrymen—A writer appeared, not long ago, informing you how to redrefs grievances.* He givs excellent advice. Let every man make a little box, and put into it *four pence* every day. This in a year will amount to fix pounds one fhilling and eight pence, a fum more than fufficient to pay any poor man's tax. Any man can pay three or four pence a day, though no poor man can, at the end of a year, pay fix pounds. Take my advice, every man of you, and you will hardly feel your taxes.

But further, a *tender law* is the *devil.* When I truft a man a fum of money, I expect he will return the full value. That Legiflature which fays my debtor may pay me with *one third* of the value he received, commits a deliberate act of villany ; an act for which an *individual*, in any government, would be honored
with

* See page 125.   K.

with a whipping poſt, and in moſt governments, with
a gallows. When a man makes dollars, one third of
which only is ſilver, and paſſes them for good coin, he
muſt loſe his ears, &c.

But Legiſlatures can, with the ſolemn face of rulers,
and guardians of juſtice, boldly give currency to an
adulterated coin, enjoin it upon debtors to cheat their
creditors, and enforce their ſyſtematic knavery with legal penalties. The differences between the man who
makes and paſſes counterfeit money, and the man who
tenders his creditor one third of the value of the debt,
and demands a diſcharge, is the ſame as between a
thief and a robber. The firſt cheats his neighbor in
the dark; and takes his property without his knowlege :
The laſt boldly meets him at noon day, tells him he is
a raſcal, and demands his purſe.

My countrymen, the devil is among you. Make
paper as much as you pleaſe ; make it a tender in all
future contracts, or let it reſt on its own bottom : But
remember that paſt contracts are *ſacred things* ; that
Legiſlatures have no right to interfere with them ; they
have no right to ſay, a debt ſhall be paid at a diſcount,
or in any manner which the parties never intended. It
is the buſineſs of juſtice to fulfil the intention of parties in contracts, not to defeat them. To pay *bona
fide* contracts for caſh, in paper of little value, or in old
horſes, would be a diſhoneſt attempt in an individual ;
but for Legiſlatures to frame laws to ſupport and encourage ſuch deteſtable villany, is like a judge who
ſhould inſcribe the arms of a rogue over the ſeat of juſtice, or clergymen who ſhould convert into bawdy-
houſes the temples of Jehovah. My countrymen, the
world ſays, the devil is in you : Mankind deteſt you as
they would a neſt of robbers.

But laſtly, mobs and conventions are devils. Good
men love law and legal meaſures. Knaves only fear
law, and try to deſtroy it. My countrymen, if a conſtitutional Legiſlature cannot redreſs a grievance, a
mob never can. Laws are the ſecurity of life and
property ; nay, what is more, of liberty. The man
who

who encourages a mob to prevent the operation of law, ceafes to be *free or fafe* ; for the fame principle which leads a man to put a bayonet to the breaft of a judge, will lead him to take property where he can find it ; and when the judge dare not act, where is the lofer's remedy ? Alas, my friends, too much liberty is no liberty at all. Giv me any thing but mobs ; for mobs are the devil in his worft fhape. I would fhoot the leader of a mob, fooner than a midnight ruffian. People may have grievances, perhaps, and no man would more readily hold up his hand to redrefs them than myfelf ; but mobs rebel againft laws of their own, and rebellion is a crime which admits of no palliation.

My countrymen, I am a private, peaceable man. I have nothing to win or to lofe by the game of paper currency ; but *I revere juftice.* I would fooner pick oakum all my life, than ftain my reputation, or pay my creditor one farthing lefs than his honeft demands.

While you attempt to trade to advantage, without a *head* to combine all the States into fyftematic, uniform meafures, the world will laugh at you for fools. While merchants take and giv credit, the world will call them idiots, and laugh at their ruin. While farmers get credit, borrow money, and mortgage their farms, the world will call them fools, and laugh at their embarraffments. While all men liv beyond their income, and are harraffed with duns and fheriffs, no man will pity them, or giv them relief. But when mobs and conventions oppofe the courts of juftice, and Legiflatures make paper or old horfes a legal tender in all cafes, the world will exclaim with one voice—*Ye are rogues, and the devil is in you !*

No.

No. XI.

NEW LONDON, OCTOBER, 1786.

DESULTORY THOUGHTS.

NO government has preferved more general and uninterrupted tranquillity for a long period, than that of Connecticut. This is a ftrong proof of the force of habit, and the danger that ever attends great alterations of government or a fufpenfion of law. Every fyftem of civil policy muft take its complexion from the fpirit and manners of the people.

Whatever political conftitutions may be formed on paper, or in the philofopher's clofet, thofe only can be permanent which arife out of the genius of the people.

A jealous uneafy temper has fometimes appeared, among the people of this State ; but as this has always proceeded from reftlefs, ambitious men, whofe defigns have been reprobated as foon as detected, this uneafinefs has always fubfided without any violence to the Conftitution. We do not advert to the time when the courfe of law has been forcibly obftructed in Connecticut.

In the middle and fouthern States the corrupt Englifh mode of elections has been adopted : We fee men meanly ftoop to advertife for an office, or beg the votes of their countrymen. In thofe States elections are often mere riots ; almoft always attended with difputes and bloody nofes, and fometimes with greater violence. In Connecticut, a man never advertifes for an office, nor do we know that a man ever folicited a vote for himfelf. We cannot name the election that produced a difpute, even in words.

It belongs to the unprincipled of other States and countries to deride religion and its preachers. It belongs to the coxcombs of courts, the productions of dancing fchools and playhoufes, to ridicule our bafhful
deportment

deportment and fimplicity of manners. We revere the ancient inftitutions of fchools and churches in this State. We revere the difcipline which has given fuch a mild complexion to the manners of its inhabitants, and fecured private fatisfaction and public tranquillity.

Paper money is the prefent hobby horfe of the States, and every State has more or lefs of the *paper madnefs*. What a pity it is mankind will not difcern their right hands from their left. *Cafh is fcarce*, is the general cry. Well, this proves nothing more than that the balance of trade is againft us, and that we eat, drink, and wear more foreign commodities than we can pay for in produce : That is, we fpend more than we earn ; or in other words, *we are poor*.

But nothing fhows the folly of people more, than their attempts to remedy the evil by a *paper currency*. This is *ignorance*, it is *abfurdity* in the extreme. Do not people know that the addition of millions and millions of money does not increafe the value of a circulating medium one farthing. Do they not know that the value of a medium ought not to be increafed beyond a certain ratio, even if it could be ? and that to increafe the circulating cafh of one State beyond the circulating cafh of other States, is a material injury to it. Thefe propofitions are as demonftrable as any problem in Euclid. Ten millions of dollars in fpecie were fuppofed to be the medium in America before the war. Congrefs iffued at firft five millions in bills. As thefe came *into* circulation, fpecie went *out* ; confequently they held their nominal and real value on par, for the nominal value of the medium was not much increafed. Congrefs fent out another fum in bills ; the nominal value of the medium was doubled, the bills funk one half, and the real value of the medium remained the fame. This was the fubfequent progrefs ; every emiffion funk the real value of bills, and two hundred millions of dollars were, in the end, worth juft ten millions in fpecie, and no more. Towards the clofe of the war, the fpecie in America was more than doubled ; it funk to lefs than half its former value,

ue, and the paper bills funk in the fame proportion ;
from forty to eighty for one, nearly. We had too
much fpecie in the country, in the years 1782 and
1783 ; it ruined hundreds of merchants, and injured
the community.

But it is faid, we want a circulating medium. This
is not true ; we have too much in circulation. The
fpecie and paper now circulating in America, amounts
to fifty or fixty millions of dollars ; whereas we want
not more than ten or fifteen millions. The paper is
therefore funk in real value, fo as to reduce the real
value of the whole medium to that fum which is wanted. We may make millions of paper if we pleafe ;
but we fhall not add one farthing to the property of the
State. Money is not wealth in a State, but the reprefentativ of wealth. A paper currency may anfwer a
temporary purpofe of enabling people to pay debts ;
but it is not an advantage even to the debtor, unlefs it
is depreciated ; and in this cafe it is an injury to the
creditor. If the paper retains its value, the debtor
muft fooner or later purchafe it with the produce of
his labor ; and if it depreciates, it is the tool of knaves
while it circulates ; it ruins thoufands of honeft unfufpecting people ; it gives the game to the idle fpecu-
lator, who is a nuifance to the State ; it ftabs public
credit and private confidence ; and what is worfe than
all, it unhinges the obligations which unite mankind.
A fluctuation of medium in a State makes more fatal
ravages among the morals of people, than a peftilence
among their lives. O America ! happy would it have
been for thy peace, thy morals, thy induftry, if, inftead
of a depreciation of paper bills and fecurities, ftamped
with public faith, millions of infernal fpirits had been
let loofe among thy inhabitants ! Never, never wilt
thou experience the return of induftry, economy, private confidence and public content, till every fpecies of
depreciated and fluctuating medium fhall be annihilat-
ed ; till Legiflatures learn to revere juftice, and dread a
breach of faith more than the vengeance of vindictiv
heaven !

Americans !

Americans! you talk of a scarcity of cash. Well, the only remedy is, to enable Congress to place our commerce on a footing with the trade of other nations. Foreign States have nothing to do with Massachusetts or New York. They must make treaties with *United America*, or not make them at all. And while we boast of the independence of particular States, we lose all the benefits of independence. For fear that Congress would abuse their powers and enrich themselves, we, like the dog in the manger, will not even enrich ourselves. We complain of poverty, and yet *giv* the profits of our trade to foreign nations. Infatuated men! We have one truth to learn—*That nothing but the absolute power of regulating our commerce, vested in some federal head,* can ever restore to us cash, or turn the balance of trade in our favor. New York alone, by its advantageous situation, is growing rich upon the spoils of her neighbors, and impoverishing the continent to fill her own treasury.

Lawyers, you say, O deluded Americans! are an evil. Will you always be fools? Why lawyers are as good men as others: I venture to say further, that lawyers in this country have devised and brought about the wisest public measures that any State has adopted. My countrymen, the expense of supporting a hundred lawyers is a very great and a very needless expense. You pay to lawyers and courts every year thirty or forty thousand pounds. A great expense, indeed! But courts and lawyers are not to be blamed. The people are the cause of the evil, and they alone, as individuals, are able to remedy it. And yet the remedy is very simple. *Cease to run in debt,* or *pay your debts punctually*; then lawyers will cease to exist, and court houses will be shut. If you wish or expect any other remedy than this, you certainly will be disappointed. A man, who purposely rushes down a precipice and breaks his arm, has no right to say, that surgeons are an evil in society. A Legislature may unjustly limit the surgeon's fee; but the broken arm must be healed, and a surgeon is the only man to do it.

My

My friends, learn wifdom. You are peaceable yet, and let the diftractions of your neighbors teach you to preferve your tranquillity.

Spend lefs money than you earn, and you will every day grow richer. Never run in debt, and lawyers will become farmers. Never make paper money, and you will not cheat your citizens, nor have it to redeem. Above all, pay your public debts, for independence and the confederation require it.

No.

No. XII.

ADVICE to CONNECTICUT FOLKS.

MY FRIENDS,

TIMES are hard ; money is fcarce ; taxes are high, and private debts pufh us. What fhall we do ? Why, hear a few facts, ftubborn facts, and then take a bit of advice.

In the year 1637, our good forefathers declared an offenfiv war againft the Pequot Indians. Their troops were ninety men. Weathersfield was ordered to furn-ifh a hog for this army, Windfor a ram goat, and Hartford a hogfhead of beer, and four or five gallons of ftrong water.*

This was ancient fimplicity ! Let us make a little eftimation of the expenfes annually incurred in Connecticut. (I fay incurred, for we can contract debts, though we cannot pay them.)

I will juft make a diftinction between neceffary and unneceffary expenfes.

	Neceffary.	Unneceffary.
	£.	£.	£.
Governor's falary,	300	300	
Lieutenant governor's,	100	100	
Upper houfe, attendance and travel, 60 days a year, at 10l. a day,	600	600	
Lower houfe, attendance and travel, 170 members, at 6s. a day, 60 days,	3,060	1,530	1,530
Carried over,	4,060	2,530	1,530

* See the records of this State, where rum is called ftrong water. This was foon after the firft diftilling of fpirits, and rum was not then named. It feems, however, that our pious anceftors had a tafte for it, which their pofterity have carefully improved.

	Neceffary.	Unneceffary.
	£.	£.	£.
Brought over,	4,060	2,530	1,530
Five judges of the Superior Court, at 24s. a day, fuppofe 150 days,	900	900	
Forty judges of Inferior Courts, at 9s. a day, fuppofe 40 days,	720	720	
Six thoufand actions in the year, the legal expenfe of each, fuppofe 3l.	18,000	1,000	17,000
Gratuities to 120 lawyers, fuppofe 50l. each,	6,000	1,000	5,000
Two hundred clergymen, at 100l. each,	20,000	20,000	
Five hundred fchools, at 20l. a year,	10,000	10,000	
Support of poor,	10,000	10,000	
Bridges and other town expenfes,	10,000	10,000	
Contingencies and articles not enumerated,	10,000	10,000	
	£.89,680	£.66,150	£.23,530

. Now comes RUM, my friends.

	£.
400,000 gallons of rum, at 4s. a gallon,	80,000
Allow for rum drank, on which excife is not paid, 50,000 gallons, at 4s.	10,000
	£. 90,000

Ninety nine hundredths unneceffary.

This is a fact: Deny it if you can, good folks. Now, fay not a word about taxes, judges, lawyers, courts, and women's extravagance. Your government, your courts, your lawyers, your clergymen, your fchools, and your poor, do not all coft you fo much as one

one paltry article, which does you little or no good,
but is as deftructiv of your lives as fire and brimftone.
But let us proceed.

	£.
A million of pounds of fugar, eftimated by the returns of excife mafters, at 8d.	33,333

(This is double the quantity we want; but
as it is pernicious neither to health nor
morals, I let it pafs.)

200,000lb. of tea, at 3s. 6d.	35,000
2,000 ditto hyfon, at 14s.	1,400

(Moft of thefe unneceffary.)

Coffee, molaffes, fpices, &c.	10,000
Dry goods,	250,000
	£. 329,733

The whole fettlement will ftand thus :

	£.
Neceffary expenfes,	66,150
Unneceffary, ditto,	23,530
Rum, and other diftilled fpirits,	90,000
Other foreign articles,	329,733
	£. 510,413

Intereft of the federal and State debts,	£. 130,000

Now, good people, I have a word of advice for you.
I will tell you how to pay your taxes and debts, without feeling them.

ift. Fee no lawyers.

You fay lawyers have too high fees. I fay they
have not. They coft me not one farthing. Do as I
have always done, and lawyers' fees will be no trouble
at all. If I want a new coat, or my wife wants a new
gown, we have agreed to wear the old ones until we
have got cafh or produce to pay for them. When we
buy, we pay in hand ; we get things cheaper than our
neighbors ; merchants never dun us, and we have no
lawyers' fees to pay. When we fee fheriffs and duns
                                        knocking

knocking at the doors of our neighbors, we laugh at their folly. Befides, I keep a little drawer in my defk, with money enough in it to pay the next tax ; and I never touch a farthing until the collector calls. Now, good folks, if you will take the fame method, you will fave out of lawyers' fees and court charges, on the moft moderate calculations, 20,000l. a year.

2dly. I allow my family but two gallons of rum a year. This is enough for any family, and too much for moft of them. I drink cyder and beer of my own manufacture ; and my wife makes excellent beer, I affure you. I advife you all to do the fame. I am aftonifhed at you, good folks. Not a mechanic or a laborer goes to work for a merchant, but he carries home a bottle of rum. Not a load of wood comes to town, but a gallon bottle is tied to the cart ftake to be filled with rum. Scarcely a woman comes to town with tow cloth, but fhe has a wooden gallon bottle in one fide of her faddle bags, to fill with rum. A ftranger would think you to be a nation of Indians by your thirft for this paltry liquor. Take a bit of advice from a good friend of yours. Get two gallons of rum in a year ; have two or three frolics of innocent mirth ; keep a little fpirit for a medicine, and let your common drink be the produce or manufacture of this country. This will make a faving of almoft 400,000 gallons of rum, or 80,000l. a year.

3dly. Never buy any ufelefs clothing.

Keep a good fuit for Sundays and other public days ; but let your common wearing apparel be good fubftantial cloths, and linens of your own manufacture. Let your wives and daughters lay afide their plumes. Feathers and tripperies fuit the Cherokees or the wench in your kitchen ; but they little become the fair daughters of America.* Out of the dry goods imported, you may fave 50,000l. a year.

Thefe

---

* I would juft mention to my fair readers, whom I love and efteem, that feathers and other frippery of the head, are difreputable in Europe.

Thefe favings amount to 150,000l. a year. This is more than enough to pay the intereft of all our public debts.

My countrymen, I am not trifling with you : I am ferious. You feel the facts I ftate ; you know you are poor, and ought to know, the fault is all your own. Are you not fatisfied with the food and drink which this country affords-? The beef, the pork, the wheat, the corn, the butter, the cheefe, the cyder, the beer, thofe luxuries which are heaped in profufion upon your tables ? If not, you muft expect to be poor. In vain do you wifh for mines of gold and filver. A mine would be the greateft curfe that could befal this country. There is gold and filver enough in the world, and if you have not enough of it, it is becaufe you confume all you earn in ufelefs food and drink. In vain do you wifh to increafe the quantity of cafh by a mint, or by paper emiffions. Should it rain millions of joes into your chimnies, on your prefent fyftem of expenfes, you would ftill have no money. It would leave the country in ftreams. Trifle not with ferious fubjects, nor fpend your breath in empty wifhes. Reform ; economize. This is the whole of your political duty. You may reafon, fpeculate, complain, raife mobs, fpend life in railing at Congrefs and your rulers ; but unlefs you import lefs than you export, unlefs you fpend lefs than you earn, you will eternally be poor.

N2.

No. XIII.

NEW YORK, DECEMBER, 1787.

To the DISSENTING MEMBERS *of the late* CONVENTION *of* PENNSYLVANIA.

GENTLEMEN,

YOUR long and elaborate publication, affigning the reafons for your refuſing to ſubſcribe the ratification of the *new Federal Conſtitution,* has made its appearance in the public papers, and, I flatter myſelf, will be read throughout the United States. It will feed the flame of oppoſition among the weak, the wicked, the deſigning, and the factious; but it will make many new converts to the propoſed government, and furniſh the old friends of it with new weapons of defence. The very attempt to excite uneaſineſs and diſturbance in a State, about a meaſure legally and conſtitutionally adopted, after a long and ample diſcuſſion in a convention of the people's delegates, will create ſuſpicions of the goodneſs of your cauſe. My addreſs to you will not be ſo lengthy as your publication; your arguments are *few*, altho your harangue is *long* and *inſidious.*

You begin with telling the world, that *no defect was diſcovered in the preſent confederation, till after the war.* Why did you not publiſh the truth? You know, gentlemen, that during ſix years of the war, we had *no confederation at all.* You know that the war commenced in April, 1775, and that we had *no confederation* till March, 1781. You know (for ſome of you are men of abilities and reading) or ought to know, a principle of *fear*, in time of war, operates more powerfully in binding together the States which have a common intereſt, than all the parchment compacts on earth. Could we, then, diſcover the defects of our

preſent

prefent confederation, with *two years'* experience only, and an enemy in our country? You know we could not.

I will not undertake to detect the falfehood of every affertion, or the fallacy of all your reafoning on each article. In the moft of them the public will anticipate any thing I could fay, and confute your arguments as faft as they read them. But, gentlemen, your reafoning againft the *new Conftitution* refembles that of Mr. Hume on miracles. You begin with fome *gratis dicta*, which are denied; you affume *premifes* which are *totally falfe*, and then reafon on them with great addrefs. Your whole reafoning, and that of all the oppofers of the federal government, is built on this *falfe principle*, that the *federal Legiflature* will be a body *diftinct from* and *independent of* the people. Unlefs your oppofition is grounded on *that principle*, it ftands on *nothing*; and on any *other* fuppofition, your arguments are but *declamatory nonfenfe*.

But the principle is falfe. The Congrefs, under the propofed conftitution, will have the *fame intereft* as the people; they are *a part* of the people; their intereft is *infeparable* from that of the people; and this union of intereft will eternally remain, while the right of election fhall continue in the people. Over this right Congrefs will have no controul: The time and manner of exercifing that right are very wifely vefted in Congrefs; otherwife a delinquent State might embarrafs the meafures of the Union. The fafety of the public requires that the federal body fhould prevent any particular delinquency; but the *right of election* is above their control; it *muft* remain in the people, and be exercifed once in two, four or fix years. A body thus organized, with thirteen Legiflatures watching their meafures, and feveral millions of jealous eyes infpecting their conduct, would not be apt to betray their conftituents. Yet this is not the beft ground of fafety. The firft and almoft only principle that governs men, is *intereft*. *Love of our country* is a powerful auxiliary motiv to patriotic actions; but rarely or never

operates

operates against *private interest*. The only requisit to secure liberty, is to connect the *interest* of the *governors* with that of the *governed*. Blend these interests; make them inseparable, and both are safe from voluntary invasion. How shall this union be formed? This question is answered. The union is formed by the equal principles on which the people of these States hold their property and their rights. But how shall this union of interests be perpetuated? The answer is easy; bar all perpetuities of estates; prevent any exclusiv rights; preserve all preferment dependent on the choice of the people; suffer no power to exist independent of the people or their representativs. While there exists no power in a State, which is independent on the will of the electors, the rights of the people are secure. The only barrier against tyranny, that is necessary in any State, is *the election of legislators* by the yeomanry of that State. Preserve *that*, and every privilege is safe. The legislators thus chosen to represent the people, should have all the power that the people would have, were they assembled in one body to deliberate upon public measures. The distinction between the powers of the *people* and of their *representativs* in the Legislature, is as absurd in *theory*, as it proves pernicious in *practice*. A distinction, which has already countenanced and supported *one rebellion* in America; has prevented many *good* measures; has produced many *bad*; has created animosities in many States, and embarrassments in all.* It has taught the people a lesson, which, if they continue to practise, will bring laws into contempt, and frequently mark our country with blood.

You object, gentlemen, to the powers vested in Congress. Permit me, to ask you, where will you limit
their

---

* Some of the bills of rights in America declare, that the people have a right to meet together, and consult for the public safety; that their legislators are responsible to them; that they are servants, &c. Such declarations give people an idea, that as individuals, or in town meetings, they have a power paramount to that of the Legislature. No wonder, that with such ideas, they attempt to resist law.

their powers ? What bounds will you prefcribe ? You
will reply—*we will referve certain rights, which we deem
invaluable, and reftrain our rulers from abridging them.*
But, gentlemen, let me afk you, how will you define
thefe rights ? would you fay, *the liberty of the prefs fhall
not be reftrained ?* Well, what is this liberty of the
prefs ? Is it an unlimited licence to publifh *any thing
and every thing* with impunity ? If fo, the author and
printer of any treatife, however obfcene and blafphemous, will be fcreened from punifhment. You know,
gentlemen, that there are books extant, fo fhockingly
and infamoufly obfcene and fo daringly blafphemous,
that no fociety on earth would be vindicable in fuffering the publifhers to pafs unpunifhed. You certainly
know that fuch cafes *have* happened, and *may* happen
again : Nay, you know that they are *probable.* Would
not that indefinite expreffion, *the liberty of the prefs,* extend to the juftification of every *poffible publication?*
Yes, gentlemen, you know, that under fuch a general
licenfe, a man who fhould publifh a treatife to *prove
his Maker a knave,* muft be fcreened from legal punifhment. I fhudder at the thought ! But the truth muft
not be concealed. The conftitutions of feveral States
guarantee that very licenfe.

But if you attempt to define the *liberty of the prefs,*
and afcertain what cafes fhall fall within that privilege,
during the courfe of centuries, where will you *begin ?*
Or rather, where will you *end?* Here, gentlemen, you
will be puzzled. Some publications certainly *may* be
a breach of civil law : You will not have the effront-
ery to deny a truth fo obvious and intuitivly evident.
Admit that principle ; and unlefs you can define precifely the cafes, which are, and are not a breach of law,
you have no right to fay, the liberty of the prefs fhall
not be reftrained ; for fuch a licenfe would warrant
any breach of law. Rather than hazard fuch an abufe
of privilege, is it not better to leave the right altogether
with your rulers and your pofterity ? No attempts
have ever been made by a legiflativ body in America,
to abridge that privilege ; and in this free enlightened

country, no attempts could fucceed, unleſs the public
ſhould be convinced that an abuſe of it would warrant
the reſtriction.   Should this ever be the caſe, you have
no right to ſay, that a future Legiſlature, or that poſterity ſhall not abridge the privilege, or puniſh its a-
buſes.

But you ſay, that trial by jury is an unalienable
right, that ought not to be truſted with our rulers.
Why not ? If it is fuch a darling privilege, will not
Congreſs be as fond of it, as their conſtituents ? An
elevation into that council, does not render a man in-
ſenſible to his privileges, nor place him beyond the neceſſity of ſecuring them.   A member of Congreſs is
liable to all the operations of law, except during his
attendance on public buſineſs ; and ſhould he conſent
to a law, annihilating any right whatever, he deprives
himſelf, his family and eſtate, of the benefit reſulting
from that right, as well as his conſtituents.   This circumſtance alone, is a ſufficient ſecurity.

But, why this outcry about juries ? If the people
eſteem them fo highly, why do they ever neglect them,
and ſuffer the trial by them to go into difuſe ? In ſome
States, *Courts of Admiralty* have no juries, nor Courts of
Chancery at all.   In the City Courts of ſome States,
juries are rarely or never called, altho the parties may
demand them ; and one State, at leaſt, has lately paſſed an act, empowering the parties to ſubmit both *law*
and *fact* to the court.   It is found, that the judgment
of a court gives as much ſatisfaction, as the verdict of
a jury ; for the court are as good judges of fact, as juries, and much better judges of law. I have no deſire to
aboliſh trials by jury, altho the original deſign and excellence of them, is in many caſes ſuperſeded.   While
the people remain attached to this mode of deciding
cauſes, I am confident, that no Congreſs can wreſt the
privilege from them.

But, gentlemen, our legal proceedings want a reform.   Involved in all the mazes of perplexity, which
the chicanery of lawyers could invent, in the courſe of
five thouſand years, our road to juſtice and redreſs is
tedious,

tedious, fatiguing and expensiv. Our judicial proceedings are capable of being simplified, and improved
in almost every particular. For mercy's fake, gentlemen, do not shut the door against improvement. If
the people of America, should ever spurn the shackles
of opinion, and venture to leave the road, which is so
overgrown with briers and thorns, as to strip a man's
clothes from his back as he passes, I am certain they
can devise a more easy, safe, and expeditious mode of
administering the laws, than that which harasses every
poor mortal, that is wretched enough to want *legal*
justice. In States where very respectable merchants,
have repeatedly told me, they had rather lose a debt of
fifty pounds, than attempt to recover it by a legal
process, one would think that men, who value liberty
and property, would not restrain any government from
suggesting a remedy for such disorders.

Another right, which you would place beyond the
reach of Congress, is the writ of *habeas corpus*. Will
you say that this right may not be suspended in *any*
case? You dare not. If it may be suspended in any
case, and the Congress are to judge of the necessity,
what security have you in a declaration in its favor?
You had much better say nothing upon the subject.

But you are frightened at a standing army. I beg
you, gentlemen, to define a *standing army*. If you
would refuse to giv Congress power to raise troops, to
guard our frontiers, and garrison forts, or in short, to
enlist men for any purpose, then we understand you;
you tie the hands of your rulers, so that they cannot
defend you against any invasion. This is protection,
indeed! But if Congress can raise a body of troops for
a year, they can raise them for a *hundred years*, and
your declaration against *standing armies* can have no
other effect, than to prevent Congress from denomi-
nating their troops, a *standing army*. You would only
introduce into this country the English farce of mechanically passing an annual bill for the support of
troops which are never disbanded.

You

L. 2

You object to the indefinite power of taxation in Congrefs. You muft then limit the exercife of that power by the fums of money to be raifed ; or leaving the fums indefinite, muft prefcribe the *particular mode* in which, and the *articles* on which the money is to be raifed. But the fums cannot be afcertained, becaufe the neceffities of the States cannot be forefeen nor defined. It is beyond even *your* wifdom and profound knowlege, gentlemen, to afcertain the public exigencies, and reduce them to the provifions of a conftitution. And if you would prefcribe the mode of raifing money, you will meet with equal difficulty. The different States have different modes of taxation, and I queftion much whether even *your* fkill, gentlemen, could invent a uniform fyftem that would fit eafy upon every State. It muft therefore be left to experiment, with a power that can correct the errors of a fyftem, and fuit it to the habits of the people. And if no uniform mode will anfwer this purpofe, it will be in the power of Congrefs to lay taxes in each State, according to its particular practice.

You know that requifitions on the States are ineffectual ; that they cannot be rendered effectual, but by a compulfory power in Congrefs ; that without an efficient power to raife money, government cannot fecure perfon, property or juftice ; that fuch power is as fafely lodged in your *Reprefentativs* in Congrefs, as it is in your *Reprefentativs* in your diftinct Legiflatures.

You would likewife reftrain Congrefs from requiring *exceffiv bail* or impofing *exceffiv fines* and *unufual punifhment*. But unlefs you can, in every poffible inftance, previoufly define the words *exceffiv* and *unufual* ; if you leave the difcretion of Congrefs to define them on occafion, any reftriction of their power by a general indefinit expreffion, is a nullity—mere *formal nonfenfe*. What confummate arrogance muft you poffefs, to prefume you can *now* make *better* provifion for the government of thefe States, during the courfe of ages and centuries, than the future Legiflatures can, on the fpur of the occafion ! Yet your whole reafoning on the
                                             fubject

fubject implies this arrogance, and a prefumption that you have a right to legiflate for pofterity!'

But to complete the lift of unalienable rights, you would infert a claufe in your declaration, *that every body fhall, in good weather, hunt on his own land, and catch fifh in rivers that are public property.* Here, gentlemen, you muft have exerted the whole force of your genius! Not even the *all important* fubject of *legiflating for a world,* can reftrain my laughter at this claufe! As a fupplement to that article of your bill of rights, I would fuggeft the following reftriction:—" That Congrefs fhall never reftrain any inhabitant of America from eating and drinking, *at feafonable times*, or prevent his lying on his *left fide*, in a long winter's night, or even on his back, when he is fatigued by lying on his *right*." This article is of juft as much confequence as the eighth claufe of your propofed bill of rights.

But to be more ferious, gentlemen, you muft have had in idea the foreft laws in Europe, when you inferted that article; for no circumftance that ever took place in America, could have fuggefted the thought of a declaration in favor of hunting and fifhing. Will you forever perfift in error? Do you not reflect that the ftate of property in America, is directly the reverfe of what it is in Europe? Do you not confider, that the foreft laws in Europe originated in *feudal tyranny*, of which not a trace is to be found in America? Do you not know that in this country almoft every farmer is lord of his own foil? That inftead of fuffering under the oppreffion of a monarch and nobles, a clafs of haughty mafters, totally independent of the people, almoft every man in America is a *lord himfelf,* enjoying his property in fee? Where then the neceffity of laws to fecure hunting and fifhing? You may juft as well afk for a claufe, giving licenfe for every man to till *his own land*, or milk *his own cows.* The barons in Europe procured foreft laws to fecure the right of hunting on *their own land*, from the intrufion of thofe who had no property in lands. But the diftribution of land in America, not only fuperfedes the neceffity of any laws

upon

upon this fubject, but renders them abfolutely trifling.
The fame laws which fecure the property in land, fecure to the owner the right of ufing it as he pleafes.

But you are frightened at the profpect of a *confolida-*
tion of the States. I differ from you very widely. I am
afraid, after all our attempts to unite the States, that
contending interefts, and the pride of State fovereignties, will either prevent our union, or render our federal
government weak, flow and inefficient. The danger
is all on this fide. If any thing under heaven now endangers our liberties and independence, it is that fingle
circumftance.

You harp upon that claufe of the new conftitution,
which declares, that the laws of the United States, &c.
fhall be the fupreme law of the land ; when you know
that the powers of the Congrefs are defined, to extend
only to thofe matters which are in their nature and effects, *general.* You know, the Congrefs cannot meddle with the internal police of any State, or abridge its
fovereignty. And you know, at the fame time, that in
all general concerns, the laws of Congrefs muft be *fu-*
preme, or they muft be *nothing.*

No. XIV.

PHILADELPHIA, MARCH, 1787.

On TEST LAWS, OATHS of ALLEGI-ANCE and ABJURATION, and PAR-TIAL EXCLUSIONS from OFFICE.

TO change the current of opinion, is a moft diffi-cult tafk, and the attempt is often ridiculed. For this reafon, I expect the following remarks will be paffed over with a flight reading, and all attention to them ceafe with a hum.

The revifal of the teft law has at length paffed by a refpectable majority of the Reprefentativs of this State. This is a prelude to wifer meafures ; people are juft a-waking from delufion. The time will come (and may the day be near !) when all teft laws, oaths of allegiance, abjuration, and partial exclufions from civil offices, will be profcribed from this land of freedom.

Americans ! what was the origin of thefe difcrimi-nations ? What is their ufe ?

They originated in favage ignorance, and they are the inftruments of flavery. Emperors and generals, who wifhed to attach their fubjects to their perfons and government ; who wifhed to exercife defpotic fway over them, or profecute villanous wars, (for mankind have always been butchering each other) found the fo-lemnity of oaths had an excellent effect on poor fuper-ftitious foldiers and vaffals ; oracles, demons, eclipfes ; all the terrifying phenomena of nature, have at times had remarkable effects in fecuring the obedience of men to tyrants. Oaths of fealty, and farcical ceremo-nies of homage, were very neceffary to rivet the chains of feudal vaffals ; for the whole fyftem of European tenures was erected on jurifdiction, and is fupported folely by ignorance, fuperftition, artifice, or military force,

force. Oaths of allegiance may poſſibly be ſtill neceſſary in Europe, where there are ſo many contending
powers contiguous to each other : But what is their
uſe in America ? To ſecure fidelity to the State, it will
be anſwered.   But where is the danger of defeɥion ?
Will the inhabitants join the Britiſh in Nova Scotia or
Canada ? Will they rebel ? Will they join the ſavages,
and overthrow the State ? No ; all theſe are viſionary
dangers.   My countrymen, if a State has any thing to
fear from its inhabitants, the conſtitution or the laws
muſt be wrong.   Danger cannot poſſibly ariſe from
any other cauſe.

Permit me to offer a few ideas to your minds ; and
let them be the ſubjeɥ of more than one hour's reflection.

An oath creates no new obligation. A witneſs, who
ſwears to tell the whole truth, is under no new obligation to tell the whole truth.   An oath reminds him of
his duty ; he ſwears to do as he ought to do ; that is,
he adds an expreſs promiſe to an implied one.   A moral obligation is not capable of addition or diminution.

When a man ſteps his foot into a State, he becomes
ſubjeɥ to its general laws.   When he joins it as a
member, he is ſubjeɥ to all its laws.   The aɥ of en-
tering into ſociety, binds him to ſubmit to its laws,
and to promote its intereſt.   Every man, who livs under a government, is under allegiance to that government.   Ten thouſand oaths do not increaſe the obligation upon him to be a faithful ſubjeɥ.

But, it will be aſked, how ſhall we diſtinguiſh between the friends and enemies of the government ? I
anſwer, by annihilating all diſtinɥions.   A good conſtitution, and good laws, make good ſubjeɥs.   I challenge the hiſtory of mankind to produce an inſtance of
bad ſubjeɥs under a good government.   The teſt law
in Penſylvania has produced more diſorder, by making
enemies in this State, than have curſed all the union
beſides.   During the war, every thing gave way to
force ; but the feelings and principles of war ought to
be forgotten in peace.

                              Abjuration !

Abjuration! a badge of folly, borrowed from the dark ages of bigotry. If the government of Penſylvavia is better than that of Great Britain, the ſubjects will prefer it, and abjuration is perfectly nugatory. If not, the ſubject will have his partialities in ſpite of any ſolemn renunciation of a foreign power.

But what right has even the Legiſlature to deprive any claſs of citizens of the benefits and emoluments of civil government? If any men have forfeited their lives or eſtates, they are no longer ſubjects; they ought to be baniſhed or hung. If not, no law ought to exclude them from civil emoluments. If any have committed public crimes, they are puniſhable; if any have been guilty, and have not been detected, the oath, as it now ſtands, obliges them to confeſs their guilt. To take the oath, is an implicit acknowlegement of innocence; to refuſe it, is an implicit confeſſion that the perſon has aided and abetted the enemy. This is rank deſpotiſm. The inquiſition can do no more than force confeſſion from the accuſed.

I pray God to enlighten the minds of the Americans. I wiſh they would ſhake off every badge of tyranny. Americans!—The beſt way to make men honeſt, is to let them enjoy equal rights and privileges; never ſuſpect a ſet of men will be rogues, and make laws proclaiming that ſuſpicion. Leave force to govern the wretched vaſſals of European nabobs, and reconcile ſubjects to your own conſtitutions by their excellent nature and beneficial effects. No man will commence enemy to a government which givs him as many privileges as his neighbors enjoy.

No.

No. XV.

SKETCHES *of the* RISE, PROGRESS *and* CONSEQUENCES *of the late* REVOLUTION.

Written in the years 1787, 1788, and 1789; now republished, with material corrections, and a LETTER from the late COMMANDER in CHIEF, explaining the Circumstances and Proceedings, preparatory to the Capture of Lord CORNWALLIS.

AMERICA was originally peopled by uncivilized nations, which lived mostly by hunting and fishing. The Europeans, who first visited these shores, treating the nativs as wild beasts of the forest, which have no property in the woods where they roam, planted the standard of their respectiv masters where they first landed, and in their names claimed the country by *right of discovery*.* Prior to any settlement in North America numerous titles of this kind were acquired by the English, French, Spanish, and Dutch navigators, who came hither for the purposes of fishing and trading with the nativs. Slight as such titles were, they were afterwards the causes of contention between the European nations. The subjects of different princes often laid claim to the same tract of country, because both had discovered the same river or promontary; or because the extent of their respectiv claims was indeterminate.

While the settlements in this vast uncultivated country were inconsiderable and scattered, and the trade of it confined to the bartering of a few trinkets for furs, a trade carried on by a few adventurers, the interfering of claims produced no important controversy among
the

---

* As well may the New Zealanders, who have not yet discovered Europe, fit out a ship, land on the coast of England or France, and, finding no inhabitants but poor fishermen and peasants, claim the whole country by *right of discovery*.

the fettlers or the nations of Europe. But in proportion to the progrefs of population, and the growth of the American trade, the jealoufies of the nations, which had made early difcoveries and fettlements on this coaft, were alarmed; ancient claims were revived; and each power took meafures to extend and fecure its own poffeffions at the expenfe of a rival.

By the treaty of Utrecht in 1713, the Englifh claimed a right of cutting logwood in the Bay of Campeachy, in South America. In the exercife of this right, the Englifh merchants had frequent opportunities of carrying on a contraband trade with the Spanifh fettlements on the continent. To remedy this evil, the Spaniards refolved to annihilate a claim, which, though often acknowleged, had never been clearly afcertained. To effect this defign, they captured the Englifh veffels, which they found along the Spanifh Main, and many of the Britifh fubjects were doomed to work in the mines of Potofi.

Repeated feverities of this kind at length (1739) produced a war between England and Spain. Porto Bello was taken from the Spaniards, by Admiral Vernon. Commodore Anfon, with a fquadron of fhips, failed to the South Seas, diftreffed the Spanifh fettlements on the weftern fhore of America, and took a galleon, laden with immenfe riches. But in 1741 a formidable armament, deftined to attack Carthagena, under the command of Lord Cathcart, returned unfuccefsful, with the lofs of upwards of twelve thoufand Britifh foldiers and feamen; and the defeat of the expedition, raifed a clamor againft the minifter, Sir Robert Walpole, which produced a change in the adminiftration. This change removed the fcene of war to Europe, fo that America was not immediately affected by the fubfequent tranfactions; except that Louifburgh, the principal fortrefs of Cape Breton, was taken from the French by General Pepperell, affifted by Commodore Warren and a body of New England troops.

This

This war was ended in 1748 by the treaty of peace signed at Aix la Chapelle, by which restitution was made on both sides of all places taken during the war.

Peace, however, was of short duration. The French possessed Canada, and had made considerable settlements in Florida, claiming the country on both sides of the Mississippi, by right of discovery. To secure and extend their claims, they established a line of forts, on the English possessions, from Canada to Florida. They had secured the important pass at Niagara, and erected a fort at the junction of the Allegany and Monongahela rivers, called Fort Du Quesne. They took pains to secure the friendship and assistance of the nativs, encroachments were made upon the English possessions, and mutual injuries succeeded. The disputes among the settlers in America, and the measures taken by the French to command all the trade of the St. Lawrence river on the north, and of the Mississippi on the south, excited a jealousy in the English nation, which soon broke forth in open war.

In 1756, four expeditions were undertaken in America against the French. One was conducted by General Monckton, who had orders to drive the French from the encroachments on the province of Nova Scotia. This expedition was attended with success. General Johnson was ordered, with a body of troops, to take possession of Crown Point, but he did not succeed. General Shirley commanded an expedition against the fort at Niagara, but lost the season by delay. General Braddock marched against fort Du Quesne, but in penetrating through the wilderness, he incautiously fell into an ambuscade and suffered a total defeat. General Braddock was killed, but a part of his troops were saved by the prudence and bravery of General Washington, at this time a Colonel, who then began to exhibit proofs of those military talents, by which he afterwards conducted the armies of America to victory, and his country to independence. The ill
                                                            success

succefs of thefe expeditions left the Englifh settlements in America expofed to the depredations of both the French and Indians.   But the war now raged in Europe and the Eaft Indies, and engaged the attention of both nations in thofe quarters.

It was not until the campaign in 1758, that affairs affumed a more favorable afpect in America.   But upon a change of adminiftration, Mr. Pitt was appointed Prime Minifter, and the operations of war became more vigorous and fuccefsful.   General Amherft was fent to take poffeffion of Cape Breton ; and after a warm fiege, the garrifon of Louifburgh furrendered by capitulation.   General Forbes was fuccefsful in taking poffeffion of fort Du Quefne, which the French thought fit to abandon.   But General Abercrombie, who commanded the troops deftined to act againft the French at Crown Point and Ticonderoga, attacked the lines at Ticonderoga, where the enemy were ftrongly entrenched, and was defeated with a terrible flaughter of his troops.   After his defeat, he returned to his camp at Lake George.

The next year, more effectual meafures were taken to fubdue the French in America.   General Prideaux and Sir William Johnfon began the operations of the campaign by taking the French fort near Niagara.*   General Amherft took poffeffion of the forts at Crown Point and Ticonderoga, which the French had abandoned.

But the decifiv blow, which proved fatal to the French interefts in America, was the defeat of the French army, and the taking of Quebec, by the brave general Wolfe.   This hero was flain in the beginning of the action, on the plains of Abram, and Monfieur Montcalm, the French commander, likewife loft his life.   The lofs of Quebec was foon followed by the capture of Montreal, by General Amherft, and Canada has remained ever fince in poffeffion of the Englifh.

Colonel

* General Prideaux was killed by the burfting of a mortar, before the furrender of the French.

Colonel Grant, in 1761, defeated the Cherokees in Carolina, and obliged them to fue for peace. The next year, Martinico was taken by Admiral Rodney and General Monkton ; and alfo the iflands of Grenada, St. Vincents, and others. The capture of thefe was foon followed by the furrender of the Havanna, the capital of the ifland of Cuba.

In 1763, a definitiv treaty of peace was concluded at Paris, between Great Britain, France and Spain, by which the Englifh ceded to the French feveral iflands in the Weft Indies, but were confirmed in the poffeffion of all North America on this fide the Miffifippi, except New Orleans, and a fmall diftrict of the neighboring country.

But this war, however brilliant the fuccefs, and glorious the event, proved the caufe of great and unexpected misfortunes to Great Britain. Engaged with the combined powers of France and Spain, during feveral years, her exertions were furprifing, and her expenfe immenfe. To difcharge the debts of the nation, the parliament was obliged to have recourfe to new expedients for raifing money. Previous to the laft treaty in 1763, the parliament had been fatisfied to raife a revenue from the American Colonies by monopoly of their trade.

At the beginning of the laft war with France, commiffioners from many of the colonies had affembled at Albany, and propofed that a great council fhould be formed by deputies from the feveral colonies, which, with a general Governor to be appointed by the crown, fhould be empowered to take meafures for the common fafety, and to raife money for the execution of their defigns. This propofal was not relifhed by the Britifh miniftry ; but in place of this plan, it was propofed, that the Governors of the colonies, with the affiftance of one or two of their council, fhould affemble and concert meafures for the general defence ; erect forts, levy troops, and draw on the treafury of England for monies that fhould be wanted ; but the treafury to be reimburfed by a tax on the colonies, to be laid by

the

the Englifh parliament.   To this plan, which would
imply an avowal of the right of parliament to tax the
colonies, the provincial affemblies objected with un-
fhaken firmnefs.   It feems, therefore, that the Britifh
parliament, *before* the war, had it in contemplation to
exercife the right they claimed of taxing the colonies at
pleafure, without permitting them to be reprefented.
Indeed it is obvious that they laid hold of the alarming
fituation of the colonies about the year 1754, and 1755,
to force them into an acknowlegement of the right, or
to the adoption of meafures that might afterwards be
drawn into precedent.   The colonies however, with
an uncommon forefight and firmnefs, defeated all their
attempts.   The war was carried on by requifitions on
the colonies for fupplies of men and money, or by voluntary contributions.

But no fooner was peace concluded, than the Englifh parliament refumed the plan of taxing the colonies ; and to juftify their attempts, faid, that the money
to be raifed, was to be appropriated to defray the expenfe of defending them in the late war.

The firft attempt to raife a revenue in America appeared in the memorable *ftamp act*, paffed March 22,
1765 ; by which it was enacted that certain inftruments
of writing, as bills, bonds, &c. fhould not be valid in
law, unlefs drawn on ftamped paper, on which a duty
was laid.   No fooner was this act publifhed in America, than it raifed a general alarm.   The people were
filled with apprehenfions at an act which they fuppofed an attack on their conftitutional rights.   The colonies petitioned the king and parliament for a redrefs of
the grievance, and formed affociations for the purpofe
of preventing the importation and ufe of Britifh manufactures, until the act fhould be repealed.   This fpirited and unanimous oppofition of the Americans produced the defired effect ; and on the 18th of March,
1766, the ftamp act was repealed.   The news of the
repeal was received in the colonies with univerfal joy,
and the trade between them and Great Britain was renewed on the moft liberal footing.

The

The parliament, by repealing this act, so obnoxious to their American brethren, did not intend to lay aside the scheme of raising a revenue in the colonies, but merely to change the mode. Accordingly the next year, they passed an act, laying a certain duty on glass, tea, paper, and painters' colors ; articles which were much wanted, and not manufactured, in America. This act kindled the resentment of the Americans, and excited a general opposition to the measure ; so that parliament thought proper in 1770, to take off these duties, except three pence a pound on tea. Yet this duty, however trifling, kept alive the jealousy of the colonists, and their opposition to parliamentary taxation continued and increased.

But it must be remembered that the inconvenience of paying the duty was not the sole, nor principal cause of the opposition, it was the *principle* which, once admitted, would have subjected the colonies to unlimitted parliamentary taxation, without the privilege of being represented. The . right, abstractly considered, was denied ; and the smallest attempt to establish the claim by precedent, was uniformly resisted. The Americans could not be deceived as to the views of parliament ; for the repeal of the stamp act was accompanied with an unequivocal declaration, " that the parliament had a right to make laws of sufficient validity to bind the colonies in all cases whatsoever."

The colonies therefore entered into measures to encourage their own manufactures, and home productions, and to retrench the use of foreign superfluities ; while the importation of tea was prohibited. In the royal and proprietary governments, the Governors and people were in a state of continual warfare. Assemblies were repeatedly called, and suddenly dissolved. While sitting, the assemblies employed the time in stating grievances and framing remonstrances. To inflame these discontents, an act of parliament was passed, ordaining that the Governors and Judges should receive their salaries of the crown ; thus making them 'independent of the provincial assemblies, and removeable only at the pleasure of the king. These

'Thefe arbitrary proceedings, with many others not here mentioned, could not fail of producing a rupture. The firft act of violence, was the maffacre at Bofton, on the evening of the fifth of March, 1770. A body of Britifh troops had been ftationed in Bofton to awe the inhabitants, and enforce the meafures of parliament. On the fatal day, when blood was to be fhed, as a prelude to more tragic fcenes, a riot was raifed among fome foldiers and boys ; the former aggreffing by throwing fnow balls at the latter. The bickerings and jealoufies between the inhabitants and foldiers, which had been frequent before, now became ferious. A multitude was foon collected, and the controverfy became fo warm, that to difperfe the people, the troops were embodied and ordered to fire upon the inhabitants. This fatal order was executed, and feveral perfons fell a facrifice. The people reftrained their vengeance at the time; but this wanton act of cruelty and military defpotifm fanned the flame of liberty; a flame that was not to be extinguifhed but by a total feparation of the colonies from their oppreffiv and hoftile parent.

In 1773, the fpirit of the Americans broke out into open violence. The Gafpee, an armed fchooner, belonging to his Britannic Majefty, had been ftationed at Providence, in Rhode Ifland, to prevent fmuggling. The vigilance of the commander irritated the inhabitants to that degree, that about two hundred armed men entered the veffel at night, compelled the officers and men to go on fhore, and fet fire to the fchooner. A reward of five hundred pounds, offered by government for apprehending any of the perfons concerned in this daring act, produced no effectual difcovery.

About this time, the difcovery and publication of fome private confidential letters, written by the royal officers in Bofton, to perfons in office in England, ferved to confirm the apprehenfions of the Americans, with refpect to the defigns of the Britifh government. It was now made obvious that more effectual meafures would be taken to eftablifh the fupremacy of the Britifh parliament over the colonies. The letters rec-

M   ommended

ommended decifiv meafures, and the writers were charged, by the exafperated Americans, with betraying their truft and the people they governed.

As the refolutions of the colonies not to import or confume tea, had, in a great meafure, deprived the Englifh government of a revenue from this quarter, the parliament formed a fcheme of introducing tea into America, under cover of the Eaft India company. For this purpofe an act was paffed, enabling the company to export all forts of teas, duty free, to any place whatever. The company departed from their ufual mode of bufinefs and became their own exporters. Several fhips were freighted with teas, and fent to the American colonies, and factors were appointed to receive and difpofe of their cargoes.

The Americans, determined to oppofe the revenue fyftem of the Englifh parliament in every poffible fhape, confidered the attempt of the Eaft India company to evade the refolutions of the colonies, and difpofe of teas in America, as an indirect mode of taxation, fanctioned by the authority of parliament. The people affembled in various places, and in the large commercial towns, took meafures to prevent the landing of the teas. Committees were appointed, and armed with extenfiv powers to infpect merchants' books, to propofe tefts, and make ufe of other expedients to fruftrate the defigns of the Eaft India company. The fame fpirit pervaded the people from New Hampfhire to Georgia. In fome places, the confignees of the teas were intimidated fo far as to relinquifh their appointments, or to enter into engagements not to act in that capacity. The cargo fent to South Carolina was ftored, the confignees being reftrained from offering the tea for fale. In other provinces, the fhips were fent back without difcharging their cargoes.

But in Bofton the tea fhared a more violent fate. Senfible that no legal meafures could prevent its being landed, and that if once landed, it would be difpofed of ; a number of men in difguife, on the 18th of December 1773, entered the fhips and threw overboard
three

three hundred and forty chefts of it, which was the proportion belonging to the Eaft India company. No fooner did the news of this deftruction of the tea reach Great Britain, than the parliament determined to pun-ifh that devoted town.   On the king's laying the A-merican papers before them, a bill was brought in and paffed, " to difcontinue the landing and difcharging, lading and fhipping of goods, wares and merchandizes at the town of Bofton, or within the harbor."

This act, paffed March 25, 1774, called the Bofton port bill, threw the inhabitants of Maffachufetts into the greateft confternation.   The town of Bofton paffed a refolution, expreffing their fenfe of this oppreffiv meafure, and a defire that all the colonies would con-cur to ftop all importation from Great Britain.   Moft of the colonies entered into fpirited refolutions, on this occafion, to unite with Maffachufetts in a firm oppofi-tion to the unconftitutional meafures of the parliament. The firft of June, the day on which the port bill was to take place, was appointed to be kept as a day of hu-miliation, fafting and prayer throughout the colonies, to feek the divine direction and aid, in that critical and gloomy juncture of affairs.

During the height of the confternation and confufion which the Bofton port bill occafioned ; at the very time when a town meeting was fitting to confider of it, Gen-eral Gage, who had been appointed to the government of Maffachufetts, arrived in the harbor.   His arrival however did not allay the popular ferment, or check the progrefs of the meafures then taking, to unite the col-onies in oppofition to the oppreffiv act of parliament.

But the port bill was not the only act that alarmed the apprehenfions of the Americans.   Determined to compel the province of Maffachufetts to fubmit to their laws, parliament paffed an act for " the better regulat-ing government in the province of Maffachufetts Bay." The object of this act was to alter the government, as it ftood on the charter of king William, to take the ap-pointment of the executiv out of the hands of the peo-ple, and place it in the crown ; thus making even the

judges

judges and sheriffs dependent on the king, and removeable only at his pleasure.

This act was soon followed by another, which ordained that any person, indicted for murder, or other capital offence, committed in aiding the magistrates in executing the laws, might be sent by the governor either to another colony, or to Great Britain for his trial.

This was soon followed by the Quebec bill ; which extended the bounds of that province, and granted many privileges to the Roman Catholics. The object of this bill was, to secure the attachment of that province to the crown of England, and prevent its joining the colonies in their resistance to the laws of parliament.

But these measures did not intimidate the Americans. On the other hand they served to confirm their former apprehensions of the evil designs of government, and to unite the colonies in their opposition. A correspondence of opinion with respect to the unconstitutional acts of parliament, produced a uniformity of proceedings in the colonies. The people generally concurrred in a proposition for holding a Congress by deputation from the several colonies, in order to concert measures for the preservation of their rights. Deputies were accordingly appointed, and met at Philadelphia, on the 26th of October, 1774.

In this first Congress, the proceedings were cool, deliberate and loyal ; but marked with unanimity and firmness. Their first act was a declaration, or state of their claims as to the enjoyment of all the rights of British subjects, and particularly that of taxing themselves exclusivly, and of regulating the internal police of the colonies. They also drew up a petition to the king, complaining of their grievances and praying for a repeal of the unconstitutional and oppressiv acts of parliament. They signed an association to suspend the importation of British goods, and the exportation of American produce, until their grievances should be redressed. They sent an address to the inhabitants of Great Britain, and another to the people of America ;

in

in the former of which they enumerated the oppreffiv fteps of parliament, and called on their Britifh brethren not to aid the miniftry in cnflaving their American fubjects ; and in the latter, they endeavored to confirm the people in a fpirited and unanimous determination to defend their conftitutional rights.

In the mean time, every thing in Maffachufetts wore the appearance of oppofition by force. A new council for the Governor had been appointed by the crown. New judges were appointed, and attempted to proceed in the execution of their office. But the juries refufed to be fworn under them ; in fome counties, the people af- fembled to prevent the courts from proceeding to buf- inefs ; and in Berkfhire they fucceeded, fetting an ex- ample of refiftance that has fince been followed, in vio- lation of the laws of the State.

In this fituation of affairs, the day for the annual mufter of the militia approached. General Gage, ap- prehenfiv of fome violence, had the precaution to feize the magazines of ammunition and ftores at Cambridge and Charleftown, and lodged them in Bofton. This meafure, with the fortifying of that neck of land which joins Bofton to the main land at Roxbury, caufed a univerfal alarm and ferment. Several thoufand people affembled, and it was with difficulty they could be re- ftrained from falling upon the Britifh troops.

On this occafion, an affembly of delegates from all the towns in Suffolk county, was called ; and feveral fpirited refolutions were agreed to. Thefe refolutions were prefaced with a declaration of allegiance ; but they breathed a fpirit of freedom that does honor to the delegates. They declared that the late acts of par- liament and the proceedings of General Gage, were glaring infractions of their rights and liberties, which their duty called them to defend by all lawful means.

This affembly remonftrated againft the fortification of Bofton neck, and againft the Quebec bill ; and re- folved upon a fufpenfion of commerce, and encourage- ment of arts and manufactures, the holding of a pro- vincial Congrefs, and a fubmiffion to the meafures which

which fhould be recommended by the Continental Congrefs. They recommended that the collectors of taxes fhould not pay any money into the treafury, without further orders ; they alfo recommended peace and good order, as they meant to act merely upon the defenfiv.

In anfwer to their remonftrance, General Gage affured them that he had no intention to prevent the free egrefs and regrefs of the inhabitants to and from the town of Bofton, and that he would not fuffer any perfon under his command to injure the perfon or property of any of his majefty's fubjects.

Previous to this, a General Affembly had been fummoned to meet ; and notwithftanding the writs had been countermanded by the Governor's proclamation, on account of the violence of the times and the refignation of feveral of the new counfellors, yet reprefentativs were chofen by the people, who met at Salem, refolved themfelves into a provincial Congrefs, and adjourned to Concord.

This Congrefs addreffed the Governor with a rehearfal of their diftreffes, and took the neceffary fteps for defending their rights. They regulated the militia, made provifion for fupplying the treafury, and furnifhing the people with arms ; and fuch was the enthufiafm and union of the people, that the recommendations of the provincial Congrefs had the force of laws.

General Gage was incenfed at thefe meafures ; he declared, in his anfwer to the addrefs, that Britain could never harbor the black defign of enflaving her fubjects, and publifhed a proclamation in which he infinuated that fuch proceedings amounted to rebellion. He alfo ordered barracks to be erected for the foldiers ; but he found difficulty in procuring laborers, either in Bofton or New York.

In the beginning of 1775, the fifhery bills were paffed in parliament, by which the colonies were prohibited to trade with Great Britain, Ireland or the Weft Indies, or to take fifh on the banks of Newfoundland.

In

In the diftreffes to which thefe acts of parliament reduced the town of Bofton, the unanimity of the colonies was remarkable, in the large fupplies of provifion, furnifhed by the inhabitants of different towns from New Hampfhire to Georgia, and fhipped to the relief of the fufferers.

Preparations began to be made, to oppofe by force, the execution of thefe acts of parliament. The militia of the country were trained to the ufe of arms; great encouragement was given for the manufacture of gunpowder, and meafures were taken to obtain all kinds of military ftores.

In February, Colonel Leflie was fent with a detachment of troops from Bofton, to take poffeffion of fome cannon at Salem. But the people had intelligence of the defign, took up the draw bridge in that town, and prevented the troops from paffing, until the cannon were fecured; fo that the expedition failed.

In April, Colonel Smith, and Major Pitcairn were fent with a body of about nine hundred troops, to deftroy the military ftores which had been collected at Concord, about twenty miles from Bofton. It is believed, that another object of this expedition, was to feize on the perfons of Meffrs. Hancock and Adams, who, by their fpirited exertions, had rendered themfelves very obnoxious to General Gage. At Lexington, the militia were collected on a green, to oppofe the incurfion of the Britifh forces. Thefe were fired upon by the Britifh troops, and eight men killed on the fpot.

The militia were difperfed, and the troops proceeded to Concord; where they deftroyed a few ftores. But on their return, they were inceffantly harraffed by the Americans, who, inflamed with juft refentment, fired upon them from houfes and fences, and purfued them to Bofton. The lofs of the Britifh in this expedition, in killed, wounded and prifoners, was two hundred and feventy three men.

Here was fpilt the *firft blood* in the late war; a war which fevered America from the Britifh empire. *Lex-*
ington

ington opened the firſt ſcene of this great drama, which, in its progreſs, exhibited the moſt illuſtrious characters and events, and cloſed with a revolution, equally glorious for the actors, and important in its conſequences to mankind.

This battle rouſed all America. The militia collected from all quarters, and Boſton, in a few days was beſieged by twenty thouſand men. A ſtop was put to all intercourſe between the town and country, and the inhabitants were reduced to great want of proviſions. General Gage promiſed to let the people depart, if they would deliver up their arms. The people complied; but when the General had obtained their arms, the perfidious man refuſed to let the people go.

In the mean time, a ſmall number of men, to the amount of about two hundred and forty, under the command of Colonel Allen, and Colonel Eaſton, without any public orders, ſurpriſed and took the Britiſh garriſons at Ticonderoga and Crown Point, without the loſs of a man on either ſide.

During theſe tranſactions, the Generals Howe, Burgoyne, and Clinton, arrived at Boſton from England, with a number of troops. In June following, our troops attempted to fortify Bunker's hill, which lies near Charleſtown, and but a mile and an half from Boſton. They had, during the night, thrown up a ſmall breaſt work, which ſheltered them from the fire of the Britiſh cannon. But the next morning, the Britiſh army was ſent to drive them from the hill, and, landing under cover of their cannon, they ſet fire to Charleſtown, which was conſumed, and marched to attack our troops in the entrenchments. A ſevere engagement enſued, in which the Britiſh, according to their own accounts, had ſeven hundred and forty killed, and eleven hundred and fifty wounded. They were repulſed at firſt, and thrown into diſorder; but they finally carried the fortification, with the point of the bayonet. The Americans ſuffered a ſmall loſs, compared with the Britiſh; the whole loſs in killed, wounded, and priſoners, being but about four hundred and fifty.   The

The lofs moft lamented on this bloody day, was that of Dr. Warren, who was at this time a Major General, and commanded the troops on this occafion. He died like a brave man, fighting valiantly at the head of his party, in a little redoubt at the right of our lines.

General Warren, who had rendered himfelf con-fpicuous by his univerfal merit, abilities, and eloquence, had been a delegate to the firft general Congrefs, and was at this time Prefident of the provincial Congrefs of Maffachufetts. But quitting the humane and peace-able walk of his profeffion as a phyfician, and breaking through the endearing ties of family connexions, he proved himfelf equally calculated for the field, as for public bufinefs or private ftudy.

About this time, the Continental Congrefs appoint-ed George Wafhington, Efq. a nativ of Virginia, to the chief command of the American army. This gentleman had been a diftinguifhed and fuccefsful of-ficer in the preceding war, and he feemed deftined by heaven to be the favior of his country. He accepted the appointment with a diffidence which was a proof of his prudence and his greatnefs. He refufed any pay for eight years laborious and arduous fervice; and by his matchlefs fkill, fortitude and perfeverance, conduct-ed America thro indefcribeable difficulties, to inde-pendence and peace.

While true merit is efteemed, or virtue honored, mankind will never ceafe to revere the memory of this Hero; and while gratitude remains in the human breaft, the praifes of WASHINGTON fhall dwell on ev-ery American tongue.

General Wafhington, with other officers appointed by Congrefs, arrived at Cambridge, and took com-mand of the American army in July. From this time, the affairs of America began to affume the ap-pearance of a regular and general oppofition to the forces of Great Britain.

In autumn, a body of troops, under the command of General Montgomery, befieged and took the gar-

rifon

rifon at St. John's, which commands the entrance into Canada. The prifoners amounted to about feven hundred. General Montgomery purfued his fuccefs, and took Montreal; and defigned to pufh his victories to Quebec.

A body of troops, commanded by General Arnold, was ordered to march to Canada, by the river Kennebeck, and through the wildernefs. After fuffering every hardfhip, and the moft diftreffing hunger, they arrived in Canada, and were joined by General Montgomery, before Quebec. This city, which was commanded by Governor Carleton, was immediately befieged. But there being little hope of taking the town by a fiege, it was determined to ftorm it.

The attack was made on the laft day of December, but proved unfuccefsful, and fatal to the brave General, who, with his aid, was killed in attempting to fcale the walls.

Of the three divifions which attacked the town, one only entered, and that was obliged to furrender to fuperior force. After this defeat, General Arnold, who now commanded the troops, continued fome months before Quebec, altho his troops fuffered incredibly by cold and ficknefs. But the next fpring, the Americans were obliged to retreat from Canada.

About this time, the large and flourifhing town of Norfolk, in Virginia, was wantonly burnt by order of lord Dunmore, the then royal Governor of that province.

General Gage went to England in September, and was fucceeded in the command, by General Howe.

Falmouth, a confiderable town in the province of Maine, in Maffachufetts, fhared the fate of Norfolk; being laid in afhes by order of the Britifh admiral.

The Britifh king entered into treaties with fome of the German princes for about feventeen thoufand men, who were to be fent to America the next year, to affift in fubduing the colonies. The parliament alfo paffed an act, forbidding all intercourfe with America; and while they repealed the Bofton port and fifhery bills, they declared all American property on the high feas,
forfeited!

forfeited to the captors. This act induced Congrefs to change the mode of carrying on the war ; and meaf- ures were taken to annoy the enemy in Boiton. For this purpofe, batteries were opened cn feveral hills, from whence fhot and bombs were thrown into the town.   But the batteries which were opened on Dor- chefter point had the beft effect, and foon obliged Gen- eral Howe to abandon the town. In March, 1776, the Britifh troops embarked for Halifax, and General Wafhington entered the town in triumph.

In the enfuing fummer, a fmall fquadron of fhips commanded by Sir Peter Parker, and a body of troops under the Generals Clinton and Cornwallis, attempted to take Charlefton, the capital of South Carolina. The fhips made a violent attack upon the fort on Sullivan's Ifland, but were repulfed with great lofs, and the ex- pedition was abandoned.

In July, Congrefs publifhed their declaration of in- dependence, which feparated America from Great Britain. This great event took place two hundred and eighty four years after the firft difcovery of America by Columbus ; one hundred and fixty fix, from the firft effectual fettlement in Virginia ; and one hundred and fifty fix from the firft fettlement of Plymouth, in Maf- fachufetts, which were the earlieft Englifh fettlements in America.

Juft after this declaration, General Howe with a powerful force arrived near New York, and landed the troops upon Staten Ifland.   General Wafhington was ih New York with about thirteen thoufand men, who were encamped either in the city or the neighboring fortifications.

The operations of the Britifh began by the action on Long Ifland, in the month of Auguft. The Ameri- cans were defeated, and General Sullivan and lord Sterling, with a large body of men, were made prifon- ers. The night after the engagement, a retreat was ordered, and executed with fuch filence, that the A- mericans left the ifland without alarming their ene- mies, and without lofs.

In

In September, the city of New York was abandoned by the American army, and taken by the Britifh.

In November, Fort Wafhington, on York Ifland, was taken, and more than two thoufand men made prifoners. Fort Lee, oppofit to Fort Wafhington, on the Jerfey fhore, was foon after taken, but the garrifon efcaped.

About the fame time, General Clinton was fent with a body of troops to take poffeffion of Rhode Ifland ; and fucceeded. In addition to all thefe loffes and defeats, the American army fuffered by defertion, and more by ficknefs, which was epidemic, and very mortal.

The northern army at Ticonderoga, was in a difagreeable fituation, particularly after the battle on Lake Champlain, in which the American force, confifting of a few light veffels, under the command of Generals Arnold and Waterbury, was totally difperfed. But General Carleton, inftead of purfuing his victory, landed at Crown Point, reconnoitered our pofts at Ticonderoga and Mount Independence, and returned to winter quarters in Canada.

The American army might now be faid to be no more. All that now remained of an army, which at the opening of the campaign, amounted to at leaft twenty five thoufand men, did not now exceed three thoufand. The term of their engagements being expired, they returned, in large bodies, to their families and friends ; the few, who from perfonal attachment, local circumftances, or fuperior perfeverance and bravery, continued with the Generals Wafhington and Lee, were too inconfiderable to appear formidable in the view of a powerful and victorious enemy.

In this alarming and critical fituation of affairs, General Lee, through an imprudent careleffnefs, which ill became a man in his important ftation, was captured by a party of the Britifh light horfe, commanded by Colonel Harcourt ; this unfortunate circumftance gave a fevere fhock to the remaining hopes of the little army, and rendered their fituation truly diftreffing.

While

While thefe things were tranfacting in New Jerfey, General Wafhington, far from being difcouraged by the lofs of General Lee, and always ready to improve every advantage to raife the drooping fpirits of his handful of men, had made a ftand on the Penfylvania fide of the Delaware.   Here he collected his fcattered forces, called in the affiftance of the Penfylvania militia, and on the night of the 25th of December, (1776) when the enemy were lulled into fecurity by the idea of his weaknefs, and by the inclemency of the night, which was remarkably boifterous, as well as by the fumes of a Chriftmas eve, he croffed the river, and at the breaking of day, marched down to Trenton, and fo completely furprifed them, that the greater part of the detachment which were ftationed at this place, furrendered after a fhort refiftance.   The horfemen and a few others made their efcape at the oppofit end of the town.   Upwards of nine hundred Heffians were taken prifoners at this time.

This fuccefsful expedition firft gave a favorable turn to our affairs, which, after this, feemed to brighten thro the whole courfe of the war.   Soon after, General Wafhington attacked the Britifh troops at Princeton, and obtained a complete victory ; not, however, without being bravely oppofed by Colonel Mawhood.

The addrefs in planning and executing thefe enterprifes, reflected the higheft honor on the commander, and the fuccefs revived the defponding hopes of America.   The lofs of General Mercer, a gallant officer, at Princeton, was the principal circumftance that allayed the joys of victory.

The following year, 1777, was diftinguifhed by very memorable events, in favor of America.   On the opening of the campaign, Governor Tryon was fent with a body of troops, to deftroy the ftores at Danbury, in Connecticut.   This plan was executed, and the town moftly burnt.   The enemy fuffered in their retreat, and the Americans loft General Woofter, a brave and experienced officer.

General

General Prefcot was taken from his quarters, on Rhode Ifland, by the addrefs and enterprife of Colonel Barton, and conveyed prifoner to the continent.

General Burgoyne, who commanded the northern Britifh army, took pofieffion of Ticonderoga, which had been abandoned by the Americans. He pufhed his fucceffes, croffed Lake George, and encamped upon the banks of the Hudfon, near Saratoga. His progrefs, however, was checked, by the defeat of Colonel Baum, near Bennington, in which the undifciplined militia of Vermont, under General Stark, difplayed unexampled bravery, and captured almoft the whole detachment.

The militia affembled from all parts of New England, to ftop the progrefs of General Burgoyne.

Thefe, with the regular troops, formed a refpeftable army, commanded by General Gates. After two fevere actions, in which the Generals Lincoln and Arnold, behaved with uncommon gallantry, and were wounded, General Burgoyne found himfelf enclofed with brave troops, and was forced to furrender his whole army, amounting, according to fome, to ten thoufand, and according to others, to five thoufand feven hundred and fifty two men, into the hands of the Americans. This memorable event happened on the 17th of October, 1777 ; and diffufed an univerfal joy over America, and laid a foundation for the treaty with France.

But before thefe tranfactions, the main body of the Britifh forces had embarked at New York, failed up the Chefapeak, and landed at the head of Elk river. The army foon began their march for Philadelphia. General Wafhington had determined to oppofe them, and for this purpofe made a ftand, firft at Red Clay Creek, and then upon the heights, near Brandywine Creek. Here the armies engaged, and the Americans were overpowered, and fuffered great lofs. The enemy foon purfued their march, and took pofieffion of Philadelphia towards the clofe of September.

Not long after, the two armies were again engaged at Germantown, and in the beginning of the action,

the

the Americans had the advantage ; but by fome un-lucky accident, the fortune of the day was turned in favor of the Britifh.   Both fides fuffered confiderable loffes ; on the fide of the Americans, was General Nafh.

In an attack upon the forts at Mud Ifland and Red Bank, the Heffians were unfuccefsful, and their com-mander, Colonel Donop, killed.   The Britifh alfo loft the Augufta, a fhip of the line.   But the forts were afterwards taken, and the navigation of the Delaware opened.   General Wafhington was reinforced, with part of the troops which had compofed the northern army, under General Gates ; and both armies retired to winter quarters.

In October, the fame month in which General Bur-goyne was taken at Saratoga, General Vaughan, with a fmall fleet, failed up Hudfon's river, and wantonly burnt Kingfton, a beautiful Dutch fettlement, on the weft fide of the river.

The beginning of the next year, 1778, was diftin-guifhed by a treaty of alliance between France and A-merica ; by which we obtained a powerful and gen-erous ally.   When the Englifh miniftry were in-formed that this treaty was on foot, they difpatch-ed commiffioners to America, to attempt a recon-ciliation.   But America would not now accept their offers.   Early in the fpring, Count de Eftaing, with a fleet of fifteen fail of the line, was fent by the court of France to affift America.

General Howe left the army, and returned to Eng-land ; the command then devolved upon Sir Henry Clinton.

In June, the Britifh army left Philadelphia, and marched for New York.   On their march they were annoyed by the Americans ; and at Monmouth, a very regular action took place, between part of the armies ; the enemy were repulfed with great lofs, and had Gen-eral Lee obeyed his orders, a fignal victory muft have been obtained.   General Lee, for his ill conduct that

day,

day, was suspended, and was never afterwards permitted to join the army.

General Lee's conduct, at several times before this, had been very suspicious. In December 1776, he lay at Chatham, about eleven miles from Elizabeth Town, with a brigade of troops, when a great quantity of baggage was stored at Elizabeth Town, under a guard of only five hundred Hessians. General Lee was apprised of this, and might have surprised the guard and taken the baggage. But he neglected the opportunity, and after several marches and counter marches between Troy, Chatham and Morristown, he took up his quarters at or near White's tavern, where he was surprised and taken prisoner by a party of the British horse. He was heard to say repeatedly, that General Washington would ruin a fine army. It was suspected that he had designs to supplant the General, and his friends attempted to place him at the head of the army. General Washington's prudent delays and cautious movements afforded General Lee's friends many opportunities to spread reports unfavorable to his character. It was insinuated, with some success, that General Washington wanted courage and abilities. Reports of this kind, at one time, rendered General Lee very popular, and it is supposed he wished to frustrate General Washington's plans, in order to increase the suspicions already entertained of his generalship, and turn the public clamor in his own favor. His conduct at Monmouth, must have proceeded from such a design ; for he commanded the flower of the American army, and was not destitute of courage.

In August, General Sullivan, with a large body of troops, attempted to take possession of Rhode Island, but did not succeed. Soon after, the stores and shipping at Bedford in Massachusetts, were burnt by a party of the British troops. The same year, Savannah, then the capital of Georgia, was taken by the British, under the command of Colonel Campbell.

In the following year (1779) General Lincoln was appointed to the command of the southern army.

Governor

Governor Tryon and Sir George Collier made an incurfion into Connecticut, and burnt, with wanton barbarity, the towns of Fairfield and Norwalk. But the American arms were crowned with fuccefs, in a bold attack upon Stoney Point, which was furprifed and taken by General Wayne, in the night of the 15th of July. Five hundred men were made prifoners, with little lofs on either fide.

A party of Britifh forces attempted this fummer, to build a fort on Penobfcot river, for the purpofe of cutting timber in the neighboring forefts. A plan was laid by Maffachufetts, to diflodge them, and a confiderable fleet collected for the purpofe. But the plan failed of fuccefs, and the whole marine force fell into the hands of the Britifh, except fome veffels which were burnt by the Americans themfelves.

In October, General Lincoln and Count de Eftaing made an affault upon Savannah; but they were repulfed with confiderable lofs. In this action, the celebrated Polifh Count Pulafki, who had acquired the reputation of a brave foldier, was mortally wounded.

In this fummer, General Sullivan marched with a body of troops, into the Indians' country, and burnt and deftroyed all their provifions and fettlements that fell in their way.

On the opening of the campaign, the next year, (1780) the Britifh troops left Rhode Ifland. An expedition under General Clinton and Lord Cornwallis, was undertaken againft Charlefton, South Carolina, where General Lincoln commanded. This town, after a clofe fiege of about fix weeks, was furrendered to the Britifh commander; and General Lincoln, and the whole American garrifon were made prifoners.

General Gates was appointed to the command in the fouthern department, and another army collected. In Auguft, Lord Cornwallis attacked the American troops at Camden, in South Carolina, and routed them with confiderable lofs. He afterwards marched through the fouthern States, and fuppofed them entirely fubdued.

N   The

The fame fummer, the Britifh troops made frequent incurfions from New York into the Jerfies ; ravaging and plundering the country.

In July, a French fleet, under Monfieur d'Ternay, with a body of land forces, commanded by Count de Rochambeau, arrived at Rhode Ifland, to the great joy of the Americans.

This year was alfo diftinguifhed by the infamous treafon of General Arnold. General Wafhington having fome bufinefs to tranfact at Wethersfield, in Connecticut, left Arnold to command the important poft of Weft Point ; which guards a pafs in Hudfon's river, about fixty miles from New York. Arnold's conduct in the city of Philadelphia, the preceding winter, had been cenfured ; and the treatment he received in confequence, had given him offence.

He determined to take revenge ; and for this purpofe, he entered into a negociation with Sir Henry Clinton, to deliver Weft Point, and the army, into the hands of the Britifh. While General Wafhington was abfent, he difmounted the cannon in fome of the forts, and took other fteps to render the taking of the poft eafy for the enemy.

But by a providential difcovery, the whole plan was defeated. Major Andre, aid to General Clinton, a brave officer, who had been fent up the river as a fpy, to concert the plan of operations with Arnold, was taken, condemned by a court martial, and executed. Arnold made his efcape, by getting on board the Vulture, a Britifh veffel, which lay in the river. His conduct has ftamped him with infamy ; and, like all traitors, he is defpifed by all mankind. General Wafhington arrived in camp juft after Arnold had made his efcape, and reftored order in the garrifon.

After the defeat of General Gates in Carolina, General Greene was appointed to the command in the fouthern department. From this period, things in that quarter wore a more favorable afpect. Colonel Tarleton, the activ commander of the Britifh legion, was defeated by General Morgan, the intrepid commander of the rifle men.   After

After a variety of movements, the two armies met at Guilford, in Carolina. Here was one of the beft fought actions during the war. General Greene and Lord Cornwallis exerted themfelves at the head of their refpectiv armies ; and although the Americans were obliged to retire from the field of battle, yet the Britifh army fuffered an immenfe lofs, and could not purfue the victory. This action happened on the 15th March, 1781.

In the fpring, Arnold the traitor, who was made a Brigadier General in the Britifh fervice, with a fmall number of troops, failed for Virginia, and plundered the country. This called the attention of the French fleet to that quarter ; and a naval engagement took place between the Englifh and French, in which fome of the Englifh fhips were much damaged, and one entirely difabled.

After the battle of Guilford, General Greene moved towards South Carolina, to drive the Britifh from their pofts in that State. Here Lord Rawdon obtained an inconfiderable advantage over the Americans, near Camden. But General Greene more than recovered this advantage, by the brilliant and fuccefsful action at the Eutaw Springs ; where General Marian diftinguifhed himfelf, and the brave Colonel Wafhington was wounded and taken prifoner.

Lord Cornwallis, finding General Greene fuccefsful in Carolina, marched to Virginia, collected his forces, and fortified himfelf in Yorktown. In the mean time Arnold made an incurfion into Connecticut, burnt a part of New London, took Fort Grifwold by ftorm, and put the garrifon to the fword. The garrifon confifted chiefly of men fuddenly collected from the little town of Groton, which, by the favage cruelty of the Britifh officer who commanded the attack, loft, in one hour, almoft all its heads of families. The brave Colonel Ledyard, who commanded the fort, was flain with his own fword, after he had furrendered.

The Marquis de la Fayette, the brave and generous nobleman, whofe fervices command the gratitude of

every

every American, had been difpatched with about two thoufand light infantry, from the main army, to watch the motions of lord Cornwallis in Virginia. He profecuted this expedition with the greateft military ability. Although his force was much inferior to that of the enemy, he obliged them to leave Richmond and Williamfburgh, and to feek protection under their fhipping.

About the laft of Auguft, Count de Graffe arrived with a large fleet in the Chefapeak, and blocked up the Britifh troops at Yorktown. Admiral Greaves, with a Britifh fleet, appeared off the Capes, and an action fucceeded ; but it was not decifiv.

General Wafhington had before this time moved the main body of his army, together with the French troops, to the fouthward ; and as foon as he heard of the arrival of the French fleet in the Chefapeak, he made rapid marches to the head of Elk, where embarking, the troops foon arrived at Yorktown.

A clofe fiege immediately commenced, and was carried on with fuch vigor, by the combined forces of America and France, that lord Cornwallis was obliged to furrender. This glorious event which took place on the 19th of October, 1781, decided the conteft in favor of America ; and laid the foundation of a general peace.*

A few

* It has been controverted whether the capture of General Cornwallis was the refult of a plan preconcerted between General Wafhington and Count de Graffe ; or rather whether the arrival of the Count in the Chefapeak was predetermined and expected by General Wafhington, and confequently all the preparations to attack New York a mere fineffe to deceive the enemy ; or whether the real intention was againft New York, and the fiege of Yorktown planned upon the unexpected arrival of the French fleet in the bay. The following letter will fet the matter in its true light.

Sir,   *Mount Vernon, July* 31, 1788.

' I DULY received your letter of the 14th inftant, and can only anfwer you briefly and generally from memory ; that a combined operation of the land and naval forces of France in America, for the year 1781, was preconcerted the year before ;
that

A few months after the furrender of Cornwallis, the Britifh evacuated all their pofts in South Carolina and Georgia, and retired to the main army in New York.

The next fpring, (1782) Sir Guy Carleton arrived in New York, and took the command of the Britifh army, in America.   Immediately on his arrival, he acquainted General Wafhington and Congrefs, that negociations for a peace had been commenced at Paris.

On the 30th of November, 1782, the provifional articles of peace were figned at Paris ; by which Great Britain acknowleged the independence and fovereignty of the United States of America ; and thefe articles were afterwards ratified by a definitiv treaty.

Thus

that the point of attack was not abfolutely agreed upon,* becaufe it could not be foreknown where the enemy would be moft fufceptible of impreffion ; and becaufe we (having the command of the water with fufficient means of conveyance) could tranfport ourfelves to any fpot with the greateft celerity ; that it was determined by me, nearly twelve months before hand, at all hazards, to give out and caufe it to be believed by the higheft military as well as civil officers, that New York was the deftined place of attack, for the important purpofe of inducing the eaftern and middle States to make greater exertions in furnifhing fpecific fupplies, than they otherwife would have done, as well as for the interefting purpofe of rendering the enemy lefs prepared elfewhere ; that by thefe means, and thefe alone, artillery, boats, ftores, and provifions, were in feafonable preparation to move with the utmoft rapidity to any part of the continent ; for the difficulty confifted more in providing, than knowing how to apply the military apparatus ; that before the arrival of the Count de Graffe, it was the fixed determination *to ftrike the enemy in the moft vulnerable quarter*, fo as to enfure fuccefs with moral certainty, as our affairs were then in the moft ruinous train imaginable ; that New York was thought to be beyond our effort, and confequently that the only hefitation that remained, was between an attack upon the Britifh army in Virginia and that in Charlefton : And finally, that, by the intervention of feveral communications, and fome incidents which cannot be detailed in a letter, the hoftile poft in Virginia, from being a *provifional and ftrongly expected*, became the *definitiv and certain object* of the campaign.   I only

* Becaufe it would be eafy for the Count de Graffe, in good time before his departure from the Weft Indies, to giv notice, by exprefs, at what place he could moft conveniently firft touch to receive advice.

Thus ended a long and arduous conflict, in which Great Britain expended near an hundred millions of money, with an hundred thousand lives, and won nothing. America endured every cruelty and diftrefs from her enemies; loft many lives and much treafure; but delivered herfelf from a foreign dominion, and gained a rank among the nations of the earth.

Holland acknowleged the independence of the United States on the 19th of April, 1782; Sweden, February 5th, 1783; Denmark, the 25th of February; Spain, in March, and Ruffia in July, 1783.

No

I only add, that it never was in contemplation to attack New York, unlefs the garrifon fhould firft have been fo far degarrifhed to carry on the fouthern operations, as to render our fuccefs in the fiege of that place, as infallible as any future military event can ever be made. For I repeat it, and dwell upon it again, fome fplendid advantage (whether upon a larger or fmaller fcale was almoft immaterial) was fo effentially neceffary, to revive the expiring hopes and languid exertions of the country, at the crifis in queftion, that I never would have confented to embark in any enterprife, wherein, from the moft rational plan and accurate calculations, the favorable iffue fhould not have appeared as clear to my view as a ray of light. The failure of an attempt againft the pofts of the enemy, could, in no other poffible fituation during the war, have been fo fatal to our caufe.

That much trouble was taken and fineffe ufed to mifguide and bewilder Sir Henry Clinton, in regard to the real object, by fictitious communications, as well as by making a deceptiv provifion of ovens, forage, and boats, in his neighborhood, is certain: Nor were lefs pains taken to deceive our own army; for I had always conceived, where the impofition did not completely take place at home, it could never fufficiently fucceed abroad.

Your defire of obtaining truth, is very laudable; I wifh I had more leifure to gratify it, as I am equally folicitous the undifguifed verity fhould be known. Many circumftances will unavoidably be mifconceived and mifreprefented. Notwithftanding moft of the papers, which may properly be deemed official, are preferved; yet the knowlege of innumerable things, of a more delicate and fecret nature, is confined to the perifhable remembrance of fome few of the prefent generation.

With efteem, I am, Sir, your moft obedient humble fervant,

G. WASHINGTON.

To ———.

No fooner was peace reftored by the definitiv treaty, and the Britifh troops withdrawn from the country, than fhe United States began to experience the defects of their general government.   While an enemy was in the country, fear, which had firft impelled the colonies to affociate in mutual defence, continued to operate as a band of political union.   It gave to the refolutions and recommendations of Congrefs the force of laws, and generally commanded a ready acquiefcence on the part of the State legiflatures.   Articles of confederation and perpetual union had been framed in Congrefs, and fubmitted to the confideration of the States, in the year 1778.   Some of the States immediately acceded to them ; but others, which had not unappropriated lands, hefitated to fubfcribe a compact, which would giv an advantage to the States which poffeffed large tracts of unlocated lands, and were thus capable of a great fuperiority in wealth and population.   All objections however had been overcome, and by the acceffion of Maryland in March, 1781, the articles of confederation were ratified, as the frame of government for the United States.

These articles, however were framed during the rage of war, when a principle of common fafety fupplied the place of a coerciv power in government ; by men who could have had no experience in the art of governing an extenfiv country, and under circumftances the moft critical and embarraffing.   To have offered to the people at that time, a fyftem of government armed with the powers neceffary to regulate and control the contending interefts of thirteen States, and the poffeffions of millions of people, might have raifed a jealoufy between the States or in the minds of the people at large, that would have weakened the operations of war, and perhaps have rendered a union impracticable.   Hence the numerous defects of the confederation.

On the conclufion of peace, thefe defects began to be felt.   Each State affumed the right of difputing the propriety of the refolutions of Congrefs, and the interest tereft of an individual State was placed in oppofition to the common intereft of the union. In addition to this fource of divifion, a jealoufy of the powers of Congrefs began to be excited in the minds of people.

This jealoufy of the privileges of freemen, had been roufed by the oppreffiv acts of the Britifh parliament ; and no fooner had the danger from this quarter ceafed, than the fears of people changed their object, and were turned againft their own rulers.

In this fituation, there were not wanting men of induftry and talents, who had been enemies to the revolution, and who embraced the opportunity to multiply the apprehenfions of people and increafe the popular difcontents. A remarkable inftance of this happened in Connecticut. As foon as the tumults of war had fubfided, an attempt was made to convince the people, that the act of Congrefs paffed in 1778, granting to the officers of the army, half pay for life, was highly unjuft and tyrannical ; and that it was but the firft ftep towards the eftablifhment of penfions and an uncontrolable defpotifm. The act of Congrefs, paffed in 1783, commuting half pay for life for five years full pay, was defigned to appeafe the apprehenfions of people, and to convince them that this gratuity was intended merely to indemnify the officers for their loffes by the depreciation of the paper currency ; and not to eftablifh a precedent for the granting of penfions. This act, however, did not fatisfy the people, who fuppofed that the officers had been generally indemnified for the lofs of their pay, by the grants made them from time to time by the legiflatures of the feveral States. Befides the act, while it gave five years full pay to the officers, allowed but one year's pay to the privates ; a diftinction which had great influence in exciting and continuing the popular ferment, and one that turned a large fhare of the public rage againft the officers themfelves.

The moment an alarm was raifed refpecting this act of Congrefs, the enemies of our independence became activ in blowing up the flame, by fpreading reports unfavorable to the general government, and tending to
create

create public diffenfions. Newfpapers, in fome parts
of the country, were filled with inflammatory publications; while falfe reports and groundlefs infinuations
were induftrioufly circulated to the prejudice of Congrefs and the officers of the late army. Among a people feelingly alive to every thing that could affect the
rights for which they had been contending, thefe reports could not fail of having a powerful effect; the
clamor foon became general; the officers of the army,
it was believed, had attempted to raife their fortunes on
the diftreffes of their fellow citizens, and Congrefs become the tyrants of their country.

Connecticut was the feat of this uneafinefs; altho
other States were much agitated on the occafion. But
the inhabitants of that State, accuftomed to order and
a due fubordination to the laws, did not proceed to
outrages; they took their ufual mode of collecting the
fenfe of the State; affembled in town meetings; appointed committees to meet in convention, and confult
what meafures fhould be adopted to procure a redrefs
of their grievances. In this convention, which was
held at Middletown, fome nugatory refolves were paffed, expreffing a difapprobation of the half pay act, and
the fubfequent commutation of the grant for five years
whole pay. The fame fpirit alfo difcovered itfelf in
the affembly, at their October feffion, in 1783. A remonftrance againft the acts in favor of the officers, was
framed in the houfe of reprefentativs, and notwithftanding the upper houfe refufed to concur in the meafure, it was fent to Congrefs.

During this fituation of affairs, the public odium
againft the officers, was augmented by another circumftance. The officers, juft before the difbanding of the
army, had formed a fociety, called by the name of the
Cincinnati, after the Roman Dictator, Cincinnatus,
which, it was faid, was intended to perpetuate the memory of the revolution, the friendfhip of the officers, and
the union of the States; and alfo to raife a fund for
the relief of poor widows and orphans, whofe hufbands
and fathers had fallen during the war, and for their
                                    defcendants.

defcendants. The fociety was divided into State focieties, which were to meet on the 4th of July, and
with other bufinefs, depute a number of their members
to convene annually in general meeting. The members of the inftitution were to be diftinguifhed by wearing a medal, emblematical of the defign of the fociety,
and the honors and advantages were to be hereditary
in the eldeft male heirs, and in default of male iffue, in
the collateral male heirs. Honorary members were to
be admitted, but without the hereditary advantages of
the fociety, and provided their number fhould never
exceed the ratio of one to four of the officers or their
defcendants.

Whatever were the real views of the framers of this
inftitution, its defign was generally underftood to be
harmlefs and honorable. The oftenfible views of the
fociety could not however fkreen it from popular jealoufy. A fpirited pamphlet appeared in South Carolina, the avowed production of Mr. Burke, one of the
judges of the fupreme court in that State, in which the
author attempted to prove that the principles, on which
the fociety was formed, would, in procefs of time,
originate and eftablifh an order of nobility in this country, which would be repugnant to the genius of our
republican governments, and dangerous to liberty.
This pamphlet appeared in Connecticut, during the
commotions raifed by the half pay and commutation
acts, and contributed not a little to fpread the flame of
oppofition. Nothing could exceed the odium which
prevailed at this time, againft the men who had haz-
arded their perfons and properties in the revolution.

Notwithftanding the difcontents of the people were
general, and ready to burft forth in fedition, yet men
of information, viz. the officers of government, the
clergy, and perfons of liberal education, were moftly
oppofed to the unconftitutional fteps taken by the committees and convention at Middletown. They fupported the propriety of the meafures of Congrefs, both
by converfation and writing, proved that fuch grants
to the army were neceffary to keep the troops together,

and

and that the expenfe would not be enormous nor oppreffiv.   During the clofe of the year 1783, every poffible exertion was made to enlighten the people, and
fuch was the effect of the arguments ufed by the minority, that in the beginning of the following year, the
oppofition fubfided, the committees were difmiffed, and
tranquillity reftored to the State.   In May, the legiflature were able to carry feveral meafures which had before been extremely unpopular.   An act was paffed,
granting the impoft of five per cent. to Congrefs ; another giving great encouragement to commerce, and
feveral towns were incorporated with extenfiv privileges, for the purpofe of regulating the exports of the
State, and facilitating the collection of debts.

The oppofition to the Congreffional acts in favor of
the officers, and to the order of the Cincinnati, did not
rife to the fame pitch in the other States as in Connecticut ; yet it produced much difturbance in Maffachufetts, and fome others.   Jealoufy of power had been
univerfally fpread among the people of the United
States.   The deftruction of the old forms of governments, and the licentioufnefs of war had, in a great
meafure, broken their habits of obedience ; their paffions had been inflamed by the cry of defpotifm ; and
like centinels, who have been fuddenly furprifed by the
approach of an enemy, the ruftling of a leaf was fufficient to giv them an alarm.   This fpirit of jealoufy,
which has not yet fubfided, and which will probably
continue vifible during the prefent generation, operated
with other caufes to relax the energy of our federal
operations.

During the war, vaft fums of paper currency had
been emitted by Congrefs, and large quantities of fpecie had been introduced, towards the clofe of the war,
by the French army, and the Spanifh trade.   This
plenty of money enabled the States to comply with the
firft requifitions of Congrefs ; fo that during two or
three years, the federal treafury was, in fome meafure,
fupplied.   But when the danger of war had ceafed, and
the vaft importations of foreign goods had leffened the
                                          quantity

quantity of circulating fpecie, the States began to be very remifs in furnishing their proportion of monies. The annihilation of the credit of the paper bills had totally ftopped their circulation, and the fpecie was leaving the country in cargoes, for remittances to Great Britain ; ftill the luxurious habits of the people, con- tracted during the war, called for new fupplies of goods, and private gratification feconded the narrow policy of State intereft in defeating the operations of the general government.

Thus the revenues of Congrefs were annually di- minifhing ; fome of the States wholly neglecting to make provifion for paying the intereft of the national debt ; others making but a partial provifion, until the fcanty fupplies received from a few of the rich States, would hardly fatisfy the demands of the civil lift.

This weaknefs of the federal government, in con- junction with the flood of certificates or public fecuri- ties, which Congrefs could neither fund nor pay, occa- fioned them to depreciate to a very inconfiderable val- ue. The officers and foldiers of the late army were obliged to receive for wages thefe certificates, or prom- iffary notes, which paffed at a fifth, or eighth, or a tenth of their nominal value ; being thus deprived at once of the greateft part of the reward due for their fervices. Some indeed profited by fpeculations in thefe evidences of the public debt ; but fuch as were under a neceffity of parting with them, were robbed of that fupport which they had a right to expect and demand from their countrymen.

Penfylvania indeed made provifion for paying the in- tereft of her debts, both State and federal ; affuming her fuppofed proportion of the continental debt, and giving the creditors her own State notes in exchange for thofe of the United States. The refources of that State are immenfe, but fhe has not been able to make punctual payments, even in a depreciated paper cur- rency.

Maffachufetts, in her zeal to comply fully with the requifitions of Congrefs, and fatisfy the demands of
her

her own creditors, laid a heavy tax upon the people.
This was the immediate caufe of the rebellion in that
State, in 1786.　But a heavy debt lying on the State,
added to burdens of the fame nature, upon almoft
every incorporation within it ; a decline, or rather an
extinction of public credit ; a relaxation and corruption
of manners, and a free ufe of foreign luxuries ; a decay
of trade and manufactures, with a prevailing fcarcity of
money ; and, above all, individuals involved in debt to
each other : Thefe were the real, though more remote
caufes of the infurrection.　It was the tax which the people were required to pay, that caufed them to feel evils
which we have enumerated : This called forth all their
other grievances ; and the firft act of violence committed, was the burning or deftroying of a tax bill.　This
fedition threw the State into a convulfion which lafted
about a year ; courts of juftice were violently obftructed ; the collection of debts was fufpended ; and a body
of armed troops, under the command of General Lincoln, was employed during the winter of 1786, to difperfe the infurgents.　Yet fo numerous were the latter
in the counties of Worcefter, Hampfhire and Berkfhire, and fo obftinately combined to oppofe the execution of law by force, that the Governor and Council
of the State thought proper not to intruft General Lincoln with military powers, except to act on the defenfiv, and to repel force with force, in cafe the infurgents
fhould attack him.　The leaders of the rebels however
were not men of talents ; they were defperate, but
without fortitude ; and while they were fupported with
a fuperior force, they appeared to be impreffed with
that confcioufnefs of guilt, which awes the moft daring
wretch, and makes him fhrink from his purpofe.　This
appears by the conduct of a large party of the rebels
before the magazine at Springfield ; where General
Shepard with a fmall guard, was ftationed to protect
the continental ftores.　The infurgents appeared upon
the plain, with a vaft fuperiority of numbers, but a few
fhot from the artillery made the multitude retreat in
diforder, with the lofs of four men.　This fpirited conduct

duct of General Shepard, with the induſtry, perſeverance and prudent firmneſs of General Lincoln, diſperſed the rebels, drove the leaders from the State, and reſtored tranquillity. An act of indemnity was paſſed in the Legiſlature for all the inſurgents, except a few leaders, on condition they ſhould become peaceable ſubjects, and take the oath of allegiance. The leaders afterwards petitioned for pardon, which, from motivs of policy, was granted by the Legiſlature.

But the loſs of public credit, popular diſturbances, and inſurrections, were not the only evils which were generated by the peculiar circumſtances of the times. The emiſſions of bills of credit and tender laws, were added to the black catalogue of political diſorders.

The expedient of ſupplying the deficiencies of ſpecie, by emiſſions of paper bills, was adopted very early in the colonies. The expedient was obvious and produced good effects. In a new country, where population is rapid, and the value of lands increaſing, the farmer finds an advantage in paying legal intereſt for money ; for if he can pay the intereſt by his profits, the increaſing value of his lands will, in a few years, diſcharge the principal.

In no colony was this advantage more ſenſibly experienced than in Penſylvania. The emigrants to that province were numerous ; the natural population rapid ; and theſe circumſtances combined, advanced the value of real property to an aſtoniſhing degree. As the firſt ſettlers there, as well as in other provinces, were poor, the purchaſe of a few foreign articles drained them of ſpecie. Indeed for many years, the balance of trade muſt have neceſſarily been greatly againſt the colonies.

But bills of credit, emitted by the State and loaned to the induſtrious inhabitants, ſupplied the want of ſpecie, and enabled the farmer to purchaſe ſtock. Theſe bills were generally a legal tender in all colonial or private contracts, and the ſums iſſued did not generally exceed the quantity requiſit for a medium of trade ; they retained their full nominal value in the purchaſe

of

of commodities. But as they were not received by the British merchants, in payment for goods, there was a great demand for fpecie and bills, which occafioned the latter at various times to appreciate. Thus was introduced a difference between the Englifh fterling money and the currencies of the colonies which remains to this day.*

The advantages the colonies had derived from bills of credit, under the Britifh government, fuggefted to Congrefs, in 1775, the idea of iffuing bills for the purpofe of carrying on the war. And this was perhaps their only expedient. Money could not be raifed by taxation ; it could not be borrowed. The firft emiffions had no other effect upon the medium of commerce, than to drive the fpecie from circulation. But when the paper fubftituted for fpecie, had, by repeated emiffions, augmented the fum in circulation, much beyond the ufual fum of fpecie, the bills began to lofe their value. The depreciation continued in proportion to the fums emitted, until feventy, and even one hundred and fifty nominal paper dollars, were hardly an equivalent for one Spanifh milled dollar. Still from the year 1775 to 1781, this depreciating paper currency was almoft the only medium of trade. It fupplied the place of fpecie, and enabled Congrefs to fupport a numerous army ; until the fum in circulation amounted to two hundred millions of dollars. But about the year 1780, fpecie began to be plentiful, being introduced by the French army, a private trade with the Spanifh iflands, and an illicit intercourfe with the Britifh garrifon at New York. This circumftance accelerated the depreciation of the paper bills, until their value had funk almoft to nothing. In 1781, the merchants and
'brokers

---

* A dollar, in fterling money, is 4/6. But the price of a dollar rofe in New England currency to 6/ ; in New York to 8/ ; in New Jerfey, Penfylvania and Maryland to 7/6 ; in Virginia to 6/; in North Carolina to 8/; in South Carolina and Georgia to 4/8. This difference, originating between paper and fpecie, or bills, continued afterwards to exift in the nominal eftimation of gold and filver.

Franklin's Mifcel. Works, p. 217.

brokers in the southern States, apprehensiv of the approaching fate of the currency, pushed immense quantities of it suddenly into New England, made vast purchases of goods in Boston, and instantly the bills vanished from circulation.

The whole history of this continental paper is a history of public and private frauds. Old specie debts were often paid in a depreciated currency, and even new contracts for a few weeks or days were often discharged with a small part of the value received. From this plenty and fluctuating state of the medium, sprung hosts of speculators and itinerant traders, who left their honest occupations for the prospect of immense gains, in a fraudulent business, that depended on no fixed principles, and the profits of which could be reduced to no certain calculations.

To increase these evils, a project was formed to fix the prices of articles, and restrain persons from giving or receiving more for any commodity than the price stated by authority. These regulating acts were reprobated by every man acquainted with commerce and finance ; as they were intended to prevent an effect without removing the cause. To attempt to fix the value of money, while streams of bills were incessantly flowing from the treasury of the United States, was as ridiculous as an attempt to restrain the rising of water in rivers amidst showers of rain.

Notwithstanding all opposition, some States framed and attempted to enforce these regulating acts. The effect was, a momentary apparent stand in the price of articles ; innumerable acts of collusion and evasion among the dishonest ; numberless injuries done to the honest ; and finally a total disregard of all such regulations, and the consequential contempt of laws and the authority of the magistrate.

During these fluctuations of business, occasioned by the variable value of money, people lost sight, in some measure, of the steady principles which had before governed their intercourse with each other. Speculations followed and relaxed the rigor of commercial obligations.   Industry

Induſtry likewiſe had ſuffered by the flood of money
which had deluged the States.   The prices of produce
had riſen in proportion to the quantity of money in
circulation, and the demand for the commodities of the
country.   This made the acquiſition of money eaſy,
and indolence and luxury, with their train of deſolating
conſequences, ſpread themſelves among all deſcriptions
of people.

But as ſoon as hoſtilities between Great Britain and
America were ſuſpended, the ſcene was changed.   The
bills emitted by Congreſs had long before ceaſed to circulate ; and the ſpecie of the country was ſoon drained
off to pay for foreign goods, the importations of which
exceeded all calculation.   Within two years from the
cloſe of the war, *a ſcarcity of money* was the general cry.
The merchants found it impoſſible to collect their
debts, and make punctual remittances to their creditors
in Great Britain ; and the conſumers were driven to
the neceſſity of retrenching their ſuperfluities in living
and of returning to their ancient habits of induſtry and
economy.

This change was however progreſſiv and ſlow.   In
many of the States which ſuffered by the numerous
debts they had contracted, and by the diſtreſſes of war,
the people called aloud for emiſſions of paper bills to
ſupply the deficiency of a medium.   The depreciation
of the continental bills, was a recent example of the
ill effects of ſuch an expedient, and the impoſſibility of
ſupporting the credit of paper, was urged by the oppoſ-
ers of the meaſure as a ſubſtantial argument againſt
adopting it.   But nothing would ſilence the popular
clamor ; and many men of the firſt talents and eminence, united their voices with that of the populace.
Paper money had formerly maintained its credit, and
been of ſingular utility ; and paſt experience, notwith-
ſtanding a change of circumſtances, was an argument
in its favor that bore down all oppoſition.

Penſylvania, although one of the richeſt States in
the union, was the firſt to emit bills of credit, as a ſub-
ſtitute for ſpecie.   But the revolution had removed the

neceſſity

neceffity of it, at the fame time that it had deftroyed the means by which its former credit had been fupported. Lands, at the clofe of the war, were not rifing in value; bills on London could not fo readily be purchafed, as while the province was dependent on Great Britain; the State was fplit into parties, one of which attempted to defeat the meafures moft popular with the other; and the depreciation of continental bills, with the injuries which it had done to individuals, infpired a general diftruft of all public promifes.

Notwithftanding a part of the money was loaned on good landed fecurity, and the faith of that wealthy State pledged for the redemption of the whole at its nominal value, yet the advantages of fpecie as a medium of commerce, efpecially as an article of remittance to London, foon made a difference of ten per cent. between the bills of credit and fpecie. This difference may be confidered rather as an appreciation of gold and filver, than a depreciation of paper; but its effects, in a commercial State, muft be highly prejudicial. It opens the door to frauds of all kinds, and frauds are ufually practifed on the honeft and unfufpecting, efpecially upon all claffes of laborers.

This currency of Penfylvania is receivable in all payments at the cuftom houfe, and for certain taxes, at its nominal value; yet it has funk to two thirds of this value, in the few commercial tranfactions where it is received.

North Carolina, South Carolina, and Georgia, had recourfe to the fame wretched expedient to fupply themfelves with money; not reflecting that induftry, frugality, and good commercial laws are the only means of turning the balance of trade in favor of a country, and that this balance is the only permanent fource of folid wealth and ready money. But the bills they emitted fhared a worfe fate than thofe of Penfylvania; they expelled almoft all the circulating cafh from the States; they loft a great part of their nominal value; they impoverifhed the merchants, and embarraffed the planters.

The

. The State of Virginia had too much wifdom to emit bills ; but tolerated a practice among the inhabitants of cutting dollars and fmaller pieces of filver, in order to prevent it from leaving the State. This pernicious practice prevailed alfo in Georgia.*

Maryland efcaped the calamity of a paper currency. The houfe of delegates brought forward a bill for the emiffion of bills of credit to a large amount ; but the fenate firmly and fuccefsfully refifted the pernicious fcheme. The oppofition between the two houfes was violent and tumultuous ; it threatened the State with anarchy ; but the queftion was carried to the people, and the good fenfe of the fenate finally prevailed.

New Jerfey is fituated between two of the largeft commercial towns in America, and confequently drained of fpecie.. This State alfo emitted a large fum in bills of credit, which ferved to pay the intereft of the public debt ; but the currency depreciated, as in other States.

Rhode Ifland exhibits a melancholy proof of that licentioufnefs and anarchy which always follows a re-laxation of the moral principles. In a rage for fup-plying the State with money, and filling every man's pocket without obliging him to earn it by his diligence, the Legiflature paffed an act for making one hundred thoufand pounds in bills ; a fum much more than fuf-ficient for a medium of trade in that State, even with-out any fpecie. The merchants in Newport and Providence oppofed the act with firmnefs ; their oppo-fition added frefh vigour to the refolution of the affem-bly, and induced them to inforce the fcheme by a legal tender of a moft extraordinary nature. They paffed an act, ordaining that if any creditor fhould refufe to take their bills, for any debt whatever, the debtor might lodge the fum due, with a juftice of the peace, who

fhould

---

* A dollar was ufually cut in five pieces, and each paffed by toll for a quarter ; fo that the man who cut it gained a quarter, or rather a fifth. If the State fhould recoin this fil-ver, it muft lofe a fifth.

fhould giv notice of it in the public papers ; and if the
creditor did not appear and receive the money within
fix months from the firft notice, his debt fhould be forfeited. This act aftonifhed all honeft men ; and even
the promoters of paper money making in other States,
and on other principles, reprobated this act of Rhode
Ifland, as wicked and oppreffiv. But the State was
governed by faction. During the cry for paper money,
a number of boifterous ignorant men, were elected into
the Legiflature, from the fmaller towns in the State.
Finding themfelves united with a majority in opinion,
they formed and executed any plan their inclination
fuggefted ; they oppofed every meafure that was agreeable to the mercantile intereft ; they not only made bad
laws to fuit their own wicked purpofes, but appointed
their own corrupt creatures to fill the judicial and executiv departments. Their money depreciated fufficiently to anfwer all their vile purpofes in the difcharge
of debts ; bufinefs almoft totally ceafed ; all confidence
was loft ; the State was thrown into confufion at home,
and was execrated abroad.

Maffachufetts Bay had the good fortune, amidft her
political calamities, to prevent an emiffion of bills of
credit. New Hampfhire made no paper ; but in the
diftreffes which followed her lofs of bufinefs after the
war, the Legiflature made horfes, lumber, and moft articles of produce a legal tender in the fulfilment of
contracts. It is doubtlefs unjuft to oblige a creditor to
receive any thing for his debt, which he had not in contemplation at the time of the contract. But as the
commodities which were to be a tender by the law of
New Hampfhire, were of an intrific value, bearing
fome proportion to the amount of the debt, the injuftice of the law was lefs flagrant, than that which enforced the tender of paper in Rhode Ifland. Indeed a
fimilar law prevailed for fome time in Maffachufetts ;
and in Connecticut it is optional with the creditor, either to imprifon the debtor, or take land on an execution, at a price to be fixed by three indifferent freeholders ; provided no other means of payment fhall appear

10

to fatisfy the demand. It muft not however be omitted, that while the moft flourifhing commercial States
introduced a paper medium, to the great injury of honeft men, a bill for an emiffion of paper in Connecticut,
where there is very little fpecie, could never command
more than one eighth of the votes of the Legiflature.
The movers of the bill have hardly efcaped ridicule ;
fo generally is the meafure reprobated as a fource of
fraud and public mifchief.

The Legiflature of New York, a State that had the
leaft neceffity and apology for making paper money, as
her commercial advantages always furnifh her with
fpecie fufficient for a medium, iffued a large fum in
bills of credit, which fupport their value better than the
currency of any other State. Still the paper has raifed
the value of fpecie, which is always in demand for exportation, and this difference of exchange between paper and fpecie, expofes commerce to moft of the inconveniencies refulting from a depreciated medium.

Such is the hiftory of paper money thus far ; a miferable fubftitute for real coin, in a country where the
reins of government are too weak to compel the fulfilment of public engagements ; and where all confidence in public faith is totally deftroyed.

While the States were thus endeavoring to repair the
lofs of fpecie, by empty promifes, and to fupport their
bufinefs by fhadows, rather than by reality, the Britifh
miniftry formed fome commercial regulations that deprived them of the profits of their trade to the Weft
Indies and to Great Britain. Heavy duties were laid
upon fuch articles as were remitted to the London
merchants for their goods, and fuch were the duties upon American bottoms, that the States were almoft
wholly deprived of the carrying trade. A prohibition
was laid upon the produce of the United States, fhipped to the Englifh Weft India Iflands in American
built veffels, and in thofe manned by American feamen. Thefe reftrictions fell heavy upon the eaftern
States, which depended much upon fhip building for
the

the fupport of their trade; and they materially injured
the bufinefs of the other States.

Without a union that was able to form and execute
a general fyftem of commercial regulations, fome of
the States attempted to impofe reftraints upon the Britifh trade that fhould indemnify the merchant for the
loffes he had fuffered, or induce the Britifh miniftry to
enter into a commercial treaty, and relax the rigor of
their navigation laws. Thefe meafures however produced nothing but mifchief. The States did not act
in concert, and the reftraints laid on the trade of one
State operated to throw the bufinefs into the hands of
its neighbor. Maffachufetts, in her zeal to counteract
the effect of the Englifh navigation laws, laid enormous
duties upon Britifh goods imported into that State;
but the other States did not adopt a fimilar meafure;
and the lofs of bufinefs foon obliged that State to repeal or fufpend the law. Thus when Penfylvania laid
heavy duties on Britifh goods, Delaware and New Jerfey made a number of free ports to encourage the landing of goods within the limits of thofe States; and the
duties in Penfylvania ferved no purpofe, but to create
fmuggling.

Thus divided, the States began to feel their weaknefs. Moft of the Legiflatures had neglected to comply with the requifitions of Congrefs for furnifhing the
federal treafury; the refolves of Congrefs were difre-
garded; the propofition for a general impoft to be laid
and collected by Congrefs was negatived firft by Rhode
Ifland, and afterwards by New York. The Britifh
troops continued, under pretence of a breach of treaty
on the part of America, to hold poffeffion of the forts
on the frontiers of the States, and thus commanded
the fur trade. Many of the States individually were
infefted with popular commotions or iniquitous tender
laws, while they were oppreffed with public debts; the
certificates or public notes had loft moft of their value,
and circulated merely as the objects of fpeculation;
Congrefs loft their refpectability, and the United States
their credit and importance.

In

In the midft of thefe calamities, a propofition was made in 1785, in the houfe of delegates, in Virginia, to appoint commiffioners, to meet fuch as might be appointed in the other States, who fhould form a fyftem of commercial regulations for the United States, and recommend it to the feveral Legiflatures for adoption. Commiffioners were accordingly appointed and a requeft was made to the Legiflatures of the other States to accede to the propofition. Accordingly feveral of the States appointed commiffioners, who met at Annapolis in the fummer of 1786, to confult what meafures fhould be taken to unite the States in fome general and efficient commercial fyftem. But as the States were not all reprefented, and the powers of the commiffioners were, in their opinion, too limited to propofe a fyftem of regulations adequate to the purpofes of government, they agreed to recommend a general convention to be held at Philadelphia the next year, with powers to frame a general plan of government for the United States. This meafure appeared to the commiffioners abfolutely neceffary. The old confederation was effentially defectiv. It was deftitute of almoft every principle neceffary to giv effect to legiflation.

It was defectiv in the article of legiflating over States, inftead of individuals. All hiftory teftifies that recommendations will not operate as laws, and compulfion cannot be exercifed over States, without violence, war and anarchy. The confederation was alfo deftitute of a fanction to its laws. When refolutions were paffed in Congrefs, there was no power to compel obedience by fine, by fufpenfion of privileges or other means. It was alfo deftitute of a guarantee for the State governments. Had one State been invaded by its neighbor, the union was not conftitutionally bound to affift in repelling the invafion, and fupporting the conftitution of the invaded State. The confederation was further deficient in the principle of apportioning the quotas of money to be furnifhed by each State ; in a want of power to form commercial laws, and to raife troops for the defence and fecurity of the union ; in the equal
                                                                suffrage

fuffrage of the States, which placed Rhode Ifland on a footing in Congrefs with Virginia ; and to crown all the defects, we may add the want of a judiciary power, to define the laws of the union, and to reconcile the contradictory decifions of a number of independent judicatories.

Thefe and many inferior defects were obvious to the commiffioners, and therefore they urged a general convention, with powers to form and offer to the confideration of the States, a fyftem of general government that fhould be lefs exceptionable. Accordingly in May, 1787, delegates from all the States, except Rhode Ifland, affembled at Philadelphia ; and chofe General Wafhington for their prefident. After four months deliberation, in which the clafhing interefts of the feveral States, appeared in all their force, the convention agreed to recommend a plan of federal government, &c.

As foon as the plan of the federal conftitution was fubmitted to the Legiflatures of the feveral States, they proceeded to take meafures for collecting the fenfe of the people upon the propriety of adopting it. In the fmall State of Delaware, a convention was called in November, which, after a few days deliberation, ratified the conftitution, without a diffenting voice.

In the convention of Penfylvania, held the fame month, there was a fpirited oppofition to the new form of government. The debates were long and interefting. Great abilities and firmnefs were difplayed on both fides ; but, on the 13th of December, the conftitution was received by two thirds of the members. The minority were diffatisfied, and with an obftinacy that ill became the reprefentativs of a free people, publifhed their reafons of diffent, which were calculated to inflame a party already violent, and which, in fact, produced fome difturbances in the weftern parts of the State. But the oppofition has fince fubfided.

In New Jerfey, the convention which met in December, were unanimous in adopting the conftitution ; as was likewife that of Georgia.

In

In Connecticut there was fome oppofition ; but the conftitution was, on the 9th of January, 1788, ratified by three fourths of the votes in convention, and the minority peaceably acquiefced in the decifion.

In Maffachufetts, the oppofition was large and refpectable. The convention, confifting of more than three hundred delegates, were affembled in January, and continued their debates, with great candor and liberality, about five weeks. At length the queftion was carried for the conftitution by a fmall majority, and the minority, with that manly condefcenfion which becomes great minds, fubmitted to the meafure, and united to fupport the government.

In New Hampfhire, the federal caufe was, for fome time doubtful. The greateft number of the delegates in convention, were at firft on the fide of the oppofition ; and fome, who might have had their objections removed by the difcuffion of the fubject, inftructed to reject the conftitution. Altho the inftructions of conftituents cannot, on the true principles of reprefentation, be binding upon a deputy, in any legiflativ affembly, becaufe his conftituents are but a *part* of the State, and have not heard the arguments and objections of the *whole* ; whereas, his act is to affect the *whole* State, and therefore is to be directed by the fenfe or wifdom of the whole, collected in the legiflativ affembly ; yet the delegates in the New Hampfhire convention conceived, very erroneoufly, that the fenfe of the freemen in the towns, thofe little diftricts, where no act of legiflation can be performed, impofed a reftraint upon their own wills.* An adjournment was therefore moved, and carried. This gave the people opportunity to gain a farther knowlege of the merits of the conftitution, and at the fecond meeting of the convention, it was ratified by a refpectable majority.

In Maryland, feveral men of abilities appeared in the oppofition, and were unremitted in their endeavors to perfuade the people, that the propofed plan of government

---

* This pernicious opinion has prevailed in all the States, and done infinit mifchief.

ment was artfully calculated to deprive them of their
deareft rights ; yet in convention it appeared that five
fixths of the voices were in favor of it.

In South Carolina, the oppofition was refpectable ;
but two thirds of the convention appeared to advocate
and vote for the conftitution.

In Virginia, many of the principal characters oppofed the ratification of the conftitution with great a-
bilities and induftry.   But after a full difcuffion of the
fubject, a fmall majority, of a numerous convention,
appeared for its adoption.

In New York, two thirds of the delegates in convention were, at their firft meeting, determined to reject the conftitution.   Here, therefore, the debates
were the moft interefting, and the event extremely
doubtful.   The argument was managed with uncommon addrefs and abilities on both fides of the queftion.
But during the feffion, the ninth and tenth States had
acceded to the propofed plan, fo that by the conftitution, Congrefs were empowered to iffue an ordinance
for organizing the new government.   This event
placed the oppofition on new ground ; and the expediency of uniting with the other States ; the generous
motivs of conciliating all differences, and the danger of
a rejection, influenced a refpectable number, who were
originally oppofed to the conftitution, to join the federal intereft.   The conftitution was accordingly ratified by a fmall majority ; but the ratification was accompanied here, as in Virginia, with a bill of rights,
declaratory of the fenfe of the convention, as to certain
great principles, and with a catalogue of amendments,
which were to be recommended to the confideration of
the new Congrefs, and the feveral State Legiflatures.

North Carolina met in convention in July, to deliberate on the new conftitution.   After a fhort feffion
they rejected it, by a majority of one hundred and feventy fix, againft feventy fix.

Rhode Ifland was doomed to be the fport of a blind
and fingular policy.   The Legiflature, in confiftency
with the meafures which had been before purfued, did

                                        not

not call a convention, to collect the fenfe of the State upon the propofed conftitution ; but in an unconftitutional and abfurd manner, fubmitted the plan of government to the confideration of the people. Accordingly it was brought before town meetings, and in moft of them rejected. In fome of the large towns, particularly in Newport and Providence, the people collected and refolved, with great propriety, that they could not take up the fubject ; and that the propofition for embracing or rejecting the federal conftitution, could come before no tribunal but that of the *State* in convention or legiflature.

From the moment the proceedings of the general convention at Philadelphia tranfpired, the public mind was exceedingly agitated, and fufpended between hope and fear, until nine States had ratified the plan of a federal government. Indeed, the anxiety continued until Virginia and New York had acceded to the fyftem. But this did not prevent the demonftrations of joy, on the acceffion of each State.

On the ratification in Maffachufetts, the citizens of Bofton, in the elevation of their joy, formed a proceffion in honor of the happy event, which was novel, fplendid and magnificent. This example was afterwards followed, and in fome inftances improved upon, in Baltimore, Charlefton, Philadelphia, New Haven, Portfmouth and New York, fucceffivly. Nothing could equal the beauty and grandeur of thefe exhibitions. A fhip was mounted upon wheels, and drawn thro the ftreets ; mechanics erected ftages, and exhibited fpecimens of labor in their feveral occupations, as they moved along the road ; flags with emblems, defcriptiv of all the arts and of the federal union, were invented and difplayed in honor of the government ; multitudes of all ranks in life affembled to view the majeftic fcenes ; while fobriety, joy and harmony marked the brilliant exhibitions, by which the Americans celebrated the eftablifhment of their empire.

In March, 1789, the delegates from the eleven ratifying States, convened in New York, where convenient
and

and elegant accommodations had been furnished by the citizens.   On opening the ballots for Prefident, it appeared that the late Commander in Chief of our armies was unanimoufly elected to the dignified office. This event diffufed univerfal joy among the friends to the union.

The deliberations of the firft American Legiflature were marked with wifdom, fpirit, and generally with candor.   The eftablifhment of a revenue and judiciary fyftem, with other national meafures; the wife appointments to offices ; the promptnefs and energy of the executiv, with a growing popular attachment to the general government, open the faireft profpect of peace, union and profperity to thefe States ; a profpect that is brightened by the acceffion of North Carolina to the government in November, 1789.

No.

REMARKS *on the* METHOD *of* BURYING *the* DEAD *among the* NATIVS *of this* COUNTRY ; *compared with that among the ancient* BRITONS.

Being an Extract of a Letter to the Rev. Dr. STILES, Prefident of Yale College, dated New York, January 20, 1788.

[NOTE. *I had embraced the idea, that the remarkable fortifications on the Muskingum, might be justly ascribed to the Spaniards, under Ferdinand de Soto, who penetrated into Florida, about the year* 1540 ; *which opinion I endeavored to maintain as probably well founded, and wrote three or four letters on the subject, to Dr. Stiles, which were published in* 1789. *It is now very clear that my opinion was not well founded ; but that* Chicaca, *which I had supposed to be Muskingum, ought to have been written* Chicaça, *with a cedilla, as it is in the original Spanish ; and pronounced* Chikesaw. *This determins the place of Soto's winter quarters, the second year after landing, to be in the territories of the present* Chikesaws. *Those letters, therefore, are not worth republishing ; but the following extract, on a different subject, may be considered as worthy of preservation.*]

BUT how shall we account for the mounts, caves, graves, &c. and for the contents, which evince the existence of the custom of burning the dead or their bones ; can these be ascribed to the Spaniards ? I presume, Sir, you will be of opinion they cannot. Capt. Heart says,* these graves are small mounts of earth, from some of which human bones have been taken ; in one were found bones in the natural position of a man, buried nearly east and west, and a quantity of ising glass on his breast ; in the other graves, the bones were irregular, some calcined by fire, others burnt only to a

certain

* Columbian Magazine for May, 1787.

certain degree, fo as to render them more durable ; in others the mouldered bones retain their fhape, without any fubftance ; others are partly rotten and partly the remains of decayed bones ; in moft of the graves were found ftones evidently burnt, pieces of charcoal, Indian arrows and pieces of earthen ware, which appeared to be a compofition of fhells and cement.

That thefe mounts and graves are the works of the nativ Indians, is very evident, for fuch fmall mounts are fcattered over every part of North America. " It was cuftomary with the Indians of the Weft Jerfey," fays Mr. Smith, page 137, " when they buried the dead, to put family utenfils, bows and arrows, and fometimes wampum into the grave, as tokens of their affection. When a perfon of note died far from the place of his own refidence; they would carry his bones to be buried there. They wafhed and perfumed the dead, painted the face, and followed fingly ; left the dead in a fitting pofture, and covered the grave pyramidically. They were very curious in preferving and repairing the graves of their dead, and penfivly vifited them;"

It is faid by the Englifh, who are beft acquainted with the manners of the nativs, that they had a cuftom of collecting, at certain ftated periods, all the bones of their deceafed friends, and burying them in fome common grave. Over thefe cemetaries or general repofitories of the dead, were erected thofe vaft heaps of earth or mounts, fimilar to thofe which are called in England *barrows*, and which are difcovered in every part of the United States.

The Indians feem to have had two methods of burying the dead ; one was, to depofit one body (or at moft but a fmall number of bodies) in a place, and cover it with ftones, thrown together in a carelefs manner. The pile thus formed would naturally be nearly circular, but thofe piles that are difcovered are fomething oval. In the neighborhood of my father's houfe, about feven miles from Hartford, on the public road to Farmington, there is one of thofe *Carrnedds* or heaps of ftone.

ftone. I often paffed by it in the early part of my youth, but never meafured its circumference or examined its contents. My prefent opinion is, that its circumference is about twenty five feet. The inhabitants in the neighborhood report, as a tradition received from the nativs, that an Indian was buried there, and that it is the cuftom for every Indian that paffes by to caft a ftone upon the heap. This cuftom I have never feen practifed, but have no doubt of its exiftence ; as it is confirmed by the general teftimony of the firft American fettlers.*

The other mode of burying the dead, was to depofit a vaft number of bodies, or the bones which were taken from the fingle fcattered graves, in a common cemetary, and over them raife vaft *tumuli* or barrows, fuch as the mount at Mufkingum, which is 390 feet in circumference, and 50 feet high. The beft account of thefe cemetaries may be found in Mr. Jefferfon's Notes on Virginia, which will appear the moft fatisfactory to the reader in his own words.

" I know of no fuch thing exifting as an Indian monument, for I would not honor with that name, arrow points, ftone hatchets, ftone pipes, and half fhapen images. Of labor on the large fcale, I think there are no remains as refpectable as would be a common ditch for the draining of lands, unlefs it be the barrows, of which
　　　　　　　　　　　　　　　　　　many

* The exiftence of a cuftom of paying refpect to thefe *Indian beaps*, as they are called, is proved by a ludicrous practice, that prevails among the Anglo Americans in the vicinity, of making ftrangers pull off their hats as they pafs by this grave. A man paffing by with one who is a ftranger to the cuftom, never fails to practife a jeft upon him, by telling him that a fpider, a caterpillar, or fome other infect is upon his hat ; the unfulpecting traveller immediately takes off his hat, to brufh away the offending infect, and finds by a roar of laughter, that a trick is put upon him. I have often feen this trick played upon ftrangers, and upon the neighbors who happen to be off their guard, to the great amufement of the country people. The jeft, however, is a proof that the aborigines paid a refpect to thefe rude monuments, and in ridicule of that refpect, probably, originated the vulgar practice of the Englifh, which exifts to this day.

many are to be found all over this country. There
are of different fizes, fome of them conftructed of earth,
and fome of loofe ftones.   That they were repofitories
of the dead has been obvious to all ; but on what particular occafion conftructed, was matter of doubt. Some
have thought they covered the bones of thofe who have
fallen in battles, fought on the fpot of interment.
Some afcribe them to the cuftom, faid to prevail among
the Indians, of collecting at certain periods the bones
of all their dead, wherever depofited at the time of death.
Others again fuppofed them the general fepulchre for
towns, conjectured to have been on or near thefe grounds,
and this opinion was fupported by the quality of the
lands in which they are found, (thofe conftructed of
earth being generally in the softeft and moft fertile
meadow grounds on river fides) and by a tradition faid
to be handed down from the aboriginal Indians, that
when they fettled in a town, the firft perfon who died
was placed erect, and earth put about him fo as to cover and fupport him ; that when another died, a narrow
paffage was dug to the firft, the fecond reclined againft
him, and the cover of earth replaced, and fo on. There
being one of thefe in my neighborhood, I wifhed to
fatisfy myfelf whether any, and which of thefe opinions
were juft ; for this purpofe I determined to open and
examin it thoroughly.   It was fituated on the low
grounds of the Rivanna, about two miles above its
principal fork, and oppofit to fome hills on which had
been an Indian town.   It was of a fpheroidical form,
of about forty feet diameter at the bafe, and had been
of about twelve feet altitude, tho now reduced by the
plow to feven and a half ; having been under cultivation
about a dozen years.

    " Before this, it was covered with trees of twelve
inches diameter, and round the bafe was an excavation
of five feet depth and width, from whence the earth
had been taken, of which the hillock was formed.   I
firft dug fuperficially in feveral parts of it, and came to
collections of human bones at different depths, from
fix inches to three feet, below the furface. Thefe were
                                            lying

lying in the utmoſt confuſion ; ſome vertical, ſome ob-
-lique, ſome horizontal, and directed to every point of
the compaſs, entangled and held together in cluſters by
the earth. Bones of the moſt diſtant parts were found
together ; as for inſtance, the ſmall bones of the foot
in the hollow of a ſcull ; many ſculls were ſometimes
in contact, lying on the face, on the ſide, on the back,
top or bottom, ſo as on the whole, to giv the idea of
bones emptied promiſcuouſly from a bag or baſket,
and covered over with earth, without any attention to
their order. The bones, of which the greateſt numbers remained, were ſculls, jaw bones, teeth, the bones
of the arms, thighs, legs, feet and hands. A few ribs
remained, ſome vertibræ of the neck and ſpine, without their proceſſes, and one inſtance only of the bone
which ſerves as the baſe to the vertebral column (the
os ſacrum)."

' After making ſome remarks on the ſtate of putrefaction in which the bones appeared, and on the diſcovery of the bones of infants, Mr. Jefferſon goes on,
" I proceeded then to make a perpendicular cut thro
the body of the barrow, that I might examin its internal ſtructure. This paſſed about three feet from its
center, was opened to the former ſurface of earth, and
was wide enough for a man to walk thro and examin
its ſides.

" At the bottom, that is on the level of the circum-
jacent plain, I found bones ; above theſe a few ſtones
brought from a cliff, a quarter of a mile off, and from
the river one eighth of a mile off. Then a large interval of earth, then a ſtratum of bones, and ſo on. At
one end of the ſection, were four ſtrata of bones plainly
diſtinguiſhable ; at the other, three ; the ſtrata in one
part not ranging with thoſe in another. The bones
neareſt the ſurface were leaſt decayed. No holes were
diſcovered in any of them, as if made with bullets, arrows or other weapons. I conjectured that in this
barrow might have been a thouſand ſkeletons. Every
one will readily ſeize the circumſtances above related,
which militate againſt the opinion, that it covered the

bones

bones only of perfons fallen in battle ; and againft the tradition alfo which would make it the common fepulchre of a town, in which the bodies were placed upright, and touching each other. Appearances certainly indicate, that it has derived both origin and growth from the accuftomary collection of bones and depofition of them together ; that the firft collection had been depofited on the common furface of the earth, that a few ftones were put over it, and then a covering of earth, that the fecond had been laid on this, had covered more or lefs of it in proportion to the number of bones, and was then alfo covered with earth, and fo on. The following are the particular circumftances, which giv it this afpect. 1 The number of bones. 2 The ftrata in one part having no correfpondence with thofe in another. 3 The different ftates of decay in thefe ftrata, which feem to indicate a difference in the time of inhumation. 4 The exiftence of infant bones among them.

" But on whatever occafion they may have been made, they are of confiderable notoriety among the Indians ; for a party paffing about thirty years ago, thro the part of the country where this barrow is, went thro the woods directly to it, without any inftructions or inquiry, and having ftaid about it fome time, with expreffions which were conftrued to be thofe of forrow, they returned to the high road which they had left about half a dozen miles, to pay this vifit, and purfued their journey. There is another barrow, much refembling this, in the low grounds of the fouth branch of the Shenandoah, where it is croffed by the road leading from the Rockfifh Gap to Staunton. Both of thefe have within thefe dozen years, been cleared of their trees and put under cultivation, are much reduced in their height, and fpread in width, by the plow, and will probably difappear in time. There is another on a hill in the blue ridge of mountains, a few miles north of Wood's Gap, which is made up of fmall ftones thrown together. This has been opened, and found

to

to contain human bones, as the others do. There are alſo others in other parts of the country."

From this account of Mr. Jefferſon, to whoſe induſtry and talents the ſciences and his country will ever be indebted, we may fairly conclude that the mounts at Muſkingum are the work of the nativ Indians. It is however neceſſary to notice two or three particulars, in the appearance of thoſe at Muſkingum, which are not diſcovered (or not mentioned by Mr. Jefferſon) in the ſtructure of that which he examined. Theſe are the iſing glaſs, the earthen ware, the charcoal, and the calcination of the bones by fire. As to the firſt it is well known that the iſing glaſs is found only in particular parts of America, and the ſavages in other parts could not obtain it. Mr. Jefferſon mentions no diſcovery of earthen ware, but it was uſed by the Indians in every part of America. The piece you once ſhewed me, ſir, is a ſpecimen of what is found wherever there has been an Indian town. Pieces of it are dug up frequently in the meadows on Connecticut river. It appears to be formed of pure clay, or of ſhells and cement, hardened by fire, and as we might naturally ſuppoſe, without glazing. By ſections of veſſels which remain, it is evident they were wrought with great ingenuity, and into beautiful and convenient forms.

The charcoal and calcination of ſome bones are a proof that there has exiſted, among the ſavages of America, a cuſtom of burning the dead, or their bones, after the diſſolution of the fleſh. It does not appear that this cuſtom was general, but it is not at all ſurpriſing to find that ſuch a practice has exiſted in this country; ſince it has been frequent among the uncivilized nations on the eaſtern continent.

I am ſenſible, ſir, that you have entertained an opinion that the ſtory of Madoc, the Welch Prince, may be true, and that it is poſſible the fortifications at Muſkingum may be the work of his colony. Of the truth of this concluſion there is perhaps no direct evidence, and yet collateral evidence may be obtained, that it is not chimerical. There is ſuch a ſurpriſing affinity be-

tween

tween the Indian mounts and the barrows or cemetaries which are remaining in England, but particularly in Wales and Anglesey, the last retreat of the original Britons, that we can hardly resolve it into a common principle of analogy that subsists between nations in the same stage of society; but incredulity itself will acknowlege the probability, that the primitiv inhabitants of Britain and America had a common stock from which they were derived, long since the age of the first parent : Not that I believe North America to be peopled so late as the twelfth century, the period of Madoc's migration, but supposing America to have been settled two or three thousand years before that period, a subsequent colony might pass the Atlantic and bring the Roman improvements in fortification.

Waving further conjectures, I beg leave to describe the analogy between the barrows in England and Wales, and in America. This will be striking, and cannot fail to entertain a curious reader, because it is attended with positiv proofs.

In England, Scotland, Wales, and the island Anglesey, there are numbers of monuments erected by the ancients; but the most remarkable are generally found in the two latter, whither the old Britons retreated from their Roman and Saxon conquerors; and *Anglesey*, the ancient *Mona*, is supposed to have been the chief seat of the Druids: The remains of most consequence are the *cromlechs*, the *tumuli*, and the *cumuli* or *carrnedds*. *Cromlech*, if the word is derived from the British roots *krom laech*, signifies a *bending stone.*[*] This is the common opinion, as Rowland observes.[†] If we trace the origin to the Hebrew, the root of the old British,[‡] we shall find it not less significativ;

* Camden's Britannia, volume II, page 759.
† Mona Antiq. Restaur, page 47.
‡ That the primitiv Britons may claim a very direct descent from the ancient inhabitants of Syria and Phenicia, whose languages were but branches from the same common stock, with as Hebrew, may be made to appear probable by a comparison of their customs ; but may be almost demonstrated by a collation of the old British language with the Hebrew roots. *See my Dissertations on the English Language, Appendix.*

¡cativ; for *cærem luach* fignify *devoted ftone*, or *altar*. Thefe *cromlechs* confift of large ftones, pitched on end in the earth, as fupporters, upon which is laid a broad ftone of a vaft fize.   The fupporters ftand in a bending pofture, and are from three to feven feet high.   The top ftone is often found to be of twenty, or thirty tons weight, and remains to this day on the pillars.   Numbers of thefe are found in Wales and Anglefey ; but none is more remarkable than that in Wiltfhire, called *ftone henge*, for a full defcription of which I muft beg leave to refer you to Camden's Britannia, vol. I, page 119.   Thefe cromlechs are doubtlefs works of great antiquity ; but for what purpofe they were erected, at fuch an immenfe expenfe of time and labor as would be neceffary to convey ftones of thirty tons weight a confiderable diftance, and raife them feveral feet, is not eafily determined.   The probability is that they were altars for facrifice, as pieces of burnt bones and afhes are found near them.   They might alfo be ufed in other ceremonies, under the druidical fyftem, as the ratification of covenants, &c.   As this kind of monuments is not found in America, I will wave a further confideration of it ; obferving only, that it was an ancient practice among the eaftern nations, to raife heaps of ftones, as witneffes of agreements, and facrifice upon them, as a folemn ratification of the act of the parties.   Many inftances of this ceremony are mentioned in the old teftament.   The covenant between Jacob and Laban was witneffed by a heap of ftones, which ferved alfo as a boundary between their refpectiv claims.   " *And Jacob offered facrifice upon the mount,* that is, the heap, *and called his brethren to eat bread.*" Gen. xxxi, 54.   A fimilar cuftom feems to have prevailed among the primitiv Britons.

But the *tumuli*, barrows or mounts of earth, which remain in multitudes in England and Wales, are conftructed exactly in the manner of the barrows, defcribed by Mr. Jefferfon and Mr. Heart.   One of thefe in Wiltfhire, Camden thus defcribes.*   " Here Selbury, a round

* Britannia, volume I, page 127.

a round hill, rifes to a confiderable height, and feems by the fafhion of it, and the fliding down of the earth about it, to have been caft up by mens hands. Of this fort there are many in this country, round and copped, which are called *burrows* or *barrows* ; perhaps raifed in memory of the foldiers flain there. For *bones are found in them*, and I have read, it was a cuftom among the northern people, that every foldier who furvived a battle, fhould bring a helmet full of earth towards the raifing of monuments for their flain fellows."

This is faid to be the largeft and moft uniform bar-row in the country, and perhaps in England ; and I regret that the height and circumference are not men-tioned. I am however informed verbally by a gentle-man who has vifited England, that fome of thefe tumuli appear to have been nearly one hundred feet high.* There are alfo in the fame country feveral kinds of bar-rows of different fizes ; fome furrounded with trench-es ; others not ; fome with ftones fet round them, oth-ers without any ; the general figure of them is nearly circular, but a little oval.

In Penbrokefhire, in Wales, Camden informs us†
" there are divers ancient tumuli, or artificial mounts for urn burial, whereof the moft notable I have feen, are thofe four, called *krigeu kemaes*, or the burrows of *kemeas*. One of thefe a gentlemen of the neighbor-hood, out of curiofity, and for the fatisfaction of fome friends, caufed lately to be dug ; and difcovered therein five urns, which contained a confiderable quantity of burnt bones and afhes." If there is any difference be-tween thefe barrows, and thofe at Mufkingum, it is this, that in Wales the bones were lodged in urns ; probably this was the fate of the bodies of eminent men only, or it proves a greater degree of improvement in Britain than appears among the American favages.

In Caermardhinfhire, there is a barrow of a fingular kind. It is called, *krig y dyrn* (probably the king's barrow.)

---

* One as large as that is faid to be found at Grave Creek, about eighty miles above Mufkingum.

† Volume II, page 763.

barrow*.) The circumference at bottom is fixty paces, and its height about fix yards. It rifes by an eafy afcent to the top, which is hollow. This is a heap of earth, raifed over a *carrnedd* or pile of ftones. In the center of the cavity on the top, there is a large flat ftone, about nine feet by five ; beneath this was found a *kift vaen*, a kind of ftone cheft, four feet and a half by three, and made up of ftones, and within and about it were found a few pieces of brick and ftones. This might have been the tomb of a druid, or prince.

The *cumuli* of ftones or *caernedds*, as they are called by the Welfh, from *keren nedh*, a *coped heap*, are fcattered over the weft of England and Wales, and appear to have been raifed in the manner of our Indian heaps, and for the fame purpofe, viz. to preferve the memory of the dead. Every Indian in this country that paffes one of thefe heaps, throws a ftone upon it. · Rowland remarks that the fame cuftom exifts among the vulgar Welch to this day ; and if I miftake not, Camden takes notice of the fame practice. Rowland fays, " in thefe *coel ceithic*, (certain feftivals) people ufe, even to this day, to throw and offer each one his ftone, tho they know not the reafon. The common tradition is, that thefe heaps cover the graves of men, fignal either for eminent virtues, or notorious villanies, on which every perfon looked on himfelf obliged as he paffed by, to beftow a ftone, in veneration of his good life, or in deteftation of his vilenefs." This practice now prevails in Wales and Anglefey, merely as a mark of contempt.

The *carrnedds* in America anfwer exactly the defcription of thofe in Wales, and the practice of throwing upon the heap each man his ftone as he paffes by, exifts among the Indians, in its purity ; that is, as *a mark of refpect*.

It is faid by authors that mounts and piles of ftones, are found likewife in Denmark and Sweden ; but in conftruction they differ from thofe found in Britain. Yet from the foregoing defcriptions, taken from authentic teftimony, it appears, that between the barrows

in

* Camden, volume II, page 751.

in England and America, the manner of conftructing
them in both, and the purpofes to which they were applied, there is an analogy, rarely to be traced in works
of fuch confequer c, among nations whofe intercourfe
ceafed at Babel; an analogy that we could hardly fuppofe would exift among nations defcended from different ftocks.   This analogy however, without better evidence, will not demonftrate the direct defcent of the
Indians from the ancient Celts or Britons.   But as all
the primitiv inhabitants of the weft of Europe were
evidently of the fame ftock, it is natural to fuppofe they
might pafs from Norway to Iceland, from Iceland to
Greenland, and from thence to Labrador; and thus
the North American favages may claim a common
origin with the primitiv Britons and Celts.   This fuppofition has fome foundation, and is by no means ob-
viated by Cook's late difcoveries in the Pacific ocean.*

    Thefe are however but conjectures.   Future difcov-
eries may throw more light upon thefe fubjects.   At
prefent, a few facts only can be collected to amufe a
contemplativ mind, and perhaps lead to inquiries which
will refult in a fatisfactory account of the firft peopling
of America, and of the few remains of antiquity which
it affords.

    * Monf. Mallet, in his Northern Antiquities, has produced
unqueftionable teftimony, from the Chronicles of Iceland and
others hiftories of the north, that the American continent was
difcovered about the tenth century; and the efquimaux are
clearly of the fame race as the Greenlanders.

No.

No. XVII.

NEW YORK, FEBRUARY, 1788.

On the REGULARITY of the CITY of PHILADELPHIA.

"WELL, how do you like Boston?" said an American to a Londoner, who had juft arrived, and walked thro the town. "Extremely," replied the Englifhman; "it refembles London in the crookednefs and narrownefs of the ftreets; I am always pleafed with a carelefs irregularity and variety."

"How do you like Bofton," fays a nativ of the town to a Philadelphian. "I am much pleafed with the people," replies the gentleman; "but the ftreets are fo crooked, narrow and irregular, that I have good luck to find my way, and keep my ftockings clean."

An Englifhman and a Boftonian, walking together in Philadelphia, were heard to fay, "how fatiguing it is to pafs thro this town! fuch a famenefs in the whole! no variety! when you have feen one ftreet, you have feen the whole town!"

Thefe remarks, which are heard every day, illuftrate moft ftrikingly the force of habit and tradition. The influence of habit is every where known and felt; any prepoffeffions therefore in favor of our nativ town, is not a matter of furprife. But that a traditionary remark or opinion fhould be handed from one generation to another, and lead nations into error, without a detection of its falfity, is a fact as aftonifhing as it is real. Such is the opinion of the writers on the fine arts; "that variety is pleafing;" an opinion embraced without exception, and applied promifcuoufly to the works of nature and of art. I have rarely met with a perfon, not an inhabitant of Philadelphia, who would not fay he was difgufted with its regularity; and I am confident that the opinion muft proceed from that common

place

place remark, *that variety is pleafing* ; otherwife men could notǀſo unanimoufly condemn what conftitutes its *greateft beauty.*

That in the productions of nature, variety conftitutes a principal part of beauty, and a fruitful fource of pleaſure, will not be denied : But the beauty and agreeableneſs of works of art depend on another principle, viz. *utility or convenience.* The *defign* of the work, or the end propoſed by it, muſt be attentivly confidered before we are qualified to judge of its *beauty.*

This kind of beauty is called by Lord Kaim,* *relativ beauty.* He obſerves very juftly, that " *intrinſic* beauty is a perception of fenſe merely ; for to perceive the beauty of a fpreading oak, or of a flowing river, no more is required but fingly an act of vifion. *Relativ beauty* is accompanied with an act of underſtanding and reflection ; for of a fine inftrument or engine, we perceive not the *relativ* beauty, until we are made acquainted with its uſe and deſtination." A plow has not the leaft *intrinſic* beauty ; but when we attend to its *uſe,* we are conftrained to confider it as a *beautiful inſtrument,* and ſuch a view of it furniſhes us with agreeable ſenſations.

The fingle queftion therefore, with reſpect to a town or city, is this : *Is it planned and conftructed for the greateft poſſible convenience ?* If ſo, it is completely beautiful. If wide and regular ftreets are more uſeful and convenient than thoſe that are narrow and crooked, then a city conftructed upon a regular plan is the moft beautiful, however uniform the ftreets in their directions and appearance.

I have often heard a compariſon made between the level roads of Holland and the uniform ftreets of Philadelphia. A *dull ſameneſs* is ſaid to render both diſagreeable. Yet if a perſon will attentivly confider the difference, I am perſuaded he will be convinced that his taſte is but *half correct* ; that is, that a juſt remark with reſpect to a level open country, is improperly applied to a commercial city. *Variety* in the works of nature is
.   pleaſing ;

* Elements of Criticiſm. Vol. I, page 198.

pleasing ; but never in the productions of art, unless in copies of nature, or when that variety does not interfere with *utility*. A level champaign country is rarely convenient or useful ; on the other hand, it is generally more barren than a country diversified with hills and vales. There is not generally any advantage to be derived from a wide extended plain ; the principle of *utility*; therefore does not oppose and supersede the taste for variety, and a tedious *sameness* is left to have its full effect upon the mind of a spectator. This is the fact with respect to the roads in Holland.

But it is otherwise in a city, which is built for the express purpose of accommodating men in business. We do not consider it as we do a landscape, an imitation of a natural scene, and designed to please the eye ; but we attend to its uses in artificial society, and if it appears to be calculated for the convenience of all classes of citizens, the plan and construction must certainly be beautiful, and afford us agreeable sensations.

The regularly built towns in America are Philadelphia, Charleston, in South Carolina, and New Haven. All these may be esteemed beautiful, tho not perfectly so. Philadelphia wants a public square or place of resort for men of business, with a spacious building for an exchange. This should be near Market street, in the center of business. The gardens at the State House are too small for a public walk in that large city. The whole line of bank houses* is the effect of ill timed parsimony. The houses are inconvenient, and therefore not pleasing to the eye ; at the same time they render Water street too narrow.

But whatever faults may be found in the construction or plan of the city, its general appearance is agreeable, and its *regularity* is its greatest beauty. Whenever I hear a person exclaim against the uniformity that pervades that city, I suppose him the dupe of a common place remark, or that he believes a city built merely to please the eye of a spectator.

Charleston

---

* A line of houses built on the descent of land to the river, with a street adjacent to the houses on both sides.

Charleſton is ſituated upon low ground; but juſt a-
bove high water mark.   The ſoil is ſand, which, with
a ſcarcity of ſtone, has prevented the ſtreets from being
paved.   The plan of the city is regular, but ſome of
the ſtreets are too narrow.   As it is almoſt ſurrounded
with water and low marſhy ground, it was neceſſary to
attend to every circumſtance that ſhould contribute to
preſerve a pure air.   For this purpoſe, it was the original deſign of the citizens, to prevent any buildings
from being erected, on the wharves, in front of the
town ; thus leaving a principal ſtreet, called the bay,
open to the ſea breezes.   Since the revolution, this deſign has been partially diſpenſed with ; and ſome buildings erected on the water ſide of the bay, and particu-
ularly one in front of the Exchange, which ſtands at
the head of Broad ſtreet, and commands an extenſiv
view of the town on one ſide, and of the harbor on the
other.   Should ſtores and warehouſes be raiſed on the
wharves, to ſuch a height as to intercept a view of the
harbor from the bay, they would diminiſh the beauty
of the town, and in ſome degree prevent the agreeable
effect of the cool breezes from the ſea.

New Haven was laid out on a moſt beautiful plan,
which has however ſuffered in the execution.   The
ſtreets croſs each other at right angles, as in Philadelphia ; and divide the city into convenient ſquares.   But
in the center is a large public ſquare, the ſides of which
are more than three hundred yards in length, and
adorned with rows of trees.   Thro the center of this
ſquare runs a line of elegant public buildings, viz. the
ſtate houſe, two churches and a ſchool houſe.   This
ſquare is a capital ornament to the town ; but is liable
to two exceptions.   Firſt, it is too large for the popu-
louſneſs of the city, which contains about 500 buildings.   In ſo ſmall a town, it muſt generally be empty,
and conſequently givs the town an appearance of ſoli-
tude or dullneſs.   In the ſecond place, that half of the
ſquare which lies weſt of the public buildings, is occupied moſtly by the church yard, which is encloſed with
a circular fence.   This reduces the public ground on
the

the oppofit fide to a paralellogram, which is a lefs beautiful figure than a fquare ; and annihilates the beauty
of the weftern divifion which it occupies.   Nothwith-
ftanding thefe circumftances, the green or public ground
in the center of New Haven, renders it perhaps the
moft beautiful fmall fettlement in America.

No.

No. XVIII.

NEW YORK, MAY, 1788.

A DISSERTATION *concerning the* IN-FLUENCE *of* LANGUAGE *on* OPIN-IONS, *and of* OPINIONS *on* LAN-GUAGE.*

THE defign of this differtation is to fhow how far truth and accuracy of thinking are concerned in a clear underftanding of *words*. I am fenfible that in the eye of prejudice and ignorance, grammatical re-fearches are the bufinefs of fchool boys ; and hence we may deduce the reafon why philofophers have gen-erally been fo inattentiv to this fubject. But if it can be proved that the *mere ufe of words* has led nations in-to error, and ftill continues the delufion, we cannot hefitate a moment to conclude, that grammatical en-quiries are worthy of the labor of *men*.

The Greek name of the Supreme Being, *Theos*, is derived from *Theo, to run, or move one's felf*. Hence we difcover the ideas which the Greeks originally en-tertained of God, viz. that he was the *great principle of motion*. The fame word, it is faid, was primarily appropriated to the ftars, as moving bodies ; and it is probable that, in the early ages of Greece, the heaven-ly bodies might be efteemed Deities, and denominated *Theoi, moving bodies* or *principles*. The Latin word *Deus* was ufed to denote thofe inferior beings which we call *fpirits* or *angels*, or perhaps one God among fev-eral. To giv the true idea of *Deus* in French and Englifh, the word fhould be rendered *le Dieu, the God*. This at leaft may be faid of the word, in its true *orig-inal* fenfe ; however it may have been ufed in the later ages of Rome. The

* This title, and many of the following ideas, are borrowed from a treatife of Mr. Michaelis, director of the Royal Socie-ty of Gottingen.

The Englifh word *God*, is merely the old Saxon adjectiv *god*, now fpelt and pronounced *good*.

The German *Gott* is from the fame root.   The words *God* and *good* therefore are fynonimous.   The derivation of the word leads us to the notions which our anceftors entertained of the Supreme Being ; fuppofing him to be the principle or author of good, they called him, by way of eminence, *Good*, or *the Good*.   By long ufe and the progrefs of knowlege, the word is become the name of the great Creator, and we have added to it ideas of other attributes, as juftice, power, immutability, &c.   Had our heathen anceftors entertained different ideas of the Deity ; had they, for inftance, fuppofed juftice to have been his leading attribute, if I may ufe the term, they would have called him *the juft* ; and this appellation, by being uniformly appropriated to a certain invifible being, or fuppofed caufe of certain events, would in time have loft the article *the*, and *juft* would have become the *name* of the Deity. Such is the influence of opinion in the formation of language.

Let us now compare the names of the Deity in the three languages ; the Greek, *Theos*, denoting a *moving being*, or the *principle of action*, evinces to us that the Greeks gave the name to the *caufe of events*, without having very clear ideas of the nature or attributes of that caufe.   They fuppofed the great operations of nature to have each its caufe ; and hence the plurality of caufes, *theoi*, or moving principles.

The Romans borrowed the fame word, *Deus*, and ufed it to denote the celeftial *agents* or *gods* which they fuppofed to exift, and to fuperintend the affairs of the univerfe.

Our northern anceftors had an idea that all favorable events muft have an efficient caufe ; and to this caufe they gave the name of *God* or *good*.   Hence we obferve that the Englifh and German words *God* and *Got* do not convey precifely the fame idea, as the *Theos* and *Deus* of the Greeks and Romans.   The former cannot be ufed in the plural number ; as they are the

names

names of a fingle indivifible being ; the latter were ufed as names common to a number of beings.

The word *Demon*, in Greek, was ufed to fignify fubordinate deities, both good and evil. The Jews, who had more perfect ideas of the Supreme Being, fuppofed there could be but one good Deity, and confequently that all the *demons* of the Greeks muft be *evil* beings or *devils.* In this fenfe alone they ufed the word, and this reftricted fenfe has been communicated thro Chriftian countries in modern ages. The opinion of the Jews, therefore, has had a material effect upon language, and would lead us into an error refpecting the Greek mythology ; unlefs we fhould trace the word *demon* to its primitiv fignification.

The word *devil*, in Englifh, is merely a corruption of *the evil*, occafioned by a rapid pronunciation. This will not appear improbable to thofe who know, that in fome of the Saxon dialects, the character which we write *th* is almoft invariably written and pronounced *d*. Hence we learn the notion which our anceftors entertained of the *caufe of evil*, or of unfortunate events; They probably afcribed fuch events to a malignant principle, or being, which they called, by way of eminence, *the evil*; and thefe words, corrupted by common ufe, have given name to the being or principle.

I would only obferve here that the etymology of thefe two words, *God* and *devil*, proves that the Manichean doctrine of a *good* and *evil* principle prevailed among our northern anceftors. It has prevailed over moft of the eaftern countries in all ages, and Chriftianity admits the doctrine, with this improvement only, that it fuppofes the *evil* principle to be fubordinate to the *good*. The fupreme caufe of events, Chriftians believe to be *good* or *God*, for the words are radically the fame ; the *caufe of evil* they believe to be fubordinate ; yet, ftrange as it may feem, they fuppofe the *fubordinate evil* principle to be the moft prevalent.

We are informed by Ludolph, that the Ethiopeans, having but one word for *nature* and *perfon*, could not underftand the controverfy about Chrift's two natures.

This

This is not furprifing ; nations, in a favage ftate, or which have not been accuftomed to metaphyfical dif-quifitions, have no terms to communicate abftract ideas, which they never entertained ; and hence the abfurdity of attempting to chriftianize favages.   Before men can be Chriftians they muft be civilized ; nay, they muft be philofophers.   It is probable that many who are called Chriftians, are in the ftate of the Ethiopians, with refpect to the fame doctrin ; and that they pafs thro life, without ever having any clear ideas of the different natures of Chrift.   Yet the diftinction is con-ftantly made in words ; and that diftinction paffes for a difference of ideas.   Such is the influence of lan-guage on opinion.

The words *foul, mind* and *fpirit*, are conftantly ufed by people, and probably the difference of words has given rife to an opinion that there is an actual differ-ence of things.   Yet I very much queftion whether the perfons who ufe thefe words every day, annex any diftinct ideas to them ; or if they do, whether they could explain the difference.

The Greeks believed in the doctrin of tranfmigra-tion.   They had obferved the metamorphofis of the caterpillar, and fuppofing the fame foul to animate the different bodies, and believing the foul to be perpetual or immortal, they made the butterfly the hieroglyphic of the foul : Hence the Greek word for foul, *pfuke*, came to fignify alfo a *butterfly*.

For want of attending to the true etymology of the word *glory*, falfe opinions have gained an eftablifhment in the world, and it may be hazardous to difpute them. It is faid that the *glory* of God does not depend on his creatures, and that the glory of the good man depends not on the opinion of others.   But what is glory ? The Greek word *doxe* explains it.   It is derived from *dokeo, to think* ; and fignifies the *good opinion of others.* This is its *true* original meaning ; a man's glory there-fore confifts in having the good opinion of men, and this cannot generally be obtained, but by meritorious actions.   The *glory* of God confifts in the exalted ideas

Q   which

which his creatures entertain of his being and perfec-
tions. His *glory* therefore depends *wholly on his creatures*. The word is indeed often ufed to fignify the
greatnefs, fplendor or excellence of the divine character. In this fenfe the *divine glory* may be independent
of created beings ; but it is not the primitiv fenfe of
the word, nor the fenfe which anfwers to the original
meaning of the Greek *doxe*, and the Latin *gloria*.

No right in England and America is fo mnch celebrated as that of *trial by peers* ; by which is commonly
underftood, *trial by equals*. The right is valuable, but
is not derived from the primitiv cuftom of *trial by
equals* ; on the contrary, it is very queftionable whether
fuch a cuftom exifted prior to Alfred. Yet the *trial by
peers* exifted long before, and can be traced back to the
date of the Chriftian era. The truth is, the word *peer*
is not derived from the Latin *par*, equal ; but from the
German, or Teutonic *bar* or *par*, which fignified a
landholder, freeman or judge. The *bars* were that clafs
of men who held the *fees* or property in eftates ; and
from whom the word *baron* and the attendant privileges are derived. We have the fame root in *baron*,
baronet, *parliament*, *parifh*, and many other words, all im-
plying fome degree of authority, eminence or jurifdiction. From the fame word *bar* or *par*, (for *B* and *P*
are convertible letters) the word *peer* is derived, as it is
ufed in the common expreffions *houfe of peers*, *trial by
peers*. It fignified originally, not *equals*, but *judges* or
barons. The *houfe of peers* in England derives its appellation and its jurifdiction from the ancient mode of
trial by *bars* or barons ; for it is the final refort in all
judicial cafes. Yet the ancient Englifh lawyers, fuppofing the word to be from the Latin *par*, equal, have
explained it in that fenfe, and multiplied encomiums
without end upon the excellence of the privilege. The
privilege is valuable, but its excellence, if it confifts in a
trial by equals, is modern, compared with the original
cuftom, which was a *trial by barons*, or principal landholders.

It

It is probable that our modern writers, mifunder-
ftanding the term *voluptas*, have paffed too fevere cen-
fures upon epicures. The true primitiv meaning of
voluptas was that of *pleafurable fenfations* arifing from innocent gratifications. Our modern word *voluptuoufnefs*
carries with it a much ftronger idea, and hence we are
led into an error refpecting the doctrine of Epicurus,
who might confine his ideas of pleafure to innocent
gratifications.

We have been accuftomed from childhood to hear
the expreffions, *the dew falls* ; *the dews of heaven* ; and it
is probable that nine people out of ten, have never fufpected the inaccuracy of the phrafes. But *dew* is
merely the perfpiration of the earth ; it *rifes* inftead of
falling, and rifes during the night.*

It was alfo fuppofed that *manna* in the eaftern countries, came from above, and it is called in fcripture
bread from heaven. Yet *manna* is a gum, exuding from
plants, trees and bufhes, when pierced by certain in-
fects. The truth of this fact was not difcovered, till
the middle of the fixteenth century.

Every man knows, when the prices of goods rife, it
is faid they become *dear* ; yet when the prices rife in
confequence of an overflowing fum of money in circulation, the fact is that the *value of money falls*, and the
value of goods remains the fame. This erroneous
opinion had an amazing effect in raifing popular clam-
or, at the commencement of the late revolution.

I will

* Any perfon may prove this by a trifling experiment. Let
him place a glafs receiver or bowl over the grafs in a fummer's
day, and the next morning he will find as much dew *under* it
as around it.

The truth is this ; the particles of water are conftantly exhaled from the earth by the heat of the fun. During the day
time, thefe particles afcend in an imperceptible manner, and
furnifh the atmofphere with the materials of clouds and rain.
But in the night, the atmofphere grows cool, while the earth,
retaining a fuperior degree of heat, continues to throw off the
particles of water. Thefe particles, meeting the colder atmofphere, are condenfed, and lodge upon the furface of the earth,
grafs, trees and other objects. So that the expreffion, *the dew
falls*, is in a degree true, altho it *firft rifes* from the earth.

I will name but one other inftance, which has a material influence upon our moral and religious opinions. It is faid in fcripture that *God hardened Pharaoh's heart*. How ? Was there a miracle in the cafe ? By no means. The manner of fpeaking leads us into the miftake. The firft caufe is mentioned, and not the intermediate caufe or caufes.   So we fhould fay, that *General Wafhington attacked the Britifh troops at Monmouth* ; altho he was at a great diftance when the attack was commenced, and only *ordered* the attack.   I fufpect that fimilar modes of fpeaking in fcripture often lead fuperficial minds into miftakes, and in fome inftances, giv occafion to infidels to fcoff at paffages, which, if rightly underftood, would filence all objections.

This is a fruitful theme, and would lead an ingenious inquirer into a wide field of inveftigation.   But I have neither time nor talents to do it juftice ; the few hints here fuggefted may have fome effect in convincing my readers of the importance and utility of all candid refearches into the origin and ftructure of fpeech ; and pave the way for further inveftigations, which may affift us in correcting our ideas and afcertaining the force and beauty of our own language.

No.

No. XIX.

PHILADELPHIA, 1787.

On VOCAL MUSIC.

THE eftablifhment of fchools for teaching pfalmody in this city is a pleafing inftitution ; but people feem not to underftand the defign, or rather are not
aware of the advantages which may refult from it, if
properly conducted and encouraged. Moft people confider mufic merely as a fource of pleafure ; not attending to its influence on the human mind, and its confequent effects on fociety. But it fhould be regarded as
an article of education, *ufeful* as well as ornamental.

The human mind is formed for activity ; and will
ever be employed in bufinefs or diverfions. Children
are perpetually in motion, and all the ingenuity of their
parents and guardians fhould be exerted to devife
methods for reftraining this activ principle, and direct-
ing it to fome *ufeful* object, or to *harmlefs trifles*. If
this is not done, their propenfity to action, even without a vicious motiv, will hurry them into follies and
crimes. Every thing innocent, that attracts the attention of children, and will employ their minds in
leifure hours, when idlenefs might otherwife open the
way to vice, muft be confidered as a valuable employment. Of this kind is vocal mufic. There were inftances of youth, the laft winter, who voluntarily attended a finging fchool in preference to the theatre. It
is but reafonable to fuppofe, that if they would neglect
a theatre for finging, they would neglect a thoufand
amufements, lefs engaging, and more pernicious.

Inftrumental mufic is generally prefered to vocal,
and confidered as an elegant accomplifhment. It is
indeed a pleafing accomplifhment ; but the preference
given to it, is a fpecies of the fame falfe tafte, which
places a fon under the tuition of a *drunken clown*, to
make him a gentleman of *ftrict morals*.

Inftrumental

Inftrumental mufic may exceed vocal in fome nice touches and diftinctions of found ; but when regarded as to its effects upon the mind and upon fociety, it is as inferior to vocal, as found is inferior to fenfe. It is very eafy for a fpruce beau to difplay a contempt for vocal mufic, and to fay that human invention has gone beyond the works of God Almighty. But till the fyftem of creation fhall be new modelled, the human voice properly cultivated will be capable of making the moft perfect mufic. It is neglected ; fol faing is un-fafhionable, and that is enough to damn it : But people who have not been acquainted with the perfection of pfalmody, are incapable of making a fuitable com-parifon between vocal and inftrumental mufic. I have often heard the beft vocal concerts in America, and the beft inftrumental concerts ; and can declare, that the mufic of the latter is as inferior to that of the former, as the merit of a *band box macaroni* is to that of a Cato.

Inftrumental mufic affords an agreeable amufe-ment ; and as an amufement it ought to be cultivated. But the advantage is private and limited ; it pleafes the ear, but leaves no impreffion upon the heart.

The defign of mufic is to awaken the paffions, to foften the heart for the reception of fentiment. To awaken paffion is within the power of inftruments, and this may afford a temporary pleafure ; but fociety de-rives no advantage from it, unlefs fome ufeful fentiment is left upon the heart.

Inftruments are fecondary in their ufe ; they were invented originally, not to fupercede, but to affift the voice. The firft hiftories of all nations were written in verfe, and fung by their bards. In later ages, the *oaten reed*, the *harp* and the *lyre*, were found to improve the pleafures of mufic ; but the neglect of the voice and of fentiment was referved for modern corruption. Ignorant indeed is the man, and poffeffed of a wretch-ed tafte, who can ferioufly defpife the humble pleafures of vocal mufic, and prefer the bare harmony of founds. Sentiment fhould ever accompany mufic ; the founds fhould ever correfpond with the ideas, otherwife mufic

lofes

lofes all its force.   Union of fentiment, with harmony
of founds, is the perfection of mufic.   Every ftring of
the human heart may be touched ; every paffion roufed by the different kinds of founds ; the courage of the
warrior ; the cruelty of the tyrant ; anger ; grief; love,
with all its fenfibilities, are fubject to the influence of
mufic.   Even brutes acknowlege its effects ; but while
they in common with man feel the effects of a harmony of mere founds, man enjoys the fuperior felicity of
receiving fentiment ; and while he relifhes the pleafures
of chords in found, he imbibes a difpolition to communicate happinefs to fociety.

Seldom indeed do men reflect on the connexion between the chords of mufic and the focial affections.
Morality is to immorality, what harmony is to difcord.
Society detects vice, and the ear is offended with difcordant founds.   Society is pleafed and happified with
virtue, and the ear is delighted with harmony.   This
beautiful analogy points out the utility of cultivating
mufic as a fcience.   Harfh difcordant founds excite
the peevifh malevolent paffions ; harmonious founds
correct and foften the rougher paffions.

Every perfon will acknowlege, that love refines the
heart, and renders it more fufceptible, and more capable of focial virtue.   It is for this reafon that men who
have particular attachments to women, or affociate
much with ladies of delicacy, are more difpofed to do
acts of kindnefs, in every fphere of life, than thofe who
feldom frequent ladies company.   On the other hand,
anger, jealoufy, envy, are diffocial paffions ; and even
when they are excited by a fingle object, they poifon
the heart, and difqualify it for exciting the focial affections towards any of the human race.   Every inftitution, therefore, calculated to prepare the human heart
for exerting the focial virtues, and to fupprefs or check
the malignant paffions, muft be highly beneficial to fociety ; and fuch I confider eftablifhments in favor of
vocal mufic.   Happy, indeed, fhould I feel, could I fee
youth devoted every where to the refinement of their
voices and morals ; to fee them prefer moral or re-

ligious

ligious pieces to the indecent fongs or low diverfions which taint the mind in early life, and diffufe their pernicious influence through fociety.

If the poifon of the tarantula may be counteracted by mufic ; if the Spanifh ladies are won by nocturnal ferenades ; if the foldier is infpired with courage by the martial founds of the trumpet, and the Chriftian impreffed with devout fentiments by the folemn tones of the organ ; what advantage may fociety derive from the foftening harmony of choirs of voices, celebrating the praifes of focial virtue ! Happy days ! when *falfe tafte* and *falfe opinions* fhall vanifh before the progrefs of *truth* ; when princes fhall refume their ancient and honorable tafk of teaching the young to be *good* and *great* ; when an Addifon fhall be preferred to a Chefterfield ; when the wealth of nations fhall be no longer lavifhed upon fiddlers and dancers ; when the characters of a *Benezet* and a WASHINGTON fhall obfcure the glories of a Cæfar ; and when no man fhall be afhamed to be *good*, becaufe it is unfafhionable.

No.

No. XX.

NEW YORK, JUNE, 1788.

On MORALITY.

" THE principles of morality are little underftood among favages," fays Lord Kaimes, " and if they arrive to maturity among enlightened nations, it is by flow degrees."

With fubmiffion to that writer, I would advance another pofition equally true, " that the principles of eating and drinking are little underftood by favages, and if they arrive to maturity among civilized nations, it is by flow degrees."

The truth is, morality confifts in difcharging the focial duties of life ; and fo far as the ftate of favages requires an intercourfe of duties, the moral principles feem to be as perfect in them as in more enlightened nations. Savages in a perfectly rude ftate have little or no commerce ; the tranfactions between man and man are confined to very few objects, and confequently the laws which regulate their intercourfe and diftribute juftice, muft be few and fimple.* But the crime of murder is as feverely punifhed by favages, as by civilized nations. Nay, I queftion whether it is poffible to name the barbarous tribe, which fuffers an individual to take the life of another, upon as eafy terms as the modern feudal Barons in Europe may do that of a vaffal ; or with the fame impunity that a planter in the Weft Indies takes the life of a flave. I fpeak of a time of peace, and of the conduct of favages towards their own tribes. As to war, every nation of favages has its

arbitrary

---

* It is a fact, fupported by unqueftionable teftimony, that the favage nations on the frontiers of thefe States, have fewer vices in proportion to their virtues, than are to be found in the beft regulated civilized focieties with which we are acquainted.

arbitrary cuſtoms, and ſo has every civilized nation. Savages are generally partial and capricious in the treatment of their priſoners; ſome they treat with a ſingular humanity; and others they put to death with the ſevereſt cruelty. Well, do not civilized people the ſame? Did a ſavage ever endure greater torments, than thouſands of priſoners during the late war? But not to mention the practice of a ſingle nation, at a ſingle period; let us advert to a general rule among civilized nations; that it is lawful to put to death priſoners taken in a garriſon by ſtorm. The practice grounded on this rule, is as direct and as enormous a violation of the laws of morality, as the ſlow deliberate tortures exerciſed by the moſt barbarous ſavages on earth.

Well, what are the ideas of ſavages reſpecting *theft*? How do they differ from thoſe of an enlightened people? Many things are poſſeſſed in common, as proviſions taken in hunting, corn, &c. Ferdinand de Soto relates, that the tribes (and he viſited hundreds in Florida) had public granaries of corn laid up for winter, which was diſtributed by authority to each family, according to its number. But for an individual to take from this common ſtock without licenſe, was conſidered as a criminal defrauding of the public. And with regard to the few articles, in which individuals acquire private property, the ſavages have as correct ideas of *meum* and *tuum*, of theft, treſpaſs, &c. and are as careful to guard private property from invaſion, by laws and penalties, as any civilized people. The laws of the Creeks, the Cherokees, the Six Nations, &c. with regard to theſe and many other crimes, in point of reaſon and equity, ſtand on a footing with thoſe of the moſt civilized nations; and in point of execution and obſervance, their adminiſtration would do honor to any government. Among moſt ſavage nations there is a kind of monarchy which is efficient in adminiſtration; and among thoſe tribes which have had no intercourſe with civilized nations, and which have not been deceived by the tricks of traders; the common arts of cheating, by which millions of enlightened people get

a living

a living or a fortune, are wholly unknown. This is an incontrovertible fact. I lately became acquainted with a lad of about twelve years old, who was taken captiv by the Indians in 1778, while a child, and had continued with them till about ten years old. He had no recollection of the time when he was taken, and consequently his mind could not have been corrupted among the Englifh.   When he was reftored, agreeable to the treaty, he was a perfect favage ; but what I relate the circumftance for, is this ; the lad was not addicted to a fingle vice. He was inftant and cheerful in obeying commands ; having not even a difpofition to refufe or evade a compliance. He had no inclination to lie or fteal ; on the other hand, he was always furprifed to find a perfon faying one thing and meaning another. In fhort, he knew not any thing but honefty and undifguifed franknefs and integrity. A fingle inftance does not indeed eftablifh a general rule ; but thofe who are acquainted with the nativs of America can teftify that this is the general character of favages who are not corrupted by the vices of civilized nations.

But it is faid favages are revengeful ; their hatred is hereditary and perpetual. How does this differ from the hatred of civilized nations ? I queftion much whether the principle of revenge is not as perfect in enlightened nations, as in favages. The difference is this ; a favage hunts the man who has offended him, like a wild beaft, and affaffinates him wherever he finds him ; the *gentleman* purfues his enemy or his rival with as much rancor as a favage, and even ftoops to notice little affronts, that a favage would overlook ; but he does not ftab him privately ; he hazards his own life with that of his enemy, and one or both are very *honorably* murdered. The principle of revenge is equally activ in both cafes ; but its operation is regulated by certain arbitrary cuftoms. A favage is open and avows his revenge, and kills privately ; the polite and well bred take revenge in a more *honorable* way, when *life* is to be the price of fatisfaction ; but in cafes of fmall affronts, they are content with privately ftabbing the

reputation

reputation or ruining the fortunes of their enemies. In
short, the paffions of a favage are under no reftraint;
the paffions of enlightened people are reftrained and
regulated by a thoufand civil laws and accidental circumftances of fociety.

But it will be objected, if favages underftood principles of morality, they would lay fuch paffions under
reftraint. Not at all: Civil and political regulations
are not made, becaufe the things prohibited are in their
own nature wrong; but becaufe they produce inconveniencies to fociety. The moft enlightened nations
do not found their laws and penalties on an abftract
regard to *wrong*; nor has government any concern
with that which has no influence on the peace and
fafety of fociety. If favages, therefore, leave every
man to take his own revenge, it is a proof that they
judge it the beft mode of preventing the neceffity of
it; that is, they think their fociety and government
fafer under fuch a licenfe, than under regulations which
fhould control the paffions of individuals. They may
have their ideas of the nature of revenge independent
of fociety; but it will be extremely difficult to prove,
that, abftracted from a regard to a Deity and to fociety, there is fuch a thing as *right* and *wrong*. I confider *morality* merely as it refpects *fociety*; for if we fu-
peradd the obligations of a divine command, we blend
it with *religion*; an article in which Chriftians have an
infinit advantage over favages.

Confidering moral duties as founded folely on the
conftitution of fociety, and as having for their fole end
the happinefs of focial beings, many of them will vary
in their nature and extent, according to the particular
ftate and circumftances of any fociety.

Among the ancient Britons, a fingular cuftom prevailed; which was, a community of wives by common
confent. Every man married one woman; but a
number, perhaps ten or twelve, relations or neighbors,
agreed to poffefs their wives in common. Every woman's children were accounted the children of her hufband; but every man had a fhare in the common defence

fence and care of this little community.* Was this any breach of morality? Not in the leaft. A Britiſh woman, in the time of Severus, having become intimate with Julia Augufta, and other ladies, at the court of Rome, had obferved what paffed behind the curtain; and being one day reproached for this cuftom of the Britons, as infamous in the women, and barbarous in the men; fhe replied, "We do that *openly* with the *beſt* of our men, which you do *privately* with the *worſt* of yours." This cuftom, fo far from being infamous or barbarous, originated in public and private convenience. It prevented jealoufy and the injuries of adultery, in a ftate where private wrongs could not eafily be prevented or redreffed. It might be an excellent fubftitute for penal laws and a regular adminiftration of juftice. But there is a better reafon for the cuftom, which writers feem to have overlooked; and this is, that a community multiplied the chances of fubfiftence and fecurity. In a favage life, fubfiftence is precarious, for it depends on contingent fupplies by hunting and fifhing. If every individual, therefore, fhould depend folely on his own good luck, and fail of fuccefs, his family muft ftarve. But in a community of twelve, the probability that fome one would procure provifions is increafed as twelve to one. Hence the community of provifions among moft favage nations.†

The Britons, when the Romans firft vifited their ifland, did not attend much to the cultivation of the earth. "Interiores plerique," fays Cæfar, "frumenta non ·

---

* Uxores habent deni, duodenique inter fe communes; et maxime fratres cum fratribus, et parentes cum liberis. Sed fi qui funt ex his nati; eorum habenter liberi a quibus primum virgines quæque ductæ funt.——*Cæfar de bell. Gall. Lib.* 5.

† Let an individual depend folely on his own exertions for food, and a fingle failure of crops fubjects him to a famin. Let a populous country depend folely on its own produce, and the probability of a famine is diminifhed; yet is ftill poffible. But a commercial intercourfe between all nations, multiplies the chances of fubfiftence, and reduces the matter to a certainty. China, a well peopled country, is fubject to a famin merely for want of a free commerce.

non ferunt, fed laƈte et carne vivunt." By eſtabliſhing
a community of goodꙷ, they fecured themfelves againſt
the hazard of want ; and by a community of wives and
offspring, they confirmed the obligations of each to fuperintend the whole; or rather, changed into a natural
obligation what might otherwife depend on the feebler
force of poſitiv compaƈt. Befides, it is very poſſible
that perfonal fafety from the invaſion of tribes or individuals, might be another motiv for eſtabliſhing thefe
fingular communities. At any rate, we muſt fuppofe
that the Britons had good civil or political reafons for
this cuſtom ; for even favages do not aƈt without reafon.   And if they found fociety more fafe and happy,
with fuch a cuſtom than without it, it was moſt undoubtedly right.

Should it be faid, that a community is prohibited by
divine command ; I would anfwer that it is not pre-
fumable that the old Britons had any poſitiv revela-
tion ; and I do not know that the law of nature will
decide againſt their praƈtice.   The commands given
to the Jews were poſitiv injunƈtions ; but they by no
means extend to all nations, farther than as they are
founded on *immutable principles* of right and wrong in
all focieties.   Many of the Mofaic precepts are of this
kind ; they are unlimited in their extent, becaufe they
ſtand on principles which are unlimited in their operation.

Adultery is forbidden in the Jewiſh laws ; and fo it
is in the codes of other nations.   But adultery may be
defined differently by different nations; and the crim-
inality of it depends on the particular poſitiv inſtitu-
tions, or accidental circumſtances of a nation.   The
fame reafons that would render a fimilar cuſtom in
civilized modern nations highly criminal, might render
it innocent and even neceſſary among the old Britons.
A prohibition to gather ſticks on the Sabbath, under a
penalty of death for difobedience, might be founded on
good reafons among the ancient Jews ; but it would
be hard to prove that a modern law of the fame kind,
would be warrantable in any nation.

No.

No. XXI.

NEW YORK, JUNE, 1788.

A LETTER *from a* LADY, *with* RE-MARKS.

SIR,

AS you have, in your writings, difcovered that you take a particular intereft in the happinefs of ladies, I hope you will not deem it a deviation from delicacy, if one of them offers you her grateful acknowlegements, and requefts you to giv your fentiments upon what will be here related.

About four years ago, I was vifited by a gentleman who profeffed an unalterable attachment for me. He being a genteel, fenfible and handfome man, I thought myfeif juftifiable in treating him with complacency. After I was convinced by his conftant attention and frequent profeffions, that I was a favorite, he ufed frequently to upbraid me, for being fo filent and referved : It fhewed, he faid, a want of confidence in him ; for I muft be fenfible he derived the greateft pleafure imaginable in my converfation, and why would I then deprive him of the greateft happinefs by abfenting myfelf, when he paid a vifit, refufing to chat with my ufual freedom. Tho he profeffed himfelf to be an admirer of candor, and a ftrict adherer to the rules of honor, ftill I could not but doubt his fincerity from the extravagance of his expreffions. This he confidered as an affront, faying that no man of *honor* would exprefs fentiments that were not genuine. I found myfeif unwilling to fay any thing that fhould be difagreeable, and difpofed to make him underftand by an attention that I fuppofed him entitled to, that he was prefered to any other perfon. He continued his vifits in this manner for about eighteen months, conducting himfelf with the greateft delicacy, affection and refpect. During this time, he

never

never expreſſed a wiſh to be united, which made me un-
eaſy, as I knew that all my friends thought us engaged.
At laſt I told him his attention was too particular ; I
knew not what conſtruction to put upon it.   He replied that I was too particular in my ideas ; it was a convincing proof to him, with my reſenting *trifling liberties*, that I had not an affection for him, and that he
was not the man I wiſhed to be connected with ; therefore he would not trouble me any longer with his company, and wiſhed me a good night.

This, Sir, you muſt ſuppoſe, diſtreſſed me greatly ;
I viewed myſelf injured and trifled with, but knew not
how to obtain redreſs.   My attachment and pride
were ſo great that I would not allow my friends to call
him to an account for his behavior ; tho I now deſpiſe
his conduct, and would refuſe him the hand of which
he has proved himſelf unworthy, ſtill I feel hurt at the
treatment I have received.   You, Sir, as a friend to
our ſex, and one who wiſhes to preſerve the peace of
mind of unſuſpecting girls, will do them an eſſential ſervice, by your animadverſions on theſe facts, and guarding our ſex from ſimilar impoſitions.

Theſe circumſtances would not have been related,
were I not rendered diſcontented and wretched at home,
in conſequence of refuſing the offers of three other
gentlemen ; either of whom would doubtleſs have
been acceptable, had not my affections been preengag-
ed to one who has proved himſelf worthleſs.   Their
characters and ſituations in life are equal to my wiſhes ;
but I cannot do them ſo much injuſtice and myſelf ſo
much injury, as to giv my hand unaccompanied with
my heart.   In conſulting my own inclinations I have
incurred the diſpleaſure of all my family ; they treat me
with great inattention, and are continually reflecting
on my want of ſpirit and reſolution.   I am confident,
Sir, that every generous mind will pity your unhappy
and diſtreſſed friend,

CONSTANTIA.

T

To CONSTANTIA.

WHILE I acknowlege myfelf honored by your correfpondence, and happy in an opportunity of rendering
you or your fex the leaft fervice, permit me, in compliance with your requeft, which fhall be to me a facred
law, to offer my fentiments with a franknefs, correfponding with that which marks the relation of your
misfortunes.   For altho I feel the warmeft indignation
at every fpecies of deception, and particularly at that
long continued inexplicitnefs which is *deliberate deception*, and which is the caufe of your wretchednefs, candor and truth require that cenfure fhould fall where it
is due.

If the flighteft blame can fall on you, it is that you
indulged the vifits of a gentleman for *eighteen months
without an explicit and honorable declaration of his intention*. A *delicate, affectionate* and *refpectful* attention to a
lady, for one quarter of that period, is fufficient to make
an impreffion on her mind, and decide her choice : At
the fame time, it might not render an attachment on
her part, fo ftrong as to make a feparation very painful ; it might not giv the world an opinion that an engagement exifts, or fubject the lady to the neceffity of
difmiffing other fuitors.   It is therefore prudent at leaft
for a lady to conduct herfelf in fuch a manner as to
bring her admirer to an explicit declaration of his defigns.   A man of *real honor* and principle would not
wait for a ftratagem on the part of the lady, or for a
frank demand of an explanation of his conduct.   A
tolerable acquaintance with the human heart would
enable him to difcover when a declaration would be
agreeable to the lady, and after this difcovery, he would
not keep her a moment in fufpenfe.   A man of generous feelings, who has a lively attachment, looks with
anxiety for fome proof that his addreffes are agreeable,
and that a declaration of his intentions will be well received. No fooner does he find this proof, than he haft-
ens to unbofom himfelf to the dear object of his wifhes,

R   and

and communicate the happinefs he fo ardently defires to receive. When therefore a man neglects fuch a decla- ration, after he has had convincing proofs that his offers would be well received, it may and fhould be taken for granted that his intentions are not honorable, and the lady fhould treat him accordingly.   If therefore, my unhappy friend, you deferve the leaft degree of cenfure, it is becaufe you delayed too long to take meafures for undeceiving yourfelf.   Yet this delay is a proof of your unfufpecting confidence and fincere attachment ; and faults, proceeding from fuch amiable caufes, are almoft changed to virtues ; in your fex, they entitle the fufferer to forgivnefs and to love.

You inform me, Conftantia, that the man who has injured you, profeffed to *adhere to the rules of honor.* Never, Conftantia, truft a man who deals largely in that hackeyned virtue, *honor*.   *Honor,* in the fafhiona- ble fenfe of the word, is but another name for *villany*. The *man of honor* would not be guilty of the leaft impro- priety in public company ; he would not for the world neglect the leaft punctilio of the cuftomary etiquette, but he would, without hefitation or remorfe, blow out the brains of a friend, for treading on his toe, or rob an amiable woman of her reputation and happinefs to gratify his vanity.

If a man talks too much of his *honor*, he is to be avoided, like the midnight ruffian.   He that really poffeffes a virtue never boafts of it, for he does not fuf- pect the world think him deftitute of it.   Numerous profeffions are commonly mere fubftitutes for what is profeffed.

The man, who has given you fo much uneafinefs, never deferved the confidence he won ; he muft be def- titute of principle, of virtue, and of attachment to you.   His deliberate ill ufage proves him to be callous to every tender emotion, and to deferve your contempt. Will not a generous pride and detefation expel the leaft fentiment of refpect for him from your breaft ? Can you not forget that you have been mifled, and will not your innocence buoy you above misfortunes ? That

you

you have refused good offers, is to be regretted ; but your friends, if they know the reason, as they ought, will not pain you by difingenuous reflections.   On the other hand, they will affift you in finding objects to a-mufe you and diffipate your own melancholy reflec-tions.   Smile away the anxiety that fhuts your heart againft other impreffions.   Bafe as men are, there may be fome found who defpife the character of him who has given even an hour's pain ; there may be one who knows *your* worth, and may be difpofed to reward your *conftancy*.

It is a mortifying reflection to an honeft mind, that *bad* hearts are fo often fuffered to giv pain to the *good* ; that the *trifling* and the *bafe* of our fex are not conftrain-ed, by neceffity, to affociate only with the *trifling* and the *bafe* of yours, and that the good, the generous and the conftant fhould be expofed to the abufes of the fic-kle and defigning.   But fuch is the conftitution of fo-ciety, and for the evils of it, we have no remedy, but cautious circumfpection to prevent, or patient fortitude to fupport the adverfe events of our conditions.

No man can entertain a more cordial deteftation of the fmalleft difpofition to annoy the peace of mind and difturb the tranquillity of mankind, than myfelf ; the defign of exiftence here is to footh the evils, and mul-tiply the felicities of each other, and he muft be a villain indeed, who can deliberately attempt to poifon the fources of pleafure, by croffing and difappointing the focial paffions.

To your fex, Conftantia, permit me to giv a word of caution ; never to make any inquiries about a man's family, fortune or accomplifhments, till you know whether he is a man of *principle*.   By *principle*, I mean, a difpofition of heart to conduct with ftrict propriety, both as a moral being and as a member of civil fociety ; that is, a difpofition to increafe the happinefs of all a-round him.   If he appears to wifh for his own gratifi-cation, at the expenfe even of a fervant's happinefs, he is an unfocial being, he is not a fit affociate for men, much lefs for amiable women.   If he is a man of *principle*, then proceed to inquire into his standing in life. *With* principle he may make a woman happy in almoſt any circumſtances ; *without* it, *birth*, *fortune* and *education* ſerve but to render his worthleſſneſs the more conſpicuous. With ſentiments of eſteem, I am your obliged friend, and humble ſervant,   E.

No.

No. XXII.

NEW YORK, JULY, 1788.

A LETTER *to the* AUTHOR, *with* RE-
MARKS.

S I R,

I BEG leave to relate to you a few circumftances
refpecting the conduct of a young friend of mine in
this city, and to requeft your own remarks and advice
on the occafion. Should any other perfon fimilarly
fituated, be difpofed to receive benefit from the advice,
I fhall be much gratified, and my defign more than anfwered.

This young friend to whom I allude, has been till
within a few years, under the watchful eyes of very attentiv parents; from whom he received much better
advice and much more of it, than the generality of
parents in this city are wont to beftow on their children; they taught him to regard truth with a fteady attachment; in fhort his education, till their deaths, was
fuch as might with propriety have been called rigidly
virtuous. Since that inftructiv period, he has been under the guidance of no one but himself; his former affociates with whom he grew up, and for whom he ftill
feels a degree of fchoolmate attachment, are almoft
univerfally debauched characters. The force of example is great, and let it be mentioned to his honor, that
in general he has had fufficient virtue to refift their im-
portunities, and to follow a line of conduct directly
contrary to the one they would gladly have marked out
for his purfuance. He poffeffes many of the focial virtues, and is warmly attached to the amiable part of the
female world. This attachment has preferved him
from the fafhionable vices of the age, and given him a
relifh for domeftic happinefs, which I think he will
never lofe. A young gentleman fo capable of making
himfelf

himfelf agreeable to good and virtuous characters, ought not, in my opinion, to indulge himfelf in any practices, that fhall tend in the leaft to depreciate his general merit. The practices I would mention, are few and not very confiderable; ftill I think he fhould difmifs them entirely, or at leaft not indulge them to his difadvantage. He fings a *good fong,* and he knows it tolerably well; he is often urged into company on that account; he can make himfelf agreeable withal, and is really a *mufical companion*; he pays fo much attention to *learning* and *finging fongs,* that he has but little leifure time on his hands; he reads part of the day, but he reads principally *novels* or *fong books.* I would not be underftood to confider *finging fongs* as criminal; far from it; I am often delighted with a fong from him; but the query with me is, whether he ought not to devote part of the time which he now employs about what may be called genteel trifling, to the improvement of his mind in a manner that may be of lafting benefit to him; I wifh you to giv him your advice, and direct him what books to read. He has another *fault,* which, altho it originates in the benevolence of his difpofition, may ftill be called a fault. He has a very fufceptible heart, and opens it with a generous freedom, fo much fo that he fometimes forgets himfelf, and opens it where he ought not to do. A ftranger with a fpecious outfide might eafily impofe on him. I juft throw out thefe hints, that he may be on his guard againft thofe whofe bufinefs it is to deceive. There are feveral fmaller faults dependant upon, or rather confequent to, thofe I have mentioned, which I at firft intended to have enumerated, but if the firft are amended, the others will forfake him of courfe.

The ANSWER.

SIR,

BY the defcription you have given of your young friend, it appears that he is rather *trifling* and *inconfiderate* than *profligate.* His faults are, *his fpending too*

much

much time in learning and singing songs; and too *much franknefs of heart*, which expofes him to impofitions. But you have not, Sir, informed me whether he was *bred to bufinefs*; and by his character, I judge that he was not. He has had good precepts indeed; but of how little weight are precepts to young people! Advice to the young fometimes does good; but perhaps never, except good habits have been previoufly formed by cor-rect difcipline in manners, or by a mechanical attention to honeft employments. The truth is, advice or feri-ous council is commonly lavifhed where it does no good, upon the young, the gay, the thoughtlefs; whofe paffions are ftrong, before reafon begins to have the fmalleft influence. I am young myfelf, but from the obfervations I have hitherto made, I venture to affirm, that grave advice never yet conquered a paffion, and rarely has reftrained one fo as to render a fprightly youth, in any degree ferious. How fhould it? In-ftructions are tranfient; they feldom touch the heart, and they generally oppofe paffions that are vigorous, and which are inceffantly urging for indulgence.

I have ever thought that advice to the young, un-accompanied by the routine of honeft employments, is like an attempt to make a fhrub grow in a certain direction, by blowing it with a bellows. The way to regulate the growth of a vegetable is to *confine* it to the propofed direction. The only effectual method per-haps is to keep young perfons from childhood bufy in fome employment of ufe and reputation. It is very immaterial what that employment is; the mind will grow in the direction given it at firft; it will bend and attach itfelf to the bufinefs, and will not eafily lofe that bent or attachment afterwards: The mind *will* attach itfelf to fomething; its natural difpofition is to pleaf-ure and amufement. This difpofition may be chang-ed or overcome by keeping the mind, from early life, bufy in fome ufeful occupation, and perhaps by *nothing elfe*. Advice will not produce the effect.

I fufpect, Sir, that your young friend has been bred a trifler; that he has had money to fupport him with-

out

out the labor of acquiring it ; that he has never been anxious about his future fubfiftence. If fo, his educa-tion muft be pronounced erroneous. Whether worth twenty pounds or twenty thoufand, it fhould make no difference in his attention to bufinefs while young. We are the creatures of habit ; a habit of *acquiring* property fhould always precede the *ufe* of it, otherwife it will not be ufed with credit and advantage. Befides, bufinefs is almoft the only fecurity we have for moral rectitude and for confequence in fociety. It keeps a young perfon out of vicious company ; it operates as a conftant check upon the paffions, and while it does not deftroy them, it reftrains their intemperance ; it ftrengthens the mind by exercife, and puts a young perfon upon exerting his reafoning faculties. In fhort, a man bred to bufinefs loves fociety, and feels the im-portance of the principles that fupport it. On the oth-er hand, mankind refpect him ; and whatever your young friend may think of the affertion, it is true that the ladies uniformly defpife a man who is always dang-ling at their apron ftrings, and whofe principal excel-lence confifts in finging a good fong.

If, Sir, your friend is ftill fo young, as to undergo the difcipline of a profeffional or other employment, his habits of trifling may be changed by this means ; but if he is fo far the gentleman as to difdain bufinefs, his friends have only to whiftle advice in his ears, and wait till old age, experience, and the death of his paf-fions, fhall change the man.

Accept of my thanks, Sir, for this communication, and be affured that my opinion on any fubject of this kind will always be at your fervice.   E.

No. XXIII.

BOSTON, MARCH, 1789.

An ENQUIRY *into the* ORIGIN *of the* WORDS DOMESDAY, PARISH, PARLIAMENT, PEER, BARON; *with* REMARKS, NEW *and* INTERESTING.

IN the courſe of my etymological inveſtigations, I hav been led to ſuſpect that all the writers on the laws and conſtitution of England, hav miſtaken the origin and primitiv ſignification of ſeveral words of high antiquity, and in conſequence of the miſtake, hav adopted ſome erroneous opinions, reſpecting the hiſtory of parliaments and trial by peers. Whether my own opinions are wel ſupported by hiſtory and etymology, muſt be hereafter decided by able and impartial judges of this ſubject.

Dome book, or *domeſday book,* iz a word wel underſtood by Engliſh lawyers. *Dome book,* or *dom bec,* az it waz formerly ſpelt, waz the name given to the Saxon code of laws compiled by Alfred. Some other codes of local cuſtoms or laws were alſo denominated *dom becs,* but theze are all loſt. After the conqueſt, a general ſurvey of all the lands in England, except a few counties, waz made by order of William, and recorded in a volum which iz ſtil extant, and called *domeſday.* This ſurvey waz begun by five juſtices aſſigned for the purpoſe in each county, in the year 1081 and completed 1086.

Our pious anceſtors were not a little frightened at the name of this book, which iz uſually pronounced *doomſday;* ſuppoſing it to hav ſome reference to the final doom, or day of judgement. In order to quiet ſuch apprehenſions, lawyers of leſs credulity undertook to refute the common opinion. Jacob, after Cowel, very gravely aſſerts, that the termination *day* in this word does not allude to the general judgement. " The

addition

addition of *day* to this dome book, waz not ment with
any allufion to the final day of judgement, az *moft perfons hav conceeved,*.but waz to_ftrengthen and confirm
it, and fignifieth the judicial decifiv record, or book of
dooming judgement and juftice."* The fame author
defines *domefmen* to be *judges*, or men appointed to
doom.

.. Cowel, a compiler of confiderable authority, fays,
" day or dey,". (for *dey* iz the true fpelling) " does not
augment the fenfe, but only doubles and confirms the
fame meening. It does not, in this compofition, really fignify the mefure of time, but the adminiftration
of juftice ; fo that *domefday* iz more emphatically the
judicial decifiv record, the book of *dooming* judgement."† According to this author, then, *domefday* iz
a judgement of judgements, for he quotes Dr. Hammond
to proov that *day*, *dies*, ημερα, in all idioms, fignifies
judgement. However tru this may be, I beleev our
Saxon forefathers could find a better name for a code
of laws, than *a judgement of judgements.*

" *Domefday,*" fays Coke, " dies judicii," day of
judgement.‡ Such is the influence of founds upon
credulous, fuperftitious minds.

The truth feems to be this ; *domefday* is a compound
of *dom*, judgement, decree or authority ; and *dey*, a
law or rule.§ Or *domes*, in the plural, may fignify
judges. The name of the book then will fignify, ether *the rules of judging*, or *deciding*, in queftions relating
to the real property of England ; or what is more probable, *the rules and determinations of the judges* who furvey-
ed the lands in the kingdom.

That *dom* had the fignification here explained iz capable of proof. The homager's oath, in the black book
of Hereford, fol. 46, ends thus, " So helpe me God at
his

* *Jacob Dict.* word, *domefday.*   † Cowel Dict. *Dayfman.*
‡ Coke Litt. 3. 248.
§ It iz fingular that the laft fyllable of this word *domefday*,
fhould hav been miftaken for *day*, a portion of time ; for the
latter in Saxon waz written *daeg* and *daegum*, az in the Saxon
verfion of the Gofpels ; whereaz the termination of *domefday*
waz formerly, and ought now to be, fpelt *dey.*

his holy *dome* (judgement) and by my trowthe," (troth, that is truth.)* This explanation coincides with the meening of the fame fyllable in other languages, and confirms the hypothefis of the common origin of the languages of Europe, laid down in the Notes to my Differtations on the Englifh Tung. We fee the fyllable in the Greek δαμαω, the Latin *dominus*, (domo) and in the Englifh word *tame*; az alfo in *doom*, *deem*, king *dom*.† In all theze words we obferve one primitiv and feveral derivativ fignifications. Its primitiv fenfe is that of power or authority, az in Greek and Latin. In Englifh, it ftands for jurifdiction, a judge, or a fentence. In *deem*, it denotes the act of the mind in judging, or forming its determinations.

The other fyllable *dey* iz probably the fame word az *ley*, law, with a different prepofitiv article; for etymologifts tel us, that the radical fyllable waz often found in the muther tung *ey*. Cowel informs us it waz not *day*, but *dey*; and another author writes it *d'ey*. The word *dayfman*, or az it ought to be fpelt *deyfman*, ftil ufed both in England and America, is compofed of *dey* and *man*, and fignifies an arbitrator or judge, appointed to reconcile differences. In this country I hav often heerd it applied to our Savior, az mediator between God and man.

The ancient lawyers tranflate the Saxon *dom bec* and *domefdey* by *liber judicialis*; words which feem not to convey the ful meening of the original. I fhould tranflate them, *liber judicum*, the Judges book; or *lex judicum*, the Judges law or rule.

The old Saxon word *ley*, before mentioned, waz, in different dialects, or at different periods, written *ley*, *lah*, *lage*, *laga* : It iz doubtlefs from the fame root az the Latin *lex*, *lege*; and it is remarkable, that the fame word anciently fignified *peeple*; and from this are derived

* Cowel, Law Dict. *dome.*

† In fome words *dom* is fubftituted for the ancient termination *rick*; and in one fenfe, it iz equivalent to *rick*, which implies jurifdiction or power. *King rick* waz ufed az late az Queen Elizabeth : *Bifhop-rick* iz ftil ufed, denoting the territory or jurifdiction of a bifhop.

rived *lay* and *laity*, the peeple az oppofed to the *clergy.**
It iz probable that the primitiv fenfe of the word, in
remote antiquity, waz *peoplé*; and az the peeple made
the laws in general affembly, fo their orders or decrees
came to be called by the fame name. This conjecture
iz not groundlefs, and is no trifling proof of the ancient
freedom of our Gothic anceftors. Tacitus fays exprefsly of the Germans, "De minoribus rebus principes confultant; de majoribus *omnes.*" De Mor
Germ. 11. The princes deliberate upon fmall matters, or perhaps decide private controverfes of fmall
moment; but laws of general concern are enacted in
an affembly of all the peeple.

The origin of *Parifhes* haz puzzled all the lawyers
and antiquaries of the Englifh nation. Johnfon, after
his ufual manner, recurs to the Greek, and derives the
word from παροικια, accolarum conventus, an affem-
blage or collection of peeple in a naborhood. Others
content themfelves with deriving it from the Latin *parochia* or French *paroiffe*. Thefe etymologies do not
fatisfy me. It is improbable that our anceftors went
to the Greek for names of places or divifions of territory, that exifted in England az erly az the Heptarchy;
efpecially az the Greek word before mentioned waz
never ufed in the fenfe of *parifh*. *Parochia* cannot be
the origin of parifh; for it waz not a Roman word;
on the other hand, it is merely a Gothic or Saxon
word latinized by the erly writers on law; and to derive *parifh* from the French *paroiffe* is trifling; for we
might as well derive *paroiffe* from *parifh*, which iz at
leeft az ancient.

"It iz uncertain at what time England waz divided
into parifhes," fay moft of the law writers. Camden,
in hiz Britannia, page 104, fays, the kingdom waz
firft divided into parifhes by Honorius, archbifhop of
Canterbury, in 636. This opinion iz controverted.

Sir

---

* Johnfon derives *lay* from the Greek λαος; as he does all
other words which hav fome refemblance to Greek words in
found or fignification. I beleev the Saxon or Gothic original
and the Greek may be the fame, and of equal antiquity.

Sir Henry Hobart thinks parifhes were erected by the
council of Lateran, in 1179. Selden, followed by
Blackftope, fuppofes both to be rong, and fhows that
the clergy lived in common, without any diftinction
of parifhes, long after the time mentioned by Camden ;
and it appeers by the Saxon laws, that parifhes were
known long before the council of Lateran.*

The truth probably iz, the kingdom was not divided
into parifhes at any one time, but the original ecclefiaftical divifion grew, in a great meafure, out of a prior
civil divifion. *Parifh* iz the moft ancient divifion of
the ecclefiaftical ftate, and originally denoted the *jurifdiction of a bifhop*, or what iz now called a *diocefe*.
For this opinion, we hav the authority of the Saxon
laws and charters. " Ego Cealwulfus, dei gratia rex
Merciorum, rogatus a Werfritho, Epifcopo Hwiccio-
rum, iftam libertatem donavi, ut *tota parochia Hwiccio-
rum* a paftu equorum, regis et eorum qui eos ducunt,
libera fit, &c." Charta Cealwulfi regis, Anno 872.
" Epifcopus, congregatis omnibus clericis totius *paro-
chiæ*, &c." in a paffage quoted by Cowel tit. *parifh*.
Here the *bifhoprick* iz explicitly called a *parifh*, parochia ;
and Blackftone remarks, " it is agreed on all hands,
that in the erly ages of chriftianity in this ifland, parifhes were unknown, or at leeft fignified the fame az a
diocefe does now." Com. Vol. I. 112.

This, being a fettled point, wil perhaps furnifh a clue
by which we may find the true origin of the word and
of the divifion.

It iz certain that there waz an ancient word among
the Gothic nations, and probably among the Celtic,
which fignified originally *a man*, afterwards a freeman,
or landholder, in oppofition to that clafs of men who
had no real property. This word waz fpelt by the
Romans *vir*, and fignified *a man*, by way of eminence,
az diftinguifhed from *homo* ; az alfo a hufband or houfe-
holder. It anfwered to the ανηρ of the Greeks, az diftinguifhed from ανθρωπος, a word denoting the human
race in general. The fame word in the Gothic or ancient

* Blackftone Com. vol. I. 112.

cient German waz fpelt *bar* ;* and probably in fome dialects *par,* for the convertibility of *b* with *p* iz obvious to every etymologift.† In the Erfe language, az Mc Pherfon teftifies, *bar* fignifies a man. The word iz alfo pronounced *fer* or *fear,* which approaches nearer to the Latin *vir: Fergus* or *Ferguth* fignifies a *man of word* or command. In modern Welfh, which iz the pureft relict of the old Celtic, *bar* is a fon, and *barn* a judge. In the ancient Irifh, *brehon* or *barhon,* which iz merely *baron* with an afpirate, fignified a judge. See Lhuyd, Mc Pherfon, Offian, p. 4. and Blackftone's Commentaries, Vol. I.

This word iz the root of the modern word *baron* ; for in ancient manufcripts, it iz fometimes fpelt *viron,* denoting its *derivation* from *vir.* For this we hav the authority of Camden and Du Cange under the word *baron.*

So far we tred on fure ground. That theze words hav exifted or do ftil exift in the fenfe above explained, wil not be denied ; and it iz almoft certain that they all had a common origin.

The

* Camden's Britannia. *Baron.*

† Let no one queftion the probability of fuch changes of confonants which are formed by the fame organs ; for to this day *b* and *v* are often ufed promifcuoufly. In the Spanifh language, we are at liberty to pronounce, *b* az *v,* or *v* az *b* ; and with us, *marble* is often pronounced *marvle.* It is alfo certain that the Roman *vir* is found in the word mentioned by Cefar. Com. 11. 19. *Vergo bretus,* an annual magiftrate a-mong the Ædui, a nation of Germany. This word iz derived from *vir,* and *guberno,* altho Cefar and Tacitus never fufpected it. The fame word iz mentioned by Mc Pherfon, az ftil exifting in the Erft language, *Fergubreth* ; and its meaning iz the fame az in Cefar's time : A decifiv argument that *vir, fer,* and *bar,* are radically the fame ; and that the ancient Celtic language had a common origin with the Latin. A fimilar change of confonants iz obfervable in the words *volo* and *bull* (the Pope's decree) which are radically the fame ; az alfo the German *woll* and the Englifh *will.* So the ancient *Pergamus* iz called by the modern Turks, *Bergamo.* See Mafheim's Eccle. Hift. Vol. I. and my Differtations on the Eng. Language, Appendix.

The word *Baron* iz evidently derived from the German *bar* or *par*, and under the feudal fyftem, came to fignify the proprietors of large tracts of land, or thoze vaffals of the Lord Paramount, who held lands by honorable fervice.*

I fhall hereafter attempt to proov that feveral modern words are derived from the fame root ; at prefent I confine my remarks to the word *parifh*, which, I conjecture, iz a compound of *par*, a landholder, and *rick* or *rich*, which haz been explained, az denoting territory or jurifdiction : *Parick* or *parich*, the jurifdiction of a par or baron.   It iz true the words *baron* and *parlia- ment* feem not to hav been ufed among the Saxons before the conqueft ; but they were ufed by moft of the nations of the fame original, on the continent ; az in Germany, Burgundy, Sweden and Normandy : And the ufe of the word *parochia* in England, before the conqueft, or at leeft by the firft lawyers and tranflators of the Saxon laws, iz to me the ftrongeft proof that fome fuch word az *parick* exifted among the erly Saxons, or which waz latinized by thoze writers.   Even if we fuppofe the word borrowed from nations on the continent, my fuppofition of the exiftence of fuch a word iz equally wel founded, for they all fpoke dialects of the fame tung.

The firft knowlege we hav of the word *parifh* or rather *parochia*, iz in the Saxon laws, copied and tranflated into Latin by thoze erly writers, Bracton, Britlon, Fleta, or others of an erlier date.   In that erly period, *parochia* waz a *diocefe* or *bifhoprick*.

I fufpect the jurifdiction of the bifhop waz originally limited by an erldom, county fhire, or territory of a great lord.   This waz probably the general divifion ; for fometimes a clergyman or bifhop, in the zerude ages,
                                                had

* The feudal fyftem iz commonly fuppofed to hav originated in the conqueft of the Roman empire by the northern nations.   The rudiments of it however may be difcovered az erly az the Cimbric invafion of Italy, a century before the Chriftian era.   Se Florus. lib. 3. c. 3.   The Cimbri and Teutones were tribes of the fame northern race, az the Germans and Saxons.

had cure of fouls in two or more adjoining lordfhips; and it often happened that a lord had much wafte land on hiz demefne, which waz not comprehended in the original *parifh*, and thus came, in later times, to be called *extraparochial*. But whatever particular exceptions there might be, the remark az a general one, will hold true, with refpect to the original jurifdiction of a bifhop.

The number of counties in England iz at prefent forty, and that of the diocefes, twenty four ; but the number of counties haz been different at different times ; and fome changes, both in the civil and ecclefiaftical ftate, hav doubtlefs, in a courfe of a thoufand years, deftroyed the primitiv divifion. It iz however fome proof of my hypothefis, that moft of the bifhops in England are ftil called by the names of counties, or of cities which are fhires of themfelves ; az the bifhop of Durham, of Worcefter, of London, of Norwich, &c. or by the names of the cheef towns in counties ; az bifhop of Winchefter, of Chichefter, &c.

Selden's account of the ancient divifions of the kingdom, confirms this opinion. See Bacon's Selden, ch. 11. The province or jurifdiction of an archbifhop, waz prior to the origin of diocefles or parifhes. Selden haz given an account of a divifion of diocefles by archbifhop Theodore in the feventh century ; by which it appears, that in fome inftances, a diocefe or parifh waz one fhire or county ; and in others, a parochia covered two, three, or more fhires : But in almoft every inftance, the limits of a parifh were the limits of a fhire or fhires. And however ftrange the reader may think it, the word *church* and *fhire* are radically the fame. The Saxon word waz *cyrick* or *cyrk* ;* and the Scotch pronounce and write it *kirk*. It iz, like *fhire*, derived from the Saxon *Sciran*, cir, or *feyre*, to divide. The church or kirk waz the ecclefiaftical divifion, anfwering to *fhire*, and come to fignify the jurifdiction of the cathedral

* So it iz fpelt in the Saxon laws ; but its root waz probably *circe*, from *fciran*, to divide. *C* before *i* and *e* was in Saxon pronounced *ch* or neerly ; hence *circe* is *chircke*.

†hedral church; the primaria ecclefia or mother church; and hençe the Saxon term *cyrick fceate,* church fcot or fees, paid by the whole diocefe.

In later times, the original *parochia* or diocefe was divided or extended by the *Mickle-mote, Witenagemote* or national affembly, by advice of the bifhops, nobles, and cheef men.

From all I can colleÆt refpeÆting this fubjéÆt, it appeers probable, that on the firft converfion of the Sax-ons to chriftianity, each *earle, earlederman,* or erl, whoze manor or jurifdiÆtion waz the origin of a county, had hiz clergyman or chaplain to perform divine fervice. Hiz refidence waz probably in the vicinity of the erl; and this waz the origin of the *cathedral,* or mother church, *primaria ecclefia,* to which the tenants of the whole. diÆtriÆt or erldom afterwards paid tithes. On the firft eftablifhment of theze churches, the tenants paid tithes where they choze; but fraud or delay on the part of the tenant, and the encreafing power of the clergy, occafioned a law of king Edgar, about the year 970, commanding all the tithes to be paid to the mother church, to which the parifh belonged.* This muft hav augmented the welth of the cathedral churches, and given them a fuperior rank in the ecclefiaftical ftate.

Previous, however, to this period, the *thanes* or infe-rior lords, had their chaplains and private chapels; and it waz a rule, that if fuch chapel had a confecrated cemetery or burying ground belonging to it, the lord might appropriate one third of the tithes to the fupport of hiz private chaplain. The clerks or bifhops who belonged to the cathedral churches, and were the of-ficiating minifters of the erls or princes, at that time the firft ranks of noblemen, acquired an influence in
                                   proportion

---

* Blackftone Com. vol. I, 112. That each fhire had its bifhop, feems to be obvious from a law of Edgar, c. 5, where, refpeÆting the county court, it iz ordered, " celeberrimo huic conventui epifcopus et aldermannus interfunto;" not *unus epifcoporum,* but *the bifhop* and *erl.*

proportion to their property and the extent of their jurisdictions. Hence the powers of modern bishops in superintending the clergy of their dioceses. In later times, they acquired large tracts of land, ether by purchase, gift or devise, and in right of their *baronies* gained a seet among the lords of the kingdom in parliament.

The inferior clergy were multiplied in proportion az the people wanted or could support them, and the jurisdiction of an earl's chaplain, being limited originally by his cure of souls, and being founded on a *parrick* or territory of a lord, afterwards gave name to all the jurisdictions of the inferior clergy. Hence the name of *parish*, as denoting the extent of a parson's * ecclesiastical authority.

The jurisdiction of a bishop lost the name of parish, parochia, at a very erly period; but stil the subordinate divisions of the ecclesiastical state continued to be regulated by prior civil divisions. For this assertion, we hav an indisputable authority, which confirms my opinion respecting the origin of parishes. "It seems pretty clear and certain," says the learned and elegant Blackstone, Com. vol. I, 114, "that the boundaries of *parishes* were originally ascertained by thoze of a *manor* or *manors*; since it very seldom happens that a manor extends itself over more parishes than one, tho there are often many manors in one parish." This iz the present state of facts, for originally the parish, like the modern diocese, covered many manors, or estates of the inferior feudatories.

Parliament iz said to be derived from the French, *parlement*, which iz composed of *parler*, to speak, and *ment* or *mens*, mind. Cowel tit. *Parliament*.

"Parliament," says Johnson, "parliamentuns, law Latin; parlement, French." Dict. fol. Edit.

. "It

---

* *Parson* iz said, by Coke and others, to be derived from *persona*, becaufe this officer reprefents the corporation or church, *vicem feu perfonam ecclefiæ gerere*. This reezon feems to be obfcure and unfatisfactory. It iz poffible the word may procced from the fame root az *parish*, viz. *par*.

" It is called parliament," fays Coke Litt. p. 110.
Ed. Lond. 1778, " becaufe every member of that
court fhould fincerely and difcretely *parler le ment*,"
(fpeek hiz mind) " for the general good of the commonwelth ; which name it alfo hath in Scotland ; and
this name before the conqueft waz uzed in the time of
Edward the Confeffor, William the Conqueror, &c.
It waz anciently, before the conqueft, called *michel-fi-
nath*,* *michel-gemote* ; *ealla*, *witena-gemote* ; that is to
fay, the great court or meeting of the king and all the
wifemen ; fometimes of the king, with the counfel of
hiz bifhops, nobles and wifeft of hiz peeple. This
court, the French men call *les eftates* ; or *l'affemble des
eftates*. In Germany it is called a diet. For thoze
other courts in France that are called *parliaments*, they
are but ordinary courts of juftice, and az Paulus Jovius
affirmeth, were firft eftablifhed with us."

The late editor of Cokes Inftitutes, remarks, in a
note on this paffage, that the latter part of this etymology iz juftly exploded, and apologizes for hiz author
by faying, " it iz to be found in preceding authors of
eminence." He difcards the *ment*, and confiders it,
not az an effential, but an adventitious part of the
word ; deeming it fufficient to derive the word from
parler, to fpeak. This opinion he receives from Lambard.

Such a definition, with great deference to theze
venerable authorities, iz a difgrace to etymology. Coke
waz a great lawyer, and Johnfon a good Latin and
Greek fcholar ; but neether of them waz verfed in the
Teutonic language and inftitutions, where alone we
fhould look for the origin of our laws and the Englifh
conftitution. Johnfon indeed waz a mere compiler of
other mens etymologies, and Cowel, Selden, Junius
and others from whom he copied, tho deeply lerned,
fometimes fell into very whimfical miftakes. I am
bold to affert that the Englifh derivation of *parliament*,
or *parlement* from the French *parler*, haz no better authority

* Great fynod—great meeting.

thority than a mere whim or notion of theze writers. We might az well derive *parler* from *parliament*, and both from a *parcel* of goſlips, becauſe they are loqua- cious.

The true etymology of the word iz *par*, or *bar*, a landholder or baron, and *le*, *mote*, the meeting. I ſay *mote*, for this waz the Saxon ſpelling of the word, after the prepoſitiv *ge* waz dropped. It waz originally *ge-mote*, az in *witena-gemote*; afterwards the *ge* waz diſuſ- ed, az in *falk-mote*. What the original French orthog- raphy waz, I am not certain; but the word came to England from France, and we find the French article preſixed, *par-le-ment*; *a meeting of the barons*. The ſame ſound waz uſed in Germany, Burgundy, and oth- er parts of Europe, and in all, it had the ſame meening, which it, in ſome meſure, retains in France to this day.

The *commune concilium* of England, before the con- queſt, conſiſted of the *witena*, or wiſe men. It retained the name of *witena-gemote*, til after the Norman inva- ſion. It iz perhaps impoſſible, at this diſtance of time, to aſcertain exactly the manner of ſummoning this na- tional aſſembly, or whether the commons or leſſer no- bility were entitled to a ſeet. In old charters, the king iz ſaid to hav paſſed laws by advice of the archbiſhops, biſhops, abbots, erls and wiſe men of the relm; ſeniorum ſapientium populi. But we are not able to determin whether theze ſeniores ſapientes were admitted on ac- count of their age and wiſdom; or whether poſſeſſion of real eſtate waz a requiſit qualification. So much iz certain, that in France and Germany, where we firſt heer of *parliaments*, all the *barons*, that iz, all the nobil- ity, were entitled to a ſeet in the national council, in right of their baronys; and this iz aſſerted to hav been the caſe in England.* This fact, ſo well atteſted in hiſtory az to be undeniable, ought long ago to hav led the critical enquirer to the true origin of the French word, parlement. The name of parliament took its riſe under the feudal ſyſtem, when the aſſembly of men, ſo called, conſiſted ſolely of barons or bars. It iz from

this

* Stuarts Engliſh Conſtitution, p. 275.

this circumſtance that the provincial aſſemblies of France are properly denominated *parliaments*. The erly Norman princes, who introduced the name into England, ſummoned none to their council but the cler-gy and nobility, and ſometimes a few only of the great-er barons. The houſe of lords iz ſtrictly a *parliament*, according to the original of the word, altho ſince the commons hav made a part of the legiſlature, the name iz extended to the whole body.

The word *peer* iz ſaid to be derived from the Latin *par* equal ; and this circumſtance haz been the occaſion of innumerable encomiums on the Engliſh *trial by peers*. So far az equality in the condition of judges and parties, iz an excellence in any judicial ſyſtem, the preſ-ent practice of trial by jury iz eſteemable among a free peeple ; for whatever may be the origin of the word *peer*, a trial by men of the naborhood may often proov a capital ſecurity againſt a court devoted to party. But it iz at leaſt doubtful whether *peers*, az uſed for jurors, came from the Latin *par* ; for it iz almoſt certain that the word *peer*, az uſed for nobles, iz derived from the German *par*, a landholder, and this iz undoubtedly the tru primitiv ſenſe of the word. That there waz ſuch a word in ancient Germany, iz unqueſtionable ; and *par-amount*, which ſignifies the lord of higheſt rank, iz from the ſame root ; *par-amount*, the *par* or *baron above* the reſt. The juriſts on the continent latinized the word, calling the lords *pares* ; and this, in later ages, waz miſtaken for the plural of the Latin *par*.

Az the pares or barons claimed almoſt excluſiv ju-riſdiction over their manors, and held courts of juſtice, ether in perſon or by their bailiffs, they came to be con-ſidered az the ſupreme judges in the laſt reſort of all civil and criminal cauſes. *Pares* or *barons* became e-quivalent to *judges*. Hence the *houſe of peers* in Eng-land iz the ſupreme judicatory of the nation. Hence the *parliaments* (meetings of peers) in France are ſu-preme courts of juſtice.

Twelv waz a favorit number with our Saxon an-ceſtors, and the king, or lord paramount, with twelv

judges,

judges, conftituted the fupreme court or council among the ancient Germans. It will hardly be confidered a digreffion to examin this inftitution with more attention ; for if I miftake not, the rudiments of it are vifible az far back az the Chriftian era ; or even az the Gothic migrations to the weft and north of Europe.

In the Edda, or fyftem of Gothic mythology, compiled by Snorro Sturlefon, fupreme judge of Iceland, about the year 1220, we may difcern the principles which would naturally giv rife to the practice of trial by *twelv men*. The Edda will indeed be faid to be a collection of fables. To this I anfwer, fable iz generally, perhaps always, founded on fact ; whatever additions may be made in a courfe of time by imperfect tradition. The Edda iz acknowledged to contain an authentic account of the opinions of the northern nations at the time it waz written. This iz all I afk.

Snorro, and Torfæus the hiftorian of the north, inform us that even in Scythia, " Odin, the fupreme god of the Goths, performed the functions of chief preeft, affifted by *twelv pontiffs, who diftributed juftice*."*

Let us attend to a fact confirming the account. Mallet, a hiftorian of credit, teftifies that the hall or feet of juftice, my be ftil feen in different parts of Sweden and Denmark. " Theze monuments, whoze rude bulk haz preferved them from the ravages of time, are only vaft

* Mallets North. Antiq. Vol. I. 61. The northern nations had, like the Greeks, *twelv* principal deities, and this article in their religious beleef might originate the inftitution of *twelv preefts, twelv judges*, &c. Many civil inftitutions among rude nations, may be traced to their religious opinions ; and perhaps the preference given to the number *twelv*, in Germany, in Greece, and in Judea, had its origin in fome circumftances az ancient az the race of the Jews.

Odin, which in Anglo Saxon, waz *Woden*, waz the fupreme god of the Goths, anfwering to the Jupiter of the Greeks : And it iz remarkable that the words, '*god, good, odin* and *woden*, all fprung from one fource. We fhall not be furprized that the fame word fhould begin with fuch different letters, when we reflect that fuch changes are very common. The Danes omit *w* in *word* ; a dictionary they call *ord-bog*, a word book ; and the Spaniards, in attempting to pronounce *w*, always articulate *g*. See my Differtations, p. 335.

vaſt unhewn ſtones, commonly *twelv* in number, ſet upright, and placed in form of a circle. In the middle iz a ſtone, much larger than the reſt, on which they made a ſeet for their king. The other ſtones ſerved az a barrier to keep off the populace, and marked the place of thoze whom the peeple had appointed to make the election (of king.) They treeted alſo in the ſame place of the moſt important affairs."* There iz one neer Lunden,† in Scania, another at Leyra, in Zealand, and a third neer Viburg, in Jutland.

This being a well atteſted fact, we are diſpoſed to beleev what iz related in the Edda, Fable 7th, where it iz aſked, " what the univerſal father do when he bilt Aſgard, (the divine abode.") It iz anſwered, a-greeable to the receeved opinion of the Goths, " he in the beginning eſtabliſhed governors, and ordered them to decide whatever differences ſhould arize among men, and to regulate the government in the plain, called Ida, wherein are *twelv* ſeets for themſelves, beſides the throne which iz occupied by the univerſal father."‡

On this paſſage, the tranſlator of Mallets Hiſtory haz the following note. " Theze judges were twelv in number. Waz this owing to there being twelv primary deities among the Gothic nations, az there were among the Greeks and Romans ? This I ſhall not take upon me to decide ; but I think one may plainly obſerve here the firſt traces of a cuſtom, which hath extended itſelf to a great many other things. Odin, the conqueror of the north, eſtabliſhed a ſupreme court in Sweden, compoſed of twelv members, to aſſiſt him in the functions of the preeſthood and govern-ment. This doubtleſs gave riſe to what waz after-wards called the ſenate. And the ſame eſtabliſhment in like manner took place in Denmark, Norway, and other northern States. Theze ſenators decided in the laſt appeal, all differences of importance ; they were, if I may ſay ſo, the aſſeſſors of the prince ; and were in number

* North. Antiq. Vol. I. 169.
† London, in England, probably had its name from this place.
‡ North. Antiq. Vol. II. 41.

number twelv, az we are exprefsly informed by Saxo, in hiz life of king Regner Lodbrog. Nor are other monuments wanting, which abundantly confirm this truth.   We find in Zealand, in Sweden, neer Upfal, and if I am not miftaken, in the county of Cornwal, large ftones, to the number of twelv, ranged in the form of a circle, and in the midft of them, one of a fuperior height.   Such in thoze rude ages, waz the hall of audience ; the ftones that formed the circumference, were the feets of the fenators ; that in the middle, the throne of the king.   The like monuments are found alfo in Perfia, neer Tauris.   Travellers frequently meet there with large circles of hewn ftones ; and the tradition of the country reports, that theze are the places where the *raous* or giants formerly held their councils.* I think one may difcover veftiges of this ancient cuftom, in the fable of the *twelv peers* of France, and in the eftablifhment of twelv jurymen in England, who are the *proper judges,* according to the ancient laws of that country."

It iz certain that fome outlines of this mode of deciding controverfies by *twelv,* may be feen in the cuftoms of the Cimbri and Teutónes, long before the Chriftian era.   But I cannot find that the idea of *equality* ever entered into the original inftitution.   On the other hand, every old authority that I hav confulted confirms me in the opinion, that the *twelv men* were chofen from among the landholders or better claffes of peeple ; that they were the *judges* of the court, and that the diftinction between judges and jury, law and fact, iz a refinement or improovment on the original conftitution, and comparativly of modern date.

It iz certain that a difference of rank exifted among the Germans in the time of Tacitus.   " Reges ex nobilitate, duces ex virtute fumunt."†   The fame writer exprefsly declares, that matters of inferior concern and private juftice came within the jurifdiction of their *princes.* " De minoribus rebus principes confultant, de
majoribus,

* See Chardin's Travels, Vol. III.

† Tac. de Mor. Germ. c. 7.

majoribus, omnes."* In another paſſage, he is more
explicit : " Principes jura per pagos vicoſque red-
dunt."† Ceſar iz ſtill more explicit : " Principes
regionum atque pagorum inter ſuos jus dicunt, contro-
verſiaſque minuunt."‡ Theze *principes regionum atque
pagorum,* Blackſtone ſays, we may fairly conſtur to be
lords of hundreds and manors ;§ they were originally
electiv, az we are informed by Tacitus, " eliguntur in
conciliis

* Tac. de Mor. Germ. c. 11.—† C. 12.——‡ De Bello
Gallico. lib. VI. c. 21.

§ Com. Vol. III. 35. This cannot be ſtrictly true ; for
the *principes* were electiv ; and therefore could not hav owned
the land (pagus) or exerciſed the office of judge in right of
their property. The kings, princes, and generals of the ancient Germans were elected ; ſome for their *nobility,* that iz,
the reſpectability of their families, ariſing from the valor and
merits of their anceſtors ; others, az their *duces,* military commanders, were choſen for their *virtues,* their perſonal bravery.
This I take to be the meening of that paſſage in Tacitus,
"Reges ex nobilitate, duces ex virtute ſumunt."
" The *Comites ex plebe,*" ſays Selden, chap. 18, " made one
rank of freemen ſuperior to the reſt in wiſdom." The Saxon
nobles were called *adelingi,* or wel born ; the freemen, *frilingi,*
or free born ; the latter might be aſſiſtants in the judicial department. The lower ranks were called *lazzi* or ſlaves ; and
indolence iz ſo neceſſary a conſequence of bondage, that this
word *lazzi,* or *lazy,* haz become ſinonimous with *indolent, ſlug-
giſh.* This word iz a living national ſatire upon every ſpecies
of ſlavery. But the effect of ſlavery iz not merely *indolence ;*
its natural tendency iz to produce *diſhoneſty ;* " almoſt every
ſlave, being, ſays Dr. Franklin, from the nature of hiz employment, a theef." Az a ſtriking proof of this, we may inſtance the change of meening in the words *villain* and *knave,*
which at firſt denoted *tenant* and *plowman,* but during the op-
preſſions of the feudal ſyſtem, come to ſignify, *a rogue. Vaſſal*
alſo denoted originally, a *tenant* or *feudatory* of a ſuperior lord.
It waz an honorable name, the barons being called the kings
vaſſals. But ſervitude iz ſo natural a conſequence of the tenure of lands under a propietor, in fee, that *vaſſal* haz become
ſinonimous with ſlave.* The change of meening in theze
words

* Blackſtone, Vol. II. 52, ſays, " we now uze the word *vaſſal* op-
probriouſly, az ſinonimous to ſlave' or bondman, on *account of the
prejudices we hav juſtly conceeved againſt the dccrins grafted on the feudal
ſyſtem.*" So good a man ought not to hav uzed the word *prejudice ;* and
ſo great a man ought to hav aſſigned a better reezon for this *opprobri-
ouſneſs* of the modern word *vaſſal.*

conciliis principis," and each had a hundred comites,
or affiftant judges, who were chofen from among the
peeple. " Centeni fingulis, explebe comites, concilium
fimul et auctoritas, adfunt."* Theze hundred affiftants, or companions, were chofen *ex plebe*; but when
chofen formed the *concilium principis*. ·The prince
waz their prefident, chofen by themfelves, *eliguntur in
conciliis principes*, and had *auctoritatem*, authority or jurifdiction in the town or diftrict.

The idea of equality iz no where fuggefted ; on the
contrary ; the hundredors when chofen became a court
or legiflature in the diftrict, competent to the general
purpofes of government. No mention iz made of a
diftinction between the legiflativ and judicial departments ; on the other hand, we may fafely conclude,
from the paffeges of Cefar and Tacitus before quoted,
that the powers of making laws and deciding caufes
were vefted in the fame men. Cefar fays, " nullus eft
in pace communis magiftratus," nor could the Germans, in their primitiv fimple mode of living, need
fuch a magiftrate. The princes *jus dicunt, controverfi-
afque minuunt*, diftributed juftice, by the affiftance of
their *comites*, and according to the circumftances of the
peeple.† This at leeft waz the cafe with refpect to
matters of fmall magnitude.

                                                            The

words iz a volum of inftruction to princes and legiflators.
Reduce men to bondage, and they hav no motiv but feer to
keep them induftrious and honeft, and of courfe, moft of them
commence rogues and drones. Why hav not the tyrants of
Europe difcovered this truth ? Good laws, and an equal diftribution of the advantages and the rights of government,
would generally be an effectual fubftitute for the bayonet and
the gallows. Look thro Europe ; . wherever we fee poverty
and oppreffion, there we find a nurfery of villains. A difference in the property, education and advantages, originates the
difference of character, between the nobleman of niceft honor,
and the culprits that fwing at Tyburn.

  * De Mor. Germ. c. 13.

  † The practice of choofing affiftant judges in the Roman
commonwealth, waz fomething fimilar to our mode of impannelling a jury. Theze affiftants were fometimes a hundred,
                                                            and

The number of *comites principis*, or affiftants, waz originally a *hundred*. This gave name to the diftrict which they governed, and which afterwards confifted of any indefinit number, ftill retaining the primitiv name. In later ages, the number of affiftant judges waz reduced ; a grand jury ftill confifts of twenty four ; a petit jury commonly confifts of twelv, but on certain occafions, and by the cuftom of particular places in England, may be compofed of fixteen, eight or fix.*

Such waz the conftitution of the ancient Germans, in which we may difcover the principles of the fyftem which they every where eftablifhed, after their conquefts in Gaul, Spain, Italy and Britain.

Twelv waz a favorit number, not only with the Saxons, but with all the nations of northern original. They had twelv principal deities ; they numbered the units up to *twelv*, inftead of ftopping at ten, like other nations ;† they had twelv judges to affift their kings or princes ; their hall for the election of their kings confifted of twelv huge ftones, placed in a circle. Hence we difcover the origin of the twelv fenators of Sweden,‡ Denmark and Norway ; the twelv counfellors of ftate in ancient times ; the fable, az it iz called, of the twelv peers in France ; the twelv judges in England, and
    the

and it iz not improbable, the Roman and German cuftoms of electing that number might be derived from the fame original.

The Prætor, (cheef juftice) or princeps judicum appointed by him, fummoned a number of perfons, who were called *judices felecti*, felect judges. Theze were to giv their verdict in criminal matters, like our juries. On the day of trial, the firft thing after opening the court, waz the *fortitio judicum*, or impannelling of the jury, performed by the *judex quæftionis* or cheef judge on the trial, who took by lot fuch a number of the *judices felecti*, or jurymen, az the law, on which the accufation waz founded, had determined. Liberty waz given to the parties to reject, (challenge) and the places of thoze rejected, were filled by new appointments.—*Kennetts Antiq. of Rome*, 138.

* See Coke Litt. and Hargraves notes on this fubject.

† Mallets North. Antiquities.

‡ Mentioned in the preceding note, copied from Mallet.

the trial by twelv peers or jurors, which waz formerly
common to all the northern nations of Europe.*

On the Gothic eftablifhments in the fouth and weft
of Europe, government took a military complection.   The kings parcelled out the conquered lands
among their generals, called *duces* or *principes*, by the
Latin writers ; and by the Saxons, *heretoga*.   The
generals of firft rank receeved or acquired whole provinces, az Burgundy, and the principalities of Germany.
Theze territories they diftributed among their inferior
officers and *comites* or retainers, of whom every lord
had great numbers about hiz perfon.   Theze conftituted a fecondary, but very numerous clafs of nobility ;
and altho there might be differences of rank and property among them, they were called by one general appellation.   In England, they were called *thanes*, from a
word fignifying *to ferve*, becaufe they held their lands
by the condition of military fervice.   On the continent, they were called *barons*, that is freemen, or tenants of land, upon condition of rendering certain military and honorable fervice to their fuperior lord, who
waz called lord *paramount*.

Blackftone remarks, that " a baron's iz the moft
general and *univerfal* title of nobility ; for originally every one of the peers of fuperior rank had alfo a barony
annexed to hiz title."†   The origin of this title haz
occafioned great enquiry among antiquaries ; but the
difficulty vanifhes upon my hypothefis, which derives
the word from *bar*, a landholder and freeman ; for on
the eftablifhment of the feudal tenures, all the lands
were held by a few men ; the proprietors were all called
barons, and this accounts for the *univerfality* of the title
juft mentioned.   Thus the bifhops, after they had obtained gifts of large tracts of land or manors, refigned
them to the conqueror, William ; accepted them again
                                                            fubject

---

* Thefe facts gave rife to Cokes quaint remarks, " that
the law delighteth herfelf in the number of twelv ;" and he
adds, " the number of twelv iz much refpected in holy writ ;
as 12 apoftles, 12 ftones, 12 tribes, &c." On juries, fol. 155.

† Com. Vol. I. 398.

fubject to the conditions of lay fees, claimed rank with the nobility, and took their feets in the Englifh houfe of lords. Actual poffeffion of a barony waz originally requifit to conftitute a lord of parliament ; but the title iz now granted by the king without the poffeffion.

Blackftone mentions the difficulty of tracing the word *baron* to its primitiv fenfe ; but confirms the foregoing explanation when he fays, " the moft probable opinion iz that *barons* were the fame az our *lords of manors.*"* The name indeed waz not ufed in England (fo far as can be collected from Englifh writers) till after the conqueft. But it iz certain that the feudal fyftcm, tho not in all its feverity, waz eftablifhed in England before that period ; and degrees of nobility were cotemporary with the Saxon eftablifhments in the ifland. The firft clafs were called in Saxon *heretoga,* that iz generals or military commanders. But the moft ancient and perhaps the moft important civil title waz that of *earles* or *ealdormen.* Theze erls were called alfo in Saxon *fchiremen,* for they exercifed fupreme jurifdiction in the *fhires.* After the conqueft they were called by the correfponding Norman title *counts,* from *comites,* becaufe they were the king's companions in war ; and their jurifdiction waz called a *county.*†

Inferior to theze in rank were the Saxon *thanes,* who were fo called from the Saxon *thanian* miniftrare, becaufe they were the *comites* or attendants of the ancient kings or earls. Theze were numerous, and after the conqueft called by the equivalent continental title, *barons.* Of theze there were different ranks, *thani majores* or *thani regis,* who ferved the king in places of high importance, and took rank next to the bifhops and abbots. Theze had inferior thanes under them, called *thani minores,* who were alfo *lords of manors.*‡ The word

* Com. Vol. I. 399.

† I am by no ineens certain that this derivation of *counts* from *comites,* iz juft ; it iz at leeft az probable az otherwife, that *contces* may be a Gothic word. But this iz conjecture.

‡ See Cowel on the word *thane* ; and in Domefday, " thanus, eft tenens, qui eft caput manerii."

word *peer* I fuppofe to be derived from the fame root az *baron*, bar or par, and to be equivalent in fenfe. It iz cleer to me that *landholder*, or man by way of eminence, waz its original meening ; and that it iz a proper name of the ancient nobility, given them az proprietors of vaft tracts of land, and that it had no reference to *equality* of rank.

But there are better proofs of this point than that drawn from this fuppofed derivation. The true original fignification of the word we hav in the phrafes, *houfe of peers, peers of the relm, peerage.* And for this affertion we hav the beft authorities in the language. Cowel, from whom Johnfon and moft modern lawyers have borrowed their definitions of law terms, after explaining the word *peer* az denoting jurors, fays exprefsly, " but this word iz *moft principally ufed for thoze that be of the nobility of the relm and lords of the parliament.*" Here the author haz mentioned a well fupported fact, and quotes ancient authorities. But he immediately leevs fact, and runs into conjecture, az to the reezon of this appellation, which he deduces from a preconceeved, but probably erroneous, opinion. " The reezon whereof iz, that altho there be a diftinction of degrees in our nobility, yet in all public actions they are equal ; az in their votes of parliament, &c." Here the author takes it for granted that the word *peer* fignifies *equal*, and affigns, az a caufe of its *moft principal* appropriation to the nobility, that the men, tho of different ranks, hav an *equal vote* in parliament. This a curious reafon indeed ! A man muft be more credulous than I am, to beleev this flight circumftance would giv rife to fuch a particular appropriation of a name. One would think that the fame reezon would hav given the name to the clergy in convocation and other ecclefiaftical courts. Yet the learned and candid Blackftone haz copied the fame reezon. " The commonalty, like the nobility, are divided into feveral degrees ; and, az the lords, tho different in rank, yet all them are *peers* in refpect of their nobility ; fo the commoners, tho fome are greatly fuperior to others, yet all are in law *peers*, in
refpect

refpect of their *want* of *nobility.*"* This appeers very extraordinary, that an *equality of fuffrage* fhould giv an appellation in preference to *difference of rank,* which iz fo much more obvious and more flattering to the haughty barons. But if the commoners are *peers* or *equals in fuffrage* az well az the lords ; that iz, on the *fame principle* ; or as Blackftone ftates it, if the *lords* are *peers* becaufe they are *noble,* and the commoners are *peers,* becaufe they are *not noble,* why hav not the commoners the fame appellations of *peers of the relm ?* The lords are not *equally* noble, by Blackftone's own ftatement, for they are of very different ranks ; and the commons are not equally *ignoble,* (this word iz ufed merely for contraft) for they are of different ranks : Yet the vote of one commoner iz az good in the houfe of commons, az that of another ; and the vote of one lord, in the other houfe, iz az good az that of another. If the *equality of fuffrage* iz a proper ground for the title of *peers* in one houfe, the reezon extends to the other. Yet commoners are not *peers of the relm* ; and until a good reezon can be affigned for the diftinction of titles between the houfes, I fhall beleev that the word *peer* had originally no reference to *equality.*†

But

---

* Com. Vol. I. 403. "But the fame author, in page 399, fays, the right of *peerage* feems to hav been originally territorial, that iz, annexed to lands, manors, &c. the proprietors of which were, in right of thoze eftates, allowed to be *peers of the relm* ;" that iz, in plain Englifh, certain men, in right of their eftates, were allowed to be *equals* of the relm. This will not pafs for reezon and truth on this fide of the Atlantic.

† Horne, in hiz Mirror of Juftices, chap. I. fect. 2. fays, "altho the king ought not to hav any *peer* (that iz, *equal*) in the land, yet becaufe he cannot be a judge in a cafe where he iz a party, it waz behovefull by the law that he fhould hav *companions* to heer and determin of all writs and plaints of all wrongs, &c. Theze companions are now called *countees, earles,* according to the Latin *comites,* &c." This iz fingular ! The king ought to hav no *equal* ; therefore he ought to hav *companions* for judges ; or, in plainer words, if poffible, the king ought not to hav *equals* in the kingdom, therefore he fhould hav *peers* to heer and determin criminal caufes. Common fenfe at leeft, if not etymology, will fay, "the king ought not to hav *equals,* but he muft hav *judges.*"

But fay the Englifh lawyers and antiquaries, "the bifhops are not in ftrictnefs held to be *peers of the relm*, but only *lords of parliament*."* Why not ? What is the diftinction ? Here our authors leev us in the dark ; but perhaps the foregoing clu will leed us to the light. Bifhops were not the original proprietors of baronies ; they were not *bars* or *pars*, the hereditary lords of manors, confequently not *peers of the relm*. This iz fuch an obvious folution of the queftion, that I am furprized it fhould hav been overlooked. Under the papal hierarchy, the clergy gained vaft influence over the minds of men, and by a variety of expedients, became poffeffed of large eftates, and fome of them, of ancient baronies. But their acquifitions were comparativly of modern date, and many of them ufurpations, altho in confequence of their eftates they obtained a feet in the houfe of lords. They are therefore *lords of parliament* ; but the ancient peers, priding themfelves upon the antiquity of their families, and claiming certain prefcriptiv rights, would not admit the clergy to an equal fhare of authority and honor ; for to this day, a vote of the temporal lords iz good againft every vote of the clergy.+

" The appellation *peer*," fays Cowel, " feems to be borrowed from France, and from thoze *twelv peers* that Charlemagne inftituted in that kingdom." The fame word waz ufed by other nations. Theze twelv peers conftituted a great council or fupreme court, and the members were all *barons*, or of the nobility.‡ Can the word, applied to the members of this council, fignify *equal* ? By no meens. Here we trace the word
to

---

* Blackftone, Vol. I. 157, from Staunford P C. 153.

+ It iz now held that *e converfa*, a vote of the fpiritual lords, if a majority, iz good againft all the temporal lords ; but Coke douts it. Suppofing this to be admitted, the privilege is modern, and makes nothing againft my fuppofition.

‡ It haz been remarked that *baron* iz the moft general title of nobility ; indeed every nobleman waz originally a *baron*. Coke. 1. 74. The lords of manors, both in England and on the continent, were the fuitors in the king's court, and called *pares curtis* or *curiæ*. The lords tenants were called the *peers* of hiz court baron. See Blackftone, Vol. I. ch. 4.

to a remote period of antiquity, and find it ufed by the emperor of Germany ; or at leeft an appellation giv-en to one of the firft councils in hiz dominions. This iz the pure primitiv fenfe of the word *peers, barons* ; that iz, in the full latitude of its fignification, all the an-cient nobility; who held lands of him ether immediately or mediately ; who formed hiz fupreme judicial court, and in fome countries, hiz legiflativ affembly ; who were hereditary councillors of the crown ; and cheef *judges* of all caufes arifing on their own manors, ex-cept fuch az were of great confequence.

This explanation accounts for what Selden has re-marked, chap. 65, that " the barons of England, be-fore the reign of Edward I, were rather the *great* and *richer fort* of men, than *peers*, altho they were of the number." That iz, the Saxon thanes, who were great landholders, but inferior to the erls, had, after the con-queft, receeved the appellation of *barons* from the con-tinent ; but, being a fecondary clafs of nobility, had not claimed or acquired the power and privileges of the German and French princes and nobles who had the title of *peers*, until the Norman kings had intro-duced, into the kingdom, the oppreffiv and invidious diftinctions of the feudal tenures, in the full extent of the fyftem.

It will be enquired, if this iz the fenfe of the word, how came juries of common freeholders to be called *peers ?* The anfwer iz eefy ; the jurors were the *judg-es* of the inferior courts, and not merely the equals of the parties, az iz commonly fuppofed. The *erl* or *baron*, in ftrictnefs ; but more commonly, the vice-comes, fheriff or lords deputy, waz the prefident or cheef juftice, and the jurors, the *affiftant judges*. For this opinion, numberlefs authorities may be produced. The barons were the affiftant judges, *peers*, in the court of the lord paramount or king, and thus became judges by prefcription ; fo the word *peer* or *baron*, in time, became equivalent to *judge*. Az the nobles were judg-es in the kings court, and decided on appeels in the laft refort, fo the freeholders who conftituted the court

T   in

in the county, hundred or manor, came to be denominated *peers*, that iz, *judges*.

Reeve, in hiz hiſtory of the Engliſh Law, remarks,
that " the adminiſtration of juſtice in the days of
William the conqueror, waz ſo commonly attendant
on the rank and character of a baron, that *baro* and
juſticiarius were often uſed *ſynonimouſly*." Blackſtone
ſays, " it iz probable the barons were the ſame az our
lords of manors, to which the name of court baron
(which iz the lords court, and incident to every manor)
givs ſome countenance." Vol. I. 398. It iz ſurpriz-
ing, theze writers ſhould approach ſo neer the tru original and meening of the word, *baron*, and not reech it.

Moſt writers on the ancient ſtate of government in
Europe, hav remarked that the nobility held the office
of judges. " Les meſmes comtes," ſays Mezeray,
" et ducs, qui jugeoint les François, les menoient a
la guerre." tom. I. p. 118. The counts and dukes
were both judges and generals.

" Duo—comitum munera fure ; unum videlicet
juſtitiæ populis miniſtrandæ, alterum militiæ ſibi ſub-
jectæ, quando in bellum eundum erat, educendæ atque
regendæ." Muratori. Antiq. Ital. tom. I. p. 399.
The counts had two offices or departments of buſineſs ; the adminiſtration of juſtice, and command of
the troops in war.

Stuart, in hiz Engliſh Conſtitution, remarks, " that
the erls preſided in the courts of law. Their juriſdiction extended over their feefs : In all cauſes, civil and
criminal, they judged without appeel, except in caſes of
the utmoſt conſequence." Part 3. Sect. 3.

I preſume it iz needleſs to multiply authorities. The
ſtrongeſt argument in favor of my opinions iz drawn
from the ſupreme judiciary powers of the houſe of
lords in England. The lords are *peers* of the relm ;
that iz, the ancient preſcriptiv judges or barons, who
claim the privilege by hereditary right or immemorial
uſuage. The *houſe of peers*, iz literally and in fact, *a
houſe of judges* ; an aſſembly of all the ancient judges in
the kingdom. So Selden relates of the Saxons, whom
he

he fuppofes to be defcended from the fame original az the Greeks, and long prior to the ages of Roman glory ; " their country they divided into counties or circuits, all under the government of *twelv lords*, like the Athenian territory under the Archorites. Theze, with the other *princes*, had the *judicial power of diftributiv juftice* committed to them, with a hundred commoners out of each divifion." Tit. Saxons. · The fame writer declares, chap. 58, that the nobles " were in their moft ordinary work, *meetings of judges*, or *courts of judicature* ; that the king and hiz barons made many laws and conftitutions which hav obtained the name of ftatutes," (which he fuppofes may hav been equitable decifions of new caufes, which afterwards had the force of laws) " that the judges of this fupreme court are the *baronage* of England ; and that the houfe of lords ftill retain their fupreme judiciary powers by ancient prefcriptiv right."

In addition to this authority, I would remark that the modern fupreme judiciary of Scotland iz copied almoft exactly from the ancient Saxon trial by laghmen or thanes. The lords of feffion, or prefident and fourteen judges, are a court of law and fact, without a jury ; and this iz exactly the *old* trial by *peers*.

The parliaments in France are juftly faid by lord Coke, to be *ordinary courts of juftice* ; another ftriking evidence of what I hav advanced. The word *parliament* came from France, where it denotes that affembly of barons, which conftitutes the fupreme *court of juftice* in each of the feveral provinces. This iz the original import of the word, and the parliaments in France ftill retain that fignification. This name waz introduced into England, under the Norman princes, and fuperfeded the Saxon name of the national affembly, *witenagemote*. Indeed, during the depreffion of the peeple, under the firft princes of the Norman line, when the military tenures were eftablifhed with rigor, national affemblies were called but feldom, and when fummoned, confifted principally of the bifhops and peers (barons) of the relm. They however acquired the name of *par-*

liament, and retain it to this day ; altho one branch of that body iz compofed of commoners. The tru meening of *parliament* iz a *meeting* of *barons* or *peers,* and their principal bufinefs waz to decide controverfies : They had original jurifdiction over caufes in which the nobles were parties, az men of rank would not feek redrefs before an inferior tribunal ; and they had an appellate jurifdiction over other caufes in the laft refort. The parliament of England iz a legiflativ body ; but the *houfe of lords* retains the primitiv privilege of finally deciding controverfies. This branch of the legiflature alone anfwers to the *parliaments* in France, which approach neer the ancient inftitution.*

So in England, the houfe of lords, and even the temporal lords alone, were called formerly a *parliament.* Blackftone, b. IV, c. 19, upon the authority of ancient books and records, repeetedly denominates the houfe of peers, when acting az a court of fupreme judicature, a *parliament,* a *full parliament* ; and the fpiritual lords are not permitted to giv any vote upon *gilty* or *not gilty,* for they are not ancient *peers* (that iz, barons, prefcriptiv judges) of the relm. It haz been douted whether the fpiritual lords had a right to fit in the houfe on the trial of a peer ; but by a determination of the lords in the erl of Danby's cafe, 1679, they were permitted " to ftay and fit in court in capital cafes, till the court proceeds to the vote of gilty or not gilty." Still they form no part of the court ; the temporal lords conftituting a *full parliament,* that iz, az I hav explained the tru primitiv meening of the word, *a meeting of barons or judges.*†

　　　　　　　　　　　　　　　I would

* The Norman princes might well call their councils *parliaments, meetings of barons* ; for they often fummoned none but the barons and clergy, and fometimes but a few of the barons. Henry the third, once fummoned but twenty five barons of two hundred and fifty, then in the kingdom, and one hundred and fifty of the clergy. Yet this meeting waz a *parliament.* Selden, chap. 67.

† Thoze who wifh to fee a more particular account of the extenfiv judicial powers of the barons in Europe, may confult Robertfon's Charles V. Vol. I. page 49, and note [Z] page 150, where the authorities are referred to.

I would juſt add on this head, that the inſtitution of *twelv judges* in England, iz copied from the ancient mode of trial in Germany. The old *Curia Regis* conſiſted of the king, hiz grand juſticiary, the officers of hiz palace and *his barons.* This court followed the kings perſon wherever he went. Out of this were formed the ſeveral courts now eſtabliſhed at Weſtminſter. But the title of *barons of the exchequer* and *barons* of the cinque ports, who are judges, furniſhes an additional argument in favor of my opinions.

The foregoing explanation of the words, *baron* and *peer*, leeds to a probable account of the *trial by peers.* It can be prooved that the jurors were the *judges* of the county, hundred and manor courts, and the probability iz that the ſuitors in theze courts receeved the appellation of *peers*, from the circumſtance of their being landholders. Several authorities ſeem at leeſt to favor this opinion.

" Concerning the inſtitution of this court by the laws and ordinances of ancient kings, and eſpecially of Alfred, it appeereth that the firſt kings of this relm had all the lands of England in demeſne, and les grand manors et royalties, they reſerved to themſelves ; and of the remnant, they, for the defence of the relm, enfeoffed the barons of the relm, with ſuch juriſdiction az the court baron now hath, and inſtituted the freeholders to be *judges of the court baron.*"*

" The manor courts are of two ſorts. The firſt iz by the common law, and iz called the court baron, az ſome hav ſaid, for that it iz the freeholders or freemens court, (for *barons* in one ſenſe ſignifie *freemen)* and of that court the *freeholders,* being ſuitors, be *judges.* The ſecond iz the copyholders court, which iz called a court baron, becauſe among the laws of king Edward the confeſſor, it iz ſaid : " Barones vero qui ſuam habent curiam de ſuis' hominibus," taking the name of the baron who waz lord of the manor, or for that properly

* Coke Litt. 74. That the freeholders were judges iz tru ; but that the barons and freeholders derived their authority from kings, iz wholly a miſtake.

erly in the eye of the law, it hath relation to the *freehold-ers who are judges of this court.* And in ancient charters and records, the *barons* of London and the cinque ports do fignify the *freemen* of London and the cinque ports."* Theze paffages are exprefs to my purpofe. Indeed it muft hav been that the freeholders, now called *jurors*, were judges ; for the lord of the manor waz cheef judge or prefident merely, and we heer nothing, at this erly period of Saxon jurifprudence, of a diftinction between law and fact.

Horne, in the Mirror of Juftices, afferts† "that by the conftitutions of Alfred, the free tenants in every county, hundred and manor, were to meet together and *judge their nabors.*" "Every free tenant hath ordinary jurifdiction in theze courts." "The lords and tenants fhall incur certain penalties by the *judgement of the fuitors.*" "Theze courts are called county courts, where the *judgement iz by the fuitors*, if there be no writ, and iz by warrant of ordinary jurifdiction." That iz, when there waz no fpecial court held by the juftices in eyre.‡ So alfo in a book called the "Diverfity of Courts," written in Henry the eighth's time, it iz faid, "in the court baron the *fuitors are the judges*, and *not* the *fteward.*"

Cowel tels us, "the court baron iz more properly *curia baronum*, i. e. the court of *freeholders*, (for fo bar-ones does alfo fignify) over whom the lord of the manor prefides. In this court the *freeholders are judges.*"§

Selden's authority confirms this fact. He fays, "neether waz the bifhops nor fheriffs work, in the folk-mote or county court, other than directory or declaratory ; for the *freemen* were judges of the fact, and the other did but *edocere jura populo.*" Here a diftinction iz cleerly made beetween the *freemen* and the *pop-ulus* ; the freemen were the judges, and the bifhop or fheriff edocuit jura, proclaimed the decifion to the multitude.

---

* 1. Coke Litt. 73.——† Cap. I. Sect. III.

‡ He muft fpeck of the ftate of things after the conqueft, otherwife *juftices in eyre* would not hav been mentioned.

§ Law Dict. *Court baron.*   ‖ Bacon's Selden. chap. 24.

multitude. The freemen, or landholders, then were the *peers* of the court ; they were not the *equals* of the multitude, for the *populus*, the laborers of all defcriptions, were confidered az belonging to an inferior clafs of men, and had no voice in the folk-mote.

To fum up the whole, we hav the authority of the correct and judicious Blackftone, who exprefsly afferts, book III. chapters IV and V, that in the court baron, the hundred court and county court, the freeholders or fuitors are *the judges*, and the fteward in the two former, and the fheriff in the latter, are *the regiftrars or minifterial officers*. Now it iz well known that before the conqueft, theze included *all the courts* that were in the kingdom, except the *witenagemote*, in which there waz nothing like a jury, feparate from the members of that council. So that the freeholders or jurors were not only *judges*, but they were the *fole judges* in all the inferior courts in the kingdom ; and of courfe there could be little or no diftinction between *law* and *fact*. Nay, more, the fuitors were the *witneffes* alfo ; and the principal reezon for fummoning *freeholders of the vicinage* waz originally this ; it waz fuppofed they were acquainted with the facts in difpute. Hence laws were made to compel the jurors to *tell the truth, if they knew the facts*, which waz always fuppofed, till the contrary appeered. In theze courts fmall caufes were decided ; and the county court had cognizance of ecclefiaftical caufes, az well az civil, and often determined difputes between the nobles, about real eftates of immenfe value.

But important matters were generally brought bebefore the *witena-gemote*, or affembly compofed of the king, bifhops, erls and wife men. This waz a national council, which united in itfelf all powers, legiflativ, judicial, civil and ecclefiaftical, in law and equity. Such a thing az a jury waz never known in this fupreme court. William the conqueror firft feparated the civil from the ecclefiaftical authority, and fubftituted the *aula regiæ*, a high court, confifting of hiz cheef officers and barons, in place of the Saxon *witena-gemote*. This court waz the fupreme judicature in the nation ; a jury

waz

waz no part of it, and it followed the king wherever
he went, till it waz fixed by Magna Charta in Weft-
minfter Hall. Afterwards, in the reigns of Henry III
and Edward I, feveral courts were carved out of the
Aula Regis ; az the common pleas; the court of kings
bench, the exchequer and chancery courts ; and it does
not appeer that a jury, diftinct from the judges, formed
any part of the important common law courts, till after this period. The diftinction therefore between
judges and jury, law and fact, feems not to hav been
known, till the diffolution of the *Aula Regis*, at the
cloze of the thirteenth century.

Let us enquire what kind of men theze freeholders
were, who were fummoned az jurors or judges at theze
courts.

Lord Coke iz exprefs, and quotes Glanvil and Bracton for authorities, that " in ancient times the jurors
were *twelv knights*," (that iz, probably, perfons holding land amounting to a knights fee.)*

Henry III iffued writs to the feveral counties to enquire into the liberties of hiz fubjects, by *twelv good and
lawful knights.*† The Saxon laws are more explicit.
" Habeantur placita in fingulis wapentachiis, ut exean-
tur *duodecem thayni* et præpofitus cum eis, et jurent fu-
per fanetuarium, quod eis dabitur in manu, quod ne-
minem innocentem velint accufare, vel noxium conce-
lare."‡ Here the law of Ethelred iz explicit in ordaining a court of twelve *thayni*, thanes or barons, with
their præpofitus or prefident, who waz the officer of
the hundred. Cowel remarks on this paffage, " that
this may feem to intend the number of *judges*, and not
of the *jury* ; but the jury themfelves, in fome cafes, are
judges, that iz, they are *judges* of the *fact*, and the judge
iz bound to giv fentence according to their verdict."

This

---

* Some fay this fee waz eight hundred akers of land ;
others, fix hundred and eighty, or 20l. a year, which, confidering the difference in the value of money, waz equal perhaps
to 300l. or 400l. at the prefent time. Here feems to be a
confufion of ancient and modern ideas. The ancient knights
fee waz a certain tract of land ; in later times that fee waz
valued at 20l. in money.

† Hale's Hift of Com. Law, 154.——‡ L L Ethel. c. 4.

This writer here fuppofes the *thayni* to be really *jurors* and *judges* ; but *judges* only of the *fact*.   This iz *the fundamental error* of moft lawyers who hav written on the fubject ; they take it for granted, that the diftinction of *law* and *fact* waz coeval with the trial by twelv free-holders.   Yet a fingle circumftance, mentioned by Cowel in the fame page, with the paffage quoted, might hav undeceeved him, which iz, that " trial by jury waz anciently called *duodecem virale judicium*," the *judgement* of twelv men.   Their fentence or decifion waz called a *judgement* ; the diftinction between the *verdict* of a jury, and the *judgement* of the court, waz unknown in the erly ages of the Saxons ; nor can I find it mentioned, till after the conqueft.

This, and fimilar paffages, hav however occafioned much difpute among other Englifh lawyers and anti-quaries.   They hav adopted the opinion, that a jury muft confift of twelv equal commoners, and cannot ex-plain what iz ment by fummoning *twelv thanes.* " Brady and Hicks," fays Stuart, " contended that theze thanes were *not jurors*, but *judges* or *lawyers.* Coke and Spelman were of a different opinion." The truth iz, they were both *jurors* and *judges* ; and a knowlege of the tru primitiv fenfe of one little mono-fyllable in our language, would hav unravelled the whole myftery to theze learned enquirers.

The moft ufual word for jurors, in the Saxon laws, iz *lahmen* or *lagemen* ; a word that haz puzzled the law writers, az it feems to meen fomething more than *equals* ; and they hav no idea of any thing in a jury, but *equality.* Hicks fuppofed them to be judges, " duo-deni jure confulti," men verfed in law.   Spelman rendered the word, *legales homines*, good and lawful men ; very inadequate words indeed ; but the error haz been copied times without number, and ftill pre-vails.   *Lahman* iz literally a *law man*, man of the law, a judge.   Law waz in a rude ftate, at that period ; but the thanes were both *lawyers* and *judges* ; *jure confulti.**

Profeffional

* We find by ancient records, that the clergy, before the conqueft, were fometimes fummoned az jurors or judges in the temporal

Profeſſional diſtinctions could not be but little known, amidſt an unlettered peeple, who had few poſitiv laws, and fewer records and precedents ; and the *lahmen*, the *ſeniores thani*, or *meliores viri*, az they were called, were ſummoned at certain times to decide controver- ſies, according to law, where a law waz provided ; oth- erwiſe according to their diſcretion. The deciſions of theze *lahmen* were held in eſteem ; many of them were preſerved and handed down by tradition, and I hav no dout, theze, rather than ſtatutes, gave riſe to the general and particular cuſtoms, which are called the common law of England.*

Coke defines *lahman* to be one, " habens ſocam et ſacam ſuper homines ſuos ;" that iz, liberty of hold- ing a court over hiz tenants : Which explanation he quotes from Bracton. " Soke, (or ſoc) ſignificat lib- ertatem curiæ tenentium quam *ſocam* appellamus."†

This

temporal courts.§ But the *thanes* were the moſt uſual judges in the courts baron. The proper Saxon name of this court waz *halimote* or *halmote*, *hallmeeting* ; " Omnis cauſa terminetur vel hundredo, vel comitatu, vel *halimote*, ſocam habentiam, vel dominorum curia."‡ And in W. Thorn, Anno 1176, the judges of this court are expreſsly ſaid to be thanes, " *tha- nenſes, qui* in *Halimcto* ſuo, in Thaneto, omnia ſua judicia ex- erceri*," (debent.) Selden, chap. 47, mentions a law of Henry I, which recites a cuſtom of that time, by which " the *biſhops* and *erls*, with *other the cheef men* of the county, were preſent in the county court az aſſiſtants in directory of judge- ment." Nothing can be more explicit. And altho Selden, in a paſſage hereafter quoted, mentions a compromiſe between Gunthrune, the Dane, and the Saxon king, that men of a rank inferior to lords ſhould be tried by their *equals*, yet this inferior rank could extend only to *freemen* ; for others were never admitted upon juries.

* " And the ſheriffs and bailiffs cauſed the free tenants of their bailiwicks to meet at the counties and hundreds, at which juſtice waz ſo done, that every one ſo judged hiz na- bor by ſuch judgement az a man could not elſewhere receev in the like caſes, until ſuch times az the cuſtoms of the relm were put in writing, and certainly eſtabliſhed."——Mirror. chap I. ſect. 3.

† Fleta. lib. I. c. 47.

§ See Selden, tit Sax. biſhops.——‡ L. L. Hen. I. cap. 10.

This word iz found in domefday and in the laws of
Edward the confeffor.   Cowel quotes a paffage from
an ancient book, where .Ulvet, the Son of Forno, iz
called *lagaman* of the city of York, where, he fays, it
doutlefs fignified fome cheef officer, az judge or re-
corder.   Thoze who had *focam* et *facam*, or jurifdiction over the perfons and eftates of their tenants, were
the *thanes* or barons ; and this iz agreed by Lambard,
Somner, Coke, Cowel, and moft writers on law.*
Lambard, whoze authority iz very refpectable, fpeeks
of a jury thus : " In fingulis Centuriis comitia funto,
atque liberæ conditionis viri duodeni ætate fuperiores
unà cum præpofito, facra tenentes juranto, &c."   Of
a jury *per medietatem leriquæ*, he fays, " Viri dacodeni
jure confulti, Angliæ fex, Walliæ totidem, Anglis et
Wallis jus dicunto."   Fol. 91. 3.   Here Lambard
not only defcribes jurors az men of *free condition* and
refpectable for age, but az *jure confulti*, the *judges* of
the court ; and *jus dicunto* ; they were men who ad-
miniftered law and juftice.   This, it appeers from all
ancient teftimonies, waz the uniform practice among
the Saxons.   The jurors were twelv *thancs* or men of
free condition ; *lahmen, jure confulti*, or judges, and
conftituted the *court* ; with the præpofitus, or proper
officer of the diftrict, az their prefident, who fat az the
deputy of the erl, in the county court ; the deputy of
the lord of the manor, in the court baron ; or az the
cheef magiftrate of the hundred.   And one fource of
error in underftanding this ancient inftitution, haz
been the wrong tranflation of *lahman*, by Spelman and
others, who rendered the word, *legalis homo* ; a good
and lawful man.   The meening iz not fo indefinit az
a *lawful man*, which could not be redily underftood or
explained.   Rude nations do not deal in fuch vague
ideas.

* *Laghman*, to this day, iz the name of a judge or magiftrate, both in Sweden and Iceland.   In theze countries it retains its primitiv and tru Englifh meening.—Mallets North.
Antiq. Vol. I.

ideas.   The meening iz, *man of law*, whoze bufinefs
it waz to know the law and adminifter juftice.*

But if we fuppofe the word to meen *legalis homo*,
and that the only requifit in a juror, iz freedom ; or
that he fhould be *liber homo* ; this would exclude a
vaft proportion of the Englifh nation from the privilege.   I know that Magna Charta repeetedly mentions
theze freemen, *liberos homines*, and fecures to them
certain rights, among which iz, trial *per pares fuos*,
which I fuppofe to hav been originally, *by their judges* ;
altho at this period, the idea of equality in the condition of judges might hav prevailed : And indeed the
freemen were moftly tried by men of equal rank.   I
am fenfible alfo that the modern conftruction of Magna
Charta extends this privilege to every man in the relm
of England ; *omnis liber homo* iz faid to comprehend
every Englifh fubject.   I rejoice that by the ftruggles
of a brave peeple, this conftruction of that compact haz
actually

---

* Selden waz forced to confefs the *jure confulti* and *ætate fuperiores*, fo often mentioned in the Saxon laws, az compofing
the homage or jury of twelv, to hav been *cheef men both for
experience and knowlege*. To fuch as *ftumble at this conceet*, as
he exprefses it, he remarks that the work of jurors requires
them to be cheef men, az they *judge of matter of fact* ; (a reezon
drawn from the modern notions of jurymen's province.) And
he adds, the jurors, who were co-aſſeſſors, with the bifhop or
fheriff in the court, were feeted in the moft eminent place, and
might hav held it to this day, az they do in Sweden, had the
cheef men ftill holden the fervice. But the great became neg-
ligent of fuch public duties, and left the bufinefs to thoze of a
meener condition, who would not or durft not take the bench ;
and therefore took their feets on the floor—(took feparate
feets.) He fays further, that the Danes, on their fettlement
in England, would not aſſociate with men of this condition ; fo
that a compromife took place between Alfred, the Saxon king,
and Gunthrune, the Dane, by which it waz decreed, that a
lord or baron fhould be tried by twelv lords, and one of inferior rank, by *eleven of his equals* and *one lord*. This waz in
the cafe of homicide only ; tho afterwards the law might extend to other cafes and civil fuits. By hiz own account of the
matter, this writer fuppofes the trial by *twelv* waz originally
a trial by the *cheef men, (thanes lahmen)* and the idea of equality
waz never fuggefted in the practice till the ninth or tenth century.

actually taken effect in a considerable degree. But I cannot think all the Englifh nation were comprehended in the words of the inftrument ; or that the privilege of *trial by peers* waz extended, or ment to be extended, to all the peeple. Magna Charta waz merely a convention between the king and hiz barons, affembled at Runing-mead ; and the laboring part of the peeple, debafed by fervitude under an oppreffiv ariftocracy, feem hardly to hav been in the contemplation of the parties. The villeins, ruftics, or tenants at will, who probably compofed a majority of the peeple, had one privilege indeed fecured to them : It waz ftipulated that they fhould not be deprived, by fine, of their carts, plows, and other inftruments of hufbandry ; that iz, they fhould not be deprived of the meens of laboring for their mafters. Further than this, a large proportion of the Englifh were not noticed in Magna

tury. But juries exifted at courts for centuries before ; and the word *peers* iz acknowleged to hav had its origin on the continent, where it fignified the lords or members of the high court inftituted by Charlemagne. In modern ufe, trial by *peers* iz trial by equals *generally* ; for men are moftly become freemen and landholders ; but this waz not the primitiv practice ; nor was *equality* the bafis of the inftitution. Even if we fuppofe the word peer to hav fignified *equal*, as uzed originally on the continent, it extended no privilege on that account to the body of the nations where it waz ufed ; for it ment only the *kings equals*, hiz *comites*, hiz dukes, erls and barons, among whom he waz merely *primus inter pares*. In England Bracton, who wrote under Henry III, declares █ king waz confidered in this light ; and that the " *erls and barons are his affociates*, who ought to bridle him, when the law does not."[*] The courts then which Charlemagne inftituted in France and Germany, confifted merely of the kings *peers* or *equals* ; and in theze countries, the courts remain moftly on the ancient footing ; fo that none but the nobility can be tried by their *equals*. In this fenfe of the word therefore juries were not ufed in England, till the compromife between Alfred and Gunthrune, about the year 900. Before that period, the jurors were not called or confidered az *equals* ; but they were *thanes, jure confulti, lahmen* and *clergymen*. A diftinction afterwards took place, and lords were tried by *their* equals, and commoners by *theirs*.

* L. 1. c. 16.

na Charta, but were confidered az a part of their lord?
property, and transferable, like moveables, at their plezure.

The *freemen,* or thoze claffes of peeple which came
within the defcription of *liberi homines* in that famous
convention, were the nobility and clergy tenants *in
capite,* or fuch at moft az had a life eftate in lands, and
could ferve on juries. The lazzi, villeins, or modern
copyholders, were not at that time capable of ferving ;
they were below the rank of freemen ; they had not
the right of trial by peers, even in the common acceptation of the word ; nor were they admitted to the
privilege till the reign of Richard III. Multitudes of
them are not *peers* of *the commons,* even on the principle
of equal fuffrage, for they hav not the property requifit
to qualify them for the privilege of voting at elections.
Blackftone's affertion therefore, that every fubject of the
kingdom haz a right by Magna Charta, to trial by hiz
equals, cannot be tru, for vaft numbers of the nations
are not, and never were, entitled to be jurors. But in
the fenfe I underfland and hav explained the word, every man haz a right to *trial by hiz peers ;* that iz, by
freeholders of the vicinity, who are *his judges.* The
propriety of calling them *hiz judges, pares fuos,* iz difcovered in the gradation of courts eftablifhed in England. The *peers of the relm,* or barons, were originally
the fuitors or judges in the kings court, where alone
the nobility were tried ; hence the barons were always
tried by *their* judges, *pares fuos.* The clergy, the thanes
of the lower clafs, or other freeholders who had life
eftates in lands, were the fuitors in the courts of the
counties, the hundreds and manors. Theze were
the *judges* of theze courts, and called *peers.* The freemen might be faid to be tried by their *equals* ; but the
villeins were not ; yet both were tried by *their* peers ;
that iz, by the peers of theze inferior courts, who were
exclufivly *the judges.**

From

---

* " The divifion of the county waz done by the *freemen,*
who are the *fole judges thereof.*" Selden, Matthew, Paris, and

others,

* Selden on the authority of Polydore.

From what haz been advanced on this fubject, if we may rely on fubftantial authorities, and at leeft probable etymologies, the following conclufions may be fafely deduced. That in ancient Germany, the *principes pagorum et regionum*, with a certain number of affiftants, originally a hundred, fometimes twenty four, but commonly twelv, elected by the peeple, (not *pro re nata*, but for a ftated period) formed a council (concilium) for the government of a diftrict : That in their military expeditions, the *duces*, or generals, had their *life guards*, or comites, who attached themfelves to the perfon of their cheef, and fought by hiz fide :[*]

That

others, teftify that the *folk-mote*, peeple's meeting or county court, waz a county parliament, invefted with legiflativ or difcretionary powers in county matters. In theze fmall diftricts, they appeer to hav been competent to decide all controverfies, and make all neceffary local regulations. The legiflativ, judicial and executiv powers, both civil and ecclefiaftical, were originally blended in the fame council ; the witena-gemote had the powers of a legiflature, of a court of law, and of a court of equity over the whole kingdom, in all matters of great and general concern. But this court waz compofed of lords, bifhops, and *majores natu* or *fapientes*, men refpected for their age and lerning, who were of the rank of *freemen*. All the freemen were bound alfo to do fuit in the lords court, and to attend the *folk-mote* on the fheriffs fummons ; but *twelv* were ufually felected to fit az judges in common cafes.

The vaft powers of the county court, when the freeholders were all fummoned and actually fat in judgement, may be underftood by two facts. Odo, the conquerors half-brother, and Lanfrank, archbifhop of Canterbury, had a difpute about certain lands and tenements in Kent. The archbifhop petitioned the king, who iffued hiz writ, and fummoned the freemen of the county, to take cognizance of the fuit. After three days trial, the freemen gave judgement for the archbifhop, and the decifion waz final.

In like manner, two peers of the relm, a Norman and an Italian, fubmitted a title in fifteen manors, two townfhips, and many liberties, to the freeholders of the county, whofe judgement waz allowed by the king.[§]

[*] " Magnaque et comitum æmulatio, quibus primus apud principem fuum locus ; et principum, cui plurimi et acerrimi comites."[†] The princes kept az many of thefe retainers in their
fervice

[§] Selden. Chap. 48.————[†] Tacitus de mor Germ. c. 13.

That theze retainers, in fome of the Teutonic dialect:
on the continent, were called *barons*, az they were called
thanes by the Saxons in England : That after the ir-
ruption of the northern nations into the fouth of
Europe, the conquered lands were divided among the
great officers and their retainers, az fees or ftipendiary
feuds, on the honorable tenure of military fervice :
That the princes, erls and barons, hav been, from time
immemorial, the affiftant judges in the kings courts, and
eech of them, a cheef judge, with power of holding courts,
on hiz own demefnes : That parliaments on the continent were *affemblies of barons*, and originally *courts of juftice*, az they are ftill in France : That the word *peers* waz
firft ufed on the continent, to denote the members of
this fupreme judicial court, and in its primitiv fenfe,
az derived from *bar* or *par*, it fignified freemen or landholders ; and thence came to denote *judges*, who were
originally the proprietors of lands or manors : That
this latter fenfe iz its tru meening, whether applied to
the houfe of lords or to a common jury, who were anciently the *judges* of the inferior courts, and are ftill, in
many cafes, judges of law az well az fact, notwithftanding the modern diftinction, which haz taken place
in confequence of an extenfiv and vaftly complicated
fyftem of jurifprudence : That the houfe of lords in
England retains the primitiv fenfe of the word *peers*, az
well az the original right of *judging* in the laft refort,
and this houfe alone iz a *parliament*, according to the
ancient meening of the word on the continent : That
the *freemen* mentioned in Magna Charta and all the old
law writers, were thoze who held their lands by honorable fervice, for term of life, or had eftates of inheritance ; and that the lazzi, villiens or bondmen, who
conftituted the major part of the nation, were not comprehended under the words *liberi homines*, were not entitled to be jurors themfelves, and confequently could
not be tried by their *equals* : That the twelv jurors
                                                among

---

fervice in time of peace, az they could fupport. " Hæc dignitas, hæ vires, magno femper electorum juvenum globo cir-
cumdari, in pace, decus, in bello, præfidium. Ibm."

among the Saxons were the *cheef men* of the county and
judges : That the idea of *equality* in the jurors or
judges waz introduced by the pride of the nobility,
and the humble condition of their tenants, under the
invidious diftinctions of ranks created by the feudal
fyftem : That this idea however haz been the meens
of preferving the rights of both in England ; while the
nations on the continent, having been lefs fuccefsful in
their ftruggles, and not having wrefted the *right of
judging* from the barons, the original *peers* or proprietors of that right, hav not acquired a privilege, inefti-
mable in a country where diftinctions of rank prevail,
and do not enjoy the bleffings of equal liberty : That
this privilege haz been confiderably extended in England, by the abolition of military tenures, and the diffufion of property among the commons : But that
America haz given the privilege its utmoft extenfion,
by making laws of inheritance that enable *every man* to
be a freeholder ; thus reducing the Englifh theory to
practice, and entitling every man literally to the right
of *trial by hiz equals*.

How far theze conclufions are fupported by the foregoing authorities and arguments, every reeder will
judge for himfelf. I hav ventured my opinions with
my ufual franknefs, in oppofition to thoze of the fages
of the law, which hav been receeved for centuries.
The vaft weight of authority, and long eftablifhed prepoffeffions of men in favor of a different theory, make
me diffident of my own opinions on this fubject ; but
there are many paffages in ancient law writings, and
many cuftoms and laws ftill exifting in the Englifh
conftitution and government, which I cannot explain
and reconcile on any other hypothefis.

The excellence of trial by peers, in ancient times,
appeers to me to hav confifted in this ; that twelv indifferent men of the naborhood, with the power of judges, were the guardians of life and property againft the
rapacity of the lord of the manor or hiz deputy. It iz
a fact well known that *fheriffs*, the deputies of the erls,
were in feveral counties hereditary officers ; but when

U   they

they were not, they had almoſt·unlimitted powers in
the ſhire, which they often abuſed to oppreſs the peeple.   Under the feudal ſyſtem they appeer to hav been
almoſt abſolute tyrants ; and the undue exerciſe of
their powers, probably gave riſe to thoze articles of
Magna Charta, which declare, that " no freeman ſhall
be taken, impriſoned, or diſeized of hiz freehold, liberties, or free cuſtoms, but by the lawful judgement of
hiz peers, or by legal proceſs ; that ſheriffs ſhould not
hold county courts above once a month ; that ſheriffs,
caſtellans, coroners, and kings bailiffs, ſhould be reſtrain-
ed from holding pleas of the crown ; that ſheriffs, who
had the management of the crown revenues, within
their ſeveral diſtricts, ſhould not raize the farms of
counties, hundreds, and tythes, according to their plezure."   Theze proviſions were evidently deſigned to
remedy actual evils ; the violence and uſurpations of
the executiv officers, who acted under the king, or the
great lords, with powers almoſt uncontrolled.* Againſt
ſuch petty tyrants, the revival or confirmation of the
right of trial by twelv freeholders of the vicinage, muſt
hav been a capital ſecurity : But freeholders alone
could be impannelled on a jury ; *freeholders* alone could
be diſeized of *freeholds* ; conſequently the privilege of
being tried by *equals*, could extend to freeholders only.
With reſpect to all others, the excellence of the inſtitution could not conſiſt in the *equality of condition* in the
jurors ; but in having twelv ſubſtantial freemen, impartial, independent men, unaccuſtomed to oppreſſion,
to check and control the miniſters of juſtice.
    Since the ſeparation of court and jury, law and fact,
juries, in civil caſes, hav become of leſs conſequence.
· Judges

* In the time of Henry II, there were in England eleven hundred and fifteen caſtles, and az many tyrants az lords of caſtles.
William of Newbury ſays, in the reign of Stephen, " Erant
in Angliaquodammodo tot reges, vel potius tyranni, quot dom-
ini caſtellorum."   It waz the tyranny of theze lords or their
deputies, which rendered the intervention of twelv judges of
the naborhood, highly neceſſary to preſerve the peeple from
the impoſitions of their ra acious maſters. Hence the privilege of this mode of trial derived an ineſtimable valu.

Judges are appointed by the reprefentativs of the peeple, ether in legiflature or fome other form, and are removeable for mifbehavior. They are ufually az good
judges of fact as a jury, and better judges of law. One
ftate* haz a ftatute empowering the parties to fubmit
fact az well az law to the court. This places the
court on its Saxon inftitution, except az to the number of judges. It iz alfo a common practice for the
parties to agree on the facts, and fubmit the law to the
court. The practice fuperfedes a jury. On commercial queftions an ordinary jury are altogether unfit to
decide ; they are incompetent judges, becaufe commerce iz regulated by peculiar laws, beft known by
merchants. Hence the inftitution of chambers of
commerce, and the practice of referring caufes to arbitrators of the mercantile profeffion.

But the principal valu and excellence of juries are
preferved in criminal caufes. Judges, by long cuftom,
become hardened in the bufinefs of condemning, and
may fometimes pronounce fentence, which, even when
legal, may be unneceffary. Jurors, lefs accuftomed to
the cruel tafk, retain thoze feelings which fometimes pleed againft evidence, in favor of humanity, and
foften the rigor of penal laws.

I fhall cloze theze remarks with two quotations from
very refpectable authors.

What Camden haz collected concerning the word
baron, ferves to illuftrate and confirm my opinions on
this fubject ; and the reeder will be pleezed with the
following paffage from his Britannia, Vol. I. page 238.

" Among the greater nobility, the barons hav next
place. And here, tho I am not ignorant what the
lerned write concerning the fignification of this word
in Cicero ; yet I am willing to cloze with the opinion
of Ifidore, and of an ancient grammarian, who will hav
barons to be mercenary foldiers. This feems to be
pretty plain from that known place of Hirtius in the
Alexandrian war ; " they run to the affiftance of Caffius ; for he always ufed to hav *barons*, and a good
number

* Connecticut.   U 2

number of foldiers for fudden occafions, with their
weapons reddy, about him, and feparate from the reft.''
Nor iz the old Latin and Greek Gloffary againft us,
when it tranflates *baro* by αντρ, a man ; az always in
the laws of the Longobards, *baro* iz ufed for a man.

The etymologies of this name which fome hav fan-
cied, do not by any meens pleafe me.   The French
heralds will hav barons to be fo called from *par-hom-
mes* in French ; that iz, of equal dignity ; the Englifh
lawyers fay it iz from *robora belli*, the finews of war ;
fome Germans think it a contraction of banner-heirs,
i. e. ftandard bearers ; and Ifidore derives it from ba-
reis, i. e. grave or weighty.   Alciatus thinks the name
comes from the *berones*, an ancient peeple of Spain,
which he fays were formerly ftipendiaries ; but that
other, from the German *bar*, i. e. *a free man*, pleezes
me better.

The precife time when this name came into our
ifland, I hav not yet difcovered : The Britons difown
it ; and there iz not the leeft mention made of it in the
Saxon laws, nor iz it reckoned in Alfrick's Gloffary
among the titles of honor ; for there, *dominus* iz tranflated *laford*, which we hav contracted into *lord*. And
among the Danes, the free lords, fuch az our barons
are at this day, were called thanes, and (and az Andreas
Velleius tells us) are termed fo ftill. In Burgundy,
the ufe of this name iz very ancient ;* for Gregory of
Tours fays thus, " the barons of Burgundy, az well
bifhops az others of the laity, &c."   The firft mention
of a baron in England, that I hav met with, iz in a
fragment of the laws of Canutus, king of England and
Denmark, and even there, according to different copies, it iz read vironus, baronus, and thani.   But that
the barons are there ment, iz plain from the laws of
William the conqueror ; in which that word in the
laws of Canutus iz tranflated by *baro*. Take the whole
paffage.   " Let the exercitals† be fo moderated, az to
be tolerable.   An erl fhall provide fuch things az are
fitting, eight horfes, four faddled and four unfaddled;

four

* About the year 580.——† Heriots or reliefs.

four ſteel caps, and four coats of mail ; eight javelins,*
and az many ſhields ; four ſwords, and two hundred
mancae† of gold. But a kings *viron* or *baron*, who iz
next to him, ſhall hav four horſes, two ſaddled and
two unſaddled ; two ſwords, four javelins, and az many
ſhields, one ſteel cap, and fifty mancae of gold."

In the beginning of the Norman times, the valvaſors
and thanes were reckoned in order and dignity, next
to the erls and barons, and the greater valvaſors (if we
may beleev thoze who hav written concerning feudal
tenures) were the ſame that barons are now. So that
baro may ſeem to hav come from that name ; which
time haz, by little and little, made ſomewhat ſmoother.
But even then it was waz not a title of any great hon-
or ; for in thoze times there were erls who had their
barons under them : And I remember, I hav red in
the ancient conſtitutions of France, that there were ten
barons under one erl, and az many cheeftans‡ under a
baron. It iz likewiſe certain, that there are charters
ſince the Norman conqueſt, wherein the erls write
thus : " To all my barons, az well French az Engliſh, greeting, &c." Nay, even citizens of the better rank
were called *barons* ; ſo in domeſday book the citizens of
Warwick are ſtiled *barons* ; and the citizens of London,
with the inhabitants of the cinque ports, had the ſame
title given them. But a few years after, az ſenators of
Rome were choſen according to their eſtates, ſo they
were accounted *barons* with us, who held their lands by
an entire barony, or thirteen knights fees, and one third
of a knights fee, every fee (az we hav had it in ancient
book) being computed at twenty pounds, which in all
make four hundred marks ; for that waz the value of
one entire barony ; and they who had land and revenues
to this value, were wont to be ſummoned to parliament.
It ſeems to *hav been a dignity, with juriſdiction, which our
court-barons in ſome mezure ſhow.§ And the great number
of barons iz an argument that they were ſuch lords who could
hold*

---

* Lancæe.——† Poſſibly for *Mancuſæ*, i. e. thirty pence.
‡ Capatanei.
§ This opinion of the lerned Camden, adds no ſmall weight
to my conjectures reſpecting the origin of trial *per parcs*.

hold pleez within their own jurisdiction, (like thoze whom the Germans call free-heirs) especially if they had their castles ; for then they answered the definition of Baldus, the famous lawyer, who calls him a baron, that had a mere and mixt government in some castle, by the grant of the prince. And (az some would hav it) all who held baronies, seem to hav claimed that honor ; so that some of our lawyers think, that baron and barony, erl and erldom, duke and dukedom, king and kingdom, were in the nature of conjugates. It iz certain, that in that age, king Henry III, reckoned one hundred and fifty baronies in England. From hence it iz, that in the charters and histories of that age, almost all noblemen are stiled barons ; a name, which in thoze times waz exceeding honorable ; the baronage of England including in a manner all the prime orders of the kingdom, dukes, marquisses, erls and barons.

But that name haz been much more honorable since king Henry III, out of such a multitude, which waz seditious and turbulent, summoned to parliament by writ, some of the best* only ; " for he," (the words are taken out of an author of considerable antiquity) " after thoze great disturbances and heart-burnings between himself, Simon de Montefort, and other barons, were laid ; appointed and ordained, that all such erls and barons of the kingom of England, to whom the king should vouchsafe to direct hiz writs of summons, should come to hiz parliament, and no others, unless their lord the king should pleeze to direct other writs to them alfo." And what he began a little before hiz deth, waz strictly observed by Edward the I, and hiz successors. From that time they were only looked on as barons of the kingdom, whom the king by such writs of summons had called to parliament ; until Richard the II, in the eleventh year of hiz reign, created John de Beauchamp of Holt, baron of Herderminster, by the delivery of a diploma, bearing date the tenth of October. From which time, the kings hav often conferred

* Optimos.

red that honor by diploma, (or rather honorary letters) and the putting on of an honorary long robe. And that way of creating barons by diploma, and the other of writs of fummons, are in ufe at this day ; tho they are mentioned therein not by the name of *baron*, but of *chevalier*. They who are thus created, are called barons of parliament, barons of the kingdom, and barons honorary, to diftinguifh them from thoze who are commonly called barons according to the ancient conftitution ; az thoze of Burford and Walton, and fuch az were barons to the counts Palatine of Chefter, and of Penbroch, who were feudal, and barons by tenure only."

This account of Camden's, iz alone fufficient to convince me, that my opinions are right refpecting the origin and fignification of the word *baron*. But this author cleerly miftakes the meening in the paffage quoted from Hirtius. "Caffius ufed to hav *barons*, and a good number of *foldiers*, for fudden occafions." Infted of mercenary foldiers, *barons* here meens the *comites*, retainers, who were chofen men, and who ferved their cheef voluntarily. Theze attached themfelves to the perfon of the cheef, az a military guard ; at the fame time, they ferved to gratify the pride of the hero : Hæc dignitas, hæ vires, fays Tacitus.

I hav before remarked that it iz probable *bar* and *vir* are the fame word. Camden tells us, the Greek Gloffary tranflates *baro* by ανηρ, and in the laws of William, the Norman, the *vironus, baronus* and *thanus*, found in the laws of Canute, are tranflated by *baron* or *viron*. *B* and *v* are convertible letters, and theze facts amount to a convincing proof that *bar* and *vir* are the fame word, or from the fame root. The progrefs of the word iz this. Firft it denoted a man or hufband, *vir* ; afterwards a freeman or proprietor of land, *bar, baron, viron* ; in proportion az the valu of lands encreefed in Europe, the proprietors acquired welth and influence ; they claimed exclufiv judicial powers on their manors, and thus the words *baron* and *peer* came to fignify *judge*. Under the feudal fyftem, theze barons

ons became princes on their territories, fubordinate only
to the king or lord paramount.   Power attends prop-
érty, and theze barons finally affumed the right of con-
trolling kings, and trampling on their tenants.   Where
the barons and princes combined, they eftablifhed def-
. potic authority over the peeple; when they quarrelled,
one party or the other had recourfe to the. commons
for affiftance, and waz compelled to grant them confiderable privileges.

The foregoing explanation of *baron* iz confirmed by
another fact now exifting.   In law, a *hufband* iz called
baron to this day, *baron* and *femme*, hufband and wife.
Agreeable to this idea, the terms ufed in ancient in-
feudations by the tenant or vaffal, were, *devenio vefter
homo* ; I become your *man* ; that iz, your *baron*, in the
feudal fenfe of the word.   And a juɾy, in conformity
with the fame idea, were anciently called *homagium*, the
homage, or manhood ; that iz, a court of *barons*, landholders or free tenants.

I would only remark further, that Camden iz probably miftaken in faying the Britons difown the word
baron.   In Welfh, *barn* fignifies a judge, and there can
be little dout that the word iz from the fame original ;
being written without the vowel *o*, agreeable to the
Hebrew manner.

Different nations are more or lefs inclined to uze
the vocal founds and afpirates, according to the different genius of their languages.   So in Irifh the word
waz pronounced with an afpirate, *barhon*, or *brehon* ;
for there iz little room to dout this old Irifh word iz
from the fame root.   At the time of the conqueft of
Ireland by Henry II, the Irifh were governed by the
brehon law, fo ftiled from *brehon*, the Irifh name of
judges.*   We are alfo told that the ancient Irifh had
a cuftom of deciding caufes by *twelv* men† ; and authors teftify that the fame practice exifted in ancient
Britain.‡   Their decifion iz called by the erly writers,
duodecem virale judicium.   In fhort the univerfality of
this

---

* Blackftone Com. Vol. I. 100.

† Lelands Introd. to Hift. of Ireland.——‡ L. L. Hoeli.

this word and the trial by twelv, iz a ftrong proof, that all the nations of Europe fprang from a common ftock.*

Sir William Temple derives *barons* from the Ruffian *boiarons*, and fuppofes the word to be of Gothic original. Hiz only inaccuracy iz, that he takes a modern derivativ for the primitiv root ; whereas the Ruffian *boiarons* itfelf iz derived from *bar*, az wel az *baron*. The authority of this judicious and lerned writer wil however confirm what I hav advanced in the foregoing pages ; I fhal therefore cloze my remarks with a paffage from hiz works, vol. III, 363.

" I know very well how much critic haz been employed by the moft lerned, az Erafmus, Selden, Spelman, az well az many others, about the two words *baro* and *feudum* ; and how much pains hav been taken to deduce them from the Latin and Greek, and even the Hebrew and Egyptian tungs ; but I find no reezon, after all they hav faid, to make any doubt of their having been both the original of the Gothic or northern language ; or of barons having been a term of dignity, of command, or of honor, among them, and feudum of a foldier's fhare of land. I find the firft ufed abuv eight hundred years ago, in the verfes mentioned of king Lodbrog, when one of hiz exploits waz to hav conquered eight *barons*. And tho fees or feuda were in ufe under later Roman emperors, yet they were derived from the Gothic cuftoms, after fo great numbers of thoze nations were introduced into the Roman armies. Az to the word *baro*, it iz not, that I find, at all agreed among the lerned, from whence to derive it ; but what that term imports, it iz eafy to collect from their feveral accounts, and confirm by what ftil remains in all the conftitutions of the Gothic government. For tho by *barons* are now ment in England fuch az are created by patent, and thereby called to the houfe of lords ; and *baron* in Spanifh fignifies only a man of worth or note, and the quality denoted by that title be different in the feveral countries of Chriftendom ; yet there

---

* See my Differtations on the Englifh language, 313.

there iz no queſtion, but they were originally ſuch perſons az, upon the conqueſt of any country, were, by
the conquering prince, inveſted in the poſſeſſion of certain tracts or proportions of free lands, or at leeſt az
they held by no other tenure but that of military ſervice, or attendance upon their prince in war with a certain number of armed men. Theze in Germany,
France, Scotland, ſeem to hav had, and ſome ſtil to retain, a ſovereign power in their territories, by the exerciſe of what iz called high and low juſtice, or the power
of judging criminal az well az civil cauſes, and in-
flicting capital puniſhments. But I hav not found
any thing of this kind recorded in England, tho the
great barons had not only great number of knights, but
even petty barons holding under them.

I think the whole relm of England waz, by William
the conqueror, divided into baronies,* however the diſtinctions may hav been long ſince worn out ; but in
Ireland they ſtill remain, and every county there iz divided into ſo many baronies, which ſeem to hav been
the ſhares of the firſt barons. And ſuch as theze
great proprietors of land, compoſed, in all the north
weſt regions (of Europe) one part of the ſtates (eſtates
general) of the country or kingdom.''

Sir William Temple proceeds then to giv hiz conjectures reſpecting the origin of the word *baron*. He
remarks that Guagini, in hiz deſcription of Sarmatia,
printed in 1581, calls all thoze perſons who were cheef
poſſeſſors of lands and dignities, next to the prince,
duke or palatine, in the vaſt empire of Muſcovy, by
the common appellation of *boiarons*, now contracted
into *boiars*. From this he ſuppoſes *baron* to be derived.
It iz however much more probable that *baron* and *boi-
aron* had a common root in ſome period of remote antiquity ; which afterwards ſpread into all parts of Europe.

                                                With

---

* This iz not accurate. The thaneſhips or lordſhips of the
Saxons, at the conqueſt, took the title of *baronies* ; but the
diviſions probably exiſted before.

With refpect to trial by jury, Sir William remarks, Vol. III. 130, that this waz undoutedly of Saxon inftitution, and continued thro all the revolutions in England. He fays there are fome traces of it in the firft inftitutions of Odin, the firft great leeder of the Afiatic Goths or Getæ into Europe. He mentions the council of twelv, eftablifhed by Odin, and thinks it probable theze twelv men were at firft both *judges* and *jurors*; that iz, they were a court of arbitrators or referees, az we fhould now ftyle them, empowered to decide all caufes according to equitable principles and the circumftances of each cafe; and their determinations afterwards grew into precedent for their fucceffors. In procefs of time and multiplicity of bufinefs, the matter of fact continued to be tried by twelv men of the naborhood; but the adjudgement of punifhment and the fentence waz committed to one or two perfons of lerning or knowlege in the ancient cuftoms, records and traditions. Thus, he obferves, in the Saxon reigns, caufes were adjudged by the aldermen and bifhop of the feveral fhires, with the affiftance of twelv men of the fame county, who are faid to hav been judges or affiftants. He allows, the terms *jury* and *verdict* were introduced by the Normans; but afferts very juftly that trials by twelv men, with that circumftance of their unanimous agreement, were ufed not only among the Saxons and Normans, but are known to hav been az ancient in Sweden, az any records or traditions in the kingdom; and the practice remained in fome provinces of that country, til the late revolution.

P O S T S C R I P T.

ON further examination of this fubject, I am led to fubjoin the following remarks, which are fupported by the indifputable authority of Glanville and Bracton.

I hav before fuggefted that the Saxons, prior to the conqueft, conducted moft of their important affairs in the county or fheriffs court, where all the free tenants
were

were bound to attend. Theze free tenants confifted of the leffer barons, the knights and fokemen, or foccage tenants who had freehold eftates. Theze freeholders, were, by the nature of their eftates, the *pares curtis* ; they were the proper and fole *judges* of all caufes triable at the county court, which included almoft all civil actions, and they were denominated in Saxon, *lahmen*, lawmen. The county court, thus compofed of all the freeholders in the fhire, waz a tribunal of great confequence, and inferior only to the witena-gemote, or national affembly. The Latin riters called theze freemen *pares curtis* and *fcctatores, peers of court* and *fuitors. Curtis* iz a Saxon word latinized,* like *warrantizo murdrum*, and hundreds of other law terms ; and there iz little dout that *pares* iz a word of fimilar origin.

But what places the point I would eftablifh, beyond controverfy, iz, the *pares curtis* were in fact of different ranks. The knights or leffer barons, az well az the common foccage tenants, were included in the term *pares curtis* ; for they were bound to do fuit and fervice in the court of the lord paramount. Another fact iz of equal weight in the argument : Theze *pares*, in the county court, tried all real actions between the nobility. In the caufe of Odo, Bifhop of Bayeux, and archbifhop Lanfranc, in the reign of William the conqueror, the king directed *totum Comitatum confidere*. Many fimilar inftances might be cited, were it neceffary. Theze noblemen were tried by the *pares curtis*, the peers of the county court ; but who ever faid they were tried by their *equals* ?

The Norman princes attempted to difcountenance theze fhire motes of the Saxons, and fubftitute the trial of facts by twelv *juratores*, men fworn to fpeek the truth. In the reign of Henry II, the trial by jurors had become common, if not general. Queftions of *feifin* were tried by twelv common freeholders ; but queftions of *right* were tried by twelv knights ; the fheriff fummoning *four* knights who elected the *twelv*.

I would

---

* *Curtis, court* and the Spanifh *Cortez* are all the fame word.

I would here remark that the principal original reezon for fummoning freeholders *of the vicinage*, waz
that of their fuppofed perfonal knowlege of the fact in
difpute. The *jurors* were properly the *witneffes*. This
iz evident from circumftances and from the pofitiv
teftimony of the erly law-riters. The firft mention of
a proper jury, in any public act, iz in the conftitutions
of Clarendon, 1164, where the fheriff iz directed, *quòd
faciat jurare duodecim legales homines de vicineto, feu de
villa, quòd inde veritatem fecundum confcientiam fuam man-
ifeftabunt.* It iz faid in old writers that the jury *muft
fpeek the truth, if they know it.* If the twelv men firft
fummoned knew the truth, they were compelled to declare it, under the penalty of perjury. If fome knew
the facts and others did not, the latter were difmiffed
and others fummoned, till twelv were found who knew
the facts, ether by what they had feen and heerd themfelves, or from fuch teftimony of their fathers and others, az gained full credit.

Without attending to juries in this light, the laws
refpecting them appeer beyond meafure abfurd and tyrannical. Their being *fworn to fpeek the truth*, would
be abfurd on any other ground; for had they judged
of facts on *teftimony*, they would hav been fworn to declare *their opinion*, and not the *truth*. Their *verdict,
vere dictum*, derives its name and propriety from the
fame circumftance; and the prefent practice of fwearing
them to " a tru verdict giv," when they judge of facts
only by the perhaps contradictory teftimony of feveral
witneffes, iz, ftrictly fpeeking, abfurd.

The keeping juries, without meet, drink or fire, can
be accounted for only on the fame idea; it waz a method to compel an agreement among men, who were *acquainted with facts*, fome of whom might at times be
obftinate, and not willing to difclofe them. But how
ridiculous would it be to punifh men for not agreeing
in opinion, about what others teftified !

All this iz ftill more evident from the manner in
which many queftions refpecting real eftates were afcertained and determined. It waz cuftomary for the
jurors,

jurors, after they were chofen, to go upon the land to find the tru ftate of the fact in queftion, and then de-liver their verdict.   Hence the propriety of the expref-fion in clofing iffues ; *and this he prays may be enquired of by the country.*

I would obferve further, that the reezon, why appeels from the yerdict of a jury were not allowed, iz fimply this, that the jurors were fuppofed to hav decided from their *own knowlege.*   It waz certainly a wife pro-vifion that the folemn declaration of men under oath, living in the naborhood, and eye or eer witneffes of the recent tranfactions between the parties, fhould not be overthrown by other teftimony ; for all other evidence muft hav neceffarily been of an inferior nature.   But the reezon haz ceefed, and there iz now nothing more facred in the verdict of a jury, given on the teftimony of others, than there iz in the opinions of arbitrators, referees or auditors under oath.   The laws refpecting juries are all founded on the idea that the men were acquainted with 'the facts in difpute.   Their verdict waz formerly a *declaration of facts* ; it iz now a mere *matter of opinion.*   In fhort, the original defign of the inftitution iz totally changed, and moftly fuperfeded. Since juries rely on teftimony, they need not be collect-ed from the *vicinage* ; it iz even fafer to hav men who are ftrangers to both plaintiff and defendant.,   Jurors cannot be punifhed for *perjury,* for how can a man *per-jure* himfelf in giving hiz *opinion?*   They cannot be ftarved to deth, nor carted about town for difagree-ment ; for how iz it poffible for twelv men always to *think alike,* when they hav to form their opinions on clafhing teftimonies? In fhort, juries do not now anfwer one of the purpofes for which they were at firft inftitut-ed ; and however neceffary they may be deemed to the prefervation of civil liberty, it appeers to me they are, in a great meafure, ufelefs.

I cannot leev this fubject without remarking the influ-ence of habit, in maintaining *forms,* when the *fubftance* no longer exifts.   This iz neerly the cafe with the whole inftitution of juries ; but particularly in the

manner

manner of adminiftering the oath to them.   The practice of fwearing the foreman and the other jurors feparately, ftill exifts in fome of theze ftates, altho the reezon no longer remains.   It originated in the manner
of delivering the verdict, which waz, for every juror
feparately to anfwer the interrogatories of the judge.
While this practice remained, it waz very proper that
eech juror fhould take a feparate oath ; altho this for-
mality iz difpenfed with, in adminiftering the oath to
witneffes, in modern courts ; the words, " *you* and
eech of you fwear," being fubftituted for a feparate adminiftration of the oath.

No.

No. XXIV.

HARTFORD, SEPTEMBER, 1789.

The INJUSTICE, ABSURDITY, *and* BAD POLICY *of* LAWS *againſt* USURY.

USURY, in the primitiv ſenſe of the word, ſigni-fies any compenſation given for the uſe of money ; but in modern legal acceptation, it iz the taking an ex-orbitant ſum for the uſe of money ; or a ſum beyond what iz permitted by law. The municipal laws of different ſtates and kingdoms hav fixed different rates of intereſt ; ſo that what iz uſury in one country or ſtate, iz legal intereſt in another. The propriety of ſuch laws iz here called in queſtion.

1. It iz preſumed that ſuch laws are *unjuſt*. Money iz a ſpecies of commercial property, in which a man haz az complete ownerſhip, az in any other chattel in-tereſt. He haz therefore the ſame *natural* right to ex-ercife every act of ownerſhip upon money, az upon any other perſonal eſtate ; and it iz contended, he ought to hav the ſame *civil* and *political* right. He ought to hav the ſame right to trade with money az with goods ; to ſell, to loan and exchange it to any advantage what-ever, provided there iz no fraud in the buſineſs, and the minds of the parties meet in the contracts. The legiſlature haz no right to interfere with private con-tracts, and ſay that a man ſhall make no more than a certain profit per cent on the ſale of hiz goods, or limit the rent of hiz houſe to the annual ſum of forty pounds. This poſition iz admitted for ſelf evident, az it reſpects every thing but money ; and it muſt extend to money alſo, unleſs it can be proved that the privi-lege of uſing money in trade or otherwiſe without re-ſtraint, and making what profit a man iz able by fair contract, with gold and ſilver, az well az with houſes and lands, will produce ſome great public inconveni-ence,

ence, which will warrant the ftate in laying the ufe of fuch gold and filver under certain reftrictions.*

The only reezon commonly given for limiting the intereft of money by law, iz, that monied men will otherwife take advantage of the diftreffes of the poor and needy, to extort from them exorbitant intereft. Admit the propofition in its utmoft latitude, and it furnifhes no argument in favor of the reftraint, *becaufe the reftraint iz no remedy for the evil.* On the other hand, it generally increafes the evil; for when the law forbids a man to take more than fix per cent. for the ufe of hiz money, it, at the fame time, leevs him the right of withholding hiz money from hiz diftreffed nabor, and actually lays before him the ftrongeft motivs for withholding it. The law tuches the pride of a man, by reftraining what he deems an unalienable right, and this confideration, added to a certainty of employing hiz money to greater advantage, impels the man to turn a deef eer to hiz nabors calamities, when he would be otherwife difpofed to afford relief. The law therefore, fo far from furnifhing a remedy, actually doubles the evil.

To proov this affertion more cleerly, let me call the attention of my reeders to facts within their knowlege. Every man knows that there are perfons in every ftate, who, thro imprudence, idlenefs or misfortune, become involved, and unable to pay their dets when du. Theze perfons feldom make provifion for difcharging their dets, till they are preffed by their creditors. When they are urged by juft demands or legal procefs,

they

* In a converfation I had at Dr. Franklin's on this fubject, the doctor admitted the principle, and remarked, that a man who haz 1000l. in cafh, can loan it for fix per cent. profit only; but he may bild a houfe with it, and if the demand for houfes iz fufficient, he may rent hiz houfe for fifteen per cent. on the value. This iz a fair ftate of the argument, and I challenge my antagonifts to giv a good reezon for the diftinction which the laws make in the two cafes; or why a man fhould hav an unreftrained right to take any fum he can get for the ufe of hiz houfe, and yet hiz right to make profit by the loan of money, be abridged by law.

W

they are under a neceffity of raifing money immediate-
iy : But money iz fcarce ; it iz in a few men's hands,
who will not pay the full valu of lands or perfonal eftate.   The. poor detor iz then obliged to fell hiz farm
or hiz cattle, or both, at private fale or at auction, for
any price they will fetch, which iz commonly but a
fmall part of the valu.   Now, if the detor could hav
borrowed a fum of money, at ten, fifteen, or even twenty per cent. he might hav been a gainer by the loan ;
for by being prohibited by law from borrowing money,
at a high intereft, he haz been obliged to facrifice twenty, perhaps fifty or a hundred per cent.   Laws againft
ufury do not help fuch men ; on the contrary they opprefs them.   Could fuch men get money even at
twenty per cent. they would often be benefited by the
loan ; they might fave their eftates and avoid mifery
and ruin.   A prohibition of high intereft only compels
the diftreffed to feek releef by facrificing property in a
way not guarded againft by law.   Nay, I beg leev to
affert that fuch laws are the very meens of producing,
fupporting and enriching a hoft of oppreffors in every
ftate in America.   There are a few men, in every
ftate, who are what iz called *beforehand* ; theze men will
not loan money at legal intereft, for this very good reezon, they *can do better with it*, az they fay ; and no man
can blame another for making the moft profitable ufe
of hiz money.   Theze men therefore keep their money,
till their diftreffed nabor iz forced by det to fell hiz
farm ; then iz the time to lay out their money ; they
get the farm at their own price, which iz generally lefs
than half its valu.   In moft ftates, lands are fold at
auction, where they are facrificed ; and the poor owner
haz all the charges of a legal fuit to pay, az wel az the
det ; and the land fold for a fmall part of its valu.
This iz the common practice, authorized by law ; fo
that laws againft ufury only *create* an evil in one way,
by endevoring to *prevent it* in another.

The evil and hardfhips of this law, of felling real
eftate on execution, hav been fo great, az to giv rife to
a different mode of fatisfying executions in Connecticut.

cut. In this ſtate, a man's perſon and eſtate are both
liable for det; but if the perſonal eſtate iz inſufficient,
the creditor haz hiz election, ether to confine the dettor in priſon, or take hiz lands. But the law, which
iz ſo far in favor of the creditor, here ſteps in to prevent
a ſacrifice of the real property at public ſale ; and ordains that the creditor ſhall take it at a value, which
ſhall be apprized by three indifferent freeholders.
This law does injuſtice to the creditor ; for it interferes
with the contract, and obliges him to take that for pay
which he did not engage to receev. But it favors the
dettor, in a ſtate where money iz ſcarce and cannot be
eezily raized on an emergency. So far one law, by
doing injuſtice to creditors, corrects ſome of the ill effects of the law againſt high intereſt in Connecticut ;
but the remedy iz partial, for men in diſtreſs for money,
generally ſell their eſtates at private ſale, for one half
their valu ; and a few monied men and rich farmers are conſtantly taking advantage of their nabors calamities, to enrich themſelves. Such men make more
than fifty per cent. per ann. on their money by theze
ſpeculations, and no law can wholly prevent them. Now
laws againſt uſury create this very evil : They drive
money from a country ; they create a neceſſity for it ;
and then a few welthy men enrich themſelves, not by
loaning at fifteen or twenty per cent. but by purchaſing
lands at half price, which are ſold to keep men from
jail, who, if they could hav got money for a few
months, at twenty per cent. might hav ſold their eſtates to advantage, or otherwiſe paid their dets. In
general then we may obzerv, when a man iz reduced
to the neceſſity of aſking money at twenty per cent, hiz
ſituation iz ſuch that it iz better to giv that intereſt,
than to riſk a ſale of property on a ſudden to raize the
money. Laws againſt uſury do not ſave ſuch men ;
it iz idle to ſuppoſe it ; on the contrary, they multiply
inſtances of oppreſſion, az all America can witneſs.

But the argument, if good, proovs too much. If
legiſlators hav a right to fix the profit on money at intereſt, to prevent exorbitant demands from injuring the

neceſſitous,

neceffitous, wil not the fame reezon warrant a reftriction on the profits of every commodity in market ? If
my rulers hav a right to fay, my annual profit on
money loaned, fhal be but fix per cent. hav they not a
right to fay the advance on my wheet fhal be but fix
per cent. ? Where iz the difference ?.A poor man may
indeed be diftreffed by a demand of high intereft, and
fo he may by the high price of flour ; and I beg leev
to fay, that diftreffes from the laft caufe are infinitely
the moft numerous, and the moft deferving of legiflativ
remedies. It wil perhaps be faid that the price of bred,
in all cities, iz fixed by law—tru ; but if the price of
wheet iz not likewife fixed, there are times of fcarcity
when the law muft vary the price, or the baker muft
be ruined, and the poor be deftitute of bred. In an
extenfiv fertile country, like America, fuch cafes may
not happen frequently ; but the actual exiftence of the
fact proovs that fuch laws rather *follow* the ftate of the
market, than *regulate* it. And indeed it iz a queftion,
whether in this country, the citizens of our large towns
would not be fupplied with bred at a cheeper rate, without any regulations at all.

2. But the *abfurdity* and *bad policy* of laws againft ufury,
are fo obvious, that it iz furprizing fcarcely an attempt
haz been made to abolifh them in any country. Such
laws are abfurd and impolitic, becaufe they actually
and always produce and multiply the diftreffes they
are defigned to remedy. It iz impoffible it fhould be
otherwife :. The very laws of nature and commerce
require that fuch reftraints fhould neceffarily counteract
their own defign. It iz neceffary that commodities
fhould be fometimes plenty and fometimes fcarce ; and
it iz equally neceffary that money, the reprefentativ of
all commodities, fhould be liable to the fame fluctuations. In the commercial world, money and commodities wil always flow to that country, where they
are moft wanted and wil command the moft profit.
The confequence iz that a high price foon produces a
low price, and vice verfa.

Let

Let us apply the principle to the preſent queſtion. When money can bear its own profit, its profit or the intereſt ariſing on loans, wil be in proportion to the profit made in commercial tranſactions. If a man can make *tivelv per cent.* on hiz ſtock, in any kind of trade or ſpeculation, he wil not convert that ſtock into caſh, and loan it at *ſix per cent.* While therefore commerce or ſpeculation wil afford a man greater profits, than the law affords him on hiz loans of caſh, he wil hav no money to lend. The conſequence iz, while the law fixes the rate of intereſt lower than the annual profits of other buſineſs, a country wil be deſtitute of money.

This iz preciſely the caſe in America. Our remittances to Europe and the Eaſt Indies require conſiderable ſums in ſpecie to be exported ; and the merchant wil not import ſpecie, except to facilitate the purchaſe of hiz cargoes in America. He will not import it for the purpoſe of loaning, becauſe hiz ſtock in trade affords a better profit. The few landholders who hav a little caſh abuv their annual expenditures, wil not loan it ; for they can make twelv, fifteen, eighteen per cent. on their money by the purchaſe of certificates, and more on the purchaſe of lands. There are therefore no motivs, no inducements, for the welthy citizens to loan money, and conſequently when a man iz diſtreſſed to make a payment, he iz compelled to ſacrifice property to perhaps five times the valu of the det ; becauſe the law will not permit hiz nabor to take twelv or fifteen per cent. per ann. for the loan of money, a few months ; when he haz the money, and would gladly releev hiz frend, if he could receev an adequate compenſation.

Thus laws againſt uſury drive caſh from a country. They really and continually create a ſcarcity of an article, and then reſtrain men from raizing the price, in proportion to that ſcarcity. They create diſtreſſes of the poor, and at the ſame time, create an impoſſibility of releef. Were money left, like all kinds of commodities, to command its own price in market ; whenever its price ſhould rize abuv the uſual cleer profit of other
buſineſs,

bufinefs, men would import fpecie, or turn their ftock
into cafh, and loan it on good fecurity ; for no man
would fubmit to the drudgery of bufinefs, if he could
make money az faft by lying ftil, with hiz money at intereft.   Had money been permitted to bear its own
price according to the demand for it in America fince
the war, it would hav been kept in the country, or introduced til the rate of intereft had fallen, even below
the legal ftandard.   Limit the profit on any article of
life, and fet the price fo low that peeple can make more
by decling in other articles, and the articles fo fixed wil
become fcarce and deer.   Were the legiflatures of the
feveral ftates to fay that our traders fhould make but
one per cent. on falt, they would not bring cargoes of
it to the country.   It would be az fcarce az money iz
now.   Let the price of wheet be fixed at half a dollar
a bufhel, and in two years we fhould not hav a bufhel
in market.   It iz the fame cafe with money.   The low
profits on the ufe of money, expel it from the country, and none can be obtained at the legal price.   Let
the intereft rize to any fum which can be obtained, and
in two years, it would be az eezy to borrow money at
a low intereft, az it iz now difficult to command it at
any price.   The laws of nature wil continue to oppe-
rate, in fpite of the feeble oppofition of human power.

Another confideration demands our notice.   The
laws againft ufury increafe the diftreffes of the needy,
by enhancing the rifk, and confequently the infurance
on loans.*   It iz fruitlefs to attempt to prevent loans of
money.   When men are preffed for money, they can
always find perfons to fupply them, upon *fome* terms.
But az a loan of money at a higher rate of intereft than
iz allowed by law, expofes the lender to a lofs of the
money, and a fine or forfiture befides, hiz demand for
the ufe of hiz money wil rize in proportion to that rifk.

                                                            This

---

* See Blackftone on this fubject, Com. Vol. II. 455, where
the author's reezoning holds good, whether againft fixing the
value of horfe hire or money lent.   All exorbitant demands
are unjuft *in foro confcientiæ* ; but what right haz a legiflature
to fix the price of money loaned, and not of houfe-rent ?

This haz always been one of the moſt pernicious effects of ſuch laws. So that the law, not only creates a ſcarcity in the firſt inſtance, but actually raizes the demand of intereſt much abuv the natural demand required by that ſcarcity. In ſhort, inſted of releeving the detter, it multiplies hiz diſtreſſes four fold.

Beſides, ſuch laws, like all national reſtrictions on trade, tend to make men diſhoneſt, in particular things, and thus weeken the powers of the moral faculty. There are ten thouſand ways of evading ſuch laws, and ſlight evaſions gradually produce a habit of violating law, and harden the mind againſt the feer of its penalties. Indeed, ſuch laws tend to undermine that confidence which iz the baſis of ſocial intercourſe. Laws which encourage *informations*, ſhould be enacted with caution. Such are laws againſt uſury. A man haz often the ſtrongeſt temptation to be a treecherous raſcal, by inducing hiz frend to loan him money, on illegal intereſt, and then betraying him. This ſpecies of villany waz lately carried ſo far in Maſſachuſetts, az to induce the legiſlature to repeel a clauze of their law againſt uſury. And a man of morality muſt ſhudder, while he reeds the legal proſecutions and adjudications in England upon their ſtatutes of uſury.

The abſurdity of attempting to *fix the valu of money* iz another objection to it of no ſmall conſequence. The valu of it depends wholly on the quantity in circulation and the demand. In this reſpect it reſembles all other articles of trade ; and who ever thought of fixing the price of goods by law ?* It iz almoſt impoſſible for a legiſlature to aſcertain exactly the valu of money at any one time ; and utterly impoſſible to ſay that the valu when aſcertained, ſhall continu the ſame for ſix months. Nay, two ſtates adjoining eech other may eſtimate the uſe of money very differently at the ſame period. In New York the legal intereſt iz ſeven per cent. in New England but ſix. A man may therefore do that legally

*The legiſlatures of ſeveral ſtates during the late war, were raſh enough to make the attempt ; and the ſucceſs of the ſcheme waz juſt equal to the wiſdom that planned it.

ly in one ftate, which in the others would expoze him
to a fevere penalty.

In ancient Rome, the intereft waz twelv per cent.
The emperor Juftinian reduced it to four, but allowed
higher intereft to be taken of merchants, on account of
the rifk.   In Holland, when Grotius wrote, the common intereft waz eight per cent. ; but twelv to merchants. In England, the ftatute 37th, Henry VIII, confined intereft to *ten* per cent.   By the 21ft James I, it
waz reduced to eight ; by the 12th Charles II, to fix ;
and by 12th Ann, to five, the prefent legal intereft in
that country.*

Poftlethwaite remarks very juftly that theze laws hav
not afcertained the real valu or intereft of money ; for
when the legal intereft haz been fix per cent. the real
intereft haz fometimes been four ; and when the legal
· intereft haz been five, the real intereft haz fometimes
been feven.   Indeed the intereft of money depends on
fuch a combination of circumftances, az the fcarcity of
money, the demand in market, and the hazard, that an
attempt to find and fix a permanent rate, iz one of the
moft vifionary fchemes that a public body can undertake.   To proov the impoffibility of fuch a fcheme, I
would only mention the continual practice of violating
laws againft ufury ; which would not be the cafe, if the
real valu of money had been afcertained and fixed.†
If legiflatures had found the tru valu of the ufe of
money, there would hav been fewer violations of their
laws : If they hav, in any cafe, fixed a rate of intereft
lower than the real valu, they hav violated the rights of
their fubjects.   This iz a ferious confideration ; and
perhaps in no inftance are the laws of England and
America more ftrongly marked with the traces of ancient

* Blackftone Vol. II. 462.

† What are marine infurances, bottomry, loans at refpon-
dentia and annuities for life, but exceptions to the general law
againft ufury ? The neceffity of higher intereft than common
iz pleeded for theze exceptions. Very good ; but they proov
the abfurdity of attempting to fix that, which the laws of nature and commerce require fhould be fluctuating. Such laws
are partial and iniquitous.

cient prejudice and barbarity, than in the prohibition which prevents a man from uſing hiz *money* az he plee-zes, while he may demand any ſum whatever for the uſe of hiz other property.

The only power, I concéev, a legiſlature haz to de-termin what intereſt ſhall arize on the uſe of money, or property, iz where the parties hav not determined it by agreement. Thus when a man haz taken up goods upon credit, or where, by any other legal meens, a man becomes poſſeſſed of anothers money or eſtate, without a ſpecific ſtipulation for intereſt, the law very properly ſteps in and aſcertains the ſum which the detter ſhall pay for the uſe of that money. But to make a law that a man ſhall not take but ſix per cent. for the uſe of money, when the borrower iz willing to giv more, and the lender cannot part with hiz money at that rate of intereſt, iz a daring violation of private rights, an injury often to both parties, and productiv of innumer-able embarraſſments to commerce.

We are told that ſuch laws are neceſſary to guard men from the oppreſſion of the rich. What an error! Waz a monied man ever compelled to aſſiſt a diſtreſſed nabor, by the forfitures incurred by ſuch laws? Iz not hiz money hiz own? Wil he lend it all, if it ſhould not be for hiz benefit? Beſides, cannot a man in neceſſity alienate hiz property for one fourth of its valu? Are not ſuch bona fide contracts made every day to raize money to anſwer a temporary purpoſe? Nay, hav not the laws of all commercial ſtates author-ized *ſales by auction*, where any man may part with hiz property for a fourth of its valu? Iz there any remedy in law againſt ſuch a ſacrifice of a man's eſtate? Wherein then conſiſts the ſecurity of laws againſt uſu-ry? In the name of common ſenſe and common equity, let legiſlators be conſiſtent. If men are improvident, lazy and careleſs, a loſs of property wil be their pun-iſhment, and no mezures of government wil prevent it.

To what then ſhall we aſcribe the ſevere laws againſt high intereſt, which hav been and ſtil are exiſting in moſt commercial countries? I preſume the cauſe may

be

be eafily affigned. The Jewifh prohibition, not to take intereft, except of ftrangers, firft gave rife to douts in the minds of our pious chriftian forefathers, with re-fpect to the legality of any intereft at all. · This pro-duced, in the dark ages, fevere ecclefiaftical laws againft taking any thing for the ufe of money ; and theze laws originated a general prejudice againft it, thro the Chrift-ian world.

In the twelfth and thirteenth centuries, commerce began to revive ; but az there waz but little money, and trade waz lucrativ, becaufe in few hands, money bore a very high intereft. In fome parts of Europe, the intereft waz forty per cent. Even with this inter-eft, certain Italian traders could make an annual profit, and therefore it waz for their benefit to giv it. It how-ever rendered them very unpopular.*

The Jews, for their infidelity, had been confidered by the Chriftians az outcafts on earth. Severe laws were enacted againft them in almoft every country ; depriving them of the rights of citizens, and forbidding them to hold real eftates. Profcribed and infulted, the poor Jews were compelled to turn their *hand againft every man* in their own defence. They commenced ftrolling traders and bankers, and by theze meens com-manded a large fhare of the money in every kingdom.

With this command of cafh, the Jews very juftly compenfated themfelves for the injuries they fuffered from the tyrannical laws which exifted againft them. They loaned money at the higheft rate of intereft they could obtain. Hence the general karacter of the Jews, and the prejudice againft them that furvives to this en-lightened period.

It iz very probable, that before the difcovery of the American mines, money waz fo fcarce in Europe, that a few brokers in eech kingdom might engrofs fuch a fhare, az to hav it in their power to opprefs people. This waz evidently the cafe in England, about the reign of Edward I, and the parliament thought proper to interfere and reftrain the evil. Laws againft ufury

were

* Robertfons Charles V. Vol. I. 280.

were doutlefs neceffary and ufeful at that time. But fince the world haz been filled with gold and filver from South America, and nations hav opened an inter-courfe with eech other, there never can be a want of fpecie, where a country can fupply produce enough to exchange for it. It haz become a mere fluid in the commercial world ; and in order to obtain a fupply, in a country abounding with produce and manufactures, the legiflature haz nothing to do, but let it bear its own price ; let it command its own valu, ether at in-tereft, or in exchange for commodities.

Laws againft ufury therefore I confider az originat-ing ether in the neceffity of the times, which long ago ceefed, or in a bigotted prejudice againft the Jews, which waz az barbarous formerly, az it iz now infa-mous. Laws reftraining the intereft of money I now confider, in the fame light, az I do laws againft free-dom of confcience. And were it not for the force of habit, I fhould az foon expect to fee a modern legifla-ture ordering a pious fectary to the ftake for hiz prin-ciples, az to fee them gravely paffing a law, to limit the profit on the ufe of hiz money. And unlefs the leg-iflatures of this enlightened age fhould repeel fuch laws, and place money on a footing with other property, they will be confidered az acceffory to a direct violation of the deereft rights of men, and will be anfwerable for more frauds, perjuries, treechery and expenfiv litiga-tions, than proceed from any other fingle caufe in foci-ety. I am fo firmly perfuaded of the truth of theze principles, that I venture to predict, the opinions of men will be changed in lefs than half a century, and pofterity will wonder that their forefathers could think of maintaining a pofition fo abfurd and contradictory, az that men hav no right to make more than fix per cent. on the *loan of money*, while they hav an indefeez-able right to make unlimited profit on their money in any other manner. They will vew laws againft ufury in the fame light that we do the inquifition in Spain, the execution of gypfies and witches in the laft century, or thoze laws' of England which make 100l. annual income neceſſary to qualify a man for killing a partridge, while they allow *forty ſhillings* only to qualify him for electing a knight of the ſhire.

No.

No. XXV.

HARTFORD, OCTOBER, 1789.

On ALLEGIANCE.

WRITERS on law divide allegiance into two kinds, *natural* and *local.* " Natural allegiance iz fuch az iz du from all men born within the kings dominions, immediately upon their berth. For immediately upon their berth, they are under the kings protection ; at a time too when (during their infancy) they are incapable of protecting themfelves. Natural allegiance iz therefore a det of gratitude, which cannot be forfeited, cancelled or altered, by any change of time, place or circumftances ; nor by any thing but the united concurrence of the legiflature. An Englifhman who remoovs to France or to China, owes the fame allegiance to the king of England there az at home, and twenty years hence az wel az now. For it iz a principle of univerfal law, that the natural born fubject of one prince cannot by any act of hiz own, no, not by fwearing allegiance to another, put off or difcharge hiz natural allegiance to the former ; for hiz natural allegiance waz intrinfic and primitiv and antecedent to the other, and cannot be devefted, without the concurrent act of that prince to whom it waz firft du. Indeed the natural born fubject of one prince, to whom he owes allegiance, may be entangled by fubjecting himfelf abfolutely to another ; but it iz hiz own act that brings him into theze ftraits and difficulties, of owing fervice to two mafters ; and it iz unreezonable that, by fuch voluntary act of hiz own, he fhould be able at plezure to unloofe thoze bands by which he iz connected to hiz natural prince."*

I miftake much, however, if the natural born fubject would be fo much *entangled with hiz ftraits and difficulties,*

* Blackftone Com. Vol. I. 369.

ties, az lord Coke, Hale and Blackſtone, would be, to
ſupport their aſſertions and obviate the abſurdities of
their reezoning.

It iz aſtoniſhing to obſerve how ſlowly men get rid
of old prejudices and opinions. The feudal ideas of
allegiance, which make *fidelity in the ſubject an obligation
or grateful return for the protection of the prince*, ſtil prevail, and are made the baſis of all modern reezoning
on the ſubject. Such ideas in the dark ages, and in
the days of feudal deſpotiſm, are not to be wondered at.
Every baron waz a tyrant on hiz manor, and az hiz
only ſafety confiſted in hiz caſtle and hiz vaſſals, it waz
neceſſary to bind hiz ſubjects to him by oaths and ſuperſtition, az wel az by a demand upon their gratitude.
But wil our ſage writers on government and law, forever think by tradition ? Wil they never examin the
grounds of receeved opinions ? Let me enquire

What iz the real ground of *allegiance ?* Iz it not
protection ? Not at all. We may juſt az wel invert
the propoſition, and ſay, that *allegiance* iz the ground
of *protection*. A prince iz the repreſentativ of a nation
or ſtate, ſo that allegiance to him, iz merely allegiance
to a ſtate or body politic.* According to our ideas, allegiance to a king, and fidelity to a ſtate, are the ſame
thing ; for detach a king from all connection with a
nation or ſtate, and he becumes a private man, and entitled only to the rights of ſuch. This at leeſt iz the
opinion of an *American*, whoſe mind iz not biaſſed by
perſonal attachments to a ſovereign.

What then iz the ground of fidelity to a ſtate ? The
anſwer iz eezy ; the *moral law*, which haz for its object
the *good of ſociety*. This iz the baſis of all obligations
in a ſtate, whether expreſs or implied ; yet writers on
this ſubject hav hardly mentioned it. Blackſtone indeed takes notice of an implied, original allegiance, antecedent to any expreſs promis ; but ſeems rather to
· conſider

---

* Blackſtone remarks that allegiance iz applicable, not
only to the political capacity of the king, or regal office, but
to hiz *natural perſon* and *blood royal*. I would aſk then what
blood royal there can be in a man, except in hiz *kingly capacity ?*

confider it az a return for the duties of the fovereign, which he owes before coronation, than az an obligation arifing from the very conftitution of fociety.

Taking the moral law or the good of fociety for the ground of all allegiance, we difcuver two fpecies of duties to be performed by every man ; the *moral duties*, which exift at all times and in all places ; and certain *political duties*, required by the municipal laws of eech ftate. The firft are the bafis of natural or perpetual allegiance ; the laft, of local allegiance. The firft or moral duties create an obligation upon every man, the moment he iz born, which cannot be cancelled or difcharged by any act of an individual, or by any agreement between prince and fubject ; the laft, or political duties, impoze an obligation upon every member of a ftate or body politic, the moment he fteps within its jurifdiction, to fubmit peaceably to fuch pofitiv injunctions of that ftate, az hav been judged neceffary for its welfare.

Now to maintain that an oath of allegiance wil bind a man to perform all the laft clafs of duties, or the pofitiv duties enjoined by a particular ftate, and not required by the general laws of fociety, when the man haz perhaps become a member of another ftate, three thoufand miles diftant, iz to defend the wildeft notions that can poffefs any man's brain. Every man iz bound always and in all places to *do right, and avoid doing rong* ; and this with, or without taking an oath of fidelity to any ftate. This iz implied allegiance, univerfal and perpetual ; and I deny that there iz any other ground of this allegiance, except the univerfal principles of right and rong.

Should it be faid, that a man may bind himfelf *by oath* to perform the pofitiv or political duties required by a ftate, altho he may remoov and become a citizen of another ftate ; I anfwer, this wil involv him in the *ftraits* and *difficulties* mentioned by Blackftone ; for the political duties of the two ftates may interfere with eech other. The truth iz, a man haz no right to take fuch an oath, nor haz a ftate any right to require it.

He

He may fwear, when he enters into any kingdom or ftate, that he wil be a good citizen, and fubmit to all the laws of the ftate, *while he iz a member of it* ; and further, that he wil obferve the moral law in hiz con-duct towards that fociety, after *he haz ceefed to be a member of it*. Further than this, he haz no right to fwear. Az to every duty, not required by the laws of fociety in general, but only by the municipal laws of a ftate, a man's allegiance commences when he enters that ftate ; and ceefes the moment he leeves it.* The doctrin of a perpetual allegiance iz wholly a feudal idea ; inculcated, when every lord waz at war with hiz nabor ; and waz compelled by felf prefervation to attach hiz vaffals to himfelf by oaths, the penalties of perjury and the forfeitures of treezon.

Blackftone fays, in the paffage already quoted, "that natural allegiance iz a det of gratitude," becaufe the fubject iz under the kings protection while an infant. He might juft az wel fay, *protection iz a det of gratitude* du from the prince, becaufe the fubject iz born in hiz dominions. On this principle of gratitude, a child iz obliged to obey and ferve hiz parent, after he haz left hiz family, and while he livs. This det, according to the fame author, cannot be cancelled, but *by "concur-rence of the legiflature."* How in the name of reezon, can an act of the legiflature diffolv a *natural tie ?* How can it *cancel a det of gratitude ?* Common fenfe looks with difdain on fuch week and futile reezoning. But if there iz fuch a thing az natural and perpetual allegiance, an Englifhman, who remoovs to France, cannot take arms to defend France againft an invafion from England. Is this agreeable to the laws of nature and fociety, that a man fhould not protect himfelf and hiz property ? It wil be faid that the man iz within the Englifh king's liegeance, and entitled to hiz protection. But the king cannot protect him ; it iz beyond hiz power, and the Englifhman iz not obliged to leev France and feek protection in England. Hiz eftate and hiz family may be in France, and if he choofes to refide there, it iz hiz unalienable right and duty to de-

fend

* Except the cafe of Ambaffadors or other agents.

fend both againft any invafion whatever.   Every war,
except a defenfiv one, iz a breech of the moral law ;
but when a natural born fubject of England, haz become a citizen of France, he iz fubject to the laws of
France, and bound to affift, if required, in defending
the kingdom againft hiz natural prince.

No.

X

No. XXVI.

HARTFORD, JULY, 1789.

EXPLANATION *of the* REEZONS, *why* MARRIAGE *iz* PROHIBITED *between* NATURAL RELATIONS.

MUCH haz been faid and written to afcertain between what relations marriage ought to be permitted. The civil, the canon, and the Englifh laws, differ az to the degrees of confanguinity neceffary to render this connection improper. A detail of the arguments on this fubject, and even a recapitulation of the decrees of ecclefiaftical councils, in the erly ages of the church, would be tedious and unintcrefting. I fhall only offer a few thoughts of my own on the queftion, with a view to illuftrate a fingle point, which haz been agitated in modern times, and on which the different American ftates hav paffed different decifions. The point iz, whether a man fhould be permitted to marry hiz former wife's fifter. In fome ftates this iz permitted ; in others, prohibited.

Thoze who favor the prohibition, ground their reezon on the Levitical law, which fays a man fhall not marry hiz wife's fifter, during the life of hiz wife, to vex her. This prohibition, while it reftrains a man from having two fifters for wives at the fame time, among a peeple where poligamy waz permitted, iz a negativ pregnant, and a ftrong argument that a man waz allowed, after the deth of a wife, to marry her fifter.

The Jewifh law, however divine, waz defigned for a particular nation, and iz no farther binding upon other nations, than it refpects the natural and focial duties. In no one particular, hav men been more miftaken, than in explaining divine commands. It haz been fufficient for them to refolv a law into the wil of God, without

without examinining into the reezons for which the law waz revealed. They seem to hav inverted the foundation of moral obligation, in suppofing the moral law to derive its propriety and fitnefs originally from the wil of Deity, rather than from the nature of things. They talk about the fitnefs and unfitnefs of things, independent, not only of fociety, but of God himfelf. Such wild notions, I prefume, are not common. There could be no fitnefs nor unfitnefs of things, before things were made ; nor could right and rong exift without focial beings. The moral duties therefore are not right, merely becaufe they are commanded by God ; but they are commanded by him, becaufe they are right. The propriety or fitnefs of them depends on the very nature of fociety ; and this fitnefs, which waz coeval with creation, waz the ground of the divine command.*

The law of Mofes, regulating marriages, waz founded on this propriety or fitnefs of things. A divine command givs a fanction to the law ; but the propriety of it exifted prior to the command. The reezons for prohibiting marriage between certain relations are important ; yet they feem not to be underftood: It haz been fufficient, in difcuffing this point, to fay, *fuch iz the law of God*; and few attempts hav been made to find the reezons of it, by which alone its extent and authority can be afcertained.

There are two rules, furnifhed by the laws of nature, for regulating matrimonial connections. The firft iz, that marriage, which iz a focial and civil connection, fhould not interfere with a natural relation, fo az to defect or deftroy its duties and rights. Thus it iz highly improper that an aunt fhould marry her nephew, or a godfather hiz grand daughter ; becaufe the duties
and

---

* It may be faid, that *moral right* and *rong* muft ultimately be refolved into the wil of Deity, becaufe fociety itfelf depends on hiz wil. This iz conceded ; I only contend that moral fitnefs and unfitnefs refult *immediately* from the ftate of created beings, with relation to eech other, and not from any arbitrary rules impofed by Deity, fubfequent to creation.

and rights of the natural relation, would be fuperfeded by the pofitiv duties and rights of the civil conneƈion.

The other rule iz much more important. It iz a law of nature that vegetables fhould degenerate, if planted continually on the fame foil. Hence the change of feeds among farmers. Animals degenerate on the fame principle. The phyfical caufes of this law of nature, are perhaps among the arcana of creation; but the effeƈts are obvious; and it iz furprizing that modern writers on law and ethics fhould pafs over al-moft the only reezons of prohibiting marriage between blood relations. Confanguinity, and not affinity, iz the ground of the prohibition.*

It iz no crime for brothers and fifters to intermarry, except the fatal confequences to fociety; for were it generally praƈtifed, men would foon become a race of pigmies. It iz no crime for brothers and fifters child-ren to intermarry, and this iz often praƈtifed; but fuch near blood conneƈtions often produce imperfeƈt children. The common peeple hav hence drawn an argument to proov fuch conneƈtions criminal; confidering weak-nefs, ficknefs and deformity in the offspring az judge-ments upon the parents. Superftition iz often awake, when reezon iz afleep. It iz juft az criminal for a man to marry hiz coufin, az it iz to fow flax every year on the fame ground; but when he does this, he muft not complain, if he haz an indifferent crop.

Here then the queftion occurs, iz it proper for a man to marry hiz wife's fifter? The anfwer iz plain. The praƈtice does not interfere with any law of nature or fociety; and there iz not the fmalleft impropriety in a man's marrying ten fifters of hiz wife in fucceffion. There iz no natural relation deftroyed; there iz no re-lation by blood; and *ceffante ratione, ceffat et ipfa Lex*; the law ceefes when the reezon of it ceefes.

* By the ancient laws of England, relations in the fame de-gree, whether by confanguinity or affinity, were placed exaƈt-ly on a footing. See the futtle reezoning by which the pro-hibitions were fupported, in Reeve's Hiftory of the Englifh Laws, Vol. IV.

No.

No. XXVII.

HARTFORD, FEBRUARY, 1790.

MISCELLANEOUS REMARKS on DI-
VIZIONS of PROPERTY, GUVERN-
MENT, EDUCATION, RELIGION,
AGRICULTURE, SLAVERY, COM-
MERCE, CLIMATE and DISEEZES in
the UNITED STATES.

THE laws which refpect property, hav, in all civilized communities, formed the moft important
branch of municipal regulations. Of theze, the laws
which direct the divifion and defent of lands, conftitute
the firft clafs ; for on theze, in a great mezure, depend
the genius of guvernment and the compleƈtion of manners.

Savages hav very few regulations refpecting property ; for theie are but few things to which their defires
or neceffities prompt them to lay claim. Some very
rude nations feem to hav no ideas of property, efpecially in lands ; but the American tribes, even when firft
difcuvered, claimed the lands on which they lived, and
the hunting grounds of eech tribe were marked from
thoze of its nabors, by rivers or other natural boundaries. The Mexican and Peruvian Indians had indeed
advanced very far towards a ftate of civilization ; and
land with them had acquired almoft an European
valu ; but the northern tribes, yet in the hunter ftate,
would often barter millions of akers for a handful of
trinkets and a few ftrings of wampum.

In the progrefs of nations, land acquires a valu, proportioned to the degree of populoufnefs ; and other objects grow into eftimation, by their utility, convenience,
or fome plezure they afford to the imagination.

In

326 MISCELLANEOUS REMARKS.

In attending to the principles of guvernment, the leeding idea that ftrikes the mind, iz, that political power depends moftly on property; confequently guvernment will take its compleʄion from the divifions of property in the ftate.

In defpotic ftates, the fubjeʄts muft not poffefs property in fee; for an excluſiv poffeffion of lands infpires ideas of independence, fatal to defpotifm. To fupport ſuch guvernments, it iz neceffary that the laws fhould giv the prince a fovereign control over the property az wel az the lives of hiz fubjeʄts. There are however very few countries, where the guvernment iz fo purely arbitrary, that the peeple can be deprived of life and eftate, without fome legal formalities. Even when the firft poffeffion waz the voluntary gift of the prince, grants or conceffions, fanʄtioned by prefcription, hav often eftablifhed rights in the fubjeʄt, of which he cannot be deprived without a judicial procefs.

In Europe the feudal fyftem of tenures haz given rife to a fingular fpecies of guvernment. Moft of the countries are faid to be guverned by *monarkies*; but many of the guvernments might, with propriety, be called *ariftocratic republics*. The barons, who poffefs the lands, hav moft of the power in their own hands. Formerly the kings were but lords of a fuperior rank, *primi inter pares*; and they were originally eleʄtiv. This iz ftil the cafe in Poland, which continues to be what other ftates in Europe were, an *ariftocratic republic*. But from the twelfth to the fixteenth century, the princes, in many countries, were ftruggling to circumfcribe the power of the barons, and their attempts, which often defolated their dominions, were attended with various fuccefs. What they could not accomplifh by force, they fometimes obtained by ftratagem. In fome countries the commons were called in to fupport the royal prerogativs, and thus obtained a fhare in legiflation, which haz fince been augmented by vaft acceffions of power and influence, from a diftribution and encreefe of welth. This haz been the cafe in England. In other countries, the prince haz combined ed with the barons to depreſs the peeple. Where the prince holds the privilege of diſpoſing of civil, military and eccleſiaſtical offices, it haz been eezy to attach the nobility to hiz intereſt, and by this coalition, peece haz often been ſecured in a kingdom ; but the peeple hav been kept in vaſſalage. Thus by the laws of the ſeudal ſyſtem, moſt of the commons in Europe are kept in a ſtate of dependence on the great landholders.

But commerce haz been favorable to mankind. Az the rules of ſucceſſion to eſtates, every where eſtabliſhed in Europe, are calculated to aggrandize the *few* at the expenſe of the *many*, commerce, by creating and accumulating perſonal eſtate, haz introduced a new ſpecies of power to ballance the influence of the landed property. Commerce found its way from Italy and the eeſt, to Germany and England, diffuſing in its progreſs freedom, knowlege and independence. Commerce iz favorable to freedom ; it fluriſhes moſt in republics ; indeed a free intercourſe by trade iz almoſt fatal to deſpotiſm ; for which reezon, ſome princes lay it under ſevere reſtrictions : In other countries it iz diſcuraged by public opinion, which renders trade diſreputable. This iz more fatal to it, than the edicts of tyrants.

The baſis of a democratic and a republican form of government, iz, a fundamental law, favoring an equal or rather a general diſtribution of property. It iz not neceſſary nor poſſible that every citizen ſhould hav exactly an equal portion of land and goods, but the laws of ſuch a ſtate ſhould require an equal diſtribution of inteſtate eſtates, and bar all perpetuities. Such laws occaſion conſtant revolutions of property, and thus hold out to all men equal motivs to vigilance and induſtry. They excite emulation, by giving every citizen an equal change of being rich and reſpectable.

In no one particular do the American ſtates differ from European nations more widely, than in the rules which regulate the tenure and diſtribution of lands. This circumſtance alone wil, for ages at leeſt, prezerve a government in the united ſtates, very different from any which now exiſts or can arize in Europe.

In

In New England, inteftate eftates defend to all the children or other heirs in equal portions, except to the oldeft fon, who haz two fhares.   This exception in favor of the oldeft fon, waz copied from the levitical code, which waz made the bafis of the firft New England inftitutions.   The legiflature of Maffachufetts, at their May feffion, 1789, abolifhed that abfurd exception ; and nothing but inveterate habit keeps it alive in the other ftates.*

In confequence of theze laws, the peeple of New England enjoy an equality of condition, unknown in any other part of the world.   To the fame caufe may be afcribed the rapid population of theze ftates ; for eftates by divifion are kept fmall, by which meens every man iz obliged to labor, and labor iz the direct caufe of population.   For the fame reezon, the peeple of theze ftates, feel and exert the pride of independence. Their equality makes them mild and condefending, capable of being convinced and guverned by perfuafion ; but their independence renders them irritable and obftinate in refifting force and oppreffion.   A man by affociating familiarly with them, may eezily coax them into hiz views, but if he affumes any airs of fuperiority, he iz treeted with az little refpect az a fervant. The principal inconvenience arizing from theze difpofitions iz, that a man who happens to be a little diftinguifhed for hiz property or fuperior education iz ever expofed to their envy, and the tung of flander iz bizzy in backbiting him.   In this manner, they oppoze diftinctions of rank, with great fuccefs.   This however iz a private inconvenience ; but there iz an evil, arifing from this jealoufy, which deeply affects their guvernment.   Averfe to diftinctions, and reddy to humble fuperiority, they become the dupes of a fet
of

* Lands in Connecticut defend to the heirs in the following manner :   Firft to children, and if none, then to brothers and fifters or their legal reprefentativs of the whole blud ; then to parents ; then to brothers and fifters of the half blud ; then to next of kin, the whole blud taking the preference when of equal degree with the half blud.

of artful men, who, with fmall talents for bufinefs
and no regard for the public intereft, are always familiar
with every clafs of peeple, flyly hinting fomething to
the difadvantage of great and honeft men, and pretend-
ing to be frends to the public welfare. The peeple
are thus guverned at times by the moft unqualified
men among them.   If a man wil fhake hands with every one he meets, attend church conftantly, and affume
a goodly countenance ; if he wil not fwear or play
cards, he may arrive to the firft offices in the guvernment, without one fingle talent for the proper difcharge
of hiz duty ; he may even defraud the public revenu
and be accufed of it on the moft indubitable evidence,
yet by laying hiz hand on hiz breft, cafting hiz eyes to
heaven, and calling God to witnefs hiz innocence, he
may wipe away the popular fufpicions, and be a fairer
candidate for preferment than before hiz accufation.
So far az the harts of the peeple are concerned, the difpofition here mentioned iz a high recommendation, for
it proves them mild, unfufpecting and humane : But
guvernment fuffers a material injury from this turn of
mind ; and were it not for a few men who are boldly
honeft, and indefatigable in detecting impofitions on
the public, the guvernment of theze ftates would always be, az it often iz, in the hands of the weekeft, or
wickedeft of the citizens.

The fame equality of condition haz produced a fingular manner of fpeeking among the peeple of New
England.* But the inhabitants of all the large towns,
wel bred citizens, are excepted from this remark.

Altho the principle iz tru that a general diftribution
of lands iz the bafis of a republican form of guvernment, yet there iz an evil arifing out of this diftribution,
which the New England ftates now feel, and which
wil increafe with the population of the country. The
tracts of land firft taken up by the fettlers, were not
very confiderable ; and theze having been repeetedly
divided among a number of heirs, hav left the prefent
proprietors almoft without fubfiftence for their families.

                                         Vaft

* See my Differtations on the Englifh Language, page 106.

Vaft numbers of men do not poffefs more than thirty or forty akers eech, and many not half the quantity. It iz with difficulty that fuch men can fupport families and pay taxes. Indeed moft of them are unable to do it ; they involve themfelves in det ; the creditors take the little land they poffefs, and the peeple are driven, poor and helplefs, into an uncultivated wildernefs. Such are the effects of an equal divifion of lands among heirs ; and fuch the caufes of emigration to the weftern territories. Emigration indeed iz a prefent remedy for the evil ; but when fettlements hav raized the valu of the weftern lands neerly to that on the Atlantic coaft, emigrations wil moftly ceefe. They wil not entirely ceefe, until the continent iz peepled to the Pacific ocean ; and that period iz diftant ; but whenever they ceefe, our republican inhabitants, unable to fubfift on the fmall portions of land, affigned them by the laws of divifion, muft hav recourfe to manufactures. The holders of land wil be fewer in number, becaufe monied men wil hav the advantage of purchafing lands very low of the neceffitous inhabitants, who wil be multiplied by the very laws of the ftate, refpecting landed property. Other laws however could not be tolerated in theze ftates. In Europe, provifion iz made for younger fons, in the army, the church, the navy, or in the numerous manufactures of the countries. But in America, fuch provifion cannot be made ; and therefore our laws eezely provide for all the children, where they are not provided for by the parents.

By extending our views to futurity, we fee confiderable changes in the condition of theze republican ftates. The laws, by barring entailments, prevent the eftablifhment of families in permanent affluence ; we are therefore in little danger of a hereditary ariftocracy. But the fame laws, by dividing inheritances, tho their firft effect iz to create equality, ultimately tend to impoverifh a great number of citizens, and thus giv a few men, who commanded money, an advantage in procuring lands at lefs than their real valu. The evil iz increafed in a ftate, where there iz a fcarcity of cafh,

occafioned

occafioned by the courfe of trade, or by laws limiting
the intereft on money loaned. Such iz the cafe in Connecticut. A man who haz money may purchafe wel
cultivated farms in that ftate for feventy, and fometimes
for fifty per cent. of the real valu. Such a fituation iz
favorable to the accumulation of great eftates, and the
creation of diftinctions ; but while alienations of real
eftates are rendered neceffary by the laws, the genius of
the guvernment wil not be materially changed.

The caufes which deftroyed the ancient republics
were numerous ; but in Rome, one principal caufe
waz, the vaft inequality of fortunes, occafioned partly
by the ftratagems of the patricians and partly by the
fpoils of their enemies, or the exactions of tribute in
their conquered provinces. Rome, with the *name* of a
republic, waz feveral ages loozing the *fpirit* and *principle*. The Gracchi endevored to check the growing
evil by an agrarian law ; but were not fuccefsful. In
Cefar's time, the Romans were ripened for a change of
guvernment ; the *fpirit* of a commonwelth waz loft,
and Cefar waz but an inftrument of altering the *form*,
when it could no longer exift. Cefar iz execrated az
the tyrant of hiz country ; and Brutus, who ftabbed
him, iz applauded az a *Roman*. But fuch waz the
ftate of things in Rome, that Cefar waz a better ruler
than Brutus would hav been ; for when the fpirit of a
guvernment iz loft, the form muft change.

Brutus would hav been a tyrannical demagogue, or
hiz zeel to reftore the commonwelth would hav pro-
tracted the civil war and factions which raged in Rome
and which finally mufthav fubfided in monarky. Cefar
waz abfolute, but hiz guvernment waz moderate, and
hiz name waz fufficient to reprefs faction and prezerve
tranquillity. The zeel of Brutus waz intemperate and
rafh ; for when abufes hav acquired a certain degree of
ftrength ; when they are interwoven with every part of
government, it iz prudence to fuffer many evils, rather than rifk the application of a violent remedy.

How far the Roman hiftory furnifhes the data, on
which the politicians of America may calculate the future

ture changes in our form of guvernment, iz left to
every man's own opinion. Our citizens now hold
lands in fee ; this renders them bold in independence :
They all labor, and therefore make hardy foldiers ; they
all reed, and of courfe underftand their rights ; they
rove uncontrolled in the foreft ; therefore they know
the ufe of arms. But wil not poor peeple multiply, and
the poffeffions of real eftates be diminifhed in number,
and increefed in fize ? Muft not a great proportion of
our citizens becum manufacturers and thus looz the
bodies and the fpirit of foldiers ? While the mafs of
knowlege wil be increefed by difcuvcries and experience, wil it not be confined to fewer men ? In fhort,
wil not our forefts be levelled, or confined to a few
proprietors ? and when our peeple ccefe to hunt, will
not the body of them neglect the ufe of arms ? Theze
are queftions of magnitude ; but the prefent generation can anfwer them only in profpect and fpeculation.
At any rate, the genius of every guvernment muft ad-
dapt itfelf to the peculiar ftate and fpirit of the peeple
who compofe the ftate, and when the Americans looz
the *principles* of a free guvernment, it follows that they
wil fpeedily looz the *form.* Such a change would, az in
Rome, be afcribed to *bad* men ; but it is more rational to afcribe it to an imperceptible progrefs of corruption, or thoze infenfible changes which fteel into the
beft conftitutions of government.

New England waz originally fettled by a religious
fect, denominated *puritans,* who fled from the fevere
reftraints impofed upon diffenters in the reign of king
James I. Placed beyond the feer of control, they formed fiftems of civil and ecclefiaftical government, exactly fuited to their rigid notions. All their inftitutions
wear mafks of an enthufiaftic zeel for religion. Removed from the tyranny of one church, they vibrated
to the other extreme, and with an ardor to bild up
Chrift's kingdom, in what they quaintly call, *a howl-
ing wildernefs,* they eftablifhed a tyranny of the fevereft
kind over the conficienctes and rights of their own fociety, and by arbitrary decrees banifhed thoze who
                                                diffented

diſſented from them upon the moſt metaphiſical points. It waz a law of the firſt ſettlers at Boſton, 'that none could be free men and entitled to vote for civil rulers, who were not in full communion with the church; and none could be admitted to full communion, without the recommendation of a clergyman. Theze laws threw all the power of the ſtate into the hands of the clergy.* It iz equally aſtoniſhing and ridiculous to the poſterity of thoze godly peeple, to find the church and ſtate, in the infancy of the ſettlement in America, rent with diſcord upon the ſimple queſtion, whether "ſanc-"tification preceeds juſtification." Yet hundreds of councils were held upon this or ſimilar points, and a diſſent from the common opinion on ſuch trifling queſtions, waz hereſy, puniſhable with excommunication and baniſhment.

But candor requires ſome apology to be made for our anceſtors. Bigotry waz not confined to the New England ſettlers; it waz the characteriſtic of the age. The firſt ſettlers in New Jerſey, Virginia and Penſyl-vania, and indeed in moſt of the colonies, prohibited witchcraft under penalty of deth; tho the laws ſeem not to have been executed any where except in Maſſa-chuſetts. But the ſame gloomy ſuperſtition reigned in England. The ſtatues of Henry VIII. and James I. making witchcraft and ſorcery felony without benefit of clergy, upon which many perſons ſuffered deth, were not repeeled, till the ninth yeer of George II. or about 1736. Juſt before the reſtoration in 1660, no leſs than thirteen *gypſies* were condemned at one Suf-folk aſſizes, and executed.

But why ſhould I go to former times and other ſtates for apologies? Iz it not eezy to find ſuperſtition and prejudices among ourſelves equally abſurd and indefen-ſible? Does not a law againſt playing with cards pro-ceed from theze prejudices? What iz the difference between playing with *ſpotted papers and ſpotted boards?* Chequers, back-gammon and cheſs are not prohibited, and the games are az enticing az thoze which are pro-hibited.

* See Winthrop's Journal, Mather's Magnalia, and Hutch-iſons Collection of papers.

hited.   Are not fuch games az capable of conceelment
az any domeſtic concerns ? Wil laws ever reech them ?
Haz the legiſlature any right to control my family a-
muzements ? In ſhort, do laws ever ſuppreſs or reſtrain
any ſpecies of game ? By no meens ; on the other
hand, I can teſtify from actual obſervation, that prohibited games are practized az much az others, and
in ſtates where penalties againſt them are moſt ſevere,
gaming iz the moſt frequent.

Again, are laws againſt witchcraft more abſurd than
laws againſt uſury ? Did not both originate in ages of
monkiſh bigotry, and in the ſame religious ſcruples ?
Iz it not az illiberal a prejudice to ſay, that a man ſhall
hav but ſix per cent. profit on money loaned, yet may
make fifty per cent. if he can, on the ſame valu in
goods, houſes or lands ; az it iz to ſay, that a man
ſhal not be a fanatic, or a woman hav the hyſterics ?
Haz not any man az good a right to be whimſical or ſu-
perſtitious, az a legiſlature to be inconſiſtent ? Az to
the right, I ſee no difference.   A man who iz oppreſ-
ſed to an obvious degree by a rich creditor, wil find releef againſt the oppreſſor.   In a court of equity, a fanatic, who ſhould keep a naborhood in an uproar by
hiz religious worſhip, would be puniſhable for a miſ-
demeenor.   But when two men can make a voluntary
contract for eight per cent. intereſt, a contract which
eech deems favorable for himſelf, that he ſhould be
puniſhable with a hevvy forfiture, iz a curoſity in legiſlation, which ought to be placed on the catalog of
papal bulls.

Superſtition appeers in all ages under different aſ-
pects.   The ſailor who repozes confidence in the horſe-
ſhoe on hiz maſt, the Roman who counts hiz beeds,
the judge who gravely ſentences a witch to the gallows,
and the legiſlator who thinks it a crime to receev great
profits for the uſe of money, may be equally conſcien-
tious, and to poſterity in ſome future time, wil appeer to be equally miſtaken.

But while we contemplate the cenſurable laws of the
firſt New England ſettlers, let us not paſs by many
                                              excellent

excellent regulations which proceed from their religious zeel, and which hav been the bafis of inftitutions the moft favorable to morals, to freedom and happinefs.

In the firft place, our anceftors made provifion for fupporting preechers of the gofpel in every village. Abating fome rigid maxims, which were propagated and maintained for the firft century, with too much zeel, the influence of the clergy, in NewEngland, haz been productiv of the happieft effects.   The clergy, being wel informed men, and fcattered among the peeple at large, hav been inftrumental in diffufing knowlege.   Frends to order, and refpected by their parifhioners, they hav at times faved the ftates from turbulence and diforder.   The advocates of liberty, they efpoufed the American revolution with firmnefs, and contributed to unite the peeple in a fteddy oppofition to Britifh mezures ; and fince the eftablifhment of peece, they hav had no fmall influence in oppozing mezures, fatal to good faith and the rights of freemen.

The effects of their influence are the moft generally vizible in Connecticut, where every town iz well fettled and fupports a clergyman.   This ftate never experienced an infurrection ; its oppofition to the Britifh power, during the war, waz fteddy and unanimous ; and tender laws and paper currency hav been uniformly reprobated fince the revolution.

The old fettlements in Maffachufetts may fall under the fame character ; but the weftern and northern counties are exceptions.   In a great proportion of the townfhips, which hav been lately fettled, there iz no clergyman or other perfon of fuperior information, to direct the popular councils and check a rizing oppofition.   It waz obzerved, during the late infurrections in thoze counties, that the towns which were deftitute of any wel informed men, furnifhed the moft numerous and moft turbulent hofts of infurgents.   The wel informed counties on the fee coaft furnifhed fcarcely a man.

In addition to this, it may be remarked, that the mildnefs of manners and the hofpitality which prevail

among

among the yemanry of New England, are afcribeable in a great meazure, to a general adminiftration of religious ordinances. The diftinction in this refpect, iz fo great between New England and fome other parts of America, that in travelling among the fettlers on the frontiers of Vermont, a man may afcertain where the fettlers were born and educated, merely by their manner of receeving and treeting him. This iz afferted from actual obzervation.

The ftate of Rhode Ifland furnifhes full proofs of what iz here faid in favor of the clergy. That ftate waz fettled by refugees from Maffachufetts, who were banifhed or perfecuted by the firft fettlers, for their religious tenets. Roger Williams and hiz adherents imbibed an inveterate hatred againft the colony of Maffachufetts, and in particular againft the clergy, whoze rigid zeel occafioned their expulfion from the colony. The prejudice continued among their defendants, and to this day the inhabitants boaft of their liberality of fentiment and their freedom from the bigotry of clergymen, which, they fay, enflaves the peeple of Maffachufetts and Connecticut. This averfion to the clerical order haz however had a pernicious effect in the ftate. The body of the peeple, unaccuftomed to the fobriety and decent deportment neceffary in religious worfhip, and defpizing the puritanical manners of their nabors, are educated in licentioufnefs and void of principle. To this fource may be traced the moft unjuft and tyrannical laws that ever difgraced a popular affembly, and a perfeverance in executing them, which can proceed only from obftinate ignorance and difhoneft views. The large trading towns are excepted from this defcription; the inhabitants of which are well informed, polite, liberal, and firm fupporters of good government ; *but they encourage fchools and fupport a refpectable clergy.*

In the fecond place, our anceftors difcuvered their wizdom in eftablifhing public fchools and colleges. The law of Connecticut ordains, that every town, or parifh containing feventy houfeholders, fhall keep an

English

Englifh fchool, at leeft eleven months in a yeer; and towns containing a lefs number, at leeft fix months in a yeer. Every town keeping a public fkool, iz entitled to draw from the trezury of the ftate, a certain fum of money, proportioned to its cenfus in the lift of property which furnifhes the rule of taxation. This fum might hav been originally fufficient to fupport one fkool in each town or parifh; but in modern times, iz divided among a number, and the deficiency of money to fupport the fkools iz raifed upon the eftates of the peeple, in the manner the public taxes are affeffed. To extend the benefits of this eftablifhment to all the inhabitants, large towns and parifhes are divided into diftricts; eech of which iz fuppofed able to furnifh a competent number of fkolars for one fkool. In eech diftrict a houfe iz erected for the purpofe by the inhabitants of that diftrict; who hire a mafter, furnifh wood, and tax themfelves to pay all expenfes, not provided for by the public money. The fkool iz kept during the winter months, when every farmer can fpare hiz fons. In this manner every child in the ftate haz accefs to a fchool. In the fummer, a woman iz hired to teech fmall children, who are not fit for any kind of labor. In the large towns, fkools, ether public or private, are kept the whole yeer; and in every county town, a grammar fchool iz eftablifhed by law.

The ftate of Maffachufetts haz alfo public fchools on fimilar principles. The colleges and academies are too well known to need any defcription or remarks.

The beneficial effects of theze inftitutions will be experienced for ages. Next to the eftablifhments in favor of religion, they hav been the nurferies of wel-informed citizens, brave foldiers and wize legiflators. A peeple thus informed are capable of underftanding their rights and of difcuvering the meens to fecure them.

In the next place, our forefathers took mezures to prezerve the reputation of fkools and the morals of yuth, by making the bufinefs of teeching them an honorable employment. Every town or diftrict haz a committee whoze duty iz to procure a mafter of talents

Y   and

and karacter ; and the practice iz to procure a man of the beſt character in the town or naborhood. The welthy towns apply to yung gentlemen of liberal education, who, after taking the bachelor's degree, uſually keep ſkool a yeer or two, before they enter upon a profeſſion. One of the moſt unfortunate circumſtances to education in the middle and· futhern ſtates, iz, an opinion that ſkool keeping iz a meen employment, ſit only for perſons of low karacter. The retches who keep the ſkools in thoze ſtates, very frequently degrade the employment ; but the misfortune iz, public opinion ſuppozes the employment degrades the man : Of courſe no gentleman will undertake to teech children, while, in popular eſtimation, he muſt forfit hiz rank and karacter by the employment. Until public opinion iz corrected by ſome great examples, the common ſchools, what few there are in thoze ſtates, muſt continu in the hands of ſuch vagabonds az wander about the country.

Neerly connected with the eſtabliſhment of ſkools, iz the circulation of newſpapers in New England. This iz both a conſequence and a cauſe of a general diffuſion of letters. In Connecticut, almoſt every man reeds a paper every week. In the yeer 1785, I took ſome pains to aſcertain the number of papers printed weekly in Connecticut, and in the futhern ſtates. I found the number in Connecticut to be neerly eight thouſand ; which waz equal to that publiſhed in the whole territory, ſouth of Penſylvania.* By meens of this general circulation of public papers, the peeple are informed of all political affairs ; and their repreſentativs are often prepared to deliberate on propoſitions, made to the legiſlature.

Another inſtitution favorable to knowlege, iz the eſtabliſhment of pariſh libraries. · Theze are procured by ſubſcription, but they are numerous, the expenſe not being conſiderable, and the deſire of reeding universal.

---

* During the late war, eight thouſand newſpapers were publiſhed weekly at one preſs in Hartford.

verfal. One hundred volums of books, felected from the beft writers on ethics, divinity and hiftory, and red by the principal inhabitants of a town or village, wil hav an amazing influence in fpreding knowlege, correcting the morals and foftening the manners of a nation. I am acquainted with parifhes, where almoft every houfholder haz red the works of Addifon, Sherlock, Atterbury, Watts, Young, and other fimilar writings; and wil converfe handfomely on the fubjects of which they treet.

Still further, the wifdom of the erly fettlers in New England iz remarkable in the divifion of their territorial jurifdictions into townfhips, and incorporating them with certain powers of a fubordinate nature. Every town iz a corporate body, with power to appoint, at an annual meeting, certain town magiftrates, called *felectmen*, who hav the charge of providing for the poor, fuperintending the town property, difpozing of the monies &c. rendering an account to the town at the annual meeting. The towns alfo appoint conftables, *collectors of taxes*,† furveyors of roads, tithing men, whoze bufinefs iz to prezerve order on Sundays, infpectors of various denominations, &c. The towns are obliged to bild and repair their own bridges, repair roads, and defray the expenfe by a tax impozed by themfelves. They alfo fupport their own poor. This fyftem of fubordinate legiflation haz the advantage of faving the legiflature much trubble, and the corporations can hardly abufe powers, which are limited to their own territories; nor wil they probably neglect their duty, az it iz for their intereft and convenience to perform it.

In the general organization of guvernment, the New England ftates differ widely; thoze of Maffachufetts and New Hampfhire, being formed fince the revolution, are wel known; thoze of Connecticut and Rhode Ifland are moddled upon the charters of Charles II, and have fuffered but little alteration, fince their firft eftablifhment.

The

_____

† This iz an evil of great magnitude.

The New England colonies were originally guverned by a cheef magiftrate or guvernor, a deputy, and a
certain number of affiftants, all chofen by the peeple.
They were called the court of affiftants, and for a confiderable time, exercized all powers legiflativ and judicial. The clergy were uzually affociated with them,
and they feem to hav taken cognizance likewife of ecclefiaftical matters. The rulers of peeple in fmall focieties, in erly fettlements, and in the fimple ftate of nature, uzually hav difcretionary powers to act for the
common good. This waz the cafe with the ancient
witena-gemote, and folk-motes or county meetings
in England; and with the firft legiflatures in theze colonies.

The towns foon began to fend reprefentativs to the
court; but for feveral yeers in Bofton, they fat in the
fame houfe with the affiftants; in the fame manner az
the knights of fhires, or reprefentativs of the inferior
barons, fat in parliament with the lords on their firft
introduction into the legiflature. But az the towns
multiplied, this practice waz found inconvenient, and
the deputies were feparated from the affiftants. When
this took place the affiftants rezerved to themfelves the
judiciary powers, which at firft were lodged in the
whole affembly. In Connecticut, the affiftants or upper houfe of affembly retained theze powers in effect,
till the late revolution; only for the fake of convenience, five of their number were appointed by both
houfes, to the immediate exercize of the office and to
ride the circuit. Still the affembly were a court of appeels in the laft rezort, to all intents and purpofes; for
on petition, any judgement or decree might be heerd
and reverfed by the legiflature. Since the revolution,
a fupreme court of errors iz conftituted, but on an exceptionable plan, and the legiflature continues to exercize fupreme judicial power on petitions. This iz a
remnant of the old adminiftration, which was once
harmlefs, if not neceffary; but in a large *community,
may be confidered az a faulty part of the guvernment.
The whole legiflature likewize acts az a court for the

trial of public delinquents. This iz an evil of unbounded magnitude. When charges are exhibited againſt any
public officer, or any objections made to hiz re-ap-
pointment, he iz admitted to a hearing, council iz employed, the charges are red, witneſſes examined, and the
delinquent makes hiz defence in perſon or by attorney.
This mode of impeachment and trial iz the worſt that
can be invented. It iz difficult or impoſſible for a
large popular aſſembly to be good judges ; they cannot
perfectly underſtand a caſe ; they are credulous ; and
their compaſſion eezily moved. A pathetic harang,
eſpecially from the accuſed himſelf, with teers in hiz
eyes, and the misfortunes of hiz family painted in diſ-
cription, wil ſkreen from puniſhment any knave, however numerous hiz crimes, or however convincing the
proofs of hiz gilt. A popular aſſembly ſhould not ſit
in judgement upon delinquents, for the ſame reezon
that wimen would be improper judges, and for the ſame
reezons that the mother and wife of Coriolanus were
the only perſons who could ſave Rome from his ven-
gence.*

The conſtitution of Connecticut iz if poſſible, more
defectiv in the trezury or finance department. The
trezurer iz annually appointed by the freemen in the
ſtate at large. This makes him dependent on them.
The collectors are ſcattered in every part of the ſtate ;
and if the trezurer iz not agreeable to them, az he wil
not be, if he iz rigorous in enforcing collections, they
can render him unpopular and throw him out of office.
This iz an evil ; beſides, the conſtables, who are collectors, are appointed by the towns ; if they are rigorous in their duty, they are liable to looz their office ;
or what iz worſe, they may ſet up az candidates for the
legiſlature, and by an influence arizing from their power in exacting taxes with a greater or leſs degree of rigor, procure an election to an employment for which
they

* Uxor deinde ac liberi amplexi ; fletuſque ab omni turba
mulierum ortus, et comploratio ſui patriæque, *fregere tandem*
virum.—Liv. lib ii. 40.

they are wholly unqualified.   When a confiderable
number of collectors hav obtained feets in the legiflature, they are ever reddy to delay or fufpend the collection of taxes.   This iz not the worft part of the fyftem.
The method of obtaining the money in default of the
collectors, iz tedious, expenfiv, ineffectual, and in fhort
ridiculous.   When a collector iz in arreer, a diftrefs
iffues from the trezury againft hiz eftate.   Upon a return of *non eft*, or in cafe of the collector's infolvency,
execution iffues againft the felectmen of the town,
whofe eftates are liable for the arrecrages of taxes.
The felectmen then levy a tax upon the inhabitants to
indemnify themfelves.

It would be endlefs to enumerate the evils arizing
out of this mode of collection.   If the trezurer was
appointed by the legiflature, with power to name his
collectors and call them to account ; and if collectors
were obliged to giv bonds with fufficient fecurity to
fave the ftate from lofs, which fecurity fhould be liable to diftrefs immediately on failure of the collector,
the taxes would be collected with promptitude and a
great faving of expenfe.

It may be obzerved, that the faults of the conftitution are afcribeable to the ancient fimplicity of the New
England peeple, and the corruptions of the adminiftration hav grown out of the long tranquillity of the ftate.
While the peeple had perfect confidence in their rulers,
they were not difpofed to difobey the laws ; and while
there were few opportunities of corruptions, there might
be no inftance of maladminiftration, fo obvious or atro-
cious az to alarm enquiry, and excite peeple to change
laws and forms, to which they had been familiarized.
The inconveniencies refulting from a union of the legiflativ and judicial powers in the fame hands, were
not fo great az to be fenfibly felt by the public ; and
habits of refpect for men in office, and fubmiffion to
law, had rendered men credulous and unfufpecting.
To this day, it iz difficult to make the inhabitants beleev that their rulers and magiftrates can betray a public truft.   Till within two yeers, the guvernor, deputy
guvernor, judges of the fuperior court, or two juftices
                                                            of

of the peece, could draw upon the trezury of Connecticut, without their accounts being examined by any controller or auditor.

Before the legiflature could be perfuaded to inftitute a controller's office az a check upon the trezury, it waz neceffary to exhibit to them ftrong proofs of maladminiftration in that department; and the evils arizing from the prezent mode of collecting taxes, muft be obvious and great, before they wil make any change in the fyftem. Men are guverned by habit. The firft laws of a country take their complection from the peculiar caft and circumftances of the peeple; and then the laws in turn contribute to form the manners of fucceeding generations. The ftate of Connecticut iz an illuftrious example of this truth. By its fituation, it can never be expozed to fudden changes by an influx of foreigners. It haz no great capital, no general mart where all bufinefs centers; it haz very little intercourfe with Europe; and the communication by water between New York and Rhode Ifland iz fo direct, eezy and cheep, that for nine months in the yeer, few peeple travel thro Connecticut. For theze reezons, ancient manners and habits will be prezerved longer in this ftate than in moft of the others.

There iz one article in the conftitution of this ftate that merits notice and imitation, becaufe it iz equally fingular and excellent. It iz the manner of electing the affiftants or fenators of their own legiflature, and the members of congrefs. Theze are elected by the freemen at large in the whole ftate. The number of fenators iz twelve, and chofen annually in this manner. In September, the *freemen* affemble in the towns and vote for twenty perfons, by ballot; the votes are all returned to the legiflature in October, and numbered; and the twenty names that hav the moft votes are faid to ftand in *nomination*, and are publifhed by order of affembly. The next April, the freemen affemble again, and vote by ballot for *twelv* of the *twenty*, and the *twelv* perfons who hav the moft votes, are elected. Reprefentatives in congrefs are chozen in a fimilar manner. The great excellence of this mode of choozing iz,

iz, it holds up to public view, fix months before election, the karacters who are candidates ; peeple hav an
opportunity of enquiring into their merits, that they
may felect from the whole thoze who are the leeft exceptionable.

It iz alfo a fingular advantage that one branch of the
legiflature ftands upon the fuffrages of the whole.   If
a man's nabors take a diflike to hiz public or private
conduct, they wil, if poffible, difmifs him from office.
This iz the great misfortune of fmall diftrict elections,
for it often happens that a man's integrity and independence in public mezures, are moft likely to render
him unpopular among hiz nabors ; and fometimes
fmall domeftic occurrences may turn the tide of favor
againft him.   But when a man iz elected by a large
diftrict, he iz not expozed to this evil ; and nothing
fhort of a general oppofition to popular mezures will
fhake him from hiz elevation.   Theze remarks hav
been repeetedly verified in Connecticut.   The independence of the fenate, owing moftly to this article in
the conftitution, haz feveral times faved the ftate from
the moft difgraceful acts.

The reprefentativs are chozen twice a yeer, for there
are two regular feffions of the legiflature.   This iz an
inconvenience, but not fo great, az it appears to our
futhern nabors ; for the freemen meet in towns, which
are but about fix miles fquare ; fo that they can go
from home, make a choice, and return in three hours.

The regularity of theze meetings iz incredible to
ftrangers, accuftomed to the tumultuous elections in
England and the futhern ftates.   No mân dare folic-
it for the votes of hiz nabors, nor ever offers himfelf a
candidate by advertizing.   The freemen meet in fome
public bilding, uzually a church, feet themfelves, heer
the law red refpecting elections, and proclamation iz
made that they prepare their ballots for the officer to be
chozen.   The conftables then carry a hat to every
freeman and take the votes, which are counted by the
civil authority, and the choice declared in the meeting.
Thus the reprefentativs are elected ; but the ballots
for

for guvernor, deputy guvernor, fenators, and delegates
to congrefs, are feeled up, and fent to Hartford, where
they are numbered at the annual election in May. The
choice iz conducted with neerly the fame fobriety az
public worfhip on Sunday.   How different the elections in the futhern ftates, where I hav feen candidates
march at the hed of their adherents, armed with clubs,
and force their way to the place of election, and by violence thrufting away their rivals! It is a misfortune
in thoze ftates, that the freemen of a *whole county* affemble at elections.   This iz one principal caufe, why
the elections are attended with tumults, riots, quarrels,
bloody nozes, and in a few inftances, with deth. The
laws of a republic fhould gard againft all large collections
of peeple either for good or bad purpofes :   They are
always dangerous.   Rome furnifhes innumerable lef-
fons on this fubject ; and if the futhern legiflatures attend to facts, they wil doubtlefs divide their counties
into fmall diftricts for the purpofe of election, and hav
the choice completed in one day ; that the candidates
might not be able to hed their frends in more places
than one.   It iz of infinit confequence that the pernicious influence of elections fhould be deftroyed.

Religion in Connecticut haz the fupport of law.
Contracts with clergymen are valid in law, and every
man iz compelled to pay hiz proportion of taxes to
pay the falary of the minifter of the parifh where he
refides, unlefs he produces du proof that he attends
worfhip with fome diffenting congregation ; in which
cafe he iz excuzed.   This iz confidered by ftrangers
az a hardfhip : But it produces few inconveniencies in
a ftate where there are few diffenters from the common
worfhip ; and theze few are exempted, if they attend
any religious worfhip.   Every perfon iz indulged in
worfhiping az he pleezes ; and whatever modern liberality may pretend, the regular preeching of the gofpel,
az a *civil* inftitution, iz az neceffary and ufeful, az the
eftablifhment of fkools or courts of juftice.   Without
any regard to compulfion over confciences, or any reference to a future life, a legal provifion for the moral in-
                                                    ftructors

ſtructors of men, iz az beneficial in ſociety, az any civil
or literary inſtitution whatever ; and a commonalty,
who hav not the benefit of ſuch inſtruction, wil, I preſume to aſſert, always be ignorant, and of ruf uncivil
manners.   It iz an article of ſome conſtitutions in
America, that clergymen ſhal hold no civil office.
This excluſion iz founded on juſt az good reezons, az
the old laws againſt witchcraft ; a clergyman being no
more dangerous in a civil office, than a witch in civil
ſociety.   It iz ſaid that the buſineſs of clergymen iz
divine and ſpiritual, and that they ſhould hav no concern with politics.   The objection iz equally good
againſt merchants, mechanics and farmers, who hav no
immediate concern with legiſlation.   The truth iz, every citizen haz a concern in the laws which guvern
him ; and a clergyman haz the ſame concern with
civil laws, az other men.   There hav been bad clergymen and tyrannical hierarkies in the world ; but the error lies in ſeparating the civil from the eccleſiaſtical government.   When ſeparated they become rivals ; when
united, they hav the ſame intereſt to purſu.   A clergyman's buſineſs iz to *inform* hiz peeple, and to make
them *good men*.   This iz the way to make them *good
citizens*.   The clergymen in Boſton take the right
method to accompliſh this buſineſs ; they throw aſide
all *divine airs* and imperious grave ſuperiority ; they
mingle in the moſt familiar manner, with other peeple ;
they are ſocial and facetious, and their pariſhoners de-
light to hav them at all entertainments and concerts.
This conduct remoovs the awful diſtance between
them and other deſcriptions of men ; they are not only
eſteemed and reſpected, but luved ; their decent deportment iz imitated ; their churches are crowded, and
their inſtructions liſtened to with plezure.   Such men
are bleſſings to ſociety.   That clergymen ought not to
meddle with politics, iz ſo far from truth, that they
ought to be *well* acquainted with the ſubject, and *better*
than moſt claſſes of men, in proportion to their literary
attainments.   Religion and policy ought ever to go
hand in hand ; not to raize a ſyſtem of deſpotiſm over
                                                    the

the confciences, but to enlighten the minds, foften the harts, correct the manners and reftrain the vices of men. If men are to be fitted for heaven, it *muft* be by theze meens ; there iz no other way. The feparation of religion and policy, of church and ftate, waz owing at firft to the errors of a gloomy fuperftition, which exalted the minifters of Chrift into Deities ; who, like other men, under fimilar advantages, became tyrants. The way to check their ambition, and to giv full efficacy to their adminiftrations, iz to confider them az *men* and *citizens*, entitled to all the benefits of guvernment, fubject to law, and defigned for *civil* az wel az *fpiritual* inftructors.

The ftate of New York waz fettled with views, widely different from thoze which actuated the New England puritans.   Some Dutch merchants firft eftablifhed factories at Albany and on Manhattans, now York Ifland, for the purpofe of opening a fur trade. When the province came into the poffeffion of the Englifh, feveral gentlemen of property took up large tracts of lands, which, being regulated by the Englifh laws of defcent, continued unbroken, til the late revolution.   But many of the proprietors of theze manors, efpoufing the royal caufe in the late conteft, left their eftates, which were of courfe confifcated and fold by the ftate.   This circumftance waz fatal to many large manors ; and a law of the ftate, enacted about the yeer 1781, which breaks the prefent and bars all future entailments, wil in time divide the large eftates which remain unbroken.   The Dutch poffefs the moft fertile parts of the old fettlements ; az Ulfter and Claverak counties, part of Albany and Kings county, on Long Ifland.   They are honeft and economical, but indolent, and deftitute of enterprize; fo that the ftate wil be moftly indetted to emigrants from New England, for its future population and improvements.

New York city iz the moft favorable ftand for a great commercial port on the united ftates.   Men may indulge themfelves in rapfodies, about the Potomack, the Ohio and the Miffifippi ; but no part of theze ftates, eeft of the Allegany, wil ever rival New York, and it iz doutful whether the fame conveniencies for bufinefs unite on any part of the Miffifippi. New York iz the center of the commerce of all the territory, between the weftern boundary of Rhode Ifland and the middle of New Jerfey, from the Atlantic neerly to the borders of Canada ; a diftrict of two hundred miles by two hundred and fifty. And the geography of the country tells us, that no part of Atlantic America can claim the fame extenfiv advantages. New York iz 'not eezily defended in time of war, and therefore, without a navy, iz not a fafe place for an arfenal ; but Weft Point, fixty miles abuv the city, on the Hudfon, iz the moft impregnable fortrefs in America.

Before the revolution, the guvernment of New York waz under the influence of the crown of Great Britain, the guvernor and council being appointed by the king. It waz illiberal in the preference given to the epifcopal church ; no other denomination of Chriftians being able to obtain any corporate eftablifhment. The fame illiberal preference waz difcuverable in the inftitution and guvernment of the college, now called Columbia college, in which diffenters of any defcription could not hav a fhare. The revolution haz effected a change in theze particulars. Diffenting churches, which are the moft numerous in the ftate, are or may be incorporated ; and education begins to be encuraged by the laws. A univerfity iz eftablifhed, with a power of fuperintending and regulating fkools throughout the ftate ; but provifion iz not made for maintaining common fkools in every quarter of the ftate. Ignorance ftil prevails among the yemanry ; and this enables certain defigning karacters to exercife a pernicious influence in the guvernment.

The territory of New Jerfey originally belonged to two, and afterwards to many proprietors, who appointed the guvernors. But in the reign of queen Ann, the guvernment waz rezigned to the crown, and for a number of yeers, the guvernor of New York waz alfo guvernor of the Jerfies, altho eech province had a dif-
                                                    trict

trict affembly. The heirs of the original proprietors, or their purchafers, ftil hold the foil. There are in this ftate many large eftates, but an entailment iz good only to the firft donee in tail ; the eftate, on hiz deth inteftate, being divided equally among hiz heirs. In general the laws of New Jerfey are highly republican ; but they make no provifion for a general diffufion of knowlege. Many of the yemanry are extremely ignorant. The college at Princeton iz a very valuable inftitution ; but fo little concern haz the legiflature for the intereft of lerning, that the funds of that college are taxed by law.

The prefent conftitution of New Jerfey iz liable to few exceptions ; but the ftate iz divided into two parties which often agitate the guvernment. Az the caufe and effects of the controverfy which began and ftil continues theze parties, are little known to their nabors, I beg leev here to offer a concife ftate of the facts from unqueftionable authority.

James, duke of York, in June 1664, conveyed New Jerfey to John, lord Berkeley, and Sir George Carteret, in fee. The bounds of the territory granted were, the main fee and Hudfon's river on the eeft, Delaware bay or river on the weft, Cape May on the fouth, and on the north *the northernmoft branch of Delaware bay, or river, which iz forty one degrees and forty minutes of latitude, croffing over thence in a ftrait line to Hudfon's river, in forty one degrees of latitude.*

Some intermediate conveyances of lord Berkeley's undivided half part were made, but need not be here recited. On the firft of July, 1676, waz executed a quintipartite deed, between Sir George Carteret, and the grantees of lord Berkely, by which the territory waz divided ; Sir George Carteret releefing all the weftern part to the grantees of Berkeley, and the latter releefing the eeftern part to Sir George. The line of partition, which originated all the fubfequent difputes, iz thus defcribed in the deed : " Extending eeftward and northward along the fee coaft and the faid river, called Hudfon's river, from the eeft fide of a certain place or

harbor,

harbor, lying on the futhern part of the fame tract of land, and commonly called and known in a mafs of the fame, by the name of *Little Egg Harbor*, to that part of the faid Hudfon's river, which iz in forty one degrees of latitude, being the furthermoft part of faid tract of land and premifes, which iz bounded by the faid river, and crofling over from thence in a ftrait line; extending from that part of Hudfon's river aforefaid, to the northernmoft part or branch of the before mentioned river, called Delaware river, and to the moft northerly point or boundary of the faid tract of land and premifes, granted by hiz royal highnefs, James, duke of York, to lord Berkeley and Sir George Carteret."

A difficulty aroze about the northern point of partition; the duke of York's grant making the northernmoft branch of Delaware bay or river to be in *forty one degrees and forty minutes* of latitude; and declaring a line from this point to the latitude of *forty one* on Hudfon's river, to be the northern boundary of New Jerfey. Difputes aroze, and the legiflature of New Jerfey, in 1719, paffed an act, declaring that a partition line between Eeft and Weft Jerfey, fhall be run *from the moft northerly point or boundary of the province, on the northernmoft branch of Delaware river*, to the moft futherly point of Little Egg Harbor. Commiffioners were appointed for this purpofe, and alfo for running the line between New York and New Jerfey. They met with commiffioners from New York, but could not agree, and left the bufinefs unfinifhed. In 1741, another attempt waz made by Mr. Alexander, furveyor general of both divifions, but obnoxious to the Weft Jerfey proprietors. He began to run the line, but fome errors he committed, or bad inftruments, prevented the completion of the bufinefs; he ftopped half way. Difputes ran high, and were attended with riots, till the yeers 1762 and 1764, when by a law of New York and another of New Jerfey, it waz agreed the line between the provinces fhould be run by commiffioners to be appointed by the crown. To this agreement the proprietors

prietors of Weſt Jerſey az well az Eeſt, were parties. The commiſſioners met, fixed the two ſtation points between New York and New Jerſey, one at a rock on Hudſon's river, in forty one degrees of latitude, the other at the forks of the Delaware, at the mouth of the river Makhakamak, in latitude 41°. 21′. 37″. This point on Delaware iz *eighteen minutes twenty three ſeconds*, to the ſuthward of the *northern boundary* of New Jerſey, az deſcribed in the duke of York's grant to the firſt proprietors ; which waz, on the *northernmoſt branch of Delaware river, which iz forty one degrees forty minutes* of latitude.

Both parties appeeled to the crown, but without ſucceſs. Acts were afterwards paſſed, both by New York and New Jerſey, confirming the line between the provinces, and theze acts receeved the approbation of the king in council. This waz an amicable ſettlement between the two provinces ; and it waz expected that the *northern limits of New Jerſey* and the *ſtation points* on both rivers, being fixed by law, nothing waz neceſſary to quiet all parties, but to run the line from the north ſtation point on Delaware to Little Egg Harbor.

A correſpondence for this purpoſe took place between the proprietors of Eeſt and Weſt Jerſey ; but before the matter waz completed the war commenced. Since the war, the controverſies hav been revived, and divided the ſtate into violent parties. It ſeems the proprietors of Eeſt Jerſey expected the *north ſtation point on Delaware* would hav been fixed az high az *forty one degrees forty minutes*, the point deſcribed by the original grant from the duke of York. This would hav carried the limit of the ſtate about eighteen miles further north on the Delaware ſide. Now there iz a bend in the Delaware, at the forks, ſo that the ſtation point az now fixed, iz carried further eeſt than it would be, had it been fixed in *forty one degrees forty minutes* ; ſo the deciſion of the commiſſioners waz in favor of the Weſt Jerſey proprietors. From the forks, the river bends its courſe weſterly of north, and from a point eighteen miles north, a line to Little Egg Harbor, would leev an angle

angle containing feveral thoufand akers of land, in Eeft
Jerfey. This iz a fhort ftate of the origin and progrefs
of a controverfy, which ftil agitates the ftate and dif-
turbs the peece of their guvernment ; the jealoufies between Eeft and Weft Jerfey being almoft az great az
between the northern and futhern ftates, upon a queftion refpecting the feet of guvernment, or any other
matter of little confequence to the union. The conteft however iz of magnitude to both parties in New
Jerfey, az the lands in difpute hav been fettled upon
doutful titles ; and altho an act of the legiflature may
eftablifh theze, yet the loozing party wil expect a com-
penfation.*

The commerce of New Jerfey iz almoft wholly carried on thro New York and Philadelphia. Its fituation, between two large commercial towns, refembles
that of Connecticut ; but in one refpect, the latter haz
the advantage, viz. that of a butiful navigable river,
penetrating the ftate and affording the beft conveniencies for a trade to the Weft Indies. The legiflature of
New Jerfey hav attempted to call home the trade of the
ftate, by holding out liberal encouragement for direct
importations from abroad, and making free ports.
Perth Amboy affords a fine harbor, but it iz difficult,
perhaps impoffible, to raize a rival in the naborhood of
New York. New Jerfey and Connecticut wil find
their intereft in encuraging manufactures.

Penfylvania waz fettled by a religious fect, remarkable for their fobriety, induftry and pacific difpofition.
Mr. Penn, the firft proprietor of the province, waz a
man of fuperior talents. The free indulgence given to
all religious denominations, invited fettlers from England, Germany and Ireland, and the population of the
province, with the confequential increefe of the valu of
lands, waz rapid beyond any thing known in the other
colonies. The province however waz harraffed with
difputes between the acting guvernors and the commons.

* The foregoing facts are taken from Leaming and Spicer's
Collection ; a concife view of the controverfy, &c. publifhed
in 1785 ; and from the acts of the legiflature of New Jerfey.

rions.   The proprietary, who waz the guvernor, ufually rezided in England ; appointing a deputy with a
council, to act for him in the province. · The proprietaries were often feltifh, and made demands upon the
peeple, which their fenfe of liberty and right would not
permit them to grant.   The quit-rents, paper currency, and fome other matters, were conftant fubjects of
altercation, whenever the affembly convened.*

The long and violent oppofition to the influence of
their proprietaries, who were abroad, and often confidered az hoftile to popular privileges, together with the
beneficial effects of a paper currency, during the infant
ftate of the province, may be the reezons why the conftitution of Penfylvania, formed at the revolution, verg-
ed too much towards an extreme of democracy ;† and
why the legiflature of that ftate waz the firft to iffue a
paper currency, after the war.   The old republican
patriots, who had refifted, with fuccefs, the encroachments of arbitrary guvernors and kings, determined to
frame a conftitution, which fhould prevent the inter-
férence of a guvernor and council in acts of legiflation ;
and men who had feen the *good* effects of paper currency, without its *evils,* would be the firft to recommend
it.   It iz natural ; men are guverned by habit.

At the revolution in 1776, the reprefentativs of
the province, acting on the principle that public good
tranfcends all confiderations of individual right, affumed the reigns of government, formed a conftitution
for the purpofe, and divefted the proprietaries of both
territory and jurifdiction.   They gave them however,
130,000l. fterling in lieu of all quit-rents, and rezerved
to them confiderable tracts of land.   The firft conftitution, like that of the Netherlands, waz framed upon
the

---

* See **Dr.** Franklins Review of the guvernment of Penfylvania.

† The powers of legiflation by the late conftitution, were
defigned to be vefted in the peeple ; but in fact were vefted no
where.   The pretended legiflature confifted of but one houfe ;
and no bill, except on prefling occafions, could be paffed into a
law, until it had been publifhed for the affent of the peeple.

the ruins of oppreffion, and with a too jealous atten-tion to popular rights. It waz defeɛtiv in the moſt material articles, and a few yeers experience induced the peeple to adopt another form, more analagous to thoze by which her fiſter ſtates are guverned.

The laws of Penſylvania, reſpecting inheritances, hav not barred entails ; but az entails may be docked by the Engliſh fineſſe of common recoveries ; az the diviſions of lands favor equality, az wel az the genius of the peeple, there can be no apprehenſions of an ariſ-tocratical influence from large poſſeſſions of real eſtate. A fingle man may hold real or perfonal eſtate to fuch an amount, az to hav an undu influence in politics and commerce. When a man haz become ſo powerful that hiz nabors are afraid to demand their rights of him in a legal way; or when a town or city iz ſo far under hiz control, that the citizens are generally afraid of offending him, he iz or may be a dangerous man in a free ſtate, and a *bad* man in any ſtate. A Clive and a Haſtings are az dangerous in a ſtate, az an Arnold or a Shays, if they hav the fame evil propenſities ; for thoze who oppoze law, are generally puniſhed ; but thoze who are abuv law, may do injuſtice with impu-nity.

The peeple in Penſylvania may be included under the three denominations of *Frends*, *Germans*, and *Iriſh defendants*. The *Frends* and *Germans* were the firſt ſett-lers, and for the moſt part liv between the Delaware and Suſquehanna. Theze are peeceable and induſtrious peeple. The Iriſh or their defendants, inhabit the weſtern counties ; they are induſtrious, but not ſo wel informed in general, az the inhabitants of ſome older counties, and at times hav been turbulent citizens. It waz the misfortune of this, az of all the ſuthern ſtates, that no proviſion for public ſkools waz incorporated into the original fundamental laws.

Without ſuch a proviſion, it iz not poſſible that a body of freemen ſhould hav the reeding neceſſary to form juſt notions of liberty and law. This defect wil probably be ſupplied by the new conſtitution and the
future

future laws of the ftate. The number of colleges and academies alreddy founded and endowed, proov the dif-pofition of the legiflature to encurage fcience. The only difficulty iz to perfuade an agricultural peeple to fettle in villages or ilans, for the purpofe of maintaining a clergyman and fkoolmafter ; and thus to tarry into effect the wife and benevolent defigns of their rulers.

Philadelphia iz a great commercial city ; but it iz queftioned whether commerce wil giv it a future growth equal to that of New York. The future population of the futhern part of New Jerfey, and the peninfula between the Chefapeek and the Atlantic, wil not add much to the trade of Philadelphia. The naborhood of the city and moft of the lands towards Lancafter and Bethlehem, are alreddy wel fettled. About feventy three miles weft of Philadelphia runs the Sufquehanna ; a river not indeed navigable at the mouth, but with fome portages, capable of opening a communication by water from Wioming to the Chefapeek ; and fhould canals be opened to avoid the falls and rapids, the trade of the ftate, quite to the hed of that river, wil center in Baltimore. At any rate Baltimore and Alexandria wil command moft of the trade weft of the Sufquehanna ; fo that Philadelphia muft depend moftly, for the increefe of her bufinefs, on the population northward, about the hed of the Deleware. The commerce however wil always be confiderable, and the fpirit of the citizens in eftablifhing manufactures, promifes a great extenfion of the city.

The ftate of Penfylvania waz, for many yeers, agitated by a territorial controverfy with Connecticut ; the hiftory of which iz breefly this.

King James I. in 1620, made a grant to a number of gentlemen, called the *Plimouth Company*, of all the lands in North America, included between the 40th and 48th degrees of latitude, *throughout all the main land from fee to fee*; except fuch lands az were then fettled by fome Chriftian prince or ftate. The only fettlements at that time north of Virginia, were at New York and Albany, on the Hudfon.

In

In 1628, a number of gentlemen obtained from the company a grant of lands, bounded on the north, by a line three miles north of Merrimak river, and on the fouth, by a line three miles fouth of Charles river, *throughout the main lands from the Atlantic on the eeft, to the South See, on the weft.* This waz the firft grant of Maffachufetts.

In the yeer 1631, Robert, erl of Warwick, prefident of the Plimouth company, granted to lord Say and Seal, and lord Brook, all that part of New England, extending from Naraganfet river, the ,fpace of forty leegs on a ftrait line, neer the fee coaft, north and fouth in latitude and bredth, and in length and longitude of and within all the aforefaid bredth, *throughout all the main lands from the weftern Ocean to the Szuth See.* This grant waz confirmed by the charter of Charles II. dated April 23, 1662, with a fimilar defcription of the territory.

In 1664, king Charles II. gave hiz brother a tract of land in America, the defcription of which iz not wholly confiftent or intelligible ; but one part of the grant interfered with the Connecticut patent, and difputes aroze, which were amicably fettled by commiffioners in 1683 ; the line betwcen Connecticut and New York being fixed at Byram river, about twenty miles eeft of the Hudfon.

In 1680, Sir William Penn obtained from the crown a tract of land, extending from twelv miles north of New Caftle, on the Delaware, to the forty third degree of latitude, and from the Delaware weftward five degrees of longitude. This grant interfered with the patent of Connecticut, provided the grant to the guvernor and company of Connecticut fhould be extended weft of New York, according to the words of that and the other grants of New England. Mr. Penn took care to gain a juft title to hiz patent by bona fide purchafes of the Indians, who poffeffed the foil. But the queftion iz, whether he had a right of pre-emption to lands before granted to other men ; and whether the king's grant to him could be valid, fo far az it cuvered lands alredy conveyed by

the

the crown to a company, which had begun fettlements upon the grant.

The Penfylvanians contended that, the geografy of this country being little known in England, az all the maps and charts at that time were imperfect and erroneous, it muft hav been owing to an ignorance of the diftance from the Atlantic to the South See, that the grants were made to run thro the continent : That Mr. Penn had acquired the beft of titles to the lands in difpute by fair purchafe from the nativ proprietors : And that Connecticut, by a fettlement of her boundary with New York, had fixed her weftern limits, and relinquifhed all claim to lands weft of New York.

While any part of Connecticut, eeft of New York, remained unlocated, the inhabitants fuffered their claims weftward to lie dormant. But about the yeer 1750, the whole of this territory waz located, and the peeple began to think of forming a fettlement weft of Delaware river. They however knew that the lands were claimed by Penfylvania, and to remoov all douts az to the validity of their own title, requefted the opinions of the moft eminent council in England, upon their right by charter to the lands in queftion. They receeved for anfwer, that the grant to the Plimouth company, did extend to the weftward of New York : That the fettlement of the boundary line between New York and Connecticut, did not affect their claims to lands in other parts : And that, the charter of Connecticut being of a prior date to that of Sir William Penn, there waz no ground to contend, that the crown could make an effectual grant to him of that country which had been fo recently granted to others. This anfwer waz fo decifiv and cleer in favor of their claim, that they proceeded to locate and fettle the lands on the Sufquehanna river, within the latitude of the Connecticut charter. It feems however that a few fcattering fettlements had been made within the fame latitude, on the oppofit fide of the river, under Penfylvania locations. The fettlers foon came to an open quarrel, and both ftates became interefted in the controverfy. The

difpute

difpute however fubfided a few yeers during the war, til finally both ftates fubmitted their claims to the *jurifdiftion of the territory*, to a federal court, which waz held at Trenton, in November, 1782. The decifion of this court waz in favor of Penfylvania, and Connecticut acquiefced.

Diffatisfied with this decree, the fettlers under Connecticut and individual claimants, determined to maintain their *right to the foil*, which they had poffeffed more than twenty five yeers ; and to fubmit this alfo to a federal court. No court however waz ever held for the purpofe ; the claimants not finding any fupport from the guvernment of Connecticut. The fettlers, amounting to many hundreds, remained upon the foil. Penfylvania, by a precipitancy arifing out of an imperfect frame of guvernment, refolved to take poffeffion of the lands, and fent an armed force for the purpofe. This mëzure waz rafh, efpecially az the principal fettlers had taken the oath of allegiance to that ftate, and were willing, if they could be quieted in their poffeffions, to becum good and peeceable citizens. Tumults followed ; the hiftory of which would be difagreeable to moft reeders. At length, Penfylvania paffed a law to quiet thoze who were actual fettlers before the decree at Trenton, in the poffeffion of their farms, amounting to about three hundred akers eech. The territory waz erected into a county, by the name of Luzerne, in honor of the French minifter of that name. Colonel Pickering waz appointed Prothonotary* of the county. This gentleman haz fuffered much in reconciling parties ; but hiz integrity, zeel, prudence, and indefatigable induftry, bid fair to meet with merited fuccefs in quieting diforders and eftablifhing guvernment.

In this controverfy, feveral queftions arize. Firft, What right had the crown of England to the lands in North America?

I anfwer, the *right of difcuvery*. This right, however the law of nations may hav confidered it, does not in fact entitle a prince or ftate to the foil, even of an

---

* Clerk or regifter.

an uninhabited territory ; much le's, of lands poffeffed by any of the human race. It entitles the difcuvering nation to a preference in forming fettlements or occupying vacant lands. And this right iz derived rather from the common convenience of nations, or the neceffity of fome principle by which to prevent controverfy, than from any connection between *difcuvery* and a *title to property.*

Secondly, What right could the grantees derive from a royal grant of lands in America ?

I anfwer, merely a *right of pre-emption*, or a preference in purchafing the lands of the proprietors, the nativ Indians.

Thirdly, The guvernor and company of Connecticut, by the prior date of their charter, having the right of pre-emption to all the lands cuvered by the charter, could Mr. Penn acquire a title to any of the fame lands by pre-emption ?

On legal principles he certainly could not.

The only fubftantial ground of title which Penfylvania could hav to the controverted lands, waz, that Connecticut, by neglecting to purchafe of the Indians, might forfit their right of pre-emption, and leev the territory open to any purchafer whatever ; fo that Mr. Penn or hiz heirs might acquire a good title by firft purchafe. Whether Mr. Penn actually acquired fuch a title or not, I am not poffeffed of documents to decide. That the firft grant of New England actually extended to the Weftern or Pacific Ocean, cannot be denied ; and congrefs hav admitted the claim, by accepting from Connecticut a ceffion of lands weft of Penfylvania. Connecticut however ftil holds a tract of one hundred and twenty miles, weft of that ftate, which iz now for fale. The ftate of Maffachufetts haz a fimilar claim to lands weft of New York ftate ; and the line between the two ftates haz lately been fettled by commiffioners. At any rate, the controverfy between Connecticut and Penfylvania waz finally terminated by the decree of Trenton, and it iz to be wifhed no future altercation may difturb the ftates or individual proprietors.

The

The fmall ftate of Delaware refembles Penfylvania in refpect to its hiftory and guvernment.

Maryland waz fettled by Roman Catholic emigrants, from England and Ireland, under lord Baltimore. Large grants of land were carved out to individuals, and flaves purchafed from Africa to cultivate the foil. Some of the largeft eftates in America lie in Maryland. The guvernment waz formerly in the hands of the proprietary; but the peeple, at the revolution, affumed it. Mr. Harford, the natural fon of lord Baltimore, inherited hiz property in Maryland; but being an abfentee during the war, hiz eftates were confifcated, and on petition, the legiflature refuzed him even the arreerages of rent, du at the commencement of hoftilities.*

The prefent conftitution iz in general excellent; and particularly in the eftablifhment of an independent fenate. In a popular ftate, nothing contributes fo much to ftability and fafety, az an independency and firmnefs in one branch of the legiflature. This ftate however, like its nabors, iz remarkable for tumultuous elections; a malpractice that haz exifted from its firft fettlement; a practice which wil fooner or later proov fatal to the attempts of merit in obtaining offices, and fap the foundation of a free guvernment.

The body of the peeple are ignorant. I once faw a copy of inftructions given to a reprefentativ by hiz conftituents, with more than a hundred names fubfcribed; three fifths of which were marked with a crofs, becaufe the men could not write. Two or three colleges, and fome academies and private fkools, conftitute the principal meens of inftruction in this ftate, and moft of theze are of a modern eftablifhment. A few large towns only giv good encuragement to fkools and the clergy.

Maryland continues to reccev multitudes of emigrants from Europe, and many of them are of the pooreft clafs. From feveral months rezidence in Maryland, I am inclined to beleev, there are more vagabonds

in

* See the proceedings of the legiflature of Maryland in 1785.

in Baltimore and the vicinity, than in all New England. But Maryland muſt decide upon the public
benefit derived from this unreſtrained admiſſion of
foreigners.

Virginia waz ſettled *eight* yeers before New York,
and *fourteen* before New England. This circumſtance
haz given the ſtate the quaint appellation of the *ancient
dominion*. The diviſions of property are large, and the
lands cultivated by ſlaves. Entailments of land were
barred before the revolution ; but real eſtate iz not liable
for det upon an execution. It appeers ſtrange at firſt
view, that men ſhould exempt their lands from this
liability, and at the ſame time, ſuffer their perſons to be
imprizoned for det : The ſingularity however iz eezily
accounted for, by their karaĉteriſtic attachment to *large
eſtates*, or rather to the *name* of poſſeſſing them. When
a man's conſequence and reputation depend principally
on the quantity of land and number of negroes *he iz
ſaid to poſſeſs*, he will not riſk both for the ſake of hiz
creditors. The paſſion for the *name of a planter*, ab-
ſorbs all other conſiderations. I waz once preſent at
an entertainment, given by a *yung planter* in Virginia,
who had *much land* and *many ſlaves*. He aroze at two
o'clock next morning, pawned hiz knee buckles and
ſome other articles, gave hiz landlord a note for about
ſixty dollars, and rode off without paying hiz hair-dreſſ-
er. But he waz *ſaid* to be a man of property. Many
of the planters are indeed nominally rich ; but their
dets are not paid. I waz told by wel informed planters, that ſome whole counties in Virginia would hardly
ſel for the valu of the dets du from the inhabitants.
The Virginians, it iz tru, owe immenſe ſums to Britiſh
merchants, and the difficulty of paying them might be
a principal reezon for ſuſpending the collecĉtion by law,
at the cloze of the war ; but that the real eſtates of a
whole county would not diſcharge the dets of it, iz not
to be beleeved.

A large part of the peeple in Virginia hav not the
meens of education. The diſperſed ſituation of the
planters in the ſuthern ſtates, renders it impoſſible for

all

all to hav accefs to fkools. The univerfity of Williamfburg, and a few academies in large towns, conftitute the principal meens of education in Virginia ; and
the fame remark iz applicable to all the futhern ftates.
But a fmall proportion of the white children can reep
any advantage from theze inftitutions. Since the revolution, the legiflatures of all the futhern ftates hav
fhown a difpozition to giv liberal encuragement to the
education of every rank of citizens ; but the local circumftances or habits of the peeple throw innumerable
obftacles in the way of executing their patriotic defigns. Gentlemen of property, reziding on their plantations at a diftance from a village, wil fometimes hire
a private inftructor in their families ; but theze inftructors muft be vagabonds, for the moft part ; az the
gentlemen wil not admit that a *fkoolmafter* can be a *gentleman* ; in confequence of which opinion, moft or all
teechers are excluded from genteel company. While
this iz the cafe, men of good breeding wil not be found
to teech their children. An exception muft be made
of *grammar mafters,* az they are called ; for a man who
can teech Latin, they fuppoze, may be a *decent* man,
and fit for gentlemen's company.

Religion fares worfe in Virginia than education.
Before the war, the epifcopal waz the eftablifhed religion of the province, and the churches were liberally
endowed by law. A parifh ufually contained four
churches, in eech of which a clergyman officiated in
rotation, one Sunday in a month. But this greevous
burthen waz remooved by the revolution, and great
numbers of parifhes hav no officiating minifter. A
motion waz brot forward in 1785, to make fome legal
provizion for fupporting clergymen ; but the propofition
waz fufpended til the next feffion of the legiflature.
In the meen time a pompous retorical memorial waz
circulated and fubfcribed, in oppozition to the mezure.
The arguments uzed againft any ecclefiaftical eftablifhments were fplendid, *liberal* and efficacious ; and at
the following feffion, the legiflature paffed a declaratory
argumentatiy

argumentativ refolv againft giving religion any eftablifhment and protcction.*

When men hav thrown off a reftraint that iz difagreeable and unreezonable, it iz to be expected that
they wil run into the extreme of licentioufnefs. Yet
it iz one of the moft difficult problems in the hiftory of
theze ftates, that the liberal and eminently lerned men,
who conduct the guvernment of Virginia, (and many
of their leeding karacters are of this defcription) fhould
not view the minifters of religion, in America, az deftitute of that odious and tremendous authority over human confciences, which waz affumed under the papal
hierarky. I can hardly beleev a man of reeding and
reflection to be ferious, when he afferts that legiflatures
hav no right to compel the fubject to *contribute to the
fupport of clergymen*, becaufe they hav no authority *over
men's confciences*. Neether clergymen nor human laws
hav the leeft authority over the confcience ; nor iz any
fuch power implied in a law compelling every citizen
to contribute annually to the fupport of a clergyman.
But any fovereign authority may juftly command the
citizens to eftablifh and attend religious affemblies, az
wel az to meet for the choice of reprefentativs, or fend
their children to a fkool ; powers which were never
queftioned. A man iz not bound in confcience to beleev all the inftructions of hiz preceptor ; nor are the
citizens compellable to beleev the opinions and decifions of a court of juftice ; but the legiflature haz a
right to compel every citizen to pay hiz proportion of
taxes to maintain preceptors and judges. This iz precifely the fact with refpect to a legal fupport of clergymen.

No man iz bound in law or confcience to beleev all
a preecher fays ; but the whole queftion iz this ; are
clergymen, az moral inftructors, a beneficial order of
men ? Haz their miniftration a good effect upon fociety ? If this fhould be admitted, there iz no more dout
of

---

* Virginia however iz not alone in this mezure. Rhode
Ifland formerly took the fame fteps, and ftil adheres to its *liberality*.

of the right of a legiflature to fupport fuch men by law, than there iz of their right of inftituting univer-fities or courts of juftice. That enormous error which feems to be rivetted in popular opinion, *that the func-tions of clergymen are of a fpiritual and divine nature, and that this order of men fhould hav no concern with fecular affairs*, haz laid the foundation of a feparation of in-tereft and influence between the civil and ecclefiaftical orders ; haz produced a rivalfhip az fatal to the peece of fociety az war and peftilence, and a prejudice againft *all orders* of preechers, which bids fair to banifh the " gof-pel of peece" from fome parts of our empire. The Krif-tian religion, in its purity, iz the beft inftitution on erth for foftening the ferocious tempers, and awakening the benevolent affections of men. To this religion, Eu-rope and America are indetted for half their civiliza-tion. There hav been periods, when mankind hav fuffered from ecclefiaftical tyranny ; but information iz demolifhing all fyftems of defpotifm, civil and ec-clefiaftical. And when the clergy themfelves leev all rangling about fpeculativ points, which neether they nor philofophers underftand, and confine themfelves to publifhing and enforcing the benevolent precepts of a gofpel which breethes nothing but univerfal luv and peece to all mankind, they wil remoov the prejudices againft their order, they wil be *really* the meffengers of peece, they wil conciliate affection, and thus open the harts of men to receev impreffions of virtue, they wil make men good citizens here, without which they are never prepared to be members of a heavenly fociety ; and finally they wil eftablifh a *rational moral influence* over an enlightened peeple, equally fatal to the decla-mation of ranting fanatics, and the pernicious amufe-ment of gambling at inns and horfe-races.

In the Carolinas and Georgia, we find the ftate of property, literature and religion, refembling that in Virginia and Maryland. Charlefton iz remarkable for its hofpitality and good order. But in the ftates fouth of Penfylvania and Delaware, the divifions of property, the habits of the peeple, and the difperfed

local

local fituation of the planters, are all unfavorable to improovments of any kind. Men who liv remote from fociety, furrounded only by flaves, acquire manners fingular and often difagreeably imperious, ruf and clownifh. Urbanity iz acquired only in focieties of wel bred peeple. They cannot hav the benefit of fkools and churches, without which the body of a peeple *cannot* be wel informed, and *wil* not acquire focial and virtuous habits. The manners of fettlement therefore, tho it may be neceffary and beneficial to individuals, may be confidered az highly inaufpicious in a yung country, whoze conftitutions of guvernment are founded on the principle of equality, and cannot flurifh without mildnefs of manners and a general diffufion of knowlege.

In the agricultural improovments of the united ftates, there iz a remarkable difference, which muft hav proceeded principally from the flavery of the futhern. In Virginia and Maryland, I fhould queftion whether a tenth of the land iz yet cultivated. In New England, more than half the whole iz cultivated, and in Connecticut, fcarcely a tenth remains in a wild ftate. Yet Virginia haz been fettled longer than New England.

I once heerd the *Prezident* remark, " that from the northern to the futhern ftates, the agricultural improovments are in an inverfe proportion to the number of flaves." This remark, like the actions of that illuftrious karacter, dezerves to be engraven on monuments of marble. Slaves hav no motiv to labor ; at leeft, none but what iz common to horfes and cattle. They want the only ftimulus that unites induftry with economy, viz. the profpect of a permanent advantage from their labor.

It haz been obzerved in Europe, that land rented on long leefes, iz better cultivated, than that which iz farmed on fhort leefes. A man who holds lands in fee, will uze them to the beft advantage, for he expects hiz children wil enjoy the benefit. A man who haz lands on very long leefes, haz neerly the fame motivs to improov them. Tenants for life wil make the moſt of lands for themſelves ; but wil probably leev them in the moſt impoveriſhed condition. Leſſees for a yeer hav few motivs to keep a farm in good repair ; and ſlaves are the worſt cultivaters on erth, az they hav the leeſt intereſt in the fruits of their labor. One yeman, who iz maſter of himſelf and hiz labors, and eets ſubſtantial food, wil perform the work of four ſlaves.

This iz not the whole evil. Slaves not only produce *leſs* than freemen, but they waſte *more* ; every ſlave, az Dr. Franklin haz remarked in hiz Miſcellaneous wurks, being, from the nature of ſituation, a *theef.* In addition to this, wherever ſlavery exiſts, a great proportion of inhabitants are rendered indolent, and indolence iz followed by vices and diſſipation.

' Suppoze twenty thouſand men to do no productiv buſineſs ; what an immenſe difference wil this make in the cultivation of a ſtate and in the annual income. In New England every man does ſome kind of buſineſs : In the ſuthern ſtates, the proprietors of large plantations do little or no buſineſs. The reezon why the planters make ſuch a profit on the labor of their ſlaves iz, that the ſubſiſtence of negroes iz not very expenſiv. The northern yemanry not only require more clothing than the ſuthern, but they liv on expenſiv food and drinks. Every man, even the pooreſt, makes uſe of tee, ſugar, ſpirits, and a multitude of articles, which are not conſumed by the laborers of any other country.*

But

---

* The conſumption of beef in New England iz the reezon why the exports of that article do not exceed thoze of Ireland. Moſt of the laboring peeple in New England eet meet twice a day, and az much az their appetites demand. Suppoſe eech perſon to eet but ſix ounces a day on an average, which iz a low eſtimate, and the inhabitants of New England conſume more than *one hundred million* pounds of meet, in a yeer. I do not know what proportion of this iz beef, but the greateſt part iz beef and pork, worth *two pence,* and *two pence half penny* a pound. By the beſt accounts from Ireland, it iz probable the inhabitants do not conſume a *twentieth part* of the meet, conſumed in the northern ſtates, in proport ionto their numbers.

But

But however cheep may be the fubfiftence of flaves, while every thing iz left to a mercenary unprincipled overfeer and to lazy negroes, a ftate wil never be wel cultivated.   In autumn, 1785, a gentleman in Richmond informed me he had juft carried fome manure upon a field *to make an experiment for the firft time.* This fact wil hardly be beleeved in the northern ftates. In travelling thro Virginia, from Alexandria to Williamfburg, and alfo to Peterfburg, I faw not one milldam, except what confifted of mere fand, thrown acrofs a ftreem.   The idea of conftructing ·dams of timber and planks, laid fo az to make an angle of forty five or fifty degrees with the horizon, that it might gain ftrength and ftability in proportion to the preffure of the incumbent water, feemed not, at that time, to hav prevailed in Virginia.   In a variety of particulars, the flow progrefs of invention in the futhern ftates, waz equally remarkable.

  Slavery iz an evil of the worft kind ; this iz generally acknowledged.   But what remedy can be applied ? To liberate the flaves at once would be madnefs ; it would ruin both mafters and flaves.   To liberate them gradually, and fuffer the freed men to liv with the whites, might giv rife to difcord and tumults.   Colonization, by a gradual exportation, iz an expedient that would be fafe and effectual, but cannot be put in execution.   The probability iz, that, in the lapfe of time, the blacks wil all be blended with the whites ; the mixed race wil acquire freedom, and be the predominant

But fuppoze they confume a *tenth* ; let the New England peeple reduce the confumption of meet in the fame proportion, and they would fave *ninety millions* for exportation.   This at two pence a pound makes the fum of *two million five hundred thoufand dollars,* which iz a very handfome commercial income. Let the reduction proceed to all kinds of food and clothing ; let our common peeple liv like the poor of Ireland in *all refpects,* and they would fave twice the fum.   I would not recommend this to my countrymen ; I wifh them to enjoy good eeting and drinking.   But I make theze eftimates to fhow them that they never wil hav much *money* ; for they eet and drink all they ern.

ant part of the inhabitants. This event haz taken place in Spanish America, between the nativs and Spaniards ; and, to a great degree, in some of the West India islands. The same event iz rapidly taking place in the suthern states. A propozition waz once made in the house of delegates, in Virginia, for granting the rights of freemen to the free blacks ; it waz not carried ; but I do not see how any state can deny theze rights to blacks that hav the legal qualifications of property and residence. This privilege once granted, would facilitate the intercourse between the whites and blacks, and hasten the abolition of slavery.

In the climate of the united states, there are several particulars that dezerv notice. In the first place, every circumstance in the local pozition of Atlantic America, concurs to render the wether variable. Theze states extend thro fifteen degrees of latitude, in the temperate zone ; consequently must always experience the extremes of winter and summer. Every part of this territory experiences sudden changes of wether ; but the most numerous and violent changes, are between the 36th and 43d degrees of latitude, on the Atlantic coast. Within this district, the most frequent variations seem to be in Pensylvania and Maryland. Four months in the winter season, the wether in Pensylvania, Maryland and Virginia, resembles the March wether in New England ; almost every week exhibiting the varieties of cold, heet, frost, snow and rain. For two months in the spring, and one in autumn, New England iz expozed to eesterly winds and rain ; except in theze months, the changes of wether, tho sometimes sudden and violent, are not very frequent. The eesterly winds, which uzually bring rain, ceese about the 20th of May.

The variations of wether in the united states, arizing from the latitude of their situation, are multiplied by their pozition on the ocean. Water in an ocean iz of a very uniform temperature ; whereas land iz eezily heeted and cooled. This circumstance creates an incessant contest between heet and cold, on an extensiv

see

fee coaft ; and of courfe an everlafting variablenefs of winds. This iz true in all countries. According to this theory, Atlantic America muft always hav a variable climate.

The fouth eeft winds from the ocean, falling upon the continent at right angles with the fhore, invariably produce rain ; the oppofit, or north weft winds, proceeding from the high lands in the back country, invariably produce cold cleer wether. North eeft winds, running parallel with the fhore, produce ftorms of fnow in winter, and long cold ftorms of rain in fpring and autum. Our moft violent gales blow from the north eeft. A fouth wefterly wind fometimes brings rain, and when it firft blows in winter, iz chilly ; but it foon moderates cold wether, and in fummer it iz the *gentle zepher* of the poets.

In fpeeking of winds, it iz neceffary to correct a vulgar error. It iz commonly faid, that north weft winds contract their coldnefs from the vaft lakes in the north weft regions of the united ftates. This iz an unphilofophical opinion, for water always moderates the temperature of the air ; and it iz a wel known fact that the large lakes do not freeze at all ; fo that if we were to feel the wind immediately after paffing over them, we fhould find it always temperate. The truth iz, our wefterly winds come from high mountains and high regions of the atmofphere, which are always cool. The top of the blu ridge, or firft range of mountains in Virginia, iz about four thoufand feet abuv its bafe. The top of the Allegany or middle ridge, which iz the height of land between the Atlantic and the Miffifippi, tho not fo far from its bafe, muft be much higher in the atmofphere. How far the bafe of the blu ridge iz abuv the furface of the ocean, haz not been afcertained ; but fuppoze it five thoufand feet, and the top of the Allegany, two thoufand feet abuv the blu ridge, and the greateft elevation of land iz eleven thoufand feet abuv the waters of the Atlantic.

The air on the tops of theze mountains iz never heeted to the degree it iz in the low countries. The cold regions of the atmofphere are much neerer to fuch

hights,

hights, than to a vaft extended plain. Thus the topʒ
öf mountains arc often cuvered with fnow, when the
land at the feet of them, iz fit for plowing. From the
regions of air abuv theze mountains, proceed the fe-
rene cold winds which fweep the Atlantic ftates, puri-
fying the atmofphere and bracing the bodies of animals.

I would juft remark here, that the climate of the
tranf-alleganean country, wil never be expozed to the
frequent changes of air and violent tempefts which
harrafs the inhabitants of the Atlantic fhore. The
force and difagreeable effects of eefterly winds from the
occan, are broken by the mountains ; and the northerly winds wil be tempered by paffing over the lakes ;
while the futherly winds wil be az refrefhing in fummer az on this eeftern coaft. Theze remarks are now
verified by facts ; altho by being cleered from forefts,
the country wil become more expozed to variations of
wind.

In the fecond place, it iz obzervable that the climate
cf America grows more variable, in proportion to the
cultivation of the land. Every perfon obzerves this
effect of cleering the lands in the eeftern and middle
ftates. The heet in fummer, and the cold in winter,
are not fo fteddy az formerly, being interrupted by
cool rains in fummer, and moderate wether in winter.
Our fprings and autums are longer, the former extending into fummer, and the latter into winter. The
caufe of this change iz obvious : By levelling the forefts, we lay open the erth to the fun, and it becumes
more impreffible with heet and cold. This circumftance muft multiply changes of wether. The cultivation neceffary to produce this effect, haz proceeded
about one hundred miles from the Atlantic, or perhaps
a little farther. But in Vermont and other back fettlements, the wether iz yet fteddy ; there being few
violent ftorms, efpecially in winter. The fnow falls
gently, and lies til fpring ; whereas neer the Atlantic,
moderate wether for three or four days, or a warm rain,
often fweeps away the fnow in January or February.

But

But altho the wether iz growing more variable from the cleering of lands, yet the falutary effects of cultivation are vizible in the increefing falubrity of the climaté. The agü and fever iz a diforder that infefts moft new fettlements. Cultivation wil totally remoov the caufes of this diforder, from every tract of country, which iz capable of being drained. Forty yeers ago, this difeefe prevailed in the ftate of Connecticut, in the fame manner it now does in Maryland. But for twenty or thirty yeers paft, it haz hardly been heerd of in the ftate. There are a few places expozed to the effluvia of marfhy grounds, where the diforder ftil infefts the inhabitants.

Some parts of the futhern ftates can never be drained ; the land iz fo low that the frefhes in the rivers, or the tides, are almoft conftantly cuvering it with water. Vegetable putrefaction may be confidered az furnifhing the miafmata in any country ; and the greateft quantities of putrid effluvia are exhaled from lands conftantly expozed to a flux and reflux of water.

But all countries, except the very mountanous, when firft cleered, are infefted with intermittants. Peeple on the fronteers of New York and Vermont, are trubbled with it, efpecially in low flat tracts of land. The furface of a wildernefs iz cuvered with leevs and rotten wood ; at the fame time, it iz moift, the rays of the fun being excluded by the trees. Therefore when peeple firft fettle in a wildernefs, they are not immediately attacked with intermittents. They muft lay open the furface of the erth to the action of heet and wind ; the noxious effluvia then begin to rize, and wil infect the air, til the whole furface of the erth iz dry and fweetened by the heet of the fun. The amazing difference in the ftate of a cultivated and uncultivated furface of erth, iz demonftrated by the number of fmall ftreems of water, which are dried up by cleering away forefts. The quantity of water, falling upon the furface, may be the fame ; but when land iz cuvered with trees and leevs, it retains the water ; when it iz cleered, the water runs off fuddenly into the large

ftreems.

ftreems. It iz for this reezon that frefhes in rivers hav becume larger, more frequent, fudden and deftructiv, than they were formerly. This fact fhould be attended to by the fettlers in a new country, that they may gard againft fudden and extraordinary frefhes in the erection of mills and bridges.

It iz vulgarly fuppofed that the wether in fummer iz hotter in the futhern ftates than in the northern. This opinion iz not accurate. The truth iz, at particular times, the northern ftates experience a greater degree of heet than iz ever known in the futhern. In the fummer muntlis, the mercury in Farenheit often rizes, in the middle of the day, much higher at Bofton, than at Charlefton, in South Caroiina. Thus in July, 1789, the mercury roze to 90 ° or upwards no lefs than fix days, and once to 93°, in the vicinity of Bofton; whereas at Charlfton, it roze but once to 88° during the fame munth, and but four days to 87°. Befides the meteorological obzervations I hav, were made at Bofton, at *one* o'clock, P. M. and in Charlefton, at *two* o'clock, when the heet iz ufually the greateft. In Auguft, the fame yeer, the mercury roze at Bofton* four days to 90, and once to 95°; but in Charlefton, it roze but once to 89^b. The remark then ought not to be, that the heet at the futhward iz *greater*; but that it *continus longer*; that iz, the aggregate quantity of heet in the futhern latitudes, exceeds that in the northern. I hav taken fome pains to afcertain the difference, and omitting decimals, here giv the refult of my enquiries.

The meen degree of heet for the whole munth of July, 1789, in Charlefton, South Carolina, by Farenheit's thermometer, waz az follows:

At 6 o'clock, A. M.   74°
At 2 o'clock, P. M.   83   } Total meen of the month 78.
At 10 o'clock, P. M.   77

For

---

* I fay Bofton, but I beleev the obfervations to be made at Cambridge.

For *A U G U S T*, 1789.

At 6 o'clock, A.M.   75 ⎫
At 2 o'clock, P. M.   83 ⎬ Total meen 77 neerly.
At 10 o'clock, P. M.   72 ⎭

The meen degree of heet, at Spring-Mill, a few miles from Philadelphia, for *July*, waz 74.

The meen degree of heet, at Bofton, for July, waz

At 7 o'clock, A. M.   67 ⎫ Total meen 71° neer-
At 1 o'clock, P. M.   80 ⎬ ly.
At 9 o'clock, P. M.   67 ⎭

For *A U G U S T*.

At 7 o'clock, A. M.   62 ⎫
At 1 o'clock, P. M.   77 ⎬ Total meen 68 neerly.
At 9 o'clock, P. M. · 66 ⎭

Theze facts, tho they cannot be the foundation of exact calculations, becaufe the obfervations were not made at the fame hour of the day, and perhaps the thermometers were not exactly alike or in the fame fituation az to heet, the facts I fay may ftil eftablifh the following conclufion :

That tho the middle of the days in fummer may be az warm and even warmer in New England, than in Carolina, yet the nights are much cooler.

In July, the meen temperature at Bofton, at feven o'clock in the morning, waz feven degrees lefs than at Charlefton at fix o'clock. At one o'clock, P. M. the meen heet at Bofton waz within three degrees of the heet in Charlefton at two o'clock. At ten o'clock at night, the meen heet at Charlefton, waz ten degrees abuv that at Bofton at nine o'clock. The meen temperature for the whole month in Charlefton, exceeded that in Bofton, feven degrees. Similar remarks may be made of the munth of Auguft.

Meen heet at Charlefton, for January, 1789. ·

At 7 o'clock, A.M.   50 ⎫
At 2   · P.M.   55 ⎬ Total meen 52½.
At 10   P.M.   52 ⎭

At

At Bofton, for the fame munth.

At 7 o'clock, A. M.   21 ⎫
At 1   P. M.   29 ⎬ Total meen 25 neerly.
At 9   P. M.   24 ⎭

Meen heet at Philadelphia, for January, 1789, 30°.

Here we may remark, that altho the meen heet of New England, in the fummer munths, approaches within feven, eight, or nine degrees of that in Charlefton, yet in winter, it iz lefs than *half* the heet at Charlefton ; the meen degree in Bofton being twenty five, and in Charlefton, fifty two.

The meen temperature in Charlefton, for March, 1789, waz about fixty one; and in Bofton, for the fame munth, a little lefs than thirty five, which iz more than half.   In Penfylvania, the fame munth, the meen waz forty.

So far az I am able to calculate on obzervations in my poffeffion, I find the aggregate quantity of heet in South Carolina, for a whole yeer, iz to that in New England, az twenty to eleven ; yet there are feveral days almoft every yeer, when the mercury in New England rizes higher at noon than it ever does in Carolina at any time, This may be afcribed to the fuperior length of the days in the northern latitudes.

The heet of the futhern latitude iz fuppozed to produce fevers and other fatal diforders which prevail in the Carolinas and Georgia. But heet iz not very often pernicious, unlefs when operating upon a low, wet, marfhy furface of earth. All hilly countries are helthy ; and the air of the mountanous parts of Carolina, two or three hundred miles from the fee, iz in general falubrious. But the marfh-effluvia iz not the only caufe of difeefe ; bad water iz a caufe that fhould be mentioned, and this abounds in a flat country ; whereas the water on hills and mountains iz generally pure. In a great number of towns to the futhward of the Delaware, and in fome to the northward, the want of good water iz a capital inconvenience.

On the whole, the climate of America iz az falubrious, az that of any country in the fame ftate of cultivation.

vation. The European naturalifts, with more fpleen than knowlege, hav condemned the climate of America, az unfavorable to animal growth and perfection ; but if their ideas are founded on facts, the facts muft be taken from the naborhood of an Indigo plantation. America, like all new countries, haz been expozed to certain annual epidemic diforders ; but wherever the furface of the erth haz been, for a few yeers, cultivated, theze diforders hav ceefed to rage. I am confident that Connecticut, the moft cultivated ftate in the union, iz now az helthy az the fouth of France. I am confident that the inhabitants enjoy az general helth, and liv az long. Az to fize, no part of the world can boaft of larger and more robuft men than the northern ftates. If I miftake not, the Englifh eftimate the mcen hight of their men to be *five feet, feven inches* ; but I am confident the average hight of the men in New England, iz not lefs than *five feet nine, or ten inches.*

I could wifh to afcertain the difference in the weight of the atmofphere at Bofton and Charlefton ; but hav no obzervations on the barometer from the latter place. The difference between the weight at Bofton and Philadelphia, upon an average of thirty days, appeers to be very trifling, altho at any given day or hour, it may be confiderable.

There are fome curious facts refpecting the coaft of North America, which dezerve notis.

The Miffifippi iz a river of great length, running from the high northern latitudes, in neerly a fouth direction. It iz deep and rapid. It refembles the Nile in Africa, particularly in making land where it iz difcharged into the ocean. By the moft accurate obzervations of Mr. Huchins and others, the diftance from the Balize to New Orleans, iz fomething more than two hundred miles, the whole of which iz land formed by the difcharge of the river. The Nile, in the time of Herodotus, had formed confiderable ilans, which were then inhabited. Theze ilans ftil exift, between the feveral channels by which that river iz difcharged. It iz probable, that by an accurate calculation of the

defcent

defent of the waters of the Miffifippi, in certain places, taking into account the moft rapid and moft moderate flow, and afcertaining the diftance of the mouth from the moft northerly fources, we might find, to a tolerable degree of accuracy, the elevation of the land at the fources of that river, abuv the level of the ocean.

Perhaps it wil be found that the mountains and lands at the north weft, are much higher in America than in the north of Europe. Iz not this probable from the hight of the Allegany, and the rapidity of the river Miffifippi ? And would not the fact, if prooved, in conjunction with other caufes, which are wel known, fully account for the fuperior degree of cold in America under the fame parallels ? It iz wel known that there are no confiderable mountains to the north eeft of Great Brirain, thro Denmark, Sweden and Ruffia.

On the Atlantic fhore of America, the Gulf Streem iz a curious phenomenon. It iz however wel accounted for, on the fuppozition that the trade winds drive the waters of the ocean weftward into the fpacious gulf of Mexico, where meeting the continent, they are forced between the Bahama ilans and the coaft of Florida, and take their direction along the fhore of the united ftates. Such an immenfe body of waters, flowing at the rate of three miles an hour, muft produce innumerable currents neer the fhore ; for every point of land wil occafion an eddy, which wil be in proportion to the extent of the point or cape from main coaft. Hence the variety of currents, in all directions, between the ftreem and the American coaft, which are obzerved by our feemen.

Theze currents and eddies, at the fame time *produce* and *add to*, the points of land fhooting into the ocean. The cape of Florida iz probably produced between a vaft eddy of waters in the Mexican gulf, and the ftreem which flows between the fhore and Bahamas. For theory indicates that the principal body of water, carried along the Spanifh main, or between that and the Weft India ilans, muft be forced to bend its courfe on the Mexican fhore, and by the coaft of Weft Florida, be thrown into a circular motion, fo az to form a vaft

eddy

eddy to the futhward and weftward of Eeeft Florida. Where this iz met by the ftreem, a point of land muft neceffarily be formed.

It iz not improbable that Cape Koman, Cape Fear, Cape Hatteras, and Cape Cod, may be formed by fimilar currents, within the main Gulf Streem. A confiderable extent of land on the coaft of Carolina and Georgia, appeers to be made by the wafhing down of fand from the high country, and the wafhing up of fand by the Atlantic, whoze furges almoft inceffantly beet the fhore. But this alone wil not account for the extenfion of points of fand, ten, fifteen or twenty leegs into the ocean.

It iz a fact that capes and promontories are more frequently harraffed with tempefts, lightning and thunder, than other parts of the fhore or continent. This haz been remarked of New York and Cape Hatteras. Can a philofophical reezon be affigned for this phenomenon? Perhaps there may be fome attractiv power in land thus fituated ; and perhaps tempefts are generated by the agitation of the air, produced by a flux and reflux of water, or a variety of oppofit currents. A ftorm hangs over Cape Hatteras, every day, for a confiderable part of the yeer. I hav been witnefs to the fact, for a number of days in fucceffion. This circumftance increefes the terror of navigating that coaft ; otherwize fo formidable to feemen for fhoals and breakers.*

In examining the harbors of North America, we find moft of them prezent a channel or entrance neerly at right angles with the fhore. The entrance into moft of them iz between the points of weft and north. The entrance into Newport, iz the fafeft in America, and this iz almoft the only harbor in the united ftates which can be made with a northwefterly wind. This circumftance iz highly favorable to fhips coming upon the coaft in winter. This harbor iz capacious enough to admit all the navees in Europe, and, if defenfible, may be the proper Portfmouth of America.

* I once paffed the cape at *five* or *fix* leegs from the breakers, and found but feven fathoms of water.

No.

No. XXVIII.

The following iz part of an " Essay on the Dets of the United States," written in 1787, but never before published. The question haz been ably discussed in Congress, and the proposition for a discrimination between original and purchasing holders of certificates, which I had started, without the prospect of support, haz been maintained by very powerful arguments in our federal legislature. Az the question now appeers to my mind, I should vote against the proposition, yet merely on the ground that from the manner in which the certificates were issued, it iz impossible to discriminate, without multiplying the instances of hardship and injustice. But I hav no more dout, that legislatures hav a right to interfere, in certain extreme cases, and suspend or counteract the operation of legal principles, than I hav of any reveeled truth or intuitiv proposition ; and were it possible to ascertain the original holders of certificates, I conceev our legislators could not hav neglected a provision for their losses, without violating their oaths, the constitution and public faith. The following extract iz published, becauce I am desirous my opinion on this subject should be known and recorded.

HARTFORD, MARCH, 1790.

On a DISCRIMINATION between the ORIGINAL HOLDERS and the PURCHASERS of the CERTIFICATES of the UNITED STATES.

OBJECTION I. IT iz said that *public faith* requires the payment of the certificates, according to contract ; that iz, to the bearers. Let me ask the men who contend for promise, what they meen by *public faith ?* Did the public ever promise to do rong ? The money waz du to men who erned it ; the money waz not paid. The full valu expressed on the
certificates

certificates waz du, and the certificates were worth but a fourth, or perhaps an eighth part of that valu. The public promifed the creditors their full demands ; but theze promifes, at the time of iffuing the certificates, were actually worth but a fmall part of that demand. Ought the creditors to be difmiffed with this part of their money, and then compelled to pay the full valu of the certificates to their nabors, who purchafed them at their current price ? If this iz right, my ideas of juftice are *rong.* Public faith iz fuppozed to be founded on juftice. The public engaged to do juftice to its creditors ; but this juftice *haz* not been done ; and it appeers to me az plain az the fhining of the fun, that if the certificates fhould be paid to the bearers, juftice *wil* not be done. The creditors at the time of contract, expected to receev gold and filver, or fomething equivalent ; they hav receeved neether the one nor the other. They receeved articles which were worth but a fourth part of their demands ; for the remainder of their money, the public iz ftil their detor. Public faith therefore requires, that the full valu of the alienated certificates fhould not be paid to the bearer. It appeers to me that the principles of equity, rather than of law, fhould decide this important queftion. It iz the defign of the contract, not the words, which fhould be purfued ; for it muft be remembered, that the defign of the public haz been counteracted. The intention of the public, expreffed on the certificates, haz been defeated by the public exigences ; and to purfue the words of the engagement, wil now produce an effect which waz not defigned, viz. *extenfiv injuftice.*

In this fituation the public haz an undouted right to call in the evidences of the det, and form a fyftem that fhall be effectual in the diftribution of juftice. If the public fuppoze that any arrangement for this purpoze can be made, they certainly hav a right to attempt it ; for the object of the attempt would be public juftice. The fticklers for paying the det to the prefent holders, hav the fame object in view, *national faith* ; but their ideas of this faith, feem to be derived from the practice

of

of other nations, the fituation of whoze dets bears very little analogy to that of ours. They therefore advance an argument againſt their own cauze ; for the faith of the public iz prezerved by fulfilling *the intention,* rather than the *words,* of the contraƈt.

Every dollar of old continental currency, promiſes a Spaniſh milled dollar. This promiſe waz founded on the ſuppozition that the valu would be neerly the ſame, or waz deſigned to prezerve the valu. But the depreciation of that currency, by the enormous ſums in circulation, rendered the fulfilment of the promiſe impraƈticable ; and had it been attempted, it would hav thrown the united ſtates into confuſion. The redemption of the bills, at their nominal valu, would hav done juſtice to a few, whoze money had depreciated in their hands, but would hav ruined fifty times the number. Thoze who loſt their property by continental bills, ought to be indemnified, if the perſons and ſums loſt could be aſcertained ; but this iz impoſſible. The caſe of the certificates iz different. Theze are promiſſory notes, expreſſing the ſums du, and the perſons names to whom they were given. If in ſome inſtances the purchaſers hav returned alienated certificates to the office, and taken out new ones in their own names, ſtil the public books may remedy this inconyenience.

2.   But it iz ſaid the creditors of the public parted with their certificates voluntarily. It waz at their own option, whether to keep them or not ; and if they choze to alienate them at a diſcount, the public iz not reſponſible for the loſs. *A* owes *B* 100l. he cannot make immediate payment, but haz property to ſecure *B,* who takes a promiſſory note. *B* wants the money, and rather than wait for *A's* ability to pay it, he aſſigns the note to *C* for 50l. In this caſe, *A* cannot refuſe to pay the full ſum of 100l. becauſe *C* gave but fifty for the note. This reezoning iz applied to the caſe of the public det ; and yet a ſkool boy ought to be aſhamed of the application. The caſe iz not parrallel, and the reezoning iz defeƈtiv and inapplicable in every particular.

In the firſt caſe, it iz not tru that the alienation of the certificates waz a voluntary act ; but in moſt caſes, waz an act of neceſſity. Moſt of the original creditors were ether *rich* men who loaned money, or poor men who did perſonal ſervice. In many inſtances, thoze who loaned money, loaned all their eſtates ; and when they found no provizion made for paying the intereſt, or when the intereſt waz paid in paper of leſs valu than ſpecie, they were left deſtitute of the meens of ſubſiſtence. Some of theze hav been obliged to part with their certificates at a great loſs. But a large number of creditors were poor peeple, who had little or no property, but their certificates, who had performed ſervice, and were under a neceſſity of negociating them on az good terms az they could. Moſt of the alienations hav therefore been a neceſſary conſequence of public delinquency. Many of the creditors hav experienced a degree of diſtreſs, which, in a court of chancery, would entitle them to a conſideration and redreſs. When a number of loſſes iz ſo great az to effect the public, the legiſlature then becumes a court of equity, where the ſufferers muſt ſeek reparation. The legal principle muſt be ſuſpended, and ſpecial proviſion made for this particular caſe. Thoze creditors who were able to keep their certificates, hav generally done it, and on every principle are entitled to the full nominal valu.

In the ſecond place, the caſe of an individual aſſignee of a bond wil not apply ; for *B*, in the ſuppozition, takes the bond voluntarily. *A*, the dettor, haz property, and it iz optional with *B*, whether to bring a ſuit for the money, recover a judgement, and take *A's* property, or take a bond on intereſt. This iz generally the caſe with individuals, but not with the public creditors. Theze hav no alternativ ; they muſt take promiſes, which the ſubject cannot compel the public to fulfil, when the money iz wanted. In another particular, the two caſes are widely different. *A, B,* and *C,* are three diſtinct perſons. *A* iz the dettor, and it iz indifferent whether he pays the det to *B* or *C*. But when *B* haz ſold the note for half the valu, he cannot

be

be called upon for the money, nor for any part of it.
In the other cafe, the creditors and the public are, in
fome mezure, the fame perfon. The fame perfons
who looze their property by public delinquency, are afterwards taxed to pay their proportion to the purchafers. But I wil for a moment fuppoze the two cafes
exactly fimilar ; for I am willing to giv my antagonifts
the faireft field of argument ; and what conclufion can
be drawn in favor of paying the certificates to the bearers ? Can that reezoning be juft which draws general
confequences from particular propozitions ? Such bad
logic ought not to impeech a man's heart ; but it can
do very little honor to hiz head.

Do men, who reezon in this manner, confider that
a principle with refpect to individuals, may be perfectly *juft*, and yet purfued to a certain degree, it may become entirely falfe ? That the fame principle which
may be good in a certain degree, may, in the extreme
become criminal, iz tru not only in politics, but in the
natural and moral fyftems. Heet and water, prouduce
vegetables ; but too large portions of either, deftroy
plants. Every paffion, natural to man, iz good in itfelf, and the wurk of a perfectly wife being ; but any
paffion indulged to a certain degree, becumes criminal
and deftructiv to focial happinefs. Self-love, the fpring
of all action, and in the tru fenfe of the word, the
moft neceffary principle in creation, when it becumes
exceffiv, iz az criminal and pernicious, az the moft
malignant paffion. Eeting and fleeping are effential to
helth ; but beyond a certain degree, they are hurtful,
and may be fatal to the human body.

In politices, the greateft poffible good iz the end of
guvernment. Any principle, which may be tru, in
particular inftances, but which, when extended to the
public, does not produce the greateft good to fociety, iz
certainly falfe in legiflation. A law which may be
good and neceffarily in a community, may ftil bear
hard upon individuals. This iz generally tru of all
laws. If a man takes a note of another, and fells it for
half its valu, he haz no remedy in law, nor ought the
                                                    law

law to make provifion for hiz cafe ; for laws are, in their nature and ufe, general ; they do not defend to particular cafes. The reezon iz obvious. Were laws to notice every inconvenience, which may flow from their operation, they would produce confufion rather than order, and occafion greater injuries to the public, than would refult from the loffes of individuals. But when fuch particular loffes becume general, the principle loozes its force. Sufferings, multiplied to a certain number, becume public, and then require the interference of the legiflature. If a man iz in det, and cannot pay, he iz at the difpofal of the law ; the law cannot be fufpended nor relaxed for hiz particular benefit. But when the body of a peeple becume involved, the public fafety requires a fufpenfion or relaxation of law. If an individual fettles upon land of another man, he iz confidered az a trefpaffer, and iz liable to an ejectment. But let thirty thoufand men fettle thus upon land that iz not their own, and a wize legiflature wil confirm them in their poffeffions. Neceffity or general good, in fuch cafes, fufpends the operation of legal right, or rather changes *private rongs* into *public right*. Or to exprefs the idea differently ; when evils are increefed and extended to a certain degree, it iz better to let them remain, than to rifk the application of a violent remedy. Inftances of this kind occur fo frequently, that it iz needlefs to multiply examples. Nothing betrays greater weeknefs, than the reezoning of peeple, who fay, if a principle iz juft, it extends to all cafes. I fhould however be very unhappy to hav fuch men for my legiflators. It may be afked, where iz the line of diftinction ? I anfwer, it may be impoffible to determin. Where the *right* ends, and the *rong* begins ; where the legal principle fhould ceefe to operate, and fpecial legiflativ interference becumes neceffary, it may be difficult to difcuver ; but the extreme iz always obvious. Whenever the operation of a receeved maxim or principle givs general uneafinefs, it iz a demonftrativ proof that it iz rong ; that it produces public evil ; and a wize legiflator wil

reftrain

reftrain the operation, or eftablifh a different principle;. On the fuppozition therefore that the prefent holders of the public det, are precifely in the fituation of the af- fignees of bonds, ftil the principle wil not apply nor warrant the fame conclufion in both cafes ; becauze we cannot reezon from particulars to generals, efpecial- ly on political fubjects.

Suppoze the original creditors to be five, and the prefent holders two ; more than half the number of creditors hav loft the money which waz due to them ; the lofs affects them in the firft inftance, and the hevy taxes which are neceffary to appreciate the certificates in other hands, double their injuries and complaints. Theze loozing creditors hav an idea that they are real- ly cheeted, and their murmurs foment that popular jealoufy which iz ever bizzy to check large and fudden revolutions of property.   The certificates fall into the hands of rich men, at a great difcount, and the body of the peeple fay, " we wil not fuffer our own loffes to enrich our welthy nabors."

This outcry, it iz faid, proceeds from a levelling principle, which aims to deftroy all diftinction of rank and property.   But in the prefent cafe, the popular complaints proceed from equitable principles ; nor do I know of any inftance of public jeloufy, excited by an acquizition of property in the courfe of honeft induftry. Fortunes may be fuddenly raized in private bufinefs, by commercial fpeculations, and no notice taken of the event; but when public delinquency haz thrown num- berlefs advantages into the hands of a particular clafs of men, which the peeple know are made at their own expenfe, it iz impoffible that they fhould behold fuch a change of property, without queftioning the propriety of it, and the juftnefs of the principle by which it iz defended.   When the common fenfe of mankind iz oppozed to fuch a change, it ought to be confidered az a good proof that it iz not juft.

Whatever conclufions therefore may be drawn from a principle, eftablifhed in *courts* of *law,* or among na- tions in different circumftances, the public fenfe of
juftice

juftice muft, after all, decide the queftion. A lawyer may wurk himfelf up to convictions, in wire-drawing principles ; but hiz reezoning iz oppozed to the fenfe of mankind. Peeple may not be able to *difcuver* the fallacy of the reezoning, but they can *feel* it. They may be *filenced,* but cannot be *convinced.*

One grain of common fenfe iz worth a thoufand cobweb theories ; and however peeple may be abuzed for refining upon juftice, we rarely find them generally difpozed to do rong.

The domeftic det of America furnifhes a new era in the hiftory of finance. We hav no examples to follow ; we muft purfu fome practicable fyftem, with our eyes invariably fixed on public juftice. I know it iz faid that the original creditors can purchafe certificates now, at the fame or a lefs price than they took for them. But this iz not ftrictly tru. Individuals might purchafe at a low rate ; but a general demand for them would raize their valu much abuv their current valu at any paft period : For it fhould be confidered that hitherto the fellers hav been numerous, and the purchafers, few ; that iz, a full market, with little demand for the articles. Reverfe the cafe, Let the fellers becume the purchafers ; the demand would at once raize the valu of the certificates neerly to the face of them.

But if the certificates were to pafs at their prefent low valu, few of thoze who hav alienated them, could re-purchafe ; for the fame neceffity which obliged them to fell at a lofs, now prevents their repurchafing. Peeple hav not grown rich fince the revolution ; efpecially thoze who were faithful in the fervice of their country. At any rate it iz to be wifhed that the certificates might ceefe to circulate az objects of fpeculation. They are a Pandora's box to this country.

Almoft the whole activ fpecie of the country iz employed in fpeculation. Laws prohibiting ufury, reftrain the loan of money, while the certain profits of fpeculation amount to five or ten times the legal intereft. No money can be borrowed ; no capitals can

B b   be

be raized to encurage agriculture and manufactures :
Lucrativ induſtry iz checked ; land iz ſunk to two
thirds of its real valu, and multitudes of induſtrious
peeple are embarraſſed.   From ſuch evils, good Lord
deliver us.

No.

No. XXIX.

HARTFORD, JANUARY, 1790.

An ADDRESS *to* YUNG GENTLEMEN.

AT a time of life when the paſſions are lively and ſtrong, when the reezoning powers ſcarcely begin to be exerciſed, and the judgement iz not yet ripened by experience and obzervation, it iz of infinit conſequence that yung perſons ſhould avail themſelves of the advice of their frends. It iz tru that the maxims of old age are ſometimes too rigorous to be reliſhed by the yung ; but in general they are to be valued az the leſſons of infallible experience, and ought to be the guides of youth. The opinions here offered to your conſideration hav not the advantage of great age to giv them weight, nor do they claim the authority of long experience : But they are formed from *ſome* experience, with much reeding and reflection ; and ſo far az a zeel for your welfare and reſpectability in future life merits your regard, ſo far this addreſs haz a claim to your notis.

The firſt thing recommended to your attention iz, the care of your helth and the prezervation of your bodily conſtitution. In no particular iz the neglect of parents and guardians more obvious and fatal, than in ſuffering the bodies of their children to grow without care. My remark applies in particular to thoze who deſign their children to get a living without manual labor. Let yung perſons then attend to facts, which are always before their eyes.

Nature ſeldom fails to giv both ſexes the materials of a good conſtitution ; that iz, a body complete in all its parts. But it depends moſtly on perſons themſelves to manage theze materials, ſo az to giv them ſtrength and ſolidity.

B b 2 The

The moſt criticcal period of life, in this reſpect, iʑ the age of puberty, which iz uſually between thirteen and ſeventeen, or eighteen. Before this period, you are very much in the power of parents or maſters, and if they wiſh to ſee you ſtrong and robuſt, they wil feed you with coarſe ſubſtantial food of eezy digeſtion. But at fourteen yeers old, yung perſons are capable of exerciſing their reezon, in ſome degree, and ought to be inſtructed in the mode of living, beſt calculated to ſecure helth and long life. It iz obzervable that yung perſons of both ſexes grow tall very rapidly about the age of thirteen, fourteen, fifteen or ſixteen ; but they do not acquire muſcular ſtrength in du proportion. It ſhould then be the bizzineſs of yung perſons to aſſiſt nature, and ſtrengthen the growing frame by athletic exerciſes.

Thoze perſons who leed a ſedentary life, ſhould practis ſome amuſement which requires conſiderable exertion of the lims ; az running, foot ball, quoit ; taking care not to injure themſelves by too violent exertion ; for this would defeet the ſalutary purpoſe of ſuch exercizes. But the exercize I would moſt recommend, iz *fencing* ; for the art itſelf iz highly uſeful at times, and the practice tends more to render the body firm and vigorous than almoſt any exercize whatever. It braces the muſcles of the arm, ſpreds the breſt, opens the cheſt to giv the lungs play ; an effect of great conſequence to perſons about the age of puberty. For, az waz before obzerved, perſons of this age, ſhoot up very faſt ; the body grows tall, but narrow ; the maſs of fleſh and blood iz increeſed much faſter than the tone of the veſſels and muſcular ſtrength ; the cheſt iz two narrow for the lungs to perform their office, and the blood veſſels hav not ſufficient elaſticity to produce a briſk free circulation ; the ſyſtem iz often too week to carry on the neceſſary ſecretions of the juices ; and the conſequence of the whole iz, an obſtructed circulation produces ulcers upon the lungs, which bring on a decay, or ſome infirmities of body, which laſt for many yeers, and not unfrequently for life.

T●

To avoid theze ills, much exercife of the arms and body iz not only ufeful, but neceffary ; and when it iz not the lot of yung perfons to labor, in agriculture or mekanic arts, fome laborious amufement fhould be conftantly and daily purfued az a fubftitute, and none iz preferable to fencing. A fencing fkool iz perhaps az neceffary an inftitution in a college, az a profeffor-fhip of mathematics ; for yung men ufually enter col-lege about the age of puberty ; and often leev a labori-ous occupation, to commence a fedentary life, at the very time when labor or other exercize iz the moft neceffary to giv firmnefs and vigor to their conftitu-tions. In confequence of this change and an academ-ic life, they often run up into long, flender, effeminate bodies, which a flight cold may throw into a confump-tion ; or by intenfe application to books, add, to a de-bilitated frame of body, a week nervous fyftem, which keeps them always dying, tho it may not end life til old age.

Dancing iz an excellent amufement for yung peeple, efpecially for thoze of fedentary occupations. Its ex-cellence confifts in exciting a cheerfulnefs of the mind, highly effential to helth ; in bracing the mufcles of the body, and in producing copious perfpiration. Az the two firft effects are very vifibly beneficial, they are the fubject of common obzervation ; but the laft, which iz perhaps the moft generally beneficial, iz rarely men-tioned.

Experience haz led me to the following ideas on this fubject. Our bodies are fo conftituted that a large portion of the juices fhould be thrown off by infenfi-ble perfpiration ; nor can the procefs be abated without danger, nor wholly obftructed without occafioning dif-cefe. The body muft perfpire, or muft be out of or-der. A violent cold iz a fudden obftruction of the procefs, which throws the matter, intended for evacua-tion thro the pores of the fkin, back upon the *inteftines*, taking the word, not in a tecknical, but in its original extended fenfe. All that iz neceffary to cure a cold, which iz not attended with fymptoms of inflamation, iz

to

to open the pores of the body ; which may be done by
bracing, az by drinking cold water, which excites circulation by its tonic power ; or by relaxing the fyftem,
az by the warm bath and warm teas. The firft wil
anfwer, where the body haz vigor enough to giv the
tonic its full effect ; but iz not fo efficacious, nor fo
generally practicable az the laft. It iz not fo eezy to
force thro a wall, az to open a gate.

The common houfe-wifely remedies, confifting of
butter or other oily fubftances, mixed with fpirits,
ufually hav no effect upon a cold, or a bad one. Flan-
nel, warm teas, or fimple warm water, hav the beft effect in relaxing ; but if they fail of producing a perfpiration, the patient fhould hav recourfe to exercife.
Dancing in a warm room, or other violent exercife,
wil generally throw a perfon into a copious fwet in a
few minutes ; and this, two or three times repeeted,
wil ufually releev the perfon, however obftinate the
cold. If every thing elfe fails, the warm bath fhould
be reforted to az an almoft infallible remedy.

But there iz another fpecies of obftructed perfpiration more dangerous perhaps than fudden colds, becaufe lefs perceptible ; I meen, that which proceeds
from a week habit of body. Whenever the tone of
the veffels iz loft, the circulation of the blood becumes
languid, the animal heet iz diminifhed, and the fyftem
haz not ftrength fufficient to throw off the perfpirable
matter. The confequence iz, the fkin becumes dry
and rigid, and the perfon ufually feels a dull pain in hiz
hed and the back part of hiz neck. Wimen, literary
men, clerks, &c. are moft expozed to theze fymptoms.
The remedy for them iz, free perfpiration ; but the
moft effectual remedy iz dancing, or other vigorous
exercife, which increefes, at the fame time, animal
heet and the tone of the veffels. Dancing indeed
unites to theze, the other advantage of cheerfulnefs and
good fpirits, which iz of fingular ufe to perfons accuftomed to clofe application to bizzinefs or contemplation.
The only caution to be obzerved iz, not to go into the
cold air, without confiderable additional clothing.

In

In cafes where perfons cannot hav recourfe to dancing or other exercize in a warm room, the warm bath
may be uzed to great advantage. At firft thought, one
would imagin, that the cold bath fhould be prefcribed
for giving tone to a week fyftem ; but on reflection,
this would appcer to be generally, tho not always hazardous. The truth iz, a general relaxation of the body
checks perfpiration ; and the firft effect of cold, in fuch
cafes, iz to brace the exterior parts of the body, and
throw the offending matter, lodged in the fkin by the
dcbility of the fyftem, back upon the lungs, or other
interior parts. If the fyftem haz ftrength enough, or
can receev enough by the operation of cold, to force
open the pores and produce a copious perfpiration, the
cold bath wil hav an excellent effect. But when the
perfon iz of a week frame, the experiment iz extremely
dangerous. The fafeft remedy iz the warm bath, which
remooves the obftructing matter by a gentle relaxation
of the furface ; thus enabling the veffels to recuver
their tone, in a degree, and keep up a brifk circulation.
The warm bath then iz the moft fafe and efficacious
remedy for obftructed perfpiration, occafioned by de-
bility ; and this iz an evil to which all fedentary pceple
are expozed, and by which moft of them fuffer.

I hav been often fuprized that the moderns hav fo
generally neglected the meens of prezerving helth,
which were uzed by the ancients. A little attention
to the ftructure of the human body, and the effect of
heet and cold upon it, led the ancients to the obvious
and almoft infallable meens of garding themfelves from
difeeze. Their method waz to bathe almoft daily ;
and then oil their bodies. By bathing, they kept their
perfpiration free, and their bodies of courfe, in vigor and
clenly ; and by the ufe of oil, they fecured the body
from the fatal effects of fudden cold. In the later
ages of Rome, warm baths indeed became a luxury,
and were uzed to excefs ; but this waz only an abufe
of a good thing, the excellent effects of which had
been experienced for ages. The neglect of the fame
meens, of preventing difcefe, haz obliged the moderns

to

to hav recourfe to phyfic, a fubftitute, more expenfiv
and trublefome, and not always effectual.*

Whether in bizzinefs or amufement, let your whole
conduct be guided by temperance. Are you ftudents?
Eet moderately, and let your food be of the nutritiv
kind, but not oily, high feefoned and indigeftible.
Drink but little, or rather no diftilled liquors; wine
and fermented liquors are much to be preferred. A
good cup of tee, iz fometimes a cordial; coffee may
be uzed freely; but the conftant ufe of hot liquors feldom fails to debilitate the fyftem and impair the digef-
tiv powers.

Whether you reed or rite, accuftom yourfelves to
ftand at a high defk, rather than indulge an indolent
habit of fitting, which always weekens, and fometimes
disfigures the body. The neerer you can keep every
part of the body to an eezy ftrait pofture, the more
equable wil'be the circulation of the fluids; and in order to giv them the moft unconftrained flow to the ex-
tremities of the lims, it iz very ufeful to loofen thoze
parts of drefs that bind the lims clofely.

There iz another kind of temperance which I would
warmly recommend; that iz, temperance in ftudy.
Little does a helthy robuft yuth reflect upon the delicate texture of the nervous fyftem, which iz immediately affected by clofe mental application. The full
fed mufcular man may fpurn the caution, that warns
him

---

* It iz evident, from the filence of all ancient monuments,
that the heeling art waz not cultivated, and fcarcely known
among the old Romans. For feveral ages from the bilding of
Rome, there iz hardly any mention made of a phyfician:
Pliny relates, that Rome flurifhed, fix hundred yeers, without
phyficians; that iz, the profeffion waz not honorable, being
confined to fervants or other low karacters. In Seneca's time,
many of theze had acquired eftates by the bizzinefs; but they
were ftil held in no eftimation. "Bona in arte medendi hu-
millimifque quibus contingere videmus." After the conqueft
of Greece and Afia, the manners of the Romans were corrupted by the luxuries of the eeft; difeefes multiplied, and the
practice of phyfic became more neceffary and more reputable;
but the art of furgery waz not feparated from that of medicin,
til the times of the emperors.

him againſt the danger of hypocondriacs; but it iz
next to impoſſible that the hard ſtudent, who cloſſets
himſelf ſeven or eight hours a day, in deep meditation,
ſhould eſcape the deplorable evil, which makes men
valetudinarians for life, without hope of a radical cure,
and with the wretched conſolation of being perpetually
laughed at.

Four hours of uninterrupted ſtudy in a day iz generally ſufficient to furniſh the mind with az many ideas
az can be retained, methodized and applied to practice;
and it iz wel if one half of what are run over in this
time are not loſt. It may ſometimes be neceſſary to
ſtudy or reed *more* hours in a day; but it wil az often
be found uſeful to reed *leſs*.

When you exercize at any diverſion, or go into
company, forget your ſtudies, and giv up yourſelves entirely to the amuſement. It wil do you no good to
leev your books behind, unleſs you diſmiſs your attention or train of thinking. Attend to experience.
You find it very fateeging to ſtand, ſit or even to lie
in one fixed poſture, for any length of time, and change
affords releef. The ſame iz tru of the mind. It iz
neceſſary, if I may indulge the expreſſion, to change the
pozition of the mind; that iz, vary the train of
thought; for by a variety of ideas, the mind iz releev-
ed, in the ſame degree az the body by a change of poſture.

When you reed, always endevor to reed with ſome
particular object. You wil find many books that
ought to be red in courſe; but in general when you
take up a treetis upon any ſcience, or a volum of hiſtory, without a view to inform yourſelf of ſome *particular* in that wurk, you are not likely to retain what
you reed. The object iz too general; the mind iz
not capable of embracing the whole. For inſtance, if
you reed Hume's England in courſe, with deſign to
acquaint yourſelf with the whole ſtory, you wil find, at
the end of your labor, that you are able to recollect
only a few of the moſt remarkable occurrences; the
greateſt part of the hiſtory haz eſcaped you. But if
you

you confine yourfelf to *one point of hiftory* at a time, for
example, the life and policy of Alfred, or the account
of Mary, queen of Scots, and reed what every author
you can lay your hand on, haz faid upon that fubject,
comparing their different accounts of it, you wil imprefs the hiftory upon the mind, fo az not to be eezily
effaced.   Law ftudents fhould attend to theze remarks.

There iz another kind of temperance of more confequence than thoze mentioned, viz. temperance in
plezure : For to all the perfonal evils of an exceffiv indulgence of the animal appetite, we may add innumerable evils of a moral and focial nature.   No intercourfe fhould take place between the fexes, til the body
haz attained to full ftrength and maturity.   In this refpect, ancient barbarous nations hav fet an example,
that ought to make moderns blufh for their effeminacy
of manners, and their juvenile indulgences.   The old
Germans accounted it fhameful and difreputable for
yung men to hav any intercourfe with the other fex,
before the age of twenty.*   To this continence were
they much indetted for their mufcular bodies, their
helth and longevity.   But fuch an abftinence from
plezure waz not maintained by law ; the Germans
knew that pofitiv prohibitions would be ineffectual to
reftrain this indulgence ; they had recourfe to the only
certain method ; they made it *difhonorable*.   How different iz the cafe in modern times ! So far iz debauch-
ery from being fcandalous, that it iz frequently the
boaft of men in the firft offices of ftate ; and a karacter of licentioufnefs iz little or no objection in a candidate for preferment.†

Oppozed

* Qui diutiffimè impuberes permanferunt, maximam inter
fuos ferunt laudem : Hôc ali ftaturam, ali vires, nervofque
confirmari putant. Intra annum vero xx feminæ notitiam
habuiffe, in turpiffimis habent rebus.——Cefar De Bel. Gal.
lib. 6. 19.

† The ancients were wifer than the moderns in many refpects ; and particularly in reftraining certain vices by *opinion*,
rather than by *pofitiv injunctions*. Duelling and profane fwearing

Oppozed to paffion and to falfe pride, caution wil
perhaps be unavailing. But men who wifh for permanent happinefs, fhould be perfuaded to take the
meens for fecuring it. Wil you then run the rifk of
erly indulgence in illicit plezure ? Some of you *may*
efcape the evils which generally follow ; but the chances are againft you. In nine cafes of ten, you wil deftroy the vigor of your bodies, and thus impair the
ability of enjoyment by excefs ; or what iz an additional evil, you wil contract difeefe. What iz the confequence ? Eether your tafte for the vileft plezures wil
grow into habit and make abandoned rakes of you,
averfe to the innocent enjoyments of the married life,
and of courfe bad members of fociety ; or you wil
perhaps marry amiable wimen, with your ftrength and
helth impaired, and your minds debauched, fickle,
prone to jeloufy. In this cafe, you are neether fecure

of

ing are prohibited by the laws of moft countries ; yet penalties hav no effect in preventing the crimes, whilft they are not
followed by lofs of reputation. Vices which do not immediately affect the lives, honor or property of men, which are not
ma la in fe, which are eezily conceeled, or which are fupported
by a principle of honor or reputation, are not reftrainable by
law. Under fome of theze defcription fall, duelling, profane.
fwearing, gambling, &c. To check fuch vices, public opinion
muft render them infamous.* Thoze who hav the diftribution of honors and offices, may reftrain theze vices by making
the commiffion of them an infuperable bar to preferment.
Were the *Prezident* and the executivs of the feveral ftates, to
be az particular in enquiring whether candidates for offices
are given to gambling, fwearing or debaucheries ; whether they
hav ever given or receeved a challenge, or betrayed an innocent female ; az they are in enquiring whether they are men
of abilities and integrity ; and would they, with undeviating
refolution, profcribe from their favor and their company, every man whoze karacter, in theze particulars, iz not unim-
peechable, they would diminifh the number of vices, exclude
fome wholly from fociety, banifh others from genteel company,
and confine their contagion to the herd of mankind. But
where iz the man of elevated rank, of great talents, of un-
fhaken firmnefs, of heroic virtue, to begin the glorious reformation ? America may now furnifh the man, but where fhall
hiz fucceffor be found ?

* See Vattels Law of Nations, b. I. ch. 12.

of your partners affections, nor wil you be likely to know the valu of their virtues. Having broken over the barriers of virtue, you are forever liable to ftray ; and the probability iz, you deftroy the happinefs of your wives, and the peece of your families. Perhaps with fome art, and the forgiving temper of your wives, you may conceel the family difcord, and the wretched ftate of your minds, from a cenforious world ; pride, reputation, every motiv would urge you to this pre-caution ; but iz not this a poor fubftitute for happi-nefs ? A poor confolation for the multiplied evils that follow, in an endlefs train, from the unreezonable and criminal indulgences of a few yeers ? You may be af-fured alfo that a woman of good principles cannot feel a pure fatisfaction, in the company even of a reformed hufband, when fhe reflects, az fhe frequently wil, that he haz wafted hiz helth and fubftance upon the vileft of her fex. My yung frends, it iz idle, it iz weeknefs and folly to expect any kind of happinefs or plezure, which fhal indemnify you for the trubble of feeking it, except in the purfuance of the principles which moral-ity prefcribes. Whenever you purfu an object, at the expenfe of any moral principle ; when the attainment of your end muft injure the perfon, the property, the reputation or the feelings of one child of Adam, the acquifition of that object wil not giv you happinefs ; you are purfuing a fantom. This leeds me to fay fomething on one of the moft hanous crimes a man can commit, and which the laws of fociety cannot or at leeft do not punifh ; that iz, feduction.

Fafhion, which iz often founded on moral propriety, and oftener on political convenience, iz fometimes an enemy to both ; and public opinion, enlifted in the cauze of vice, iz a greater fcurge to fociety than war or peftilence. It iz one of the evils, or rather of the curfes of civilization, that certain crimes, az malignant in their nature, and az fatal in their confequences, az murder and robbery, becume fafhionable, and to a cer-tain degree, reputable. Of this kind, iz deliberate fe-duction. It iz az malignant in its nature az murder,

for

for it iz accompanied with the fame aggravation, mal-
ice prepenfe, or a premeditated defign : It iz az fatal to
fociety ; for reputation iz az deer az life ; and the
wretched victims of deception, if they lay violent hands
on themfelves, or linger out a life of difgrace, are equally murdered, equally loft to fociety. And the only
reezon why the feducer and the murderer hav not been
placed on a footing by the laws of fociety, muft be, the
difficulty of proof, or of afcertaining the degrees of gilt,
where there iz a poffibility or a prefumtion of affent
on the part of the woman.

There are however certain inftances of this crime
which are az capable of proof az, arfon, burglary or
murder ; and why the laws of a ftate, which prohibit
under fevere penalties, the taking or giving more than
fix per cent. intereft on the loan of money, even on the
faireft contract, fhould yet permit the feducer to take
another's reputation, to doom to indelible infamy the
helplefs female, whoze reputation iz all her portion, iz
one of thoze problems in fociety, which the philofopher wil impute to human imperfection, and the Krift-
ian number among the infcrutable myfteries of providence.

But I am not addreffing legiflators ; I am reezoning
with individuals. Waving the bafenefs of the crime,
let us attend to its confequences in families and fociety. You wil doutlefs acknowlege, for I do not fee
how you can deny, that when you deliberately commit
a crime that affects your nabor, you explicitly admit
that your nabor haz an equal right to commit the fame
crime againft yourfelves ; for I prefume no man wil
arrogate to himfelf an exclufiv privilege of being a vil-
lan.

You attempt then to feduce the wife, the fifter, or
the dawter of your frend ; but hav you none of theze
relations ? Hav you not a wife, a fifter, a dawter, whoze
reputation iz deer to you ; whoze honor you would
die to defend ? You hav attacked the honor of your
nabor ; haz he not the fame right to affail your family,
in the fame delicate point ? But if you hav none of
theze

theze neer connections, hav you no female frend whoze
reputatation iz deer to you ? Now by attempting the
honor of any woman, you wage war with the whole
human race ; you break down the barriers which nature and focicty hav eftablifhed to gard your *own* family and frends, and leev *their* honor and happinefs, and
confequently your *own*, expozed to the intreegs of every unprincipled retch : You even invite an attempt
upon your family and frends ; you beet a challenge,
and bid defiance to any man who haz the fpirit to revenge the rongs of the helplefs. Theze are ferious
confiderations, in which men of principle and of no
principle are equally interefted ; for an abandoned rake
iz ufually az fond of hiz own and hiz family's honor,
az the man of the chafteft life.

Mingle with your fuperiors in age and wizdom,
whenever you can do it with propriety. If your parents are wize, they wil affociate with you az much az
poffible in your amufements ; they wil be cheerful and
facetious, and thus make you az happy az you wifh to
be at home. A morofe crabbed old man iz not inviting
company for the yung and fprightly ; and you ought
rather to fhun the illnatured, if poffible. But whenever your parents are of a cheerful difpozition, and luv
their children, they make the moft agreeable and moft
ufeful companions. They wil find amufements for
you at home, and you wil be happier there than any
where elfe. If your parents are thus difpozed to make
themfelves your principal companions, always indulge
their inclination. You wil thus avoid the contagion
of vicious company, you wil form a habit of content-
ment and fatisfaction at home ; and remember, if you
do not find happinefs there, you wil never find much
fatisfaction abroad.

In choofing fociety however, be careful not to pufh
yourfelf into company. Yung men are often impa-
tient of the reftraints which modefty and decorum impoze upon them. They are anxious to affociate with
thoze of greater age and rank than themfelves ; and
expect more notis than mankind in general fuppoze
they

they dezerv. This proceeds from the ambition and fire of youth ; the motivs I beleev to be often innocent and laudable ; the ambition therefore fhould be guverned, rather than repreffed. A little experience wil dictate patience and a modeft deportment, which, with yeers and information, wil always enfure refpectability. I once knew a man of twenty two chagrined even to petulence, becauze he could not be admitted a truftee of a college. I waz furprized at hiz fevere remarks on the venerable body of gentlemen who rejected him. He thought himfelf a man of more fcience than fome of the corporation ; and therefore better qualified to direct a literary inftitution. Admit the fact, that he excelled in fcientific attainments, yet the vexation he felt at hiz difappointment waz proof enough that he waz deftitute of the firft requifits in the overfeers of yuth, *coolnefs* and *judgement.*

In the world, avoid every fpecies of affectation, and be az fafhionable az convenience wil warrant. Yet never be the firft to invent novelty, nor run to excefs in imitation. This advice, *to be fafhionable,* fhould however be qualified, and reftrained to things indifferent, in point of morality. Az the moral karacter of men does not depend on the fhape of their garments, it iz generally beft to wear our clothes in the model that fafhion prefcribes ; unlefs your circumftances forbid, or the fafhion itfelf iz inconvenient : For if you are not able to afford the expenfe, it iz criminal in you to follow the cuftoms of the welthy ; and if the fhape of a garment makes it uneezy upon you or cumberfome, the fafhion iz ridiculous, and none but week peeple, the common coxcombs and butterflies of the world, wil adopt it. For this reezon follow lord Chefterfield's maxims with great caution. His letters contain a ftrange compound of the *beft* and *worft* inftructions ever given to a yung man ; indeed it would be expected of a man, whoze object waz not to make hiz fon *good,* but to make him *fhowy.*

Hiz lordfhip, I think, recommends to hiz fon to wear *long nails* ; in confequence of which advice, long nails are

are very fashionable wherever hiz letters are red. But a man ought to be confiftent. Why did he not at the fame time recommend long beards ? Both are very proper among favages, who hav no ideas of neetnefs ; and one would think they fhould always go together ; but among civilized peeple, both are equally flovenly. Hiz lordfhip givs an excellent reezon for hiz advice ; that mekanics pare their nails, and *gentlemen* ought to be diftinguifhed from *laborers.* Why did not he add, that az mekanics walk on two feet, gentlemen, for fake of diftinction, ought to walk on all fours ? But hiz lordfhip had better reezons for hiz advice. Long nails are a moft commodious fubftitute, or at leeft furnifh a reddy alleviation of the evils arizing from a fparing ufe of ivory. Befides, hiz lordfhip waz a courtier, fond of royal examples, &c. He found a princely one in the Affyrian monark, who, when he waz a beeft, wore hiz nails in the fame manner. Nebuchadnezzer however waz under the direction of a divine impulfe ; an au-thority that hiz lordfhip could not claim for *all* hiz in-junctions and maxims.

Never let fafhion blind you to convenience and con-gruity. Do not introduce foreign cuftoms, without reezon, or by the halves. The French feed themfelves with forks, uzing knives merely to cut their meet ; therefore knives with fharp points, are for them the moft convenient. But it iz really laughable to fee the A-mericans adopting the ufe of fharp pointed knives, without the practice of feeding themfelves with forks. They do not fee the particular convenience of the cuf-tom in France, where it originated ; but it iz *the fafhion to uze them*, and this iz all they think of. They are however well punifhed for their fervile apifhnefs, efpec-ially when they are hungry ; for a man may az wel feed himfelf with a bodkin, az with a knife of the prefent fafhion.

Be equally careful of affectation in the ufe of lan-guage. Uze words that are moft common and gener-ally underftood. Remember that fublimity and ele-gance do not confift principally in words ; az the mod-ern

ern ftile of writing would make us beleev. Sublimity
confifts in grand and elevated ideas; and elegance iz
moft generally found in a plain, neet, chafte phrafeolo-
gy. In pronunciation be very cautious of imitating
the ftage, where indeed nature *fhould be reprefented*, but
where in fact we find too much ftrutting, mouthing,
rant, and every kind of affectation. The modern pronunciation of our language on the Englifh ftage iz,
beyond mezure, affected and ridiculous. The change
of *t, d* and *f* into *ch, j* and *fh*, in fuch words az *nature, education, fuperftition,* originated in the theatrical
mouthing of words; and iz, in language, what the
ftage-ftrut iz in walking. The practice haz indeed
fpred from the ftage among our polite fpeekers, who
hav adopted it, az peeple do other fafhions, without
knowing why. Were it a matter of indifference, like
the fhape of a hat, I would recommend it to your imitation; but I hav cleerly prooved in another place,*
that the practice iz not vindicable on any good principles; that on the contrary, it materially injures the
language, both in orthography and the melody of
fpeeking. There iz fuch a thing az tru and falfe tafte,
and the latter az often directs fafhion, az the former.
The *nachure* and *edjucation* of modern times are to purity of language, what red fethers and yellow ribbons
are to elegance in drefs; and could the practice be reprefented with a pencil, it would be az boldly caricatur-
ed, az the normous hed-dreffes of 1774.

Do not adopt fuch phrafes az *averfe from, agreeably
to, going paft,* and other modern alterations of the ufual
idiom; for they are grofs violations of the principles
of the language, az might be eezily prooved, were this
the place. If you are a lawyer, do not confound fuch
terms, az, *witnefs, teftimony* and *evidence,* calling a *witnefs,* an *evidence. Witnefs* iz the perfon teftifying; *teftimony* iz what he declares in court; and *evidence* iz
the effect of that teftimony in producing conviction.
Do not confound fuch words az, *genius* and *capacity,* or
fenfe, lerning and *knowlege. Genius* iz the power of *invention;*

* See my Differtations on the Englifh Language, 4.

C c

vention ; *capacity*, the power of *receiving* ideas. *Senſe* iz the faculty of perception ; *lerning* iz what iz obtained in *books* ; *knowlege* iz what iz acquired by *obſervation*.

Attach yourſelves to bizzineſs in the erly part of life. Shun idle diſſipated karacters az you would the plague. Liſten to nature and reezon, and draw juſt ideas of things from theze pure ſources ; otherwize you wil imbibe *faſhionable ſentiments*, than which a more fatal evil cannot happen to you. You wil often heer bizzineſs condemned az drudgery and diſgrace. Deſpize the ſentiment. Nature ſpeeks a different language. Nature tells you, " that ſhe haz given you bodies, which require conſtant exerciže ; that labor or ſome other exercize iz eſſential to helth ; that employment iz neceſſary to peece of mind ; and induſtry iz the meens of acquiring property." Nature then haz rendered *bizzineſs* neceſſary to *helth and happineſs*, az wel az to *intereſt* ; and when men neglect her dictates, they are uſually puniſhed with poverty, diſeeze and retchedneſs. It ſometimes happens that a man's anceſtors hav accumulated ſuch an eſtate, that he iz wel ſecured from *poverty* ; but the very eſtate he poſſeſſes, iz the meens of entailing upon him diſeeze and all its conſequential evils : For a rich man iz ſtrongly tempted to be lazy ; and indolence, by debilitating the animal ſyſtem, deſtroys the power of enjoyment. Beſides, a man of eezy circumſtances iz very apt to looze the virtu of ſelf denial ; he indulges hiz appetite too freely ; be becumes an epicure in eeting, and perhaps a bakkanalian ; he iz then a ſlave of the worſt kind, a ſlave to hiz own deſires, and hiz faithful ſervices to himſelf are rewarded with the gout.

In addition to this, he may ſquander away hiz eſtate ; and then he iz poor indeed ! For a man who iz bred in affluence, ſeldom haz the reſolution or the knowlege requiſit to repair a broken fortune. The way to *keep an eſtate*, iz to lern in youth how to *acquire one* ; and the way to *enjoy* an eſtate, iz to be conſtantly in ſome bizzineſs which ſhal find employment for the faculties of the mind. Idleneſs and plezure fateeg az ſoon az
bizzineſs ;

bizzinefs ; and indeed when bizzinefs haz become
habitual, it iz the firft of plezures.

In forming a matrimonial connection, bridle fancy,
and reduce it to the control of reezon. You wil perhaps be in luv àt fixteen ; but remember, you cannot
rely on the continuance of the paffion. At this erly
period of life, a man's paffions are too violent to laft ;
he iz in raptures and ecftacy ; but *raptures and ecftacy*
never continu *thro life*. While a man talks of raptures and paradife on erth, he iz not fit to be married ;
for hiz paffion, or rather hiz frenzy, warps hiz judgement ; he iz az unqualified to form a juft eftimate of a
woman's karacter, az a blind man to judge of colors.
The probability iz, in all fuch cafes, that a man wil
make a bad choice ; at leeft the chances are ten to one
againft him. Before a man marries, he fhould liv long
enuf to experience the fallacy of hope, and to moderate
hiz expectations down to real life. He wil then meet
with fewer difappointments, and be better prepared to
realize the happinefs that iz within hiz power.

If you feel a *violent* paffion for a young lady, the
chance iz that the firft opportunity you hav, you wil
difcloze it, and affure her you are dying for her. Should
paffion hurry you to fuch a declaration, before you hav
much acquaintance with her, and before you hav, by
your attentions, made fome favorable impreffions on
her hart, you may be fure of a repulfe ; for your fudden profeffions frighten the lady, and ladies are never
frightened into luv. A widow wil fometimes furrender to the moft unexpected attack ; but yung coy
maidens are to be taken only by gradual approaches.
To enfure fuccefs, take the advice of a very fenfible
woman ; " firft be the frend, and then the luver." Be
polite and attentiv ; fhow yourfelf a particular frend,
for ladies are not alarmed at profeffions of efteem ; be
neether bafhful, nor difcuver uncommon folicitude ;
and the lady's hart wil probably be yours before fhe
knows it.

Do you afk, how you fhal difcuver the tru karacter
of a woman, fo az not to be deceeved ? I anfwer, this

muft

muft depend moftly on obzervations of your own, or of thoze that are more acquainted with the fex than yourfelf. The virtues of good nature, delicacy, modeft rezervednefs, prudence, &c. are difcuverable only by confiderable acquaintance. I would however advize you to be cautious of connecting yourfelves with the following karacters : Firft, wimen who hav been accuftomed to indulge familiarities, even in company, futh az kiffing, playing with their hands, and the like. Secondly, thoze who wil never be feen in the morning ; for if a lady runs out of a room, and avoids you in' a morning drefs, the fufpicion iz that fhe iz a flut, and that fhe iz confcious of her unfitnefs to be feen. A neet woman wil never be afhamed of her difhabille, for in this fhe wil fhow her neetnefs to the beft advantage. A flut may look tolerably wel in filks ; but a neet woman only wil appeer wel in a kitchen or at a brekfaft table in her own family.

Thirdly, never connect yourfelves with a very loquacious or fretful woman ; fuch a partner wil teeze you thro life. Fourthly, avoid one who haz a flanderous tung ; fhe wil keep your family and the naborhood in perpetual difcord. Fifthly, form no connection with a woman, who haz no acquaintance with a kitchen. She wil truft every thing to fervants, who wil wafte more than you confume ; fhe wil not know how to reform abufes or guvern domeftics ; the clothes wil be ill wafhed, the food wil be badly cooked ; you wil be harraffed with diforders and irregularity in the family ; and you wil be afhamed of your wife, if fhe iz not afhamed of herfelf. A mafter of a veffel fhould not come in at the cabin windows ; nor fhould a man be placed at the hed of an army, without an intimate knowlege of the duty of a private foldier. How then can a lady be qualified for the care of a family, without being acquainted with every part of domeftic bizzinefs ? Sixthly, marry, if poffible, a lady of virtu and religion ; for religion iz her beft gard from temptation and the allurements of vice. At any rate, marry. A

married

married man, efpecially a *father*, iz a better citizen than
a bachelor. Hiz benevolent affections are called in to
exercize in hiz family; and he iz thus prepared to luv
and to blefs fociety in general.

No.

No. XXX.

NEW YORK, 1788.

An ADDRESS *to* YUNG LADIES.

MY AMIABLE FRENDS,

ALTHO men in general are expozed to the fufpicion of your fex, and their opinions are often con-
ſtrued into flattery or ſtratagem, yet the tenor of the following remarks wil, it iz preſumed, bear ſuch marks
of ſincerity az to giv them a place in your confidence.
They are not the precepts of a moroſe inſtructor, nor the
opinions of a hoary ſage who haz loſt all reliſh for the
joys of life, and wiſhes to reſtrain the innocent plezures of ſenſe. They do not proceed from a peeviſh
old bachelor, whom a phlegmatic conſtitution, or re-
pected diſappointments, hav changed into a hater of
your ſex ; but they come from a heart capable of being
foftened by your charms or your misfortunes ; a heart
that never harbored a wiſh but to ſee and make you
happy. They are the ſentiments of a yung *frend* ; one
who haz lived long enuf, if not to feel his *own* faults,
at leeſt to *diſcuver* thoze of others ; and to form a tolerable eſtimate of your worth in ſocial life.

Our Saviour, when on erth, took a child in hiz
arms and ſaid, " of ſuch iz the kingdom of heaven."
I never view a circle of little miſſes without recollect-
ing the divine compariſon. A collection of ſweet little beings, with voices az melodious az the notes of the
nightingale, whoze cheeks even a whiſper wil cuver
with bluſhes, and whoze hearts are az pure az the falling ſnow drop ; iz heaven in miniature. Such iz the
deſcription of my little female frends in the bloom of
childhood. To prezerve that delicacy of mind, which
nature furniſhes ; which conſtitutes the glory of your
ſex, and forms the principal gard of your own virtue,
iz the bizzineſs of education. In this article, you hav

an opportunity to display the excellence of your character, and to exert your talents moſt ſuccefsfully in benefitting ſociety.

A woman without delicacy, iz a woman without reputation ; for chaſtity really exiſts in the mind ; and when this fountain iz pure, the words and actions that flow from it, wil be chaſte and delicate. Yung miſſes therefore ſhould be remooved az far az poſſible from all company that can taint their minds, or accuſtom them to indecency of any kind. Their nurſes, their companions, their teechers, ſhould be ſelected from peeple of at leeſt uncorrupted morals and amiable manners.

But a more advanced ſtage of life, the time when yung ladies enter into ſociety, iz, with reſpect to their future reputation, a period extremely critical. Little, my deer friends, do you reflect, how important iz the manner in which you enter into life. Prudery and coquetry are extremes equally to be ſhunned, becauze both are equally diſagreeable to our ſex, and fatal to your reputations. It haz been ſaid that coquetts often looze their reputation, while they retain their virtu ; and that prudes often prezerve their reputation, after they hav loſt their virtu. I would only add this remark, that coquetts are *generally*, but prudes *almoſt always* ſuſpected ; and ſuſpicion iz az fatal to a female karacter, az a crime. Iz this unjuſt ? Coquetry and prudery are both affectation ; every ſpecies of affectation dezerves puniſhment ; and when perſons relinquiſh their own natural karacters for thoze which are borrowed, iz it unjuſt to ſuſpect their motivs, az a puniſhment for the offence ?

You are taught to ſuſpect the man who flatters you. But your good ſenſe wil very eezily diſtinguiſh between expreſſions of mere civility and declarations of real eſteem. In general one rule holds, that the man who iz moſt laviſh in declarations of eſteem and admiration, luvs and admires you the leeſt. A profuſion of flattery iz real ground for ſuſpicion. Reel eſteem iz evinced

by

by a uniform courfe of polite refpectful behaviour. This iz a proof on which you may depend ; it iz a flattery the moft grateful to a lady of underftanding, becaufe it muft proceed from a real refpect for her karacter and virtues.

Permit me here to fuggeft one caution. You are told that unmeening flattery iz an infult to your underftandings, and fometimes you are apt to refent it. This fhould be done with great prudence. Precipitate refentment iz dangerous ; it may not be dezerved at the time ; it may make you an enemy ; it may giv uneezinefs to a frend ; it may giv your own harts pain ; it may injure you by creating a fufpicion that it iz all affectation. The common place civilities of dangling beaux may be very trifling and difagreeable, but can rarely amount to an infult, or dezerve more than indifference and neglect. Refentment of fuch trifles can hardly be a mark of tru dignity of foul.

At this period of life, let the prime excellence of your karacters, *delicacy*, be difcuvered in all your words and actions. Permit me, az one acquainted at leeft with the fentiments of my own fex, to affure you, that a man never refpects a woman, who does not refpect herfelf. The moment a woman fuffers to fall from her tung, any expreffions that indicate the leeft indelicacy of mind ; the moment fhe ceefes to blufh at fuch expreffions from our fex, fhe ceefes to be refpected ; becauze az a lady, fhe iz no longer refpectable. Whatever familiarity of converfation may be vindicable or pardonable in ether fex alone, there iz, in mixed companies, a facred decorum that fhould not be violated by one rude idea. And however difpozed the ladies may be to overlook fmall tranfgreffions in our fex, yet unforgiving man cannot eezily forget the offences of yours, efpecially when thoze offences difcuver a want of all that renders you lovely.

If your *words* are to be fo ftrictly watched, how much more attention iz neceffary to render your *conduct* unexceptionable. You charge our fex, with being the feducers, the betrayers of yours. Admit the charge

to

to be partially tru, yet let us be candid. Az profligate az many of our sex are acknowleged to be, it iz but juſtice to ſay, that very few are ſo abandoned a z to attempt deliberately the ſeduction of an artleſs and innocent lady, who ſhows, by her conduct, that ſhe iz conſcious of the worth of her reputation, and that ſhe reſpects her own karacter. I hav rarely found a libertine who had impudence enuf to aſſail virtue, that had not been expozed by ſome improprieties of conduct. There iz ſomething ſo commanding in virtu, that even villans reſpect her, and dare not approach her temples but in the karacter of her votaries.

But when a woman iz incautious, when ſhe iz reddy to fall into the arms of any man that approaches her, when ſhe ſuffers double entendres, indecent hints and converſation to flow from her lips in mixed companies, ſhe remooves the barriers of her reputation, ſhe diſarms herſelf, and thouſands conſider themſelves at liberty to commence an attack.

When ſo much depends on your principles and reputation ; when we expect to derive all the happineſs of the married life from that ſource, can it be a crime to wiſh for ſome proof of your virtu before the indiſſoluble connection iz formed ? Iz that virtu to be truſted which haz never been tempted ? Iz it abſurd to ſay that an attack may be made even with honorable intentions ? Admit the abſurdity ; but ſuch attempts are often made, and may end in your ruin. The man may then be retched in hiz miſtake becauze he iz diſappointed in hiz opinion and expectations. Be aſſured, my frends, that even vile man cannot but eſteem the woman who reſpects herſelf. We look to you, in a world of vice, for that delicacy of mind, that innocence of life, which render *you* lovely and *ourſelves* happy.

Do you wiſh for admiration ? But admiration iz az tranſient az the blaze of a meteor. Ladies who hav the moſt admirers, are often the laſt to find valuable partners.

Do

Do you wiſh to be eſteemed and luved ? It iz eezy
to render yourſelves eſteemable and lovely. It iz only
by retaining that ſoftneſs of manners, that obliging and
delicate attention to every karaꞔter, which, whether
natural or acquired, are at ſome period of life, the property of almoſt every female. Beauty and money, without
merit, will ſometimes command eligible connecꞔions ;
but ſuch connecꞔions do not anſwer the wiſhes of our
hearts ; they do not render us happy. Lerning, or an
acquaintance with books, may be a very agreeable or a
very diſagreeable accompliſhment, in proportion to the
diſcretion of the lady who poſſeſſes it. Properly employed, it iz highly ſatisfacꞔory to the lady and her connecꞔions ; but I beleev obzervation wil confirm my
conjecꞔure, that a ſtrong attachment to books in a lady,
often deters a man from approaching her with the offer of hiz heart. This iz aſcribed to the pride of our
ſex. That the imputation iz always falſe, I wil not
aver ; but I undertake to ſay, that if pride iz the cauze,
it iz ſupported by the order of nature.

One ſex iz formed for the more hardy exercizes of
the council, the field and the laborious employments of
procuring ſubſiſtence. The other, for the ſuperintend-
ance of domeſtic concerns, and for diffuſing bliſs thro
ſocial life. When a woman quits her own department, ſhe offends her huſband, not merely becauze ſhe
obtrudes herſelf upon *hiz* bizzineſs, but becauze ſhe
departs from that ſphere which iz aſſigned *her* in the
order of ſociety ; becauze ſhe neglecꞔs *her* duty, and
leeves *her own* department vacant. The ſame remark
wil apply to the man who viſits the kitchen and gets
the name of a *betty*. The ſame principle which excludes a man from an attention to domeſtic bizzineſs,
excludes a woman from law, mathematics and aſtron-
omy. Eech ſex feels a degree of pride in being beſt
qualified for a particular ſtation, and a degree of re-
ſentment when the other encroaches upon their privilege. This iz acꞔing conformably to the conſtitution
of ſociety. A woman would not willingly marry a man
who iz ſtrongly inclined to paſs hiz time in ſeeing the
house

houfe and furniture in order, in fuperintending the
cooks, or in working gauze and tiffany ; for fhe would
predict, with fome certainty, that he would neglect hiz
proper bizzinefs. In the fame manner, a man iz cautious of forming a connection with a woman, whoze
predilection for the fciences might take her attention
from neceffary family concerns.

Ladies however are not generally charged with a too
ftrong attachment to books. It iz neceffary that they
fhould be wel acquainted with every thing that refpects
life and manners ; with a knowlege of the human hart
and the graceful accomplifhments. The greateft mif-
fortune iz, that your erly ftudies are not always wel directed ; and you are permitted to devour a thoufand
volumes of fictitious nonfenfe, when a fmaller number
of books, at lefs trubble and expenfe, would furnifh
you with more valuable trezures of knowlege.

To be *lovely* then you muft be content to be *wimen* ;
to be mild, focial and fentimental ; to be acquainted
with all that belongs to your department, and leeve the
mafculine virtues, and the profound refearches of ftudy,
to the province of the other fex.

That it may be neceffary, for political purpofes, to
confider man az the fuperior in authority, iz to me
probable. I queftion whether a different maxim would
not deftroy your own happinefs.

A man iz pleezed with the deference hiz wife fhows
for hiz opinions ; he often loves her even for her want
of information, when it creates a kind of dependence
upon hiz judgement. On the other hand, a woman
always defpifes her hufband for hiz inferiority in underftanding and knowlege, and blufhes at the figure he
makes in the company of men who poffefs fuperior
talents. Do not theze facts juftify the order of fociety, and render fome difference in rank between the fexes, neceffary to the happinefs of both ? But this fuperiority iz comparativ, and in fome mezure, mutual. In
many things, the woman iz az much fuperior to her
hufband, az he iz to her, in any article of information.
They depend on eech other, and the affumption of any

prerogativ

prerogativ or fuperiority in domeftic life, iz a proof
that the union iz not perfect ; it iz a ftrong evidence
the parties *are* not, or *wil* not be happy.

Ladies are often ridiculed for their loquacioufnefs.
But ridicule iz not the worft punifhment of this fault.
However witty, fprightly and fentimental your converfation may be, depend on it, az a maxim that holds
without exception, that the perfon who talks inceffantly, wil foon ceefe to be refpected. From congrefs to
private families, the remark iz tru, that a man or woman who talks much, loozes all influence. To your fex,
talkativnefs iz very injurious ; for a man wil hardly
ever chooze a noizy loquacious woman for hiz companion. A delicate rezerv iz a becuming, a commanding characteriftic of an amiable woman ; the want of
which no brilliant accomplifhments wil fupply. A
want of ability to converfe, iz fcarcely fo much cenfured, az a want of difcretion to know when to fpeek
and when to be filent.

In the choice of hufbands, my fair reeders, what
fhall I fay ? It haz been faid or infinuated, that you
prefer men of inferior talents. This iz not tru. You
are fenfible that a good addrefs and a refpectful attention, are the qualities which moft generally recommend
to the efteem of both fexes. A philofopher, who iz
abfent and ftupid, wil not pleafe az a companion ; but
of two perfons equal in other refpects, the man of fuperior talents iz your choice. If my obzervations hav
not deceeved me, you pride yourfelves in being connected with men of eminence. I mention this to con-
tradict the opinion maintained in the Lounger, that ladies giv a fort of preference to men of inferior talents.
The opinion wants extenfion and qualification ; it extends to both fexes, when tru, but iz never tru, except
when men of talents are deftitute of focial accomplifhments.

Money iz the great object of defire with both fexes ;
but how few obtain it by marriage ? With refpect to
our fex, I confefs, it iz not much to a man's credit to
feek a fortune without any exertions of hiz own ; but

the

the ladies often make a capital miſtake in the meens of obtaining their object. They aſk, *what iz a man's fortune?* Whereas, if they are in purſuit of welth, ſolid permanent welth, they ſhould aſk, *is he a man of bizzineſs? Of talents? Of perſevering induſtry? Does he know the uſe of money?* The difference in the two caſes iz this: The man of fortune, who haz not formed a habit of acquiring property, iz generally ignorant of the uſe of it. He not only ſpends it, but he ſpends it without ſyſtem or advantage, and often dies a poor man. But the man who knows how to *acquire* property, generally keeps hiz expenditures within hiz income; in exerting hiz talents to *obtain*, he forms a habit of *uzing* hiz property to advantage, and commonly enjoys life az wel in *accumulating* an eſtate, az the man of fortune does in *diſſipating* one. My idea iz breefly this; that the woman who marries a man of bizzineſs, with very little property, haz a better chance for a fortune in middle life and old age, than one who marries a rich man who livs in idleneſs.

After all, ladies, it depends much on yourſelves to determin, whether your families ſhall enjoy eezy circumſtances. Any man may acquire ſomething by hiz application; but *economy*, the moſt difficult article in conducting domeſtic concerns, iz the womans province.

You ſee with what frankneſs and candor I tell you my opinions. This iz undoutedly the beſt mode of conducting ſocial intercourſe, and particularly our intercourſe with the faireſt part of the creation.

I rite from feeling; from obzervation; from experience. The ſexes, while eech keep their proper ſphere, cannot fail to render eech other ſocial and happy. But frail az yours iz commonly repreſented, you may not only boaſt of a ſuperior ſhare of virtu yourſelves, but of garding and cheriſhing ours. You hav not only an intereſt in being good for your *own* ſakes, but *ſociety* iz intereſted in your goodneſs; you poliſh our manners, correct our vices, and inſpire our harts with a love of virtue. Can a man who loves an amiable woman, abandon himſelf to vices which ſhe abhors?

hors? May your influence over our sex be increased;
not merely the influence of beauty and gay accom-
plishments, but the influence of your virtues, whose
dominion controls the evils, and multiplies the blessings
of society.

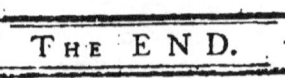

The END.